CONTINUITY AND CHANGE
IN CONTEMPORARY EUROPE

To our students

Continuity and Change in Contemporary Europe

Clive H. Church
Gisela Hendriks

*University of Kent
at Canterbury, UK*

Edward Elgar

Aldershot, UK • Brookfield, US

Published by
Edward Elgar Publishing Limited
Gower House
Croft Road
Aldershot
Hants GU11 3HR
UK

Edward Elgar Publishing Company
Old Post Road
Brookfield
Vermont 05036
US

British Library Cataloguing in Publication Data
Church, Clive H.
    Continuity and Change in Contemporary Europe
    I. Title II. Hendriks, Gisela
    320.94

Library of Congress Cataloguing in Publication Data
Church, Clive H.
    Continuity and change in contemporary Europe/Clive H. Church and
    Gisela Hendriks
    Includes bibliographical references and index.
    1. Europe—Politics and government—1945– 2. Europe—Economic
    conditions—1945– I. Hendriks, Gisela. II. Title.
    D843.C5285   1996
    940.55—dc20   95–19494
                                                              CIP

ISBN 1 85278 420 2
     1 85898 414 9 (paperback)

Printed and bound in Great Britain by
Hartnolls Limited, Bodmin, Cornwall

Contents

Illustrations

Abbreviations

ABM	Anti-Ballistic Missile
AIDS	Acquired Immune Deficiency Syndrome
APO	Extra-Parliamentary Opposition
BSP	Bulgarian Socialist Party
CAP	Common Agricultural Policy
CDA	Dutch Christian Democratic Appeal party
CDE	Conference on Disarmament in Europe
CDU	Christlich-Demokratische Union Deutschlands [Christian Democratic Union]
CE	Council of Europe
CET	Common External Tariff
CFE	Conventional Forces in Europe
CFSP	Common Foreign and Security Policy
CIS	Commonwealth of Independent States
CMEA	Council for Mutual Economic Assistance [Comecon]
COR	Committee of the Regions
CPSU	Communist Party of the Soviet Union
CSCE	Conference on Security & Cooperation in Europe [Now OSCE]
CSU	Christlich Sozial Union [Bavarian Christian Social Union]
CTB	Comprehensive Test Ban
CU	Greek Centre Party
DGB	Deutscher Gewerkschaftsbund [German TUC]
DM	Deutsch Mark
DNSF	Romanian Democratic National Salvation Front
DPA	Democratic Party of Albania
DVU	Deutsche Volksunion [German Peoples' Union]
EAEC	European Atomic Energy Community [Euratom]
EBRD	European Bank for Reconstruction and Development
EC	European Community
ECB	European Central Bank
ECJ	European Court of Justice
ECSC	European Coal and Steel Community
ECU	European Currency Unit
EDC	European Defence Community
EEA	European Economic Area
EEC	European Economic Community

EFTA	European Free Trade Area
EMI	European Monetary Institute
EMS	European Monetary System
EMU	Economic and Monetary Union
EP	European Parliament
EPC	European Political Cooperation
ERDF	European Regional Development Fund
ERM	Exchange Rate Mechanism
ERP	European Recovery Programme
ETA	Euskadi ta Azkatasuna [Basque Nation and Liberty]
EU	European Union
FDP	Freie Demokratische Partei [German Free Democratic or Liberal Party]
FN	Front National [National Front]
FRG	Federal Republic of Germany
FYROM	Former Yugoslav Republic of Macedonia
GATT	General Agreement on Tarrifs and Trade
GDP	Gross Domestic Product
GDR	German Democratic Republic
GNP	Gross National Product
GLC	Greater London Council
G7	Group of Seven Industrialized Countries
HSP	Hungarian Socialist Party
HUWP	Hungarian United Workers' Party
ICBM	Intercontinental Ballistic Missile
IGC	Intergovernmental Conference
IMF	International Monetary Fund
INF	Intermediate Nuclear Forces
JHA	Cooperation in Justice and Home Affairs
KGB	USSR Committee on State Security, the Soviet Security Agency
MAD	Mutually Assured Destruction
MBFR	Mutual and Balanced Force Reductions
MDF	Hungary: Hungarian Democratic Forum; Moldova: Moldovan Popular Front
MDS	Movement for a Democratic Slovakia
MFA	Portuguese Armed Forces Movement
NACC	North Atlantic Cooperation Council
NATO	North Atlantic Treaty Organization
NICs	Newly Industrializing Countries
NPD	National Demokratische Partei Deutschland [German National Democratic Party]
NPT	Non-Proliferation Treaty

NSF	Romanian National Salvation Front
OECD	Organization for Economic Cooperation & Development
OEEC	Organization for European Economic Cooperation
OPEC	Organization of Petroleum Exporting Countries
ÖVP	Österrichische Volkspartei [Austrian Peoples' Party]
PASOK	Greek Panhellenic Socialist Movement
PCI	Partito Communista Italiano [Italian Communist Party]
PDP	Afghan Peoples' Democratic Party
PFP	NATO's Partnership for Peace
PHARE	Economic Assistance for the Reconstruction of Central and Eastern Europe
PS	Parti Socialiste [French Socialist Party]
PSD	Partei des Demonkratischen Sozialismus [Party of Democratic Socialism]
PSI	Partito Socialista Italiano [Italian Socialist Party]
PSOE	Partido Socialista Obrero Espano [Spanish Socialist Workers Party]
PSP	Partnership for Peace
PUWP	Polish United Workers Party
RPR	Rassemblement pour la République [Rally for the French Republic]
SALT	Strategic Arms Limitation Talks
SCSE	USSR State Committee for the State of Emergency
SDI	Strategic Defence Initiative
SDP	Germany: Sozialdemokratische Partei Deutschlands [Social Democratic Party]; UK: Social Democratic Party
SEA	Single European Act
SEAT	Spanish Car Firm
SED	Sozialistiche Einheitspartei Deutschlands [Socialist Unity Party]
SFIO	Section Française de l'International Ouvrière [French Section of the First International]
SLMB	Submarine Launched Ballistic Missiles
SNF	Short Range Nuclear Forces
SPÖ	Sozialdemokratische Partei Österreichs [Austrian Socialist Party]
START	Strategic Arms Reduction Talks
SZDSZ	Hungarian Free Democratic Party
UDF	Union des Forces Démocratiques [French Centre-Right Party]
UN	United Nations
USSR	Union of Soviet Socialist Republics
WEU	Western European Union
WTO	Warsaw Treaty Organization (or sometimes 'Pact')
ZOMO	Polish Communist Security Police

Preface

This book has its origins in a course on 'Contemporary European Issues' which we jointly taught at the University of Kent. Because the course crossed the unhelpfully rigid boundaries between prevailing academic disciplines and also between past and present, it was never very easy to provide our students with adequate and up-to-date reading to support the course. When the events of 1989 then succeeded in making a vast amount of literature on recent Europe inappropriate, it seemed to us that the time had come to try and make good the damage.

This book attempts to do this in two ways. One is by trying to fill the gap between history and current affairs in European Studies. The other is by trying to re-assess the nature and evolution of post-war Europe in the light of recent events and new priorities. In other words, it seeks to introduce students to the complicated balance of changes and continuities likely to face them in the Europe of the later 1990s. However, it makes no attempt or claim to be exhaustive. It is our attempt at interpreting continuity and change in Europe since 1945.

The work is very much a joint effort. If Chapters 1, 2, 5, 6, 10, 12 and 15 were written by Clive Church and Chapters 3, 4, 7, 8, 9, 11, 13 and 14 by Gisela Hendriks, the final texts have been scrutinized, edited and agreed by both of us. So, while we are grateful to the many people who have helped us by supplying information, suggestions and criticisms, the responsibility for any faults is ours alone.

In particular we would like to thank both Edward Elgar and our copy editor for their tolerance and assistance. On the institutional level our indebtedness also extends to Anne Stevens whose willingness to shoulder administrative burdens helped to free us for writing. Our sincere thanks are due to Yvonne Latham and Nicola Cooper for all they have done to help prepare the manuscript for publication. John Hills of Canterbury Christ Church gave us tremendous help with the maps. We must also acknowledge our gratitude to our students, past and present, who have pushed us along the road to documenting our assertions and clarifying our often confused presentations. We hope that they, and their successors, will find that *Continuity and Change in Contemporary Europe* lives up to their expectations.

CHC/GH

Introduction

In January 1990 the then Prime Minister of Hungary Lajos Nemeth asked the Council of Europe whether it was 'prepared to accept – both in our spirit and in our mind – that a period of European history has ended?'. Our book is premised on this acceptance. The period that ended during the winter of 1989–90 was one in which Western Europe had been able to assume that there was no single Europe. After the Iron Curtain had come down across the continent in the 1940s Eastern Europe was, understandably enough, treated as a different, and hostile, world. Even when, in the mid-1980s, international tensions began to lessen and perestroika offered the possibility of closer and more meaningful relationships between the two parts of Europe, the essential intellectual divide remained.

However, while, consciously or unconsciously, we all assumed that real comparison between East and West was impossible and that the former could safely be abandoned to a few specialists, there was still much uniting Europe. Since 1989 it has ceased to be possible, let alone wise, to consider the centre and east of Europe to be 'far off places of which we know little' as Neville Chamberlain once tragically said. The revolutions in the old Eastern bloc have led to many countries there to try and remodel themselves on the political and economic patterns of the West, so that the concept of Western Europe as a unique area defined by its own patterns of pluralism is beginning to apply more widely. The European Union (EU) is also becoming central both to the economic revival of the newly emerging democracies, and to the creation of a broader and deeper European architecture.

The exact borders of the new Europe are, as yet, very unclear. While the former USSR remains a significant influence on Europe, and parts of it are undergoing the same processes of change, we have made no attempt to cover all developments there. Nonetheless, the first imperative of *Continuity and Change in Contemporary Europe* is to try and look at Europe west of the Urals, as a single continent with shared characteristics and interests as well as many differences.

A second imperative is to recognize that the current period of history which opened in 1989–90 is neither as new nor as unproblematic as seemed to be the case in the euphoric days of 1989–90. After such dramatic events it seemed all was changing for the better, towards a new 'golden age' in which Europe was reunited and re-integrated, and where the Cold War and nuclear confrontation gave way to a 'new world order' and disarmament. Democratic pluralism and successful integration of prosperous market economies were everywhere to be the norm.

xv

In the event, while many old problems did disappear, there were still plenty left. Equally, new crises were to emerge. Together they conspired to make the 1990s a difficult time. As a result the growing together of the continent has been much slower than had been hoped. The nature of these problems need to be spelt out.

A third imperative of *Continuity and Change* is to make clear that these present difficulties are the product not just of recent events but also of longer term causes. Although Soviet rule seemed to have changed the very nature of Eastern Europe, the reality since 1989 has been that underlying continuities have resurfaced, often in an aggravated fashion. The effects of a differential history, whether in the shape of antiquated and polluting industrial plant or in very different political and social attitudes cannot be removed as quickly as Communist party rule.

Thus, Europe in the 1990s cannot be looked at simply as something brand new, emerging from the revolutionary events of 1989–90. Events since 1989 have shown that, far from history having come to an end, history is taking its revenge on Europe. Clio is calling us back to times and processes which we thought we could ignore. Both in the East and the West events of the past, which we had imagined were irrelevant, are exerting an unexpected influence. Understanding contemporary Europe and its problems demands awareness of both continuity and change.

Conversely, it is equally wrong to think that nothing has changed, and that Europe is merely returning to where it was in the 1930s. Understanding the Europe of the 1990s means both assessing recent political changes and setting them against the background from which they have emerged. Hence a fourth imperative of *Continuity and Change* is to ensure that history is not seen as ending at some time in the 1970s or early 1980s, but that it continues unabated. Given the number of excellent studies of the earlier phases of post-war European development we have chosen to concentrate on the 1980s and the 1990s, hard though the latter are to interpret. In particular we have tried to look at the issues which have emerged.

Finally, we have tried to bring out the dialectic between what happens inside states and what happens on the wider European and institutional stage. Too often these seem to inhabit separate worlds. Thus, as well as looking at Europe as a bloc, the book also tries to provide some account of the political processes inside individual states if not of events as such. These processes seem to us the key to understanding the play of change and continuity.

To try and respond to these challenges, and to make the past, present and future of the 'new' or the restored Europe comprehensible to new generations, who came to maturity in the declining years of the 'old Europe' or who are growing up in an insecure post-Communist continent, is the purpose of this book. In particular, it is aimed at helping students on European Studies courses to come to terms with the unfolding story of the Continent. They need to be made aware that, increasingly, Europe is facing new and jointly shared policy challenges about how to respond to other parts of the world. Such challenges need to be understood if the future is to be managed effectively.

So *Continuity and Change* is a work of history, of present-day politics and of coming challenges. It is therefore divided into three parts. The first section, covering the period from the 1940s to the 1970s is designed to provide the essential background for an understanding of recent events. Hence it looks at the state of Europe in the 1940s and at crucial social and economic developments of the post-war years, stressing the way in which East and West diverged after the Second World War. The domestic development of West European countries is examined in parallel to a study of adaptation and abortive revolts in the East. Equally, the failure of Soviet attempts to integrate the societies and economies of the satellites is contrasted with the successful integration of the West. The crucial role of East–West relations which divided the two zones and prevented their resemblances from appearing, is also analysed. The conclusion is that, with the economic crisis of the 1970s, the West was merely shaken while the centre and east were fundamentally undermined.

The second section traces the story in more detail through the 1980s, leading to the climacteric of 1989. The way the West was able to maintain its continuity and renew its socio-economic and international dynamism is contrasted with the growing stresses of change in central and eastern Europe. In the West economies, broadly speaking, revived after the depression and political pluralism was reinforced, notably where Iberia was concerned. This consolidation is first of all examined at the national level. However, the latter also helped to revive the European Community (EC), giving it a new strength and dynamism, leading to institutional and economic relaunching through the Single European Act (SEA) and the 1992 Programme for the completion of the Internal Market. This is, in turn, considered.

In the centre and east of Europe these developments helped to increase the pressure for change. This showed itself first in *détente* and arms control and then in the crucial change of domestic direction brought about by Gorbachev's new policies of glasnost and perestroika. These had, as many authorities had foretold would be the case, a profound role in promoting transformation in the satellites. However, few would have thought, even as late as the summer of 1989, that the transformation would be as revolutionary, or as rapid and as peaceful as was to be the case. The revolutions which showed the revival in the East are thus examined in some detail.

In the final section an attempt is made both to continue the story as far as possible into the 1990s, and to assess the issues and challenges raised by these developments. Because both halves of Europe are already being affected by the completion of the Internal Market we start by examining the development of the EC and its economic and political implications. Then the situation in individual states, both West and East, is examined. Stress here is laid on the difficulties of responding to a new depression which hit the East particularly badly, threatening its fragile new states. Democratic governments have come under increasing strain.

Security and diplomatic questions are changing equally dramatically. Events in Europe have facilitated rapid disarmament, notably where nuclear weapons are concerned, but they have done less to produce the new kinds of security policies and institutions which seem to be needed. At the same time broader relations between European states, their institutions and peoples have only slowly became recognized as important and as interdependent as they have become. All this means that the 1990s are likely to continue as they have begun, uncertain, ambivalent and challenging. They challenge us both to rethink the history of the last 50 years or so in the light of recent events and to face the issues that they pose.

PART I

THE POST-WAR BACKGROUND

Overview

Europe in the mid-1940s was still in trauma from the past. Not merely had the continent failed to find stability after the First World War but it had been plagued by Fascism and Nazism. These then plunged the continent into a new civil war in 1939. The Second World War was a disaster for Europe, given the atrocities, destruction and divisions which it produced. Yet, despite this, Europe was to re-emerge after 1945 economically, politically and internationally.

This re-emergence went through two phases: of reconstruction and then of expansion. Both were achieved despite the new Iron Curtain in Europe which meant that they showed themselves in different ways in East and West. However, expansion was followed, in the 1970s, by a period of economic and political crisis. Both periods were to play an important role in the pattern of continuity and change in contemporary Europe.

Economic reconstruction was surprisingly rapid in both parts of Europe, even though in the East it was accompanied by a drastic change in the economic and social system. This also happened in politics whereas the West saw the redevelopment of the old nation states, albeit now in a pluralist, welfare mode. The speed of reconstruction was closely linked to the development of the Cold War, which also helped to start the first movements towards West European integration.

From the late 1940s, however, things began to change more rapidly and widely. The key factor in this was the remarkable economic growth, especially in the West. Although this remains hard to explain, it certainly transformed economy and society. Domestic politics in the West echoed these developments as, encouraged by the boom and the Cold War, most countries settled down to a striking degree of stable political pluralism. France was an exception in this and events there in 1968 were to encourage a revival of the European left.

European integration was another unexpected development. From the mid-1950s this took on new, and more successful, characteristics with the emergence of the Coal and Steel Community. This was reinforced by the development of the European Economic Community (EEC). Despite a series of crises in the 1960s, the developing EEC successfully encouraged economic growth and political stability.

In the East, however, stability was challenged by a series of revolts against the new order, facilitated by the political relaxation which followed the death of Stalin. Not surprisingly the division between the two blocs was consolidated in the 1950s and 1960s. However, following the Cuban missile crisis of 1962, things began to ease slightly. Yet it was in the affluent West that social protest against the new society emerged.

The 1970s were to be a paradoxical mixture of improving international relations and worsening domestic conditions. The slow thaw of the 1960s thus paved the way for *détente*, a combination of disarmament, resolution of the German problem and the generally better relations enshrined in the Helsinki process. *Détente* seemed to have given the satellites a new stability and legitimacy. However, this did not mean great improvements, either where the controlling organizations of Eastern integration, the Council for Mutual Economic Assistance (CMEA) and, especially, the Warsaw Pact, were concerned, or internally. Nor did *détente* do much to discourage the growing economic and political stagnation of the eastern bloc, which was reaching crisis point.

In the West, the depression which developed out of the 1973 oil crisis, struck more openly and brutally. Political movements and governments found coming to terms with the new conditions very painful. The depression also affected the successful process of European integration. So, in the 1970s, it found the momentum much harder to maintain. Along with the incipient crisis which faced the East of Europe this was another example of the way in which post-war achievements had run out of steam by the end of the 1970s. So, the post-war period ended somewhat disappointingly.

1 The economic and social background: West and East

The most significant factor in post-war European history was the dramatic economic transformation which took place over the '30 glorious years' between the late 1940s and the early 1970s. Not only did this mark a major break with previous patterns of economic growth, but the new society and economy which emerged were to remain elements of continuity into the 1990s despite the effects of the 1973 depression. The transformation, moreover, was not just a matter of economic and social change. It had considerable political implications. In the West it encouraged both consensual domestic politics and the development of integration. The fact that growth in the East was more limited meant that the political structures, both domestic and international, imposed by the Soviet Union on the new satellites, were rather more problematical.

Yet, despite its importance for the understanding of post-war Europe, the fact that there was such a boom in the first place, was rather surprising. After all, conditions in 1945 were anything but propitious for economic growth. Europe's dominant position in the world economy had been gravely undermined by the First World War and the subsequent slump inflicted further damage. The industrialized countries of the North and West saw a massive drop in output and employment together with considerable social conflict. The more agricultural countries of the South and East were also badly destabilized by falling farm prices. The economic traumas of the slump played a considerable part in weakening democracy in Europe. Only the USSR seemed to have escaped the economic crisis, thanks to its isolation and the apparent success of its economic system.

Yet the USSR, like the rest of the continent, was to be tested to breaking point when Nazism unleashed the Second World War. This proved even more destructive and horrific than the First World War, inflicting appalling losses in resources, infrastructure and, above all, human lives. The War cost anything up to 50 million lives and displaced millions more. The economies of both East and West were also grotesquely distorted by the demands of war, especially when these were imposed by Nazi racialist exploitation. Normal production virtually ground to a halt and ordinary trade dried up, further weakening Europe's position in the world economy. The cumulative result was unparalleled destruction, starvation and inflation together with a legacy of conflict, misery and psychological exhaustion.

5

Yet, as we will show in this Chapter, this unpropitious situation was to be the prelude to a 'super-boom' in the West and to significant change in the more backward East. There were, in fact, three distinct phases of economic growth in the post-war period, beginning with a period of reconstruction which was particularly painful in the East. Thereafter, growth entered a second, self-sustaining, phase in the early 1950s. In the West the resulting boom rapidly transformed Western economies. In the East, if growth was less, political engineering meant that the economic transformation was even more drastic. At the same time society also changed markedly, becoming much more mobile and organized on a larger scale.

However, despite the emergence of more modern and affluent societies, all was not well. Hence the economy entered a third phase in the late 1960s. In the West social protest around 1968 proved to be the prelude to a severe downturn in the economy in the 1970s. However, although growth was interrupted, it was not halted altogether, and structural economic change continued apace. The experience of recession was to be as painful in the East as it was in the West, although this was not always realized at the time.

Reconstruction

Despite the extreme difficulties which faced the European economies in 1945 rehabilitation followed surprisingly quickly. The first phase of economic development after the war thus lasted no more than ten years. In the West in particular there was rapid reconstruction and recovery. In the East, where the devastation of war had been even greater and the imposition of Soviet communist control meant that change went far beyond mere rebuilding, the process was more drawn out.

The countries of Western Europe needed to rebuild their shattered infrastructures, cope with the high inflation and currency depreciation caused by the war, and provide food, housing and jobs for ex-servicemen and the millions of refugees created by the war and Soviet expansion. They faced up to the task very positively. Ideas of reducing Germany to a simple agrarian economy were abandoned and generally governments found they had to intervene more actively in the economy. This echoed the ideas of the resistance and of John Maynard Keynes which saw a positive economic role for the State.

Priority was given to rebuilding the infrastructure rather than to satisfying consumption needs other than food. At the same time most countries sought to squeeze out inflation through financial controls, higher taxes and currency reform. The latter often involved wage freezes as well. Since controlling inflation added to unemployment and food shortages, there were moves to provide a whole new range of social services to offset these. The combination of deflation and social provision helped to get economies moving relatively quickly. Such new social thinking was, along with technological development, one of the positive developments resulting from the war.

An even more important stimulus to reconstruction was aid from outside, notably from the USA. Between 1947 and 1952 $23 billion[*] were made available to Europe by the USA in the form of Marshall Aid. The hard currency then provided enabled the Western European economies to consolidate their recovery by buying the capital goods needed for further reconstruction and modernization. The USA thus played an important part in helping to return the West to the world economy and encouraging affluence. Marshall Aid also, as later Chapters show, set the West of the continent on a separate road to integration.

So, while in 1946 West European production was only 8 per cent of the world total, by 1950 it accounted for almost 20 per cent. By the early 1950s national income and production levels in manufacturing and agriculture had generally risen above those prevailing in the late 1930s. Moreover, as well as making good its own losses Europe began to export again, and showed itself able to penetrate American markets. Reconstruction thus laid a solid basis for further growth.

The situation was rather different in the East. Given that the East of Europe started from a lower base and had suffered more in the war from Nazi depredations and destructive battles, reconstruction was even more important than in the West. Unfortunately, it was to prove neither as rapid nor as successful as in the West. Yet, if the West merely sought to rebuild, and modernize, traditional free market economies, in the East reconstruction meant a dramatic alteration in the prevailing type of economy. So, if needs were even greater than in the West, the priorities adopted were very different.

There was a similar surge of social and economic change, but on a wholly different ideological basis. The coalition governments, behind which the communist elite at first sheltered, seized land and redistributed it to poor peasants, and nationalized most industrial property, especially that owned by collaborators and members of the old ruling classes. By the early 1950s much private property had disappeared, along with a lot of craft production. This was the prelude to the longer term plans, on Soviet lines, which were put into operation throughout the bloc from the later 1940s. So, in a way, reconstruction continued for much longer than in the West.

One key factor in all this was that there was little parallel to the support given to Western economies by the USA. Security and ideological reasons meant that the USSR not merely sought to remodel its new satellites in its own command economy image, but also tried to use them to help rebuild its appallingly damaged economy. In 1946 Soviet output was only three quarters of what it had been in 1941. Stalin therefore provided few credits of his own to the new

---

[*] The term billion indicates a thousand million throughout.

satellites. Nor was he willing to allow the latter to accept Marshall Aid to make up for this.

Instead he sought to exploit his new territories to the full. While some states were only called on to supply manufactures and capital goods, the East of Germany was forced to make much more extreme sacrifices. All kinds of plant, even railways lines and whole factories, were dismantled and moved eastwards. Russian economic pressure remained a continuing problem even when this phase had passed.

Yet, despite all these depredations and the huge structural changes pushed through by the new regimes, things did improve somewhat. By 1949 production in the satellites was above pre-war levels, although the USSR did not achieve pre-1941 levels until 1953. Productivity and living standards remained low partly because exports remained dominated by the needs of the USSR. So, if there was recovery in the East, the styles and rates of growth were clearly different from those of the West.

The boom years in the West

Not surprisingly, when the great boom started, it was far more marked in the West than in the East. For nearly 30 years the West was to enjoy almost uninterrupted growth. This involved a huge surge in production and prosperity, which transformed most Western economies and was to be the basis for West European achievements over the next decades. Yet the reasons for this unexpected quantum leap are still not fully understood.

Once reconstruction was achieved, Western Europe experienced no real interruptions in growth until 1973. Until then there were only minor upsets such as that in 1951–2 when the Korean War temporarily pushed prices up before new trade opportunities, opened by the American re-concentration on military production, led to a new surge. At such times falls in output were only found in a few peripheral economies while Britain was then alone in experiencing a drop in gross national product (GNP), and then only briefly. For the rest there was only the occasional slackening in tempo as in 1957–8, when the Suez crisis caused 'overheating'.

As a result, average growth rates in the 1950s were about 4.4 per cent per year, which was far ahead of both 19th century figures and of post-war US performance. Countries like the Federal Republic of Germany (FRG), which had been particularly badly hit by the war, grew most. The 1960s were to see even higher growth rates of about 5.2 per cent on average. By then, however, countries which had not suffered so much from war damage grew the most rapidly. Previously backward countries like Spain also shared significantly in the process. Overall national growth rates ranged from a low of 2.6 per cent, in the case of Britain, to 7 per cent in peripheral southern countries like Spain.

So, in the West, growth was faster, more sustained and more widely spread than ever before.

Thanks to this continued growth Western Europe produced more between the 1940s and the 1970s than it had in the previous 70 years. With output soaring to 250 per cent between 1950 and 1970, unemployment was low, averaging about 2.9 per cent. Much production was concentrated in new products, like televisions, which had been virtually unknown before the war, and these new products were increasingly traded across Western Europe and beyond. In fact, trade grew even more than Gross Domestic Product (GDP), and some eight times faster than had been the case in the first half of the century. Thus, the share of exports in average GDP almost doubled. By the 1960s Western Europe was again the world's largest trading bloc.

All this was achieved without massive inflation because productivity rose enormously and capacity was fully used. Average inflation rates for the FRG were 2.9 per cent and in Britain and France just under 5 per cent. Overall GDP per head went up almost fivefold in many countries between 1950 and 1970 alone, which is an indication of the way in which growth produced a much more affluent society than ever before.

The reasons for this 'economic miracle' were manifold. Technical factors played a part, with new sources of energy, new technologies, more modern communications, new production processes and new styles of management, many derived from the war or American practice. The growing role of the state in stimulating increasingly 'mixed' economies through nationalization and demand management was also important. Some authorities tend to argue, however, that the essential dynamic was a matter of 'catching up' with more advanced economies, notably those of North America. West European economies thus sought to emulate what was already happening on the other side of the Atlantic. Certainly, high levels of capital investment, the switch of resources from agriculture to more productive sectors and the stimulus of reconstruction all played a part.

There were also social causes. Although demographic decline was expected after the war, it did not materialize. The 'baby-boom' of the war years, and enforced migration, helped to produce a larger, younger and better qualified labour force. This reflected the impact of better education, of new welfare provisions and of new attitudes. Rising demand from a growing population which, after the austerities of the 1930s and 1940s, was more willing to be consumers, was very significant. Other domestic factors such as political stability, new attitudes to economic management, and better labour relations, encouraged by the very low levels of unemployment, also helped.

Externally, Europe benefitted from initial US aid and inspiration. Over the medium to long term it also gained greatly from American protection. This encouraged freer trade and growing interdependence, both within Europe and beyond. Both helped to promote change. The fact that the Bretton Woods system provided exchange rate stability throughout the Atlantic economy until the late 1960s was also important.

Perhaps none of these factors can explain the surge in economic growth on their own. It was probably the fact that so many things came right at the same time which was crucial. Yet, even if economic historians are still uncertain as to exactly why Western Europe 'took off', the fact is that it did. This meant firstly that it increasingly diverged from the East and secondly that the character of European economies and societies also changed greatly.

Economically Western Europe was transformed by 1970. The new economy was larger not just, as already noted, in terms of output but also in organizational and geographical terms. As output and sales expanded, so firms grew larger in order to cope and attain the economies of scale provided by new technologies, mass advertising and enlarged markets. Similarly, national economies became more interrelated as previously isolated regions and countries were brought into the mainstream of the Western European economy. This in turn was part of a wider economy which began to expand beyond the Atlantic world into the Pacific.

All these factors made exports a more dominant element in many economies by the 1960s. At the same time Europe became much less agricultural than it had been. Labour increasingly shifted from the land into manufacturing, whose share of employment remained stable in percentage terms, although the actual numbers involved rose, and especially into services. Within industry there was a shift from food, textiles and heavy industries to chemicals, engineering and consumer goods, notably the new range of household appliances like refrigerators, washing machines, radiograms and televisions. Western Europe also developed large-scale oil and automobile industries. The latter were producing some 8 million vehicles a year by the 1960s encouraged by a growing process of concentration.

In the service sector communications, design, education, management, sales and public and professional employment all boomed. Transport was also a growing sector. Even agriculture became more productive and progressive thanks to the consolidation of farms, production for the market and technical improvements. Indeed the whole economy was much more technically and scientifically based. Mass production using artificial energy, new communications technologies and new machines, became the norm and the amount of capital invested per worker grew markedly. So, overall, Western economies became infinitely more modern and more affluent.

Developments in the East
The East of Europe shared in the growth and restructuring of the 1950s and 1960s. However, change there was neither as rapid nor as far reaching. This was caused by greater backwardness and, even more, by the very different dynamic

for change. In the West growth was self-sustaining because the economy was largely autonomous and grew without real interruptions. Neither was true in the East where the dictates of Marxist Leninism were the main force shaping development. This denied autonomy to the economy and proved incapable of delivering consistent and successful growth.

As already noted, reconstruction was both a longer affair than in the West and a process complicated by the first steps in reshaping the economy on communist lines. The process of transformation continued as the East moved into its second phase of economic development. This saw the communist states taking over almost total control of resources and labour. Some 90 per cent of land and industry thus passed into state control although central planning and nationalization meant that managers had neither real freedom nor incentive to innovate.

Nonetheless, industrialization moved forward on a massive scale, especially in the 1950s. Unfortunately, it focused on the heavy industries encouraged by Stalin and then maintained by the military because of the Cold War. The suspicions this generated also made it impossible to call on Western aid. The aim became to produce as much as possible, irrespective of the resources used, a process known as 'extensive production'. Factories were required to fulfil quotas without regard to efficiency, marketability or quality. Agriculture, light industry and services, like consumption needs, were all sacrificed to this drive to industrialization.

Most of the Eastern states began their second stage of economic development by implementing Five-Year Plans designed to carry forward the energy and heavy industry programmes of the 1930s and 1940s. Although this involved the elimination of the craft sector in many countries it still led to growth rates of about 6 per cent in the 1950s, albeit from a lower starting point than in the West. Conversely, the 1960s, which saw rising growth in the West, were a period of lessened expansion in both the USSR and the satellites because reconstruction and 'Sovietization' came to an end. Despite experiments with less centralized management of the economy rates fell to an average of 5 per cent. Here, too, they were highest in the more backward and peripheral states like Romania.

As a result of the drive for industrialization, industry's share of GDP rose from an average of 20 per cent to 31 per cent over the two decades to 1970. There were large increases in the output of electricity, coal and metals and many countries experienced a dramatic increase in capital investment. Yet, productivity remained low because of the extensive nature of manufacturing and the extent of underemployment, caused by the communist refusal to countenance unemployment. Quality was also low because trade was confined within the bloc. Furthermore, the domination of industry by military priorities only faded slightly.

The expansion of industry was, moreover, very much at the expense of agriculture. This was despite the way in which agriculture was also remodelled. Collectivization eliminated most private farms and concentrated production in larger units, whether co-operatively run 'collectives' of peasants or centrally run 'state farms' managed by officials. Only in Poland, where special political factors were at work, were peasant farms allowed to survive on any scale. Elsewhere only household plots were tolerated.

Aimed at increasing yields, so that the new industrial cities could be fed while rural labour and investment were reduced, collectivization brought no great improvement in output. The ineffectiveness of state and collective farms meant that rationing remained in force for a long time. Indeed, by the late 1960s, the USSR had to import grain from the West. The way living standards were thus held down in the East had disastrous political consequences, as will be seen in Chapter 5. This was despite the fact that wages and savings rose, with apparently no inflation, because the state arbitrarily fixed prices and paid large subsidies to minimize costs to the public.

The new economies which emerged were more urban and industrial than before. They underwent substantial, if painful, modernization as the index of industrialization rose over fivefold in many countries and more in the Balkan states. Output also went up, as did the scale of organization. Equally, the economic geography of Eastern Europe expanded, with new regions being brought into CMEA's economic circuits. However, the eastern economies were much less connected with the world economy and trade counted for much less.

The satellites also remained far more agricultural than the West. Over a third of the labour force worked on the land in the early 1970s, compared with an average of 55 per cent in 1950. Yet, agriculture remained inefficient. Like much else in the Eastern economies it remained much less technologically developed than its Western counterpart. Services also remained small and underdeveloped, accounting for no more than 20 per cent of GDP. This was despite the expansion of technical education.

Although, in the 1950s, Krushchev promised that the Eastern economies would overtake the West by the 1970s, this did not happen, notwithstanding the fact that officially proclaimed targets were often over-fulfilled. The lack of autonomy inherent in the communist system did not, therefore, produce equivalent growth to that in the West. Performance varied amongst the communist states but none of them outstripped the West. At best they were able to compete in limited areas. This failure to achieve either full economic maturity or equivalent growth meant that the East was to be more exposed than the West to the downturn of the 1970s and 1980s and to the resulting social strains.

The reasons both for growth and for its limitations, were much more political than in the West. It is ironic that, as already implied, centralized planning and control did not produce the consistency of growth found in the West. This was because political direction changed far more rapidly than might be imagined. Targets were raised and lowered with remarkable frequency, in line with shifts inside the party. Furthermore, the frequent revolts against the new order, discussed in Chapter 5, could also disrupt economic development.

So, although the East underwent similar economic processes to the West, growth remained dictated and not spontaneous. Moreover, the East experienced less technological change so that a clear gap between East and West emerged. The impetus from integration – as will be seen – and from other external factors was weaker. Equally, population growth was less dynamic while Eastern citizens were, by fiat, not allowed to become consumers, thus removing another force for growth. All in all there was no real affluent society in the East.

Social changes

Nonetheless, post-war economic change obviously produced a more prosperous society in both East and West. Europeans came to enjoy higher incomes and better facilities. Their numbers expanded and they became much more urban in nature. This was one aspect of the increasing mobility of European society. However, the new societies also generated strains which were to be one of the causes of economic and other difficulties from the 1970s onward.

In the West affluence showed itself in incomes which rose by some 4.5 per cent p.a. compared with no more than 1 per cent before the war. It also produced a different kind of society. In the West affluence meant more consumer durables, such as cars, and more facilities and entertainments, together with many social benefits. In the East wages fell and facilities were fewer, although they did increase and were publicly provided. Such facilities were often very cheap, even if people had to wait a long time to get them, as was the case with cars and housing.

The expansion of housing and other goods was part of a general phenomenon after the war. Society became larger and more organized than before. The overall population of Europe, excluding the USSR, grew from some 390 million at the end of the war to 462 million by 1970. A falling death rate and an initial rise in birth rates lay behind this increase. However, once affluence got under way and new forms of contraception were developed, birth rates were to fall. Nonetheless, with better medical care, and an improved diet, life expectancy began to grow, by up to 10 per cent in the West and by as much as 50 per cent in parts of the East. Family structures also changed with the extended family becoming less significant in the West because of increasing mobility and the growing role of public provision of services. Divorce also became much more common while the social position of women began to change, albeit slowly and uncertainly.

Society also became much more urban since it was in cities that jobs, facilities and entertainment were concentrated. In the West big cities grew most, partly because people moved into new suburbs. As a result of the mobility provoked by agricultural change, the urban population rose from 67 per cent of the total in 1960 to 77 per cent by 1980. In the East capitals and smaller towns benefited most. Towns also tended to set social and cultural trends in what were increasingly 'national' societies owing to new means of communication. However, the shift to the towns also meant that some rural areas were drained of people and facilities, causing new problems.

This second form of mobility meant that people moved from underdeveloped to developed regions in search of employment, as they did from the Italian Mezzogiorno to the Po valley. However, labour mobility was also international. As the northern European economies expanded they needed an increasing supply of manual labour and, once post-war migration was absorbed, this came increasingly to be provided by southern Europe. By 1970 there were some 7.5 million so-called guest-workers in Western Europe. In the USSR industrialization and political control meant that large numbers of ethnic Russians moved to new areas such as the Baltic republics and Kazakhstan. Similar trends were also seen in the satellites although the migration of labour from less successful states to the German Democratic Republic (GDR) was very limited. Governments also tried to promote industrialization in remote areas to limit political dissent. Equally they sometimes sought to limit migration to overcrowded capitals.

Social structures also showed a third kind of mobility. In the West the arrival of new immigrants who were happy to take up poorly paid and menial jobs interacted with other trends to cause a general upgrading of social classes. As a result of affluence, economic change and growing educational opportunities Western society became rather middle class. Old forms of social distinction became less significant while the growing white-collar opportunities in industry and, especially, the services provided a significant means of social promotion. This was despite the fact that far more people were employed than ran their own businesses. Similarly, new skills were expected of workers. For those who were able to benefit from these trends conditions and prospects improved greatly. However, those who, because of their outsider status or for more personal reasons, could not showed a worrying tendency to form what has been called an 'under-class'.

In the East social patterns, although more mobile, were somewhat different. This came to reflect the way the Party dominated social structures. At first, upward social mobility was provided by the systematic attacks on old elites, whether nobles, old-style bourgeois or well-off peasants. This improved the position of the old lower classes and offered some chances of promotion. Increasingly, however, mobility should have come about because of new prospects for administrative employment, whether in the State or of nationalized enterprises. Indeed, because of the Marxist ideological commitment to the proletariat, Communist regimes attempted to provide special privileges for workers and, to a lesser extent, ordinary peasants.

However, many commentators have been impressed by the limited facilities for social promotion actually provided. This was because of the dominant role of the Party. Rather than representing the workers the Party became a vested social interest in its own right, the so-called 'new class'. Not merely did it control access to power but, through the *nomenklatura* system, it even controlled nominations. The system meant that access to all key posts in society was dependent on Party approval, and approved lists of party members and sympathizers were kept for the purpose of ensuring politically correct appointments. All this made it very hard for ordinary people to gain promotion. The new elite of intellectuals and Party managers differed from elites in the West in that its strength came from privileged access to public resources such as housing, education and foreign produce, not from private wealth or occupation.

Given their dependence on the existing political order the new Eastern elites did not question the post-war social order. This was left to dissidents and discontented workers. In the West, however, increasing education and the failure of public facilities to keep pace with new expectations produced a significant, and very open, questioning of the way in which Western society was developing. This trend also drew on the first signs of economic difficulty that occurred in the late 1960s. Thereafter, it was to complicate the recession of the 1970s.

All this was symbolized by the events of May 1968 in France when, as is shown in Chapter 2, student agitation over lack of facilities in overcrowded universities sparked off massive social protests. At one stage 8 million people were on strike. The protests were directed not just at the Gaullist regime but at the very idea of the 'consumer society' and its inequalities. It was this which brought large numbers of workers briefly into the fray.

Though things in France quietened down thereafter, May 1968 gave a considerable boost to social movements on the left. This was also the case in Spain, Germany and, especially, Italy. Even the Czech revolt of that year may also have been affected. Together these events led western governments to concede even more social welfare provision, a move which came home to roost when, after 1973, the economic boom came to an end.

1973 and the recession in the West

While the new economy continued to develop in the 1970s, it was to be severely shaken. The main reasons for the sudden deterioration were economic. Thus, productivity had begun to slacken in the late 1960s partly because of the new labour and left wing militancy. Moreover, between 1968 and 1973 inflation began to creep up and overall growth rates to fall well below those of preceding years. Domestically there were further problems. One was that the European economies had not modernized as much as their competitors. Structural change, the use of new technologies and the shift into new products had not gone far enough, while the agricultural sector still remained too large and inefficient. Public sector and welfare costs were also becoming more burdensome. At the same time some of the factors that had propelled Western economic growth were no longer so effective. Thus, population growth was falling off, the flight from the land was ending and the wave of acquisitions of consumer durables and new housing was largely over owing to a process of over-accumulation.

Had the European economies been self-contained this might not have mattered. Unfortunately, external circumstances were also deteriorating. To begin with Europe was starting to face growing competition from Japan and other newly industrializing countries, where labour costs were lower, plant more modern and products more reliable; then again the Vietnam war had undermined the American economy, producing an inflation boosting budgetary deficit. This weakened the dollar, the key Western currency, forcing the Nixon administration to end the convertibility of the dollar against gold in August 1971. Together with the problems of sterling, this brought instability and inflation into the international monetary order, ending the equilibrium provided by the 1944 Bretton Woods agreement.

Then, in October 1973, following the Yom Kippur war between Israel and the Arab states, the Middle East oil producers of the Organization of Petroleum Exporting Countries (OPEC) pushed the price of oil up from $3 to $12 a barrel in 4 months. This was done in order to punish the West both for its support of Israel and for the way in which it had exploited Middle East economies. The cause of resentment were both western control of the oil industry and the inflated prices OPEC countries were forced to pay for Western manufactures.

Since at the time Europe covered 60 per cent of its energy needs with oil, and since, between 1950 and 1970, those needs had risen from 289 to 850 million tonnes of coal equivalent, the increases hit Western Europe very hard. Oil was vital to the new economy: its energy production, its transport and many aspects of manufacturing depended on it. With a further rise in prices in 1978–79, the two 'oil shocks' drove the European economy over the brink and into severe recession. This was often intensified by the austerity policies adopted to cope with it. However, though there was an acute crisis, growth was not permanently ended. Its effects and the difficulties caused by the recession were to be continuing features of Western development towards the end of the century.

In the West the effects of the crisis were all too obvious. They showed themselves in five ways. Firstly, there was a marked downturn in growth rates. In 1974 GNP growth fell to a mere 0.6 per cent. The next year, for the first time in decades, it actually fell by half a per cent. External trade also contracted as the crisis spread worldwide, hitting the Third World even more than Europe. Protectionism also became much more marked.

This largely reflected a second effect, industrial contraction. Initially, industrial output fell by 10 per cent and it did not recover. As demand fell, because of the crisis, stocks were run down and not replaced, driving many firms into bankruptcy. Investment likewise tailed off even though interest rates, though nominally high, were in fact negative. This initiated a continuing process of industrial change and decline.

Thirdly, as a result of these developments, unemployment rose to an average of 12 per cent in EEC countries despite the fact that many *gastarbeiter* had their contracts ended, forcing them to return home. Unemployment figures were especially high in Iberia. This was one example of the way in which the recession increased regional disparities. Areas with old heavy industries were particularly badly hit by the crisis. And Europe was very unsuccessful in generating sufficient new jobs to cope with the problem despite a growing shift into services.

Not surprisingly, the social climate also deteriorated. Social mobility began to decline and there was a resurgence of class conflict. Union membership began to rise and strikes and demonstrations became increasingly common. The expectations produced by the super-boom and the revival of the left combined to make workers very resistant to paying the costs of the depression.

Finally, one of the strange things about the post-1973 crisis was that, while output and employment were stagnant, prices did not fall as they normally do in a recession. Because of the hikes in oil prices firms had no alternative but to pass on the new costs, thus increasing prices. Inflation thus rose from between 4 and 8 per cent in the early 1970s to between 20 and 30 per cent in the second half of the decade, an extremely destabilizing rate. Faced with such 'stagflation', public pressure on governments built up to provide increased welfare and investment in order to offset the crisis. However, this pushed governments into deficit, forcing them to adopt austerity measures to cope with inflation, thereby intensifying the crisis. Financial markets were also badly affected as a number of bank crashes showed. Rising taxation, dwindling savings and interest rates which, though nominally high, were actually lower than the rate of inflation, all added to the overt crisis in the West. This was bitterly resented because it followed such an unprecedented period of growth.

The Eastern crisis of the late 1970s

The communist regimes of the East refused to admit that they too could be affected by a capitalist economic crisis. Yet, while prices apparently remained stable because they were fixed by the State and not by markets, and there was no visible unemployment, in reality, there were economic problems. Because of the downturn, Five-Year Plan targets were rarely met, living standards failed to rise (despite increased subsidies and a flourishing 'black economy'), and, by the end of the decade, total production was falling in some of the satellites.

These satellite states also began to resist pressures for tighter integration, as Chapter 5 shows. Even the USSR found it very galling to have to proffer large discounts on the price of its oil so as to keep the satellites afloat. It was forced to provide some $14 billion in this way, forgoing the chance of selling its oil on the hard currency markets. Such evidence of declining growth showed that the satellite economies were not exempt from the crisis.

Indeed, underneath the surface, the structural situation was in some ways worse than in the West. Politics played a large part in this. One aspect of the problem was that, in order to maintain existing price and job levels in the face of declining growth, Eastern states had to spend an ever increasing percentage of their income on subsidies. This was in addition to the growing costs of military expenditure and to the burden of the food purchases from the West necessitated by agricultural decline and bad harvests. The financing of the Eastern economies was thus very badly affected.

Another aspect was the failing management of the economy. In the 1950s and 1960s there had been much dissatisfaction with the rigidities and poor performance of command economics. This had led to a crop of decentralizing reforms linked with the Soviet economist Lieberman. Unfortunately, these were largely suspended after 1968 when there was a return to conservatism, following the Czech experiment with market socialism in 1968. This frightened the bloc back into the old centralizing ways until the very end of the 1970s.

However, this so-called Brezhnevian complacency was coupled with experiments which exposed the bloc to the worldwide economic storms. While it was considered too dangerous to carry on with reform, many countries tried to rejuvenate their economies, in which productivity and returns on investment were falling, by bringing in Western technology to sustain a 'second industrialization'. This meant trying to redirect trade to the West, encouraging joint ventures and tourism, and borrowing from Western banks and governments. Such aid was available as it seemed a means of offsetting depression in the West by opening up new markets. Owing to Brezhnev's policy of import-led growth, Soviet trade with the West rose by 50 per cent in the 1970s while countries like Poland borrowed billions of dollars to re-equip their plant. The additional short-term expenditure was expected to be offset by long-term revenues from new exports to the West.

However, this policy failed to work. The East found it had few goods which were saleable on the Western market, even when produced with newer equipment. Thus, the satellites were accumulating a mountain of debt for no real gain. By the end of the decade they were facing difficulties with repayment, despite both a forced resort to barter, or 'counter-trade', and a new squeeze on living standards at home. Subsequently, food prices went up and rationing was re-introduced in some areas. Moreover, while there could be nothing like the social unrest found in the West, there were bread riots and more signs of intellectual dissidence.

Thus, by the end of the 1970s, although many of the remarkable economic gains of the post-war period remained, especially in the West where growth never wholly ceased, Europe was facing major economic and social problems. Although a new baseline had been created, the second oil shock meant that the problems were transmitted into the 1980s. These problems also altered the evolution of integration in both parts of the continent and, more directly, that of domestic developments. This was most notable in the West where pluralist politics ensured that the vagaries of economic growth were high on the political agenda.

Further reading

Ambrosius, G. (1989), *Social and Economic History of Western Europe*, Cambridge, Mass.: Harvard University Press.

Armstrong, P. *et al.* (1991), *Capitalism Since 1945 II*, Oxford: Blackwell.

Fowkes, B. (1993), *The Rise and Fall of Communism in Europe*, London: MacMillan.

Morris, L.P. (1984), *Eastern Europe Since 1945*, London: Heineman.

Stearns, P. (1975), *Europe in Upheaval*, London: MacMillan.

Tipton, R. and Aldrich, R. (1988), *Economic and Social History of Europe II*, London: MacMillan.

Van der Wee, H. (1987), *Prosperity and Upheaval*, Harmondsworth: Penguin.

Williams, A. (1987), *West European Economy*, London: Hutchinson.

Woodall, P. and Lovenduski, J. (1987), *Politics and Society in Eastern Europe*, London: MacMillan

2   The states of Western Europe after the war

At the end of the Second World War most European states were in almost as parlous a state as was the European economy. Many of them had been undermined by the First World War, while some of the new nations created at the Peace of Versailles as indicated on Map 1(a) proved weak and divided. Hence, some succumbed to fascist or authoritarian movements. Western responses to this were muted, notably in the Spanish Civil War because the large communist involvement divided the left and alarmed liberals. As a result democracy in Western Europe in 1939 was weak and uncertain.

The Second World War then led to many states being overrun and occupied as Map 1(b) shows. Under occupation normal political life was ended in much of Western Europe even though there were not quite the same horrors as those in the East. Occupation also saw the emergence of new political divisions, as the forces of the Resistance, amongst whom communists were very active, clashed violently with Nazis and collaborationists. Although democracy survived in Britain, which had resisted the Nazi onslaughts, and elsewhere, such countries were exhausted by the conflict. Even neutral states came under pressure.

All this meant that, by 1945, the bases of democratic self-government were extremely weak. With the rise of Communism and the USSR there were fears for the survival of democracy and even of the nation state, given the way in which so many of these had failed prior to 1940. Yet, there was to be a renewal of democracy once the Second World War ended. And if this was not quite as dramatic as the economic changes, it did evolve in three phases, paralleling those in the economic sphere.

These often overlooked domestic political changes were very significant. Not only did they reinforce social and economic change and make possible the new colonial and foreign policy developments of the time, they enabled the nation states of Western Europe to re-establish and develop their position. This was partly achieved by drawing on the fact that the Allied victory restored nationhood in the West, and partly by finding new support in economic management and, especially, welfare provision. The creation of welfare services was a major element in the post-war modernization of the state in Western Europe as was the growing importance of the much debated role of the state in economic management. Equally, as Chapter 3 shows, the states found new support in integration. This was to be a third element of the post-war recovery of Western Europe.

This Chapter, however, seeks to explore these processes of political restoration and development rather than look at specific events. Initially, many Western

Europe after the First World War

NORWAY

SWEDEN

FINLAND

ESTONIA

LATVIA

LITHUANIA

U.S.S.R.

DENMARK

DANZIG

EAST PRUSSIA

GERMANY

POLAND

CZECHOSLOVAKIA

AUSTRIA

HUNGARY

ROMANIA

ITALY

YUGOSLAVIA

ALBANIA

BULGARIA

New states created from old empires. — Pre 1914 Russian frontier. Territorial gains by existing states.

Map 1 (a)

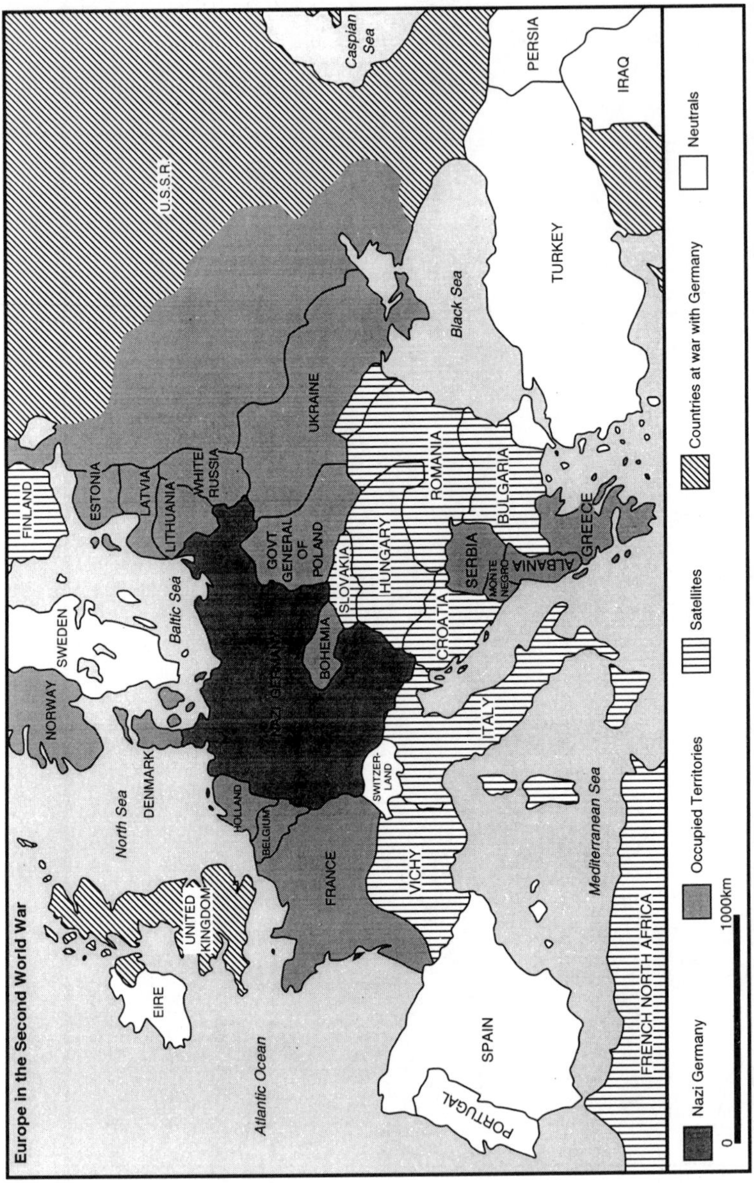

Europe in the Second World War
U.S.S.R.
Caspian Sea
PERSIA
IRAQ
TURKEY
Black Sea
UKRAINE
FINLAND
ESTONIA
LATVIA
LITHUANIA
WHITE RUSSIA
GOVT GENERAL OF POLAND
ROMANIA
BULGARIA
HUNGARY
SLOVAKIA
SERBIA
MONTE NEGRO
ALBANIA
GREECE
CROATIA
BOHEMIA
NAZI GERMANY
SWEDEN
Baltic Sea
NORWAY
DENMARK
North Sea
HOLLAND
BELGIUM
SWITZER-LAND
ITALY
FRANCE
VICHY
Mediterranean Sea
UNITED KINGDOM
EIRE
Atlantic Ocean
SPAIN
PORTUGAL
FRENCH NORTH AFRICA
Nazi Germany
Occupied Territories
Satellites
Countries at war with Germany
Neutrals
0
1000km

Map 1 (b)

states faced severe difficulties after the Second World War. So, during the period of economic reconstruction, there was a first phase of painful restoration. However, it was also a period of renewal since it was then that the democratic states acquired their new welfare basis.

Then, in a second phase, Western politics, constrained by the Cold War and encouraged by the acceptance of the state's new roles, adapted to the new conditions of the boom years by becoming more consensual. Orthodox social democratic parties in particular came to terms with the new mixed economy. However, it was to be some while before they returned to a leading role in most Western states. The return to consensus was slowest and most problematic in France, mainly because of the difficulties of decolonization.

This second phase was not to last and, from the late 1960s onwards, Western politics entered a third and more difficult phase. To begin with, the easy adaptation to the politics of consensus and affluence ironically helped to provoke new forms of left wing protest, symbolized by the events of May 1968 in France. This was to add to the renewed stresses which pluralist politics had to endure in the 1970s. Yet, it was at this time that democracy finally returned to southern Europe, after long periods of authoritarian rule.

Nonetheless, the recession meant immense stresses for Western welfare states. The latter also had to cope with new political movements, declining popular support and intensified social conflict. These developments meant that the political tone of the late 1970s was somewhat bleak, despite the coming of *détente*. Yet, if pluralist democracy came under pressure, it was never abandoned and its new foundations proved strong enough to enable it to take advantage of new opportunities in the 1980s.

The Resistance and the post-war political settlement

The frontiers of Western European states did not change greatly after 1945. As shown in Map 2, the main changes were the cession by Finland of nearly an eighth of its territory to the USSR, the transfer of Istria from Italy to Yugoslavia and, especially, the division of Germany. Returning to old borders and identities aided political reconstruction. Even so, the effects of the war and the emerging threat of the Cold War still made this difficult for most continental states.

The Cold War obviously helped to hold Western European democracy together. However, the restoration of democratic stability had at least three other political causes: the political impetus emerging from the Resistance, the constitutional changes which followed the Second World War and the appeal of new forms of economic and social management which were developed after the war. Together they rebuilt western nations on new, and more secure, pluralist bases, enabling the restored nations to survive the post-war crisis.

The Resistance generated many new political forces and ideas, thus bringing many new people into the political arena. It also helped to end the exclusion of

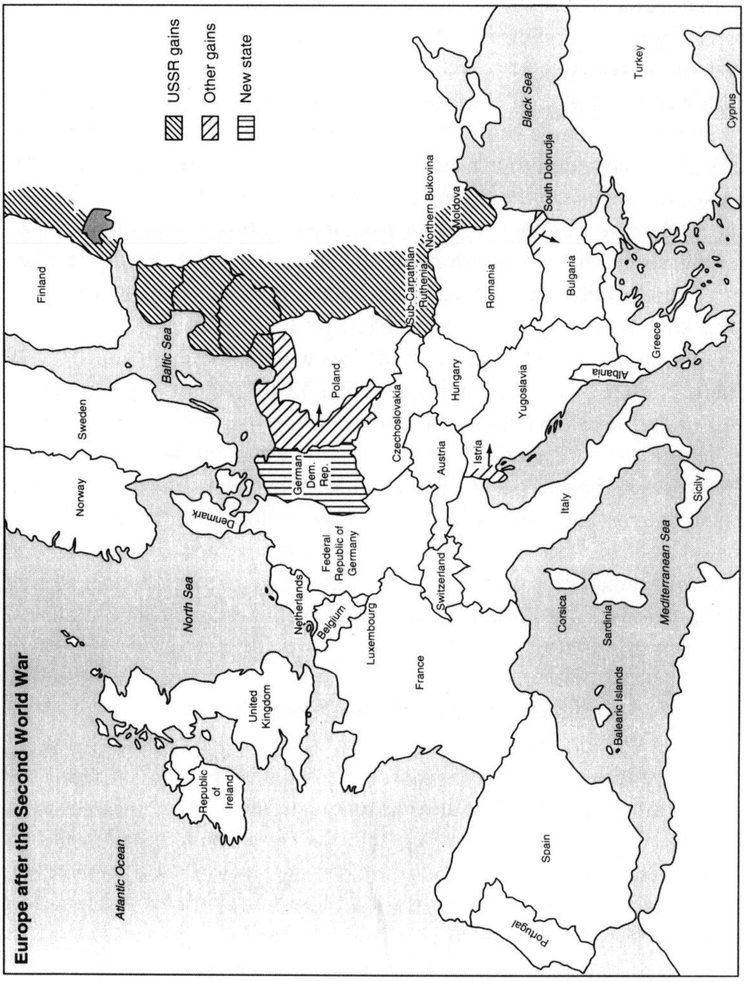
Europe after the Second World War
USSR gains
Other gains
New state
Atlantic Ocean
North Sea
Baltic Sea
Black Sea
Mediterranean Sea
Finland
Sweden
Norway
Denmark
Republic of Ireland
United Kingdom
Netherlands
Belgium
Luxembourg
France
Federal Republic of Germany
German Dem. Rep.
Poland
Czechoslovakia
Sub-Carpathian Ruthenia
Northern Bukovina
Moldova
Romania
Hungary
Austria
Switzerland
Istria
Yugoslavia
Bulgaria
South Dobrudja
Albania
Greece
Turkey
Cyprus
Italy
Corsica
Sardinia
Sicily
Balearic Islands
Spain
Portugal

Map 2

Catholics from the political mainstream, boosting Christian Democratic parties in Italy, Germany, and, more briefly, in France. In France it also generated a new patriotic force in the shape of the Gaullist RPR which questioned the return to the old political system. Nonetheless, the move helped to end the damaging alienation of the Church from political life and gave the nation states involved more appeal and legitimacy.

The Resistance and the beginnings of the Cold War also encouraged co-operation amongst democratic political forces, as well as reshaping the political landscape in other ways. To begin with traditional right wing nationalist forces lost most of their strength because they were compromised by misgovernment and collaboration. However, purges and denazification were, outside France, relatively restrained. Equally few reparations were imposed, and the defeated powers were relatively quickly restored to the Western comity of nations. This meant that extremist parties were not able to feed on post-war rancour in the way they had in the 1920s.

On the other hand, communist parties initially played a significant part in government in Austria, Finland, France and Italy. There they took part in 'tripartite' coalitions with centrist and social democratic parties. This reflected the considerable electoral strength won by communist parties, thanks to their role in the Resistance. However, this was a potential threat to pluralist democracy because the Communists, often directed by Moscow, thought in terms of one party rule.

In the event, as the need to secure Marshall Aid made itself felt, communist parties were gradually driven from office in many countries. This was because the USA was increasingly reluctant to hand over funds to governments linked to Stalin. The marginalization of communist parties, which lasted until the 1980s in some countries, limited but did not remove the threat from the left. However, it forced many Westerners to rally round existing parties and politics. Indeed, this pressure on communist parties posed real problems for Socialist parties in Germany and Italy which had been accustomed to co-operate with the communists. In the case of the latter the more moderate elements of the Socialist Party of Italy (PSI) in fact seceded to form a separate Social Democratic party.

However, in Britain, France, the Netherlands and Switzerland, orthodox socialist parties moved rapidly to drop any communist affiliations and to establish their own right to govern, normally in partnership with centre right parties. Hence, while party competition did not disappear, coalition government became much more common and accepted. Thus, in Austria there was a Grand Coalition between the conservative Österrichische Volkspartie (ÖVP) and the left wing Sozialdemokratische Partei Österreichs (SPÖ), even though, in the early 1930s, the two had fought a civil war. In Italy, the Christian Democrats won a virtual majority of the votes in 1948, but refused to form a one-party government, considering it to be wiser to form a coalition with smaller non-left wing parties. This was an important step towards making governments more representative and pluralist, and hence more acceptable.

The modernization of the state

The combined influence of the Allies and the Resistance also helped to produce a second factor for stabilization, a series of new constitutional changes. Thus, Austria returned to its 1920 constitution, while other defeated countries like Italy and Germany established wholly new and democratic regimes. In Italy, the nation voted narrowly to replace the monarchy by a republic in 1946. A new constitution followed in 1948, which stressed civic rights and regional devolution. The decisions were accepted with surprisingly little dissent. This was also true in Germany where Allied and local fears of a strong central state led in 1949 to the elaboration by a committee, on which the provinces were well represented, of the highly federalist constitutional law or *Grundgesetz*.

Countries which, after liberation, re-emerged on the winning side also underwent constitutional change. In France, where divisions over the war were very bitter, there were large-scale purges of alleged collaborators. Initially, the country was ruled by a provisional government under de Gaulle which pushed through considerable nationalization and modernization. In 1946, however, the politicians turned their backs on his ideas, and devised a constitution giving a great deal of power to a single chamber parliament. This return to the old domination by political parties was rejected by the population and a second, more balanced, constitution only gained narrow acceptance. And, in the event, the new constitution failed to remedy the failings of inter-war French politics. This false start was symbolic of the difficulties which the new IVth Republic was to encounter.

In Belgium the problem was equally acute although it centred on the problem of the monarchy. This was because the left and the French-speaking Walloons forced Leopold III to abdicate because of his alleged collusion with the German occupiers. They also staged their own purge of ordinary collaborators. Both events caused much bitterness amongst Dutch speakers who suffered disproportionately from the purge. This too was a pointer to later difficulties even though the role of the monarchy was successfully redefined by King Baudoin. Constitutional reform in Denmark, in 1953, was much smoother. Nonetheless, such changes did help to give a new tone to the political systems of many continental countries.

As well as creating new regimes there were also new attitudes to democracy and the state. This was the third element in the post-war political settlement. The new constitutions involved new democratic devices such as the new voting system in the FRG, allowing Germans to vote both for a local representative and for a party of their choice. The *Grundgesetz* also helped to provide stability by its restructuring of the Upper House and its introduction of the constructive vote of no confidence. This prevented governments being dismissed when there was no real alternative. Political reform in many Scandinavian countries also introduced single-chamber parliaments, controlled in part by popular referenda and the *ombudsman*, or citizen's representative against the state.

The role of political parties was also enhanced while voting systems were changed. Thus, there was an increasing use of proportional representation while the franchise was considerably extended, including to women in France and Belgium. In Britain, the remaining cases of multiple voting were abolished and the powers of the House of Lords curbed. Taken together, these developments gave the states of Western Europe a wider and more democratic legitimacy.

The war also promoted new attitudes towards the role of the State. Instead of being a bystander, the State was, as shown in Chapter 1, increasingly seen as an active participant in economic and social growth. Whether through planning, as in France and Sweden, nationalization as in Britain and France, collaboration with industry and labour, as in Austria and Switzerland, or in controlling prices, the State became a major factor in economic development, assuming responsibility for the management of the economy in the general interest. The outstanding example of this was the Social Market Economy in the FRG where the state provided housing and other key services in order to remedy the defects of the market forces which ran the rest of the economy.

This was one of the ways in which the State took on the characteristics of a welfare provider. Building on the rudimentary and selective provision of the pre-war years, most states moved from the mid-1940s onwards to provide universal social security as a right and not as an act of charity. Although there were different levels of provision, different ways of financing and different styles of organization, virtually all states began to budget for the provision of a range of services for their populations. Even in Ireland, where Catholic attitudes to state provision had been very hostile, opinions began to change in the 1950s.

The new welfare states embraced such financial benefits as accident insurance, income support, old age pensions, housing benefits, maternity and child allowances and unemployment benefits. They also provided not only free education and free health care, but publicly run school systems, hospitals and housing. Some even provided grants for marriage and house furnishing. By assuring such minimum standards for all social harmony was considerably enhanced. These reversals of pre-war policies were very attractive, as were state involvement in ensuring employment and consultation of workers representatives. They helped to give the political system a crucial new legitimacy and stability. People were more able to see the benefits provided by the State. They were therefore more inclined to think of it and its services as belonging to them, rather than being imposed on them.

Political adaptation in the boom years

By the time the immediate post-war crises were over, the Cold War had become institutionalized and rapid economic growth had set in. Thereafter, most Western democracies were to become increasingly placid. With the development of successful coalition governments and the new availability of social security, parties and politics seemed to count for rather less than in the past. Old political ideas and divisions also lost their bite. The mainstream left came to accept more of the changes already made, giving up their remaining ideas of drastic change. There was also a greater willingness to collaborate. Yet, if politics became somewhat more consensual in many countries, this was not true everywhere. Thus, in France, democracy was to be gravely shaken in 1958 while it was to be overthrown in Greece nine years later.

The increasing prosperity of the 1950s and 1960s meant that many Europeans began to think traditional party politics less important than they had been. The growing importance of lobbying and corporatist consultation of unions and management at home, together with the wider co-operation prevailing within the EEC and the North Atlantic Treaty Organization (NATO) enhanced this trend. Parties began to lose their hold on their electorates. Moreover, with things going well, elections too often seemed less important. Hence, even in a country like Switzerland, whose 'addiction' to its own democratic practices had been greatly strengthened by the way it had ridden out the stresses of the war, turnout at general elections and referenda began to fall.

This trend also reflected changes in the party system. The old allegiance to parties based on religious and other major cleavages began to fade, most notably in the FRG and the Netherlands. Elections became increasingly affected by the media, which tended to stress personalities and image over policies. Parties also sought to widen their appeal beyond the social classes and groups which had originally supported them. This move to broader people's parties meant that small parties could also be squeezed out as they were in Germany. Far right parties were thus marginalized. Even the Gaullist RPR faded away in the early 1950s.

The move towards consensus politics was particularly encouraged by changes on the orthodox left. Because many countries outside Scandinavia were governed by conservative parties the left was forced to adapt in order to win votes. With communism losing even more appeal after the events of 1956 many socialist parties moved away from their Marxist roots towards acceptance of both the West, in its still very real conflict with the East, and of the mixed economy. The parties of the left also began to change their often cautious stance on European integration, which had often been attacked as the product of capitalism and Christian democracy.

The Austrian Socialists renounced Marxism in favour of free market policies in 1957, followed by the Swiss and Germans in 1959. The PSI who had stayed loyal to their war-time alliance with the communists longer than anywhere else, finally broke off its entente with the communists about the same time and began to seek entry into the government circle. After a few years they finally entered the coalition government in 1963. The Danish and Norwegian parties lost their left wings because of such movements. And, in Britain, Gaitskill, and then Wilson, sought to wean the British Labour Party away from its commitment to large-scale nationalization and to move it towards a more managerial and technocratic style of government.

Such switches and remodelling led to a further blurring of ideological divisions between parties. This was a second factor making for enhanced consensus. Conservative and socialist parties thus accepted the introduction of welfare provision and state intervention in the economy as well as the broad lines of foreign policies, especially on Europe. What became crucial was their ability to manage the new society and ensure adequate levels of welfare. This facilitated the Swiss 'Magic Formula' government of 1959 and the German 'Grand Coalition' of 1966–69 which cut across the old divides. Even the Iberian dictatorships lost something of their ideological rigidity as a result of this kind of change.

The French exception

The great exception to these trends, however, came in France. This was partly because of the ineffectiveness of the IVth Republic and partly because of the traumas of decolonization. Despite a notable economic recovery the political system proved both unpopular and unable to deliver stability, producing 25 governments in 12 years. Such weak cabinets, threatened by powerful opposition from both Communists and Gaullists, could not cope with the crises thrown up by attempts to maintain the French empire.

Whereas decolonization caused surprisingly little domestic upheaval in Belgium, Britain and the Netherlands, France experienced extremely bitter political conflicts. The effects of colonial troubles, including a humiliating defeat at communist hands in Indo-China in 1954 and a massive rebellion by Arab nationalists in Algeria after 1956, became the dominant issue in French politics. As Algeria had a large French population and had been regarded as an integral part of metropolitan France since 1830, it was fiercely defended by the *colons*, as the French Algerians were called, by reviving conservative forces in metropolitan France, and by elements in the army. The latter wished to reverse earlier defeats in order to stop the tide of communism undermining the remaining French empire.

By 1958 difficulties with the other Western powers, who were keener on granting autonomy to Algeria, led the three groups to fear a sell out. In May of that year *colons* and their allies therefore swept aside the authorities in Algiers and threatened to invade France in support of a Gaullist takeover. The political parties, fearing civil war, persuaded de Gaulle to become Prime Minister. His price, however, proved to be a new constitution. Realizing their own impotence, and wishing above all to avoid violence, the parties conceded to his demands. This effectively ended the IVth Republic.

In its place emerged the Vth Republic in which parliament lost many of its powers to the executive, and proportional representation was dropped. De Gaulle became the dominant figure in an increasingly Presidentialist regime, as a result of the introduction of popular election after 1965. Yet, although he was regarded by some inside and outside France as an old fashioned authoritarian threat to democracy and decolonization, a fear enhanced by the military overthrow of the Greek state in 1967, this fear proved to be unfounded. Hence, at end of the decade, the French left began to drop its opposition to the new constitution and to embark on a rapid process of modernization. This led to the rise of François Mitterrand as leader of a new Socialist Party (PS) replacing the old movement whose title French Section of the First International still carried echoes of pre-war Marxism.

Prior to this, however, de Gaulle had, in fact, actually moved slowly but inexorably to giving independence to Algeria, a move resented by the *colons* and elements inside the army, but supported by the mass of the population. So, despite the spreading of terrorist campaigns from Algeria to mainland France the colonists were forced to accept the loss of Algeria. Most of them returned home in 1962. Although this gave rise to fears of continuing instability at home, France thereafter became highly stable domestically, with a much modernized political and social system. This owed much to the way people were able to rally round de Gaulle's vision of the primacy of French interests. This vision as shown in Chapter 3, was to play a major part in the development of the Community. It also had a somewhat destabilizing effect on the international fronts, leading to a partial loosening of links with NATO in 1966.

Problems on the left

France both mirrored and contradicted general European trends during the 1960s. On the one hand, it reflected the continuing modernization of society and politics. On the other, it brought to power a conservative regime at a time when Europe was moving somewhat in the other direction. So, while the politics of the time remained relatively calm, outside Greece, the 1960s saw first a revival of the traditional left, and then a major questioning of the new society which had emerged in the boom years. This social change was to help to undermine the authoritarian regimes in both Iberia and Greece.

During the 1960s established left wing parties, profiting from their new moderation, began to return to government as was already the case in Scandinavia. Thus, after 13 years in the wilderness, the modernized British Labour Party won two general elections in 1964 and 1966. In the FRG, Brandt's reformed Social Democratic Party (SDP) first joined a grand coalition in 1966 and then won power on its own account in 1969. The following year the Austrian Socialists under Kreisky also formed a successful majority government. Moreover, as already noted, the PSI had entered the Italian government in December 1963. Once inside it sought to move the coalitions, of which it became a regular member, towards a more social democratic stance. Ireland and Greece were two other countries where the conservative hold on power was broken at this time.

However, in Greece, although the former communist sympathizers were largely eclipsed by the new Centre Union (CU) of George Papandreou, its claims to power were resisted by conservative elements around the monarchy. Hence, although the CU won elections in 1963 and 1964, it was unable to push through its social reforms or to control the army. Subsequently, when it looked as though the 1967 elections would produce a clear majority for the increasingly radical CU, over a splinter cabinet supported by the King, the army staged a *putsch* which led to the suppression first of parliamentary democracy and then, after an abortive royalist counter coup, of the monarchy as well.

Elsewhere, the late 1960s were to see a rather different sort of challenge to the prevailing style of mainstream social democracy. This was partly because social democratic governments did not go beyond a number of liberal reforms. Such timidity was, like the growing evidence of economic difficulties, a cause of considerable disappointment to many of the younger, better educated white collar voters produced by the post-war boom. They were increasingly free of old allegiances and were beginning to question the direction society was taking. Many questioned the consensus of the 1950s and 1960s, and looked for large-scale policy changes reflecting their radically new economic and political orientation. Such unhappiness with the post-war *status quo* first showed itself in a growing willingness to vote for new parties, as people did in Britain for the reviving Liberal Party and in the Netherlands for Democrats '66.

1968 and the challenge to post-war democracy

By the end of the decade, however, things were to go much further. As already noted, student unrest over the failure of university provision to keep pace with demand sparked off a challenge to the new social order: its consumerism, its tolerance of the Vietnam War and its undemocratic nature. The first signs of this appeared in 1965–66 with difficulties in Italian universities and unease in the FRG over the Grand Coalition. Then, in 1967, troubles on the Paris-Nanterre campus began to mobilize the Parisian student body. Finally, in May 1968 there were large-scale riots in Paris following the arrival of the police on previously exempt University premises. Clashes with riot police led the students to take over and defend the whole Left Bank university quarter.

Police brutality also helped to stimulate massive labour unrest and demonstrations throughout the country. Most University Faculties were occupied and taken over by earnest 'teach ins' on alternatives to the present discontents. More significantly, some nine million workers soon went on strike because of their own economic and political needs. At the same time a range of middle class groups began to challenge the social and political *status quo*, symbolizing their alienation from the heavy handed Gaullist regime. The threat of anarchy involved in these events led many protestors to change their minds. Thus, the Gaullists actually won a huge electoral victory the next month. This and a new law on University reform helped to restore calm.

However, the events of 1968 were to have continuing effects. Even in France they helped to undermine de Gaulle's own position, leading to his manufactured resignation the following year after a defeat in an unnecessary referendum on local government reform. In the FRG the Extra-Parliamentary Opposition (APO) became a major thorn in the flesh of the SPD–FDP coalition government set up in October 1969. By the early 1970s the new government began to crack down. This encouraged the APO to feel they had to choose between accepting an unsatisfactory system or trying to overthrow it by force. It was this which was to help produce often violent terrorist groups like the Baader–Meinhoff group. Finally, in Italy there was a 'hot autumn' of often violent protest in 1969 with large-scale dislocation of universities and much industrial unrest. While this won many concessions for labour it did not, any more than in Germany, satisfy all the extremists. Some, therefore, formed the Red Brigades in August 1970 and launched a terrorist campaign against the state.

Elsewhere the effects of 1968 were somewhat less marked, though trade unions and the alternative New Left movements which emerged after 1968 did benefit from the new climate of questioning and protest. The general cultural scene began to alter with the breakdown of old certainties. Liberal social legislation was also often encouraged. This was true of much of the rest of northern Europe. However, in Belgium the wave of militancy encouraged Flemish language activism, which had begun earlier in the decade, starting an enforced process of separating the country into self-contained language communities. Some of these factors were also at work in southern Europe. In Greece, the military government had failed to attract much popular support. While some elements were willing to consider liberalization, others were not. Hence, student demonstrations in November 1973 were brutally repressed. This proved to be the beginning of the end for the junta. Public opinion was outraged and the junta disintegrated. A new hard-line leadership was brought to power by an internal coup. Its manoeuvring against President Makarios prompted a Turkish invasion of Cyprus which the army was unable and unwilling to resist. Humiliated, the regime could only beg traditional politicians to retake power. Democracy was restored fairly rapidly thereafter, with support from Europe.

In Portugal, the appalling costs of the unsuccessful wars in Angola and Mozambique alienated army and society. Both saw the need for democratization and decolonization. Faced with these decisions, Caetano's ineffective authoritarian regime peacefully surrendered in the face of a threatened *putsch* by junior officers in April 1974. The Armed Forces Movement (MFA) was welcomed with wild enthusiasm, but though it withdrew from Africa, it proved unable to achieve stable government at home. In fact, it opened the way to communist influence and prompted a social revolution in 1974–75 involving land reform and workers' control of factories. Then, in November, a coup by moderate elements in the army under General Eanes turned the tide back towards constitutional government.

In Spain socio-economic modernization, facilitated by the Francoist regime, played an important part in political change. As society developed and economic links with the rest of Europe increased, Francoist political controls became increasingly irksome. Restiveness amongst students, workers and economic interests was accompanied by a withdrawal of support by the Church. The regime's technocrats who had been responsible for pushing economic modernization also became cooler to the failing leadership. Hence, Franco's death in November 1975 was followed by a cautious liberalization under Juan Carlos, Franco's handpicked monarch. This process was speeded up in July 1976 when the King Juan Carlos opted for democracy. He appointed Adolfo Suarez as Prime Minister and thus opened the way for democratic political forces to take part in a gradual transition to constitutional democracy, which allowed Spain to come into line with general European trends. However, this Iberian revival was not to be the end of the problems of pluralist democracy in Western Europe where the recession added to the difficulties caused by the New Left.

The political impact of recession

By the time the return to democracy was underway, Western Europe was in the grip of the oil crisis. The economic effects of 1968 were thus intensified so that the 1970s were a period of new challenges and considerable stress for democratic governments. There were at least three elements to these difficulties: devising effective policy responses to the recession, facing up to continuing challenges from the left and terrorism, and trying to deliver on a whole range of new issues in a context of marked political volatility. Here the expansion of the state and the successes of the left stimulated new right wing dissidence. Pluralist politics, in other words, ensured that economic problems were both visible and much debated.

Coping with the new demands and new movements of increasingly pluralist politics, and in the midst of economic crisis, proved extraordinarily difficult. This was the first element in the new stresses on Western European states. Governments were especially tested over welfare because of the rising costs of unemployment pay. Hence, it was not surprising that there began to be talk of the State being overloaded and asked to do more than it was capable of doing.

The rapidity with which governments came and went certainly began to increase noticeably, as each one unsuccessfully sought to master the crisis.

Falling growth rates, rising inflation and spiralling unemployment called for new policies. Some governments tried to stimulate demand, as was the case with the Heath government's U-turn in 1972–73, and the Norwegian Labour minority government between 1972 and 1977. This was also the case in Ireland where governments of all complexions sought to borrow their way out of trouble. In Ireland, however, as elsewhere, this very often increased inflation and government deficits without achieving much in terms of growth. Only Sweden seemed to be coping reasonably well with the recession.

Other governments which had seen reflationary policies fail, were then forced to follow the German example and seek to control inflation through pay restraints, tax increases and the restructuring of ailing industries. This was true of the governments of Wilson in Britain and Barre in France. In neither case, however, did government policies really succeed in reversing economic decline. As the decade drew to its close the second oil shock undid much of the little progress already achieved. Government finances, for instance, remained very much in the red.

In other words, even if the State had grown as indeed it did during the 1970s, accounting for 40.5 per cent of the GDP in the Netherlands in 1980 compared with only 31.7 per cent in 1970, this did not mean it was free of problems. With the costs of unemployment pay rising and hard-hit social groups demanding further support from the State, European welfare states came under great pressure as government revenues fell because of the recession. The Dutch deficit thus rose to 10 per cent of the GDP by 1983 while many observers felt that the State was becoming overloaded. It was being asked to do too much, in unpropitious circumstances, and without the political support of previous decades.

The second element in the new situation was partly a reflection of this failure to come up with successful policies of economic management. The continuing crisis left unions and working class activists, whose position had often strengthened after 1968, extremely dissatisfied. As a result, the 1970s were a period of increased class conflict and labour unrest, Britain and Italy suffering particularly. In the case of the latter the problems were underlined by terrorism which reached a paroxysm in 1978 with the murder of former Prime Minister Aldo Moro. Governments thus had to cope with an increasingly acute problem of law and order.

At the same time the new left wing surge after 1968 was adding new issues to crowded political agendas. If few countries suffered the disruption caused by the European issue in Britain and Norway, movements in defence of the environment, feminism and peace and against nuclear power and nuclear weapons all added to pressures on government. Even more successful countries like Switzerland and the FRG experienced this in the middle years of the decade. Regional issues also flared up in the 1970s, often in violent form, as economic pressures exacerbated already bitter divisions. This was true in the Basque country, in Britain, in the Swiss Jura, in Ulster and especially in Belgium.

The surge of left wing activism and terrorism was one factor in producing a resurgence on the far right. This also derived from concern about the way the international economy and an expanding state were pressing on traditional societies, especially when this brought in large numbers of *gastarbeiter*. So, on the one hand, the Scandinavians (like the Austrians) saw the emergence of anti-tax progress parties while, on the other, movements such as Schwarzen-burg's National Action in Switzerland sought to restrict the number of immigrants in the country.

In many north-western countries migrants were seen as a threat to identity and jobs, even though they often came from south-western Europe. In the event the recession was to lead some of the major admitting countries to end contracts, thereby sending guest workers home. This reduced the number of foreign workers and helped to reduce both unemployment and the search for scapegoats. Nonetheless, the threat from the right remained as a series of bomb outrages in Italy made all too clear.

Guiding states through these difficult times was anything but easy because of the third element in the crisis, the growing electoral volatility. In the past people tended to vote consistently for parties which represented their social class. However, by the 1970s this was no longer the case. Indeed, by then one Swedish voter in five was a 'floater' whose vote could not be relied upon. Moreover, because votes could easily be switched, new parties were encouraged. Thus, in 1973, the number of parties represented in the Danish Parliament shot up from five to ten. This made it harder to obtain a solid majority. Even in Britain there were four general elections in nine years as minor parties did particularly well. They helped to bring down the Labour government in 1979 over the devolution issue. Parties had further to alter their programmes and appeal in order to cope. Thus, on the French right, the Gaullists had to share power with the Giscardians after 1974.

Because of the changes in the 1960s, socialist governments bore the brunt of these problems. This was true, for instance, in Austria, Britain, Germany, the Netherlands and Portugal. However, their hold on power was often tenuous and changing. In Britain the Labour Party unexpectedly lost the 1970 election. A similar phenomenon can be seen in Italy where the Partilo Communista Italiano (PCI) felt it necessary to try and support the Christian Democrat led coalition because of the threat from the ultra-left. More remarkably, in Scandinavia the Social Democrats lost power in Denmark, Norway and, exceptionally, in Sweden, where they had been in power since 1932. Since such uncertain socialist leadership did not lead to satisfactory solutions, other options began to be canvassed after the recession was given a new boost in 1978–79.

So, while their stability was never in real danger of disappearing, there is no doubt that the modernized Western democracies were tested by the crisis of the 1970s. And, if their post-war foundations were still intact, the economic and political strains resulting from the crisis were to carry over into the early 1980s. However, before then the general unease caused by the recession had also helped to inflict a severe check on the development of the EC. It was also to play a part in the uncertain evolution of the Eastern bloc and its relations with the West.

Further reading

Carr, R. and Fusi, J. (1981), *Spain: Dictatorship to Democracy*, London: Allen and Unwin.
Caute, D. (1988), *Sixty Eight*, London: Hamish Hamilton.
Childs, D. (1993), *Britain Since 1945*, London: Routledge.
Clogg, R. (1992), *Greece: A Brief History*, London: Cambridge Uuniversity Press.
Dorfman, G. and Duignan, P. (1991), *Politics in Western Europe*, Stanford, Cal.: Hoover Institute.
Fulbrook, M. (1991), *Concise History of Germany*, Oxford: Oxford University Press.
Ginsborg, P. (1990), *History of Contemporary Italy*, Harmondsworth: Penguin.
Keating, M. (1994), *The Politics of Modern Europe*, Aldershot: Edward Elgar.
Larkin, M. (1988), *France Since the Popular Front*, Oxford: Clarendon.
Milward, A. (1994), *The European Rescue of the Nation State*, London: Routledge.
Newton, G. (1978), *The Netherlands: An Historical and Cultural Survey*, London: Benn.
Opello, O. (1991), *Portugal from Monarchy to Liberal Democracy*, Boulder, Col.; Westview.
Smith, G. (1988), *Politics in Western Europe*, 5th edn, Aldershot: Gower.
Urwin, D. (1990), *Western Europe Since 1945*, 5th edn, London: Longman.

3   The development of European integration

The launching and development of the European Union (EU) has been a uniquely ambitious and highly complex achievement of post-1945 Europe. Although the story of European integration essentially begins in the years following the Second World War, the intellectual ancestry of the European movement can be traced back to the 14th century and has its roots in the early ideas of universalists who – as early as 1306 – suggested a federation of states as a defence against outside threats. Indeed, it can be argued that the cradle of European unity was the old Roman Empire having integrated – in a fashion – the whole of Christian Europe. However, it was not until after the First World War that the concept of 'unifying' Europe attracted widespread attention and support. During the inter-war years several attempts were made to promote European unity to overcome enmity between states, most notably by Count Coudenhove-Kalergi, an aristocrat of the Habsburg Empire, who founded the Pan-European Union in 1922. This was followed, in 1929, by a call for a European Federal Union, proposed by the French Foreign Minister, Aristide Briand and backed by his German counterpart, Gustav Stresemann. Unfortunately, their efforts were drowned by the rising wave of nationalism and fascism that gripped Europe in the 1930s. However, in 1945, in the face of unprecedented physical destruction and human loss, political leaders searched for a new European structure that would safeguard peace and provide a stable framework for the economic reconstruction of the devastated European continent.

In this Chapter the developments of European integration are traced from its beginnings in the late 1940s, when a multitude of international organizations were set up, which, though unconnected, paved the way for the Treaty of Rome, setting up the EEC in 1957. It is argued that, despite notable achievements in the 1950s and 1960s, European integration has not been an easy process. The EEC suffered a serious setback in the 1970s as a direct result of economic and monetary instability in the international world order. Disagreements about how to overcome these difficulties emerged among member states and further progress in the integration process came to an abrupt, if temporary, halt.

First moves towards European unity
The Second World War left a once powerful Europe economically crippled, psychologically demoralized and politically impotent. A combination of forces, which were not mutually exclusive but rather complemented and reinforced each other, made co-ordination and unification among former enemies a powerful

imperative. Firstly, there was the prevailing material devastation. Basic economic activities had to be reconstructed against the background of food shortages and fuel crises, exacerbated by harvest failures and a bitterly cold winter in 1946–47. It became clear that this enormous task required conjoint efforts.

Secondly, the Cold War drew West European countries closer together. Politicians became increasingly alarmed about communist subversion, particularly after the Prague coup in the spring of 1948 and following the Berlin crisis of 1948–49.

Thirdly, the political mood of the time was that of a deeply felt repugnance towards the horrors of wars. This gave rise to a new 'Europeanism' which was to replace historic rivalries between European states and overcome the unfettered nationalism of the past.

This new thinking was reflected by calls for closer co-ordination between European states and, as a result, a number of international organizations were set up in rapid succession. Following a speech by Winston Churchill in Zurich in September 1946 supporting the creation of a United States of Europe, the various movements for European unity led, in May 1948, to the Hague Congress of Europe with several hundred delegates from 18 countries (as well as the USA and Canada as observers) demonstrating clearly the widespread interest in unity among European countries. It was at this Congress, however, that a split opened between those who advocated a limited form of co-ordination as distinct from the more radical view held by 'federalists' who wanted to see nothing less than the merging of European countries in a federal United Europe with its own institutions empowered to make decisions equally binding for all member states. What eventually emerged from these debates was a compromise leading to the creation of the Council of Europe on 5 May 1949, which clearly fell short of the ambitious objectives articulated by federalists. Nevertheless, the Council provided a new forum for debate between its members on social, legal and cultural matters. Perhaps its most significant success was the creation of the 'European Convention for the Protection of Human Rights and Fundamental Freedoms', adopted in November 1950, laying down a minimum standard of human rights to be applied in member states.

First initiatives on economic co-ordination originated outside Europe. In June 1947 the USA, in the wake of the Cold War as Chapter 4 shows, attempted to establish a firm political and economic relationship between itself and Western Europe by offering a massive aid programme (Marshall Plan) to assist Europe's economic recovery. As a result, the first post-war European organ of economic co-operation, the Organization for European Economic Cooperation (OEEC), was set up by 17 countries in April 1948 to assure the distribution of the joint recovery fund and to coordinate investment programmes. While the new organization was too large and too diverse to encourage any degree of integration in Europe, it nevertheless set the stage for initial moves towards European unification and made an important contribution to the economic reconstruction of post-war Europe by progressively removing quota restrictions on trade and by liberalising exchange rate control. In 1960, the OEEC, by then having a worldwide membership, extended its activities to include development aid for Third World countries and was renamed Organization for Economic Co-operation and Development (OECD) concentrating on economic research and development.

Military integration proceeded simultaneously with the establishment of closer economic and political ties. In 1947, Britain and France signed the Treaty of Dunkirk, which, although originally targeted against threats from a reviving Germany, became the nucleus of a West European collective security system in the face of (perceived) Soviet aggression. With the extension of Anglo–French co-ordination to include the Benelux countries, the treaty soon gave birth to the Brussels Pact (1948) and was later (1954) transformed into the West European Union (WEU). The need to secure US military commitment to the defence of Western Europe led, in 1949, to the creation of NATO, originally comprising ten European countries as well as the USA and Canada. It was later to include Greece (1952), Turkey (1952), Germany (1955) and Spain (1982), as shown in Map 3 (see p. 176).

However, despite the ambitious objectives of some of these organizations, their structure remained merely intergovernmental, that is to say co-operation was clearly defined and controlled by the participating member states without impinging on national sovereignty. Consequently, the collective negotiating capacity of these organizations remained weak, because no centre of power – independent of member states – was created. As has been noted, fundamental differences between countries and individuals in their approach to European unity had already emerged at the Hague Congress, when several countries had resisted the call for 'pooling' their sovereignty in a supranational entity. The so-called 'federalists', however, believed that true integration required member states to cede their sovereignty, at least in part, to a supranational authority empowered to make decisions on behalf of participating members.

The birth of the EC
The intention to move closer together was common to all West European countries, but opinions differed as to the extent and depth of integration. For Italy, and particularly the FRG, European integration offered a way of reha-bilitating themselves and finding acceptance by their former enemies. For these countries the venture was a low-risk, high pay-off proposition. For France, a unified Europe could provide a route to establish French leadership on the continent. For the Benelux countries closer ties with their neighbours were geo-graphically unavoidable, economically sound and politically prudent. These countries already had experience in integration, having established a custom

union of their own in 1944. The affairs of virtually all these countries were handled by committed Europeans, for example Joseph Beck of Luxembourg, Paul-Henri Spaak of Belgium, Alcide de Gasperi of Italy, Robert Schuman of France and Konrad Adenauer of Germany. The latter three shared experiences: all were catholics and all had been born near the political frontiers of their respective countries. Beck, Spaak and the Dutch Foreign Minister J. W. Beyen had all been in exile. Britain and the Nordic countries, however, were reluctant to commit themselves to ties which would go beyond economic co-ordination and con-sultative political agreement. This reflected their different experiences of war, or occupation.

By the early 1950s, however, the completely new concept of pooling national sovereignty, commonly referred to as integration, had taken root. Jean Monnet, a committed European and head of the French economic planning, and Robert Schuman, the French Foreign Minister, put forward an ingenious plan, which at the same time was characterized by its beguiling simplicity: namely a proposal to pool both French and German coal and steel resources under a supranational High Authority and eliminate all tariff barriers between the two countries. These two men hoped that, by putting war-making capacity under a supranational authority, military conflict between France and Germany would not only be 'unthinkable, but materially impossible'. Although an economic project, the political objectives behind the plan were blatantly obvious. Hence the Schuman Plan – as it came to be known – was only a first step in the realization of a vision of a united Europe which had Franco–German reconciliation at its centre.

It is difficult to appreciate today both the boldness with which the plan was devised and the relative speed with which its objectives were carried out. Yet, it would be wrong to suggest that the plan, although clearly federally inspired, was solely born out of a strong belief in the values of integration. Distinct national interests were of equal importance in the creation of this common market of coal and steel with clear economic advantages for all participants. However, the demand to 'pool' national sovereignty in one crucial sector of the economy, must have come as a psychological shock to countries which had been engaged in a bloody war less than five years before.

The impact of the proposal was all the more dramatic, as Schuman – on 9 May 1950 – announced the plan to an overcrowded press conference rather than submitting it as a governmental report. Both the USA and Germany had been informed about the plan prior to the conference, although Britain had been kept in the dark. Within a few weeks, on 29 June 1950, a conference was convened, chaired by Jean Monnet. Both the Benelux countries and Italy responded positively to the invitation to join the new venture, while Great Britain declined, since she felt unable to commit herself to the principle of supranational authority. Within a year a treaty setting up the European Coal and Steel Community

(ECSC) was drawn up and signed on 18 April 1951. It came into force on 23 July 1952 and was to run for a period of 50 years.

Decision-making powers in the new organization were given to a nine-member High Authority. This, the executive organ, was jointly appointed by member states and charged with the introduction and maintaining of a common market in coal and steel. Its activities were scrutinized by a parliamentary assembly of 78 members chosen from the six national parliaments. A council of ministers, representing the six member states, decided on proposals submitted by the High Authority. A court of justice completed the first supranational structure and – as it transpired later – became the pioneer of other ventures in sectoral integration.

Encouraged by the success of the ECSC, several new proposals were put forward, all stimulated by the Schuman Plan. If integration could be successful in coal and steel, why not extend it to other economic areas, for example agriculture, transport or health? However, before any of these plans could materialize, world events put more urgent projects into sharper relief: the Soviet Union tightened its control on Eastern Europe and, with the outbreak of the Korean War in 1950, the US Secretary of State demanded that Germany should contribute to Western defence. In these circumstances the question of German re-armament, a focus of public debate since the autumn of 1949, gained a new dimension. However, the idea of a remilitarized Germany was enough to shock many Europeans, while national resistance to re-armament was equally strong.

In the event, France came up with what appeared to be a solution. It drew up plans for a European Defence Community (EDC) under joint European control. The proposal was to be known as the 'Pleven Plan' after the French Prime Minister René Pleven. The structure proposed for the EDC was a striking parallel to the ECSC in both objectives and methods: the new unified European army was to be made up of small national contingents from each member state, but was to be put under a common authority, with the institutions created under the ECSC treaty having decision-making power over them. Negotiations for the new EDC were completed in February 1951 in Paris and the treaty was signed in May 1952 pending ratification by member states. In an attempt to provide the necessary control for the army, a 'European Political Community', a project to broaden political and foreign policy cooperation, was also proposed.

Ratification took time. Finally, four countries approved the treaty. Italy and France, however, had unstable coalition governments and were fearful of provoking defeat by bringing the matter to the vote. In the event, on 30 August 1954, the French National Assembly, rejected the treaty by 319 to 264 votes. The idea of an independent German army was still unacceptable to France as was the transfer to a supranational institution of national sovereignty in a highly sensitive national area. The fate of the EDC treaty tellingly laid bare the resistance which still existed in some member states to the pooling of political and defensive capabilities. As to the question of German re-armament, an alternative approach was taken in the form of enlarging the Brussels Treaty Organization of 1948 into the WEU with Italy and Germany as new members.

The launching and development of the EC

The defeat of the EDC meant that integrationist forces had suffered a setback. In fact, Monnet, who had been President of the ECSC High Authority, resigned in February 1955, disappointed by the turn of events. However, many leading politicians in Western Europe, deeply committed to the goal of integration, were convinced that there must be no delay in giving integration a new impulse and agitated for further moves towards closer unity. In addition, world events conspired to bring home the urgency of closer ties between West European states. The uprisings in the East as Chapter 5 shows, as well as the abortive Anglo–French Suez expedition of 1956, further underlined the urgent need for concerted action. In view of the unfavourable attitude France had taken towards the EDC, it was felt by some member states, particularly the Benelux countries, that unification in the economic field was more practical – as had been shown by the success of the ECSC – and would cause less controversy than political integration.

The new impetus for a *rélance européenne* was above all due to Paul-Henri Spaak, the Belgian Foreign Minister and an active servant of European institutions, who proposed the setting up of a European Economic Community. He received enthusiastic support from both the ECSC Common Assembly as well as from Jean Monnet. The Belgian proposal was discussed at a meeting of ECSC foreign ministers held at Messina in June 1955 and it was decided to create a market free from customs duties and other restrictions. An inter-governmental committee, headed by Spaak, was established. This met over a period of nine months to develop the scheme. On the basis of its findings, a report, called after Spaak, was drawn up and presented in April 1956. At the Venice meeting in May 1956 the foreign ministers of the six member states of the ECSC approved the report and decided to begin inter-governmental negotiations to which other European countries were invited.

However, enthusiasm for the project was limited to the original 'Six'. Although Britain had sent a representative to the preliminary discussions, he was withdrawn early on. The more the talks of the 'Six' concentrated on the creation of a customs union, the more Britain grew reluctant to participate in the project. The rift became clearly apparent during the first session of the 'groups of experts' in November 1955, when Spaak insisted that only those heads of delegations who supported proposals for a customs union should take part in the discussion. Britain, unable to give any assurances to that effect, but fearing that its preferential trading system with the Commonwealth would not be sufficient, responded to the threat of a European 'common market' by proposing a much looser trading organization to include all OEEC states.

Britain believed that an industrial free trade area which would exclude agriculture would be attractive to some of the 'Six'. However, Britain had clearly misjudged the situation. The British plan was rejected as an attempt to stall negotiations for closer unity through economic integration. The 'Six' remained undeterred in their efforts to create a European Economic Community based on the principle of the existing ECSC. By the time the OEEC Council had agreed in October 1957 to conduct negotiations on Britain's plan for a wider free trade area, the EEC negotiations had been completed.

On 25 March 1957, in Rome, the 'Six' signed two treaties; the European Economic Community (EEC) and, on the same day, the European Atomic Energy Authority (EURATOM). Ratification took place by mid-December and the treaties came into force on 1 January 1958. As a direct response, Britain, Norway, Sweden, Denmark, Austria, Portugal, Ireland and Switzerland (later joined by Finland) set up the 'European Free Trade Area' (EFTA) in 1959. This was a much looser organization, based firmly on the principle of inter-governmental arrangements, never trespassing on the area of sovereignty.

The Treaty of Rome – consisting of a Preamble and six Parts which together comprise 248 articles or provisions deemed necessary for the creation and functioning of the new community – is effectively the constitution of the EEC. It is unique in that it has created the supremacy of community law over national law, thus giving birth to a new legal regime. Of prime importance is the Preamble which lays down the desire of the Treaty's 'founding fathers' for an 'ever closer union'. The immediate objectives of the Treaty of Rome were, however, economic: namely the establishment of a customs union. This implied a market resting on four fundamental freedoms: the free movements of (a) goods; (b) people; (c) capital and (d) services. It was agreed that the customs union was to be completed over a 'transitional period' of 12 years with a possible extension to 15. During that time, all internal duties and all quotas on trade were to be abolished and a Common External Tariff (CET) with non-EC countries would be established.

Rapid economic growth meant that the customs union was achieved 18 months ahead of schedule on 1 July 1968 and at the same time the CET was applied to the rest of the world. The Treaty is very rigid in respect of the customs union, laying down a timetable and spelling out the provisions necessary for the completion of the customs union. To that end the Treaty contains a backbone of precise commitments. However, all other provisions which were necessary to make the common market function properly were only given in vague outline. As to the free movement of capital, right of establishment and the creation of common or harmonized policies in certain crucial areas such as agriculture and transport, the Treaty confines itself to general statements of intent and to indications of the instruments that were to achieve the desired goal. It was left to member states to work out the precise details and to formulate and implement policies at the appropriate time. Given both the speed with which the EEC was established, following the failure of the EDC, and the already apparent difference in political philosophy amongst the member states, it was highly unlikely that, apart from the customs union, more detailed statements of actions could have been expected.

However, the Treaty did call for the development of common policies and rules in many areas of economic and social life. This required the setting up of a supranational institutional machinery which was modelled on that of the ECSC. As a result, a Commission, consisting of one or two representatives from each member state (depending on its size) was given the task of initiating proposals. A Council of Ministers (made up of representatives from member states) was established to take decisions on the Commission's proposals by majority vote or, on important issues, unanimously. An Assembly, later known as the European Parliament (EP), was created to advise and supervise, and a Court of Justice was founded as the final arbiter of EEC law. There now existed three 'communities', the ECSC, EURATOM and the EEC, all of which were administered by a separate set of 'supranational' bodies thereby duplicating some of the institutions. These institutions were later combined in the Merger Treaty of 8 April 1965 and the three communities were henceforth referred to as the European Communities (EC).

Crises in the 1960s

During the 1960s the work of the EC had been focused essentially on the progressive achievement of the customs union, the completion of which enabled the EC to negotiate as a single voice in multi-lateral trade conferences, such as the General Agreement on Trade and Tariffs (GATT). In parallel, the Common Agricultural Policy (CAP), regarded as an essential ingredient to cement European unity, was set up in 1967 based on common prices and protective devices at EC frontiers to protect EC produce against cheaper agricultural imports from abroad.

However, the early success of the first formative years of the EC also brought tensions. Three major crises took place in the 1960s: the first began in 1961 with clashes over the formulation and development of the CAP. The principle of a common agricultural policy had been included in the gambit of the Treaty of Rome as a result of French pressure, but it had been left to member states to work out and choose the specific measures of integrating agriculture during the transitional phase. While the Treaty defined the objectives of the CAP (Art. 39), offered several options for the organization of agricultural markets (Art. 44) and determined the means by which the EC institutions were to formulate guidelines and regulations for the CAP (Art. 43), it failed to address essential details. The vagueness of the Treaty in this respect made for different interpretations at a later stage leading to bitter conflicts between agricultural exporting countries and the industrial providers of the EC. This conflict was partially resolved in January

1962, after several years of intensive debate, when the following basic principles for the price and market policy of the CAP, the 'Agricultural Code', were agreed: (a) the principle of a unified internal market with common prices permitting free circulation of goods; (b) the principle of EC preference ensured by external protection; and (c) the principle of financial solidarity through a common fund to support a minimum price, export rebates and structural improvement.

The second crisis concerned British membership. The negotiations surrounding the early post-war attempts in European integration had already marked the beginning of a division between Britain and the six founding members of the EC. Very soon after the launching of the EC, Britain realized that it had declined to participate in what turned out to be a very powerful economic unit. By the early 1960s, Britain was quite isolated and caught between its declining empire on the one hand and the new powerful EC on the other from which it was excluded. However, it was not a conversion to the European ideal which prompted MacMillan in 1961 to apply for membership of the EEC, only two years after its own brainchild, EFTA, had begun to operate. National economic consideration motivated Britain to approach its European neighbours. Indeed, doubt over Britain's real intentions surfaced when Britain demanded safeguards for its agriculture and its links with the Commonwealth, as well as for the remaining EFTA states, which would not, or could not, join the EC. In the event, Britain's bid for membership to the Community was rejected by France in January 1963. Since new members required the unanimous approval of the 'Six', de Gaulle's veto could be imposed, but it did not lessen the crisis in the EC, as the other five partners were visibly angry at de Gaulle's unilateral action. Britain's second application for membership, in 1967, did not fare any better. De Gaulle, during a press conference in May of that year, made clear what his attitude was likely to be and indeed, the negotiations had hardly got off the ground when, in November 1967, the French President predicted that Britain's entry into the EEC would damage the EC structures. Although the British application was not withdrawn, it was quite clear that, as long as de Gaulle remained, British entry would be quite impossible. It was only after the transitional phase ended and de Gaulle had resigned that entry negotiations could be successfully concluded.

The third major conflict between Community member states during the 1960s is best described as a constitutional crisis since it seriously undermined the effective functioning of the EC's institutions and paralysed EC activities for several months. Between 1958 and 1965 virtually all decisions had been subject to unanimous voting. However, the Treaty of Rome provided for majority voting in certain areas, as from January 1966. This issue became embroiled with a dispute over the EC's proposal for funding the CAP for the period between July 1965 and the end of the EC's transitional period. The 'Agricultural Code' agreement mentioned previously had provided for funding only until 1965. The Commission therefore proposed a complex budgetary mechanism for the allocation of what was to be known as 'Own Resources' by which both the Commission itself and the European Parliament would enhance their power. The Council on the other hand, through the introduction of majority voting to replace unanimity in certain cases, would significantly lose in terms of influence and prestige. Although de Gaulle was very interested in provisions which would secure funding for the CAP, he perceived the Commission proposal as a clear infringement of France's sovereignty. He particularly resented the way in which the Commission had tied the funding for the CAP and budgetary powers to the move to majority voting. When on 30 June 1965, the deadline for an agreement on the new voting system, no consensus was reached, the French delegation departed from the Council and boycotted the Community's institutions for seven months.

Not until January 1966, when a special meeting of the foreign ministers of the 'Six' was convened in Luxembourg, was a solution found. At the insistence of France it was agreed that when vital national interests were at stake, in one or more member states, the members of the Council would try for a reasonable length of time to reach solutions which could be adopted by all members of the Council. In other words, discussions would have to continue until unanimous agreement was reached, thus giving each member state the right to veto a decision made by the majority. This agreement, the 'Luxembourg Compromise' of 1966, has often been called an agreement to disagree and has no constitutional validity. Strictly speaking it is illegal; it has never been accepted by the Commission and was essentially an acknowledgement of the fact that the member states could not be compelled to accept and implement decisions they regarded as contrary to vital national interests. Despite its dubious legitimacy, however, the Luxembourg Compromise had a major influence on the development of the EC. As a rule, decisions have not been made by majority voting, but by an exhausting attempt to achieve consensus. As a result, EC decision-making has been severely hampered until the system was reformed in the 1980s. Yet, the Luxembourg Compromise has survived to the present day.

The tribulations of the 1970s
Despite these crises, the first 12 years of the EC's existence – the transitional period – were eminently successful and the EC entered the 1970s in a mood of confidence and enthusiasm. The six heads of government met at a summit conference – called by de Gaulle's successor, Georges Pompidou – in December 1969 to take stock of progress made, to enable the EC to move into its final phase and, at the same time, to lay down the framework for future policies. This conference which took place in The Hague gave an important impetus to further development of the EC in a general mood of 'relaunching Europe'.

Between this famous summit meeting in December 1969 at The Hague and the two Paris summit meetings in October 1972 and December 1974, several very important decisions were taken, among them an agreement on financing common policies, in particular the CAP. Firstly, national contributions were to be replaced by the progressive introduction of a system of 'Own Resources', by which the revenues derived from customs duties and agricultural levies on imports from non-member states would be allocated to a 'common' budget. This was a major step towards a financial autonomy of the EC and, while it was not possible to introduce such a major structural change overnight, member states' contributions were gradually replaced by 'Own Resources'. Secondly, the principle of enlargement was established. Following de Gaulle's resignation in April 1969, negotiations with Britain, Denmark and Ireland opened formally on 20 June 1970 and the three countries became members on 1 January 1973. Thirdly, it had also been agreed that member states would progressively work towards full economic and monetary union (EMU) by 1980. Fourthly, at the summit meeting in Paris in 1974 it was decided to establish a 'European Union' by the end of the decade. The Tindemans Report (after its author, the then Prime Minister of Belgium Leo Tindemans) was produced in January 1976. Finally, it was also agreed at this summit meeting that the EP should be directly elected by the EC citizens and that these summit meetings of the heads of state and government should henceforth be convened on a regular basis and under its new title, the European Council. Furthermore, it was also agreed to embark on an ambitious social programme, set up a European Regional Development fund (ERDF) and launch an environmental action programme.

However, successful completion of many of these ventures was thwarted by the economic crises which hit the EC in the 1970s. If the crises of the 1960s had their roots in internal matters and the determination of de Gaulle to protect sovereign powers, the tribulations of the 1970s were caused by external pressures and called many of the achievements of the first 12 years into question as non-tariff barriers replaced the actual tariffs which the 1960s had so successfully removed. Three factors were responsible for the crises which, during the 1970s, put the EC under enormous strain and thus progress in the development stagnated.

The early 1970s were a turning point in many ways for the EC. As shown in Chapter 1, they marked the end of the post-war boom and the onset of upheaval and change. A worldwide recession, compounded by the Middle East crisis and the quadrupling of oil prices, transformed Europe's economic climate. In addition, an embargo was placed by OPEC – dominated by the oil-producing states of the Middle East – on exports to those countries which were regarded as supportive of Israel in the Middle East conflict. The countries most affected by the embargo were the Netherlands and the USA. The latter encouraged a co-ordinating response to the crisis, but Britain and Norway in particular, both being major producers of North Sea oil, preferred to take independent action.

The second major crisis in the 1970s was caused by monetary instability. The post-war world monetary system was based on fixed exchange rates at Bretton Wood in 1944 and parity changes were rare. However, the early 1970s were characterized by monetary upheaval and economic changes, all of which had a powerful impact on intra-EC relations. The EC was divided on the measures to be taken in the face of monetary upheaval. Exchange rates between the currencies of the member states diverged widely. Importantly, the economic upheaval of the early 1970s nullified the first moves towards monetary union, barely a month after agreement had been reached.

Institutional conflicts added to economic and monetary problems: when Britain, Ireland and Denmark joined the EC on 1 January 1973, thus bringing the number of member states up to nine, EC decision-making became even more difficult. Belief in the political potential of the EC waned, particularly as Britain, in 1974, sought a review of her entry terms. Entry had been effected under the Heath conservative government. However, when Labour returned to power in 1974, Prime Minister Wilson demanded a 're-negotiation' of the entry terms, which were regarded as unacceptable to the new British government. The 're-negotiations' lasted nearly a year and involved a serious disruption in the running of important EC business. The crisis over British continued membership was finally brought to an end at the Dublin Summit meeting in March 1975. The 're-negotiated' terms were put to the British people in a referendum on 5 June 1975, when 64% of the electorate voted for continued membership in the EC.

Thus, the promises of the early 1970s remained largely unfulfilled. Many of the ambitious projects, such as the Tindemans Report, went into oblivion, while the development of common policies were hampered by the persistent economic crisis and monetary chaos as well as by the attitudes of member states who, in the face of recession, rising unemployment and increasing inflation turned away from concerted action. Nevertheless, by the end of the decade some modest progress was made. Perhaps the most important achievement was the launching of the European Monetary System (EMS) in March 1979 – a much less ambitious project than had originally been intended – which created a new European Currency Unit and tried, through the Exchange Rate Mechanism, to tie participating currencies into a close band. A social action programme was launched in 1974, the Regional Development Fund, as already noted, was set up in 1975, the first elections to the EP by direct universal suffrage took place in 1979 and the regular meetings of heads of state and of government of member states were institutionalized by the establishment of the 'European Council' in 1974. The system of 'Own Resources' was progressively introduced by two amending treaties, 1970 and 1975, the latter granting the EP joint budgetary authority with the right to adopt the budget.

This was modest progress compared with what had been hoped for. Clearly, the broader move towards greater European integration was stalled in this period. It took nearly 15 years before member states had fully recovered from the economic and political stagnation of the 1970s. Nevertheless, it could be argued that the malaise of the 1970s constituted a much needed testing period to prepare the EC for the survival in and the challenges of a constantly changing international system. Little did the EC know as it passed the threshold of the 1980s, that it was about to embark on one of the most exciting, turbulent and rewarding decades of the post-war years.

Further reading

Coudenhove-Kalergi, R. (1923), *Pan-Europa*, Vienna: Pan-Europa Verlag.

El-Agraa, A.M. (1990), *Economics of the European Community*, 3rd edn, Cambridge: Cambridge University Press.

George, S. (1985), *Politics and Policy in the European Community*, Oxford: Oxford University Press.

Hallstein, W. (1972), *Europe in the Making*, London: Allen and Unwin.

Harrop, J. (1989), *The Political Economy of Integration in the European Community*, Aldershot: Gower.

Milward, A.S. (1984), *The Reconstruction of Western Europe 1945–57*, London: Methuen.

Molle, W. (1990), *The Economics of European Integration*, Aldershot: Dartmouth.

Pryce, R. (ed.) (1987), *The Dynamics of European Union*, London: Croom Helm.

Swann, D. (1988), *The Economics of the Common Market*, London: Penguin.

Urwin, D.W. (1991), *The Community of Europe*, London: Longman.

Weigall, D. and Stirk, P. (eds) (1992), *The origins and development of the European Community*, Leicester: Leicester University Press

Williams, A.M. (1991), *The European Community*, Oxford: Blackwell.

4 East–West relations in Europe

The Second World War marked the decline of Europe as a world power and the emergence of the two new superpowers, the USSR and the USA. Their meeting at the river Elbe during the defeat of Nazi Germany in 1945 symbolized the polarization of world politics in general and European affairs in particular.

Necessity of purpose and strategy had forged an alliance of different partners in the defeat of Nazi Germany and it had been assumed that this collaboration would continue into the post-war period. However, the underlying ideological differences between the two superpowers re-emerged almost as soon as hostilities ceased and the common enemy was defeated. Indeed, it was over the fate of post-war Germany that inter-Allied dispute was most pronounced.

Negotiations between the three Western Allies and the Soviet Union on post-war Europe and in particular on the fate of defeated Germany broke down as early as 1948 and the subsequent development of the Cold War resulted in the demarcation of spheres of influence: the USSR controlled the states of Eastern Europe by supporting the communist-led governments in these countries, while the West drew together by means of several international economic and political organizations. The division of Germany, with each half of the country taken into rival alliance systems by its occupiers, marked the beginning of the partition of Europe. Germany in general, and Berlin in particular, became a microcosm of the larger conflict which dominated successive East–West crises. The formation of the two hostile military alliances, NATO in 1949 and the Warsaw Pact in 1955, further institutionalized the East–West rift. It was only in the 1970s with the first major arms agreement, the launching of *Ostpolitik* and the setting up of a pan-European conference, the 'Conference on Security and Cooperation in Europe' (CSCE) that East and West came together in what became a continuous political and economic dialogue.

The origins of East–West confrontation
The basic cause for the emergence of the Cold War lay in the different political philosophies of the two new superpowers, the USA and the Soviet Union. These differences had been disguised and suppressed by the need to defeat the Nazi aggressor. No sooner had this overriding objective been achieved than an abyss opened between the former allies, which made any degree of collaboration concerning post-war issues difficult and eventually impossible.

The Second World War ended on 8 May 1945 with the unconditional surrender of German forces. At Tehran (November 1943) and Yalta (February 1945) the three principal Allied powers, the USA, Britain and the Soviet Union, had finalized their plans for defeated Germany in general terms. Then, in July/August 1945, at the first post-war conference, the 'Big Three' (i.e. the Soviet Union, Britain and the USA) in a far-reaching accord later known as the 'Potsdam Protocol', confirmed earlier agreements and resolved outstanding issues required for a durable peace settlement. Germany was to be demilitarized, denazified, decentralized and democratized.

Germany's territories were to be divided into zones of occupation: the Soviet Union was allotted the eastern part of Germany, Great Britain the north-west and the USA the south, while France was later assigned a territory (carved out of the British and American zones) in the south-west. Berlin, situated in the middle of the Russian sector, was occupied jointly by the four military commanders who together constituted the Allied Control Council, or 'Kommandatura', for the co-ordination of political and economic policies across the four occupation zones.

However, the conference, although nominally maintaining unity, revealed underlying tensions which gradually built up into open hostility. The first dispute arose over the territorial annexations of the Soviet Union. The victorious Red Army, advancing westwards, had made massive territorial gains annexing large parts of Poland and the northern part of East Prussia. As compensation for the USSR's annexation of Eastern Poland the Soviet Union, on 21 April 1945, placed the southern part of East Prussia as well as Pomerania (the Oder–Neiße line) under Polish rule, thus creating a *fait accompli*. Poland was run by a Soviet-controlled pro-communist government, the first in a series of friendly 'buffer states' against a reviving Germany.

Virtually all Germans living in these territories, 14 million people, were forcibly expelled in what for centuries had been German soil – it was the largest migration of people in modern history. Although the Western Allies, at Tehran and Yalta, had agreed to support both Russian and Polish claims for some territorial compensation at Germany's expense, this massive transfer of territory to Poland for so-called 'administrative purposes' presented a breach of earlier agreements, particularly as the Soviet Union – despite earlier assurances – appeared unwilling to allow a liberal democratic regime to be established in Poland. At Potsdam, the West took the position, therefore, that this unilateral action had to be provisional and that final delimitation had to await a peace settlement. In the event, however, the temporary demarcation line between East and West became the *de facto* frontier in the post-war European political geography.

The second reason for the emergence of conflict between East and West was Stalin's attitude to East European countries. Western concern over Soviet intention grew, as all Eastern European countries, 'liberated' by the Soviet Union, were progressively subjected to communist rule, as shown in Chapter 5. This was clearly in breach of earlier agreements at Yalta in February 1945, when the Soviet Union had consented to withdrawing its troops from Eastern Europe and to permit free elections.

This disturbing fact was clearly behind Churchill's famous speech in March 1946 at Fulton, Missouri, USA, when he said 'From Stettin in the Baltic to Trieste on the Adriatic, an iron curtain has descended across the Continent', articulating the fears of many of what appeared to be an indefinite expansion of Soviet power. This speech contributed to widening the rift between East and West and Stalin, undeterred by Churchill's speech, continued to tighten his grip on Eastern Europe. In September 1947 the USSR drew the communist parties of the Eastern countries as well as those of Western Europe into a tight network by setting up the Communist Information Bureau (Cominform) to replace the earlier Communist International (Comintern) which had been dissolved in 1943. The new Cominform became the centre of Communist propaganda. Orders were given to all Marxist parties in Western Europe to abandon peaceful negotiations and to encourage strikes, riots and even the violent overthrow of governments.

The third problem arose over occupied Germany. At both Yalta and Potsdam it had been agreed that each occupying power would extract productive facilities and raw material from its zone, although the scale of these reparations had never been conclusively settled. As the bulk of heavy industry was situated in the Western zones, it had been agreed that the Soviet Union would receive much of the dismantled factory equipment from the Western zones in return for food from the primarily agrarian Soviet sector. However, as soon as hostilities ceased, the Soviet Union carried out measures for the requisitioning of industry to pay for their own reconstruction. The dismantling and removal of stock was carried out on a large scale destroying sources of production and emphasizing the already desperate situation in the Eastern zone.

As a result, the occupiers of the Western zone were faced with severe food shortages and were forced to provide resources of their own to feed the starving German population. By May 1946 reparation removals in the American zone were suspended. This caused suspicion in the Soviet sector and hostility increased on both sides during the following months. During a particularly severe winter, food rations for the German population fell below 1000 calories per head. The economic misery caused by the shortage of food and coal in 1946–47, the division in views on the future of Germany between the occupying powers and the realization that war-devastated Europe could not be rebuilt with an economically unviable Germany in its midst, gradually changed the Western Allies' approach to the former enemy. Unable to reach agreement with the Soviet Union over reparations, the three Allied powers pressed ahead with the speedy economic rehabilitation of Germany. In July 1947 the Western Allies fused their zones into one single economic unit and transferred some measure of self-government to Germany's Western regions.

The Soviet-controlled zone experienced a different fate. Non-communist parties had been licenced as early as 1945. However, when local elections went against the communists, the Soviet Union eliminated all other political parties and in April 1946 ordered the fusion of socialists with the communists to create a single Socialist Unity Party (SED). A control commission monitored and dismissed non-communist members and Soviet nominees were installed in key positions.

A division had clearly begun to emerge between East and West. This was reflected by the different type of control exercised in the Eastern and Western sectors and led, despite earlier contrary agreements that the former enemy should be administered as an economic unit, to the de facto dismemberment of Germany and eventually to the establishment of two German states. However, the conflict over the fate and control of occupied Germany was only one, albeit a very important, aspect of the overall East–West confrontation which assumed global dimensions as early as 1947 and gradually turned into the Cold War.

The Cold War
The decisive trigger of open East–West confrontation came in Greece, where the monarchist government, backed by Britain, was attacked by communist guerillas. Britain, exhausted by its efforts in the war, could no longer shoulder the responsibility of defending the country. In an attempt to stem the communist drive which threatened not only Greece, but also Turkey, it asked the USA for military aid. As a result, the American President, made a far-reaching declaration, known as the 'Truman Doctrine', in which he pledged that military aid would not only be given to Greece and Turkey, but would be offered to any country under threat from 'outside pressures'. This was the first clear indication that the USA, perhaps reluctantly, was to be closely involved in post-war European politics. Moreover, it also signalled the fact that the Cold War had become an established reality.

Military aid was rapidly followed by a further extension of US support for West Europe's political and economic recovery. The Marshall Plan was, as Chapter 3 shows, America's contribution to the economic reconstruction of Europe in an attempt to prevent the economic and political collapse of that continent and save it from extremism. Although the programme was directed at both East and West Europe, the Soviet Union saw it as an instrument of the sharpening East–West conflict and accused the USA of interfering in the internal affairs of the states. Poland and Czechoslovakia which had been willing to accept the plan, were warned off by the USSR so that the Marshall Plan became an exclusively West European enterprise and, inadvertently, further cemented the division of Europe. Moscow's response was a series of bilateral trade agreements with the Eastern European countries paving the way for the creation of the CMEA in January 1949. Designed to centralize trade agreements, the CMEA became the (economic) extension of the military and political grip the Soviet Union exerted over its satellites, as indicated in Figure 1.

The next stage in the Cold War centred once again on Germany. On 20 March 1948 Marshal Sokolovskii, the Soviet military governor of the Soviet zone, left the meeting of the Allied Control Council in protest over intentions of the Western powers to establish a German political authority in their zones. This he declared to be a violation of the Potsdam Agreement. Under these circumstances co-operation between the four powers over Germany virtually came to an end – the Allied Control Council never met again.

The cool relationship between the former allies turned into open hostility when, on 18 June 1948, the West introduced a currency reform as part of a general package for Germany's economic rehabilitation. The Soviet Union responded immediately by announcing a currency reform for its own zone. Six days later, on 24 June, the USSR, as a 'defence measure' imposed a blockade of West Berlin sealing off railways, highways and canals. This drove Europe once again to the brink of war, especially when the Russians refused to permit military units of the Western occupying powers to pass through the Soviet zone into Berlin. The blockade, however, failed to achieve its objective of using West Berlin as a lever to secure concessions. The Western powers kept Berlin supplied by the famous 'air-lift' when food, raw material and medicine were flown into the beleaguered city for nearly a year. In May 1949, Stalin, admitting defeat, called off the blockade.

The Berlin blockade marked the sharpest conflict between East and West to date. Germany represented a stake in the struggle for power. Ultimately, neither the Western powers nor the Soviet Union were prepared to allow a united Germany lest it should fall under the influence or control of the other. Furthermore, the Soviet blockade of Berlin had convinced the West that a collective defence strategy was needed. The Berlin crisis in particular demonstrated very clearly that the West lacked an effective collective defence against any possible Soviet threat. The expansionism of the Soviet Union, particularly evident in Eastern Europe, but also in the Far East, the Russian rapid re-armament and in particular the development of Soviet nuclear capacity in 1949, highlighted the vulnerability of Western Europe. The earlier military organizations, such as the Treaty of Dunkirk (1947) between France and Britain which was originally targeted against Germany and the Treaty of Brussels (1948) negotiated by Britain, France and the Benelux (later to become the WEU) – the latter guaranteeing automatic military assistance to any member under threat – were largely ineffective in the wake of the developing Cold War. A more comprehensive military and defence pact was required.

As a result, in April 1949, representatives of the Brussels signatories as well as those of the USA, Canada, Italy, Denmark, Norway and Iceland signed the NATO agreement linking the USA with European countries in a collective military

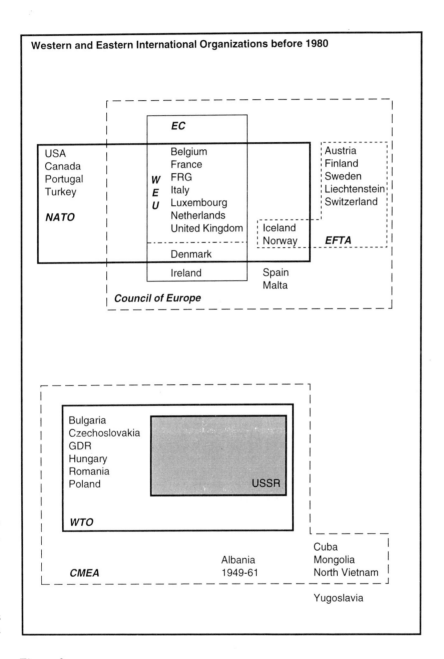

Figure 1

alliance as part of a strategy to contain communism. Military forces were supplied by each member state according to their capability. NATO was neither a 'European' army such as that which had been envisaged by the EDC, nor did it ever develop a single integrated force. The USA was clearly the military commander by virtue of its economic and military potential. During the 1950s membership was extended to include Greece, Turkey and West Germany; Spain joined in 1982.

All these events meant that any hopes of solving the future of Germany in harmony with the Soviet Union were now abandoned. This encouraged the West to go ahead and permit the setting up of a separate West German state. The FRG was founded on 23 May 1949 when its provisional constitution, the Basic Law (*Grundgesetz*), came into force. This was designed to run only until such time as the Soviet-controlled zone had acceded and a permanent constitution could be drawn up for the whole of Germany. The FRG came formally into being in September 1949 when Konrad Adenauer assumed office as the first Federal Chancellor of a conservative–liberal coalition government. The Soviet Union responded by establishing the German Democratic Republic (GDR) on 7 October 1949. A constitution was drawn up which, like the Basic Law in the West, also claimed to apply to the whole of the country.

There now existed two German states on German soil, each a loyal supporter of its respective protector. The difference was that the government of West Germany was supported by the free votes of the majority of its people, whereas the people of the GDR were prevented from expressing their free will in democratic elections. Hence, the new East German government was not recognized by the West. While the FRG embarked on a remarkable economic development and joined a number of economic, political and military organizations in the West, the unpopularity of the East German regime was demonstrated by the fact that between 1949 and 1961 3.5 million people fled to the West despite increasing border fortifications at the German–German border, as Chapter 5 shows.

The two new German states became more and more integrated into their respective systems. Originally, West Germany had been excluded from all Western post-war military organizations. However, as the Cold War progressed, and Western fears of an imminent Soviet attack reached their climax during the Korean War (1950–53), the question of German re-armament, a focus of debate since the founding of the FRG, acquired a new prominence. After the abortive attempt to establish the EDC (see Chapter 3) and after years of acrimonious debates, the Bonn and Paris Agreements (1954) officially ended the occupation of West Germany, restored its sovereignty and invited the FRG to join both the WEU and NATO. However, the three Western powers retained their rights regarding decisions on German unification, a final peace treaty and the status of Berlin. The Soviet Union reacted angrily and immediately to the FRG joining NATO by the creation of the Warsaw Pact, as a military counterpart to NATO.

The establishment of the two hostile military organizations completed the political, economic and military division of Europe.

The arms race

Nevertheless, during the mid-1950s, it seemed for a short time that relations might improve. Stalin's death in March 1953 and the end of the Korean War were followed by an interlude lasting three years during which the Soviet Union adopted a 'new European' approach. The key to the 'thaw' was Khrushchev's new political concept of 'peaceful co-existence' which implied that, although both East and West adhered to two completely different political philosophies, military confrontation should and could be avoided. This argument was used very skilfully by the new Soviet leader in an attempt to avoid major or open conflicts. The new Soviet spirit was symbolized by the four power summit conference at Geneva in 1955 – the first of its kind since Potsdam in 1945. The Soviet Union agreed to the evacuation of Austria, which, like Germany, had been placed under four-power control in 1945. As a result of the State Treaty of 1955 Austria recovered its sovereignty, subject to two conditions: it was to remain neutral and it was not to unite with Germany.

In addition, the nuclear arms race which had started in the late 1940s periodically defused further tensions between East and West, a fact which might be a little difficult to interpret in this context. Ever since the explosion of the first American nuclear bomb in 1945 which made the USA the most powerful country in the world, it had been Stalin's objective to have nuclear 'parity' with the West. This parity was achieved with the explosion of the first Russian nuclear bomb in 1949 and the development of the hydrogen bomb in 1953. By 1957 the Soviet Union had also both successfully tested an intercontinental ballistic missile and had launched the first space satellite, the Sputnik. This ought to have heightened tension. Yet, in a curious way, the arms race which now developed as both superpowers attempted to gain military advantage over the other, contributed to the relative stability of this period. The two military alliance systems, NATO and the Warsaw Pact, were locked in a framework of competitive co-existence. There was tacit recognition of each respective boundary of interest and sphere of influence. This became particularly apparent with the *de facto* recognition by the West of the division of Germany. The principle of non-interference was clearly evident during the various uprisings in the satellite states during the 1950s and 1960s when the West did little more than register a mild protest.

However, despite continued periods of mild thaws in East–West relations and the military restraints exercised by both superpowers, agreements on major issues were impossible. In 1958 Khrushchev, perhaps encouraged by Russia's apparent lead in the nuclear arms build-up, announced that the Soviet Union no longer recognized the rights of the Western powers in West Berlin. He presented the Western powers with an ultimatum for the transformation of West Berlin into a 'demilitarized free city' thus attempting to cut West Berlin's vital links with the FRG within 6 months. The West stood firm and re-affirmed its determination to remain in West Berlin. Moreover, the Eastern exodus to the West continued at an increasing rate reaching 30 000 by July 1961. The communist regime in the GDR tried to stop the damaging flow of refugees, who were generally well-trained and of working age. Soviet attempts to secure a final and irrevocable acceptance of East Germany and with it the post-war *status quo* in Europe, while also stemming the tide of refugees, culminated in the building of the Berlin Wall on 13 August 1961. This was part of a monstrous new barrier running for 500 km across Germany and developing gradually into a system of fortifications consisting of barbed wire and minefields. Berlin, Germany and Europe were thus cruelly divided, giving concrete expression to *de facto* division.

The building of the Berlin Wall in August 1961 represented an almost obscene kind of logic of the post-war division of Europe. The acceptance of both the *status quo* and the institutionalization of the division was aptly explained by the French political observer, Raymond Aron, when he said 'a clear partition of Europe is considered, rightly or wrongly, to be less dangerous than any other arrangements'. However, with the increasing complexity of the technology needed in nuclear weapon manufacture, the costs of defences in both the USA and the Soviet Union had accelerated rapidly. The pressure of these expenditures and the need to concentrate on domestic issues led to the conclusion in the 1960s that there had to be an alternative to the arms build-up. As it happened, it was not divided Germany, but the Cuban Missile Crisis of October 1962 which brought home to people both in East and West the full significance of the existential threat posed by nuclear weapons.

When the Soviet Union built a nuclear missile base in Cuba, on the doorstep of the USA, President Kennedy in October of that year, blockaded the island. Soviet actions marked a severe breach in Soviet–American understandings. The USA felt that the presence of the missiles presented an unacceptable change in the strategic *status quo*. During the following tense two weeks it became clear that the world was on the brink of nuclear war. The firm US stance eventually forced the Soviet Union to dismantle its missile site, but Cuba brought home the fact that bipolarity was not in itself a guarantee of peace. Moreover, Europe realized that a US–Soviet nuclear conflict could occur without any European control over events. It was therefore felt necessary to mitigate drastically confrontation by developing a system which would comprise communication links and regulate the build-up of arms.

The beginnings of *détente*

The most important effect of the Cuban crisis was that it ushered in an era of *détente*, which began in the early 1960s, gained momentum in the 1970s and lasted until the invasion by the Soviet Union of Afghanistan in 1979. During this time arms control negotiations were the leading influence on East–West relations. The new climate that subsequently emerged between Moscow and Washington produced, in 1963, the installation of a direct or 'hot' line of communication between the White House and the Kremlin, designed for use in urgent situations. Shortly afterwards the USA, the Soviet Union and Britain signed the 1963 Partial Test Ban Treaty (the first nuclear arms control agreement), which banned the testing of nuclear weapons in the atmosphere, in space and under water. By 1989 it had been signed by 119 countries. This was followed by a series of agreements: the Outer Space Treaty (1967), banning nuclear weapons in space and earth orbit; the 1968 Nuclear Non-Proliferation Treaty (NPT) to control the spread of nuclear weapons and technology; the Seabed Pact (1971) prohibiting nuclear arms on the ocean floors beyond a nation's 12-mile limit; and the Biological Warfare Treaty (1972) outlawing the development, production and stockpiling of biological weapons. These agreements symbolized a gradual consensus regarding the necessity to overcome tensions.

During the 1970s the process of *détente* accelerated rapidly. Pressure for a further series of arms control talks increased as the development of weapon technology and the deadliness and precision of new missiles caused renewed alarm. In 1968 agreement was reached in principle to hold Strategic Arms Limitation Talks (SALT). Strategic weapons consisted of atomic warheads targeted at the enemy's territories. These included intercontinental bomber forces, intercontinental ballistic missiles (ICBMs) and submarine-launched ballistic missiles (SLBMs). Although the plan was temporarily stalled as a result of the Soviet invasion of Czechoslovakia during the summer of 1968, negotiations were resumed in December 1969. A series of subsequent meetings led, during a Soviet–American summit meeting in Moscow in 1972, to two major arms treaties: an agreement on the Limitation of Anti-Ballistic Missile systems, known as the ABM treaty, of indefinite duration, and an interim agreement on the limitation of strategic arms (SALT 1) to run for a period of five years. The latter, the more important of the two, set specific limits on numbers and characteristics of land-based ballistic missiles. These agreements between the two superpowers were to limit the growth of their respective strategic nuclear arsenals, thus to put an end to the acceleration of the arms build-up.

The significance of the agreement lay in the recognition by the USA of the Soviet Union's achievement of strategic parity and of the mutual interest both perceived in trying to secure a strategic nuclear balance in an era still dominated by Cold War politics. While both treaties were important as first steps in limiting strategic weapons, they did not halt the arms race or deal with intermediate-range missiles and conventional forces. In that sense these achievements were limited. Nonetheless, SALT was the first step in a long-term process aimed at limiting and ultimately destroying deadly weapons. Equally importantly, the two treaties institutionalized arms control negotiations with the result that a new series of talks towards a second SALT treaty began in November 1972. Progress was laborious but, after a period of intensive East–West discussions, SALT 2 was signed by Carter and Brezhnev at their June 1979 summit meeting in Vienna.

The second major contribution to *détente* originated in West Germany. The two Germanies were both products of the Cold War and a symbol of Europe's bipolarity. In the late 1960s unification of the two Germanies, though a prime objective of the FRG's Basic Law, seemed unrealistic in the prevailing international political climate. It was therefore felt desirable to achieve *rapprochement* between the two Germanies and, by implication, between East and West Europe as a whole.

Détente – which has been defined as 'the reduction in tension in relations between states and consequent reduction of the possibilities of war' – emerged in Germany through *Ostpolitik* and was subsequently elevated at international level through the CSCE. By accepting the territorial division as a basis for improved East–West relations, the new social-democratic West German government under Willy Brandt, in a pragmatic strategy, negotiated a series of treaties which led to improved relations between the FRG and its Eastern neighbours, above all with the GDR. Thus, a *de facto* acceptance of existing European frontiers came about with the conclusion of individual treaties between the FRG and USSR (August 1970), renouncing the use of force as a means of settling disputes; with Poland (December 1970), when the FRG recognized the Oder–Neiße line as Poland's western boundary; and with the GDR (1972), when the two Germanies agreed on mutual quasi-recognition. They accepted the exchange of 'representatives' in each other's capital, since the FRG still refused to extend full diplomatic recognition, as had been demanded by the GDR. A treaty with Czechoslovakia, offering trade agreements and compensation for Nazi victims normalized the FRG's relations with this country in 1973. Finally, the four-power agreement (1972) over Berlin confirmed a permanent state of occupation by its four powers, but recognized special links of that city with the FRG. The result of Willy Brandt's Ostpolitik was *de jure* acceptance of a situation which had existed *de facto* since 1949. The permanency of Germany's division was symbolized when the FRG and the GDR became members of the United Nations (UN) as distinct sovereign states (1973).

Germany's *Ostpolitik* also opened the way to a general CSCE. The Soviet Union had encouraged the idea of multilateral negotiations on European security ever since the mid-1950s. Brandt's *Ostpolitik* was in many ways a forerunner of the CSCE. The conference was launched in Helsinki in 1973 and was attended by 35 nations (all European countries with the exception of Albania took part), including Canada and the USA. The conference concluded on 1 August 1975 with a significant 'Final Act'. This was not a legally binding treaty, but a declaration of intent. The contents of the Act were divided into separate 'baskets'.

Basket 1 dealt with security: the Helsinki Act re-affirmed the inviolability of European post-war frontiers; Basket 2 dealt with economic relations; and Basket 3, the most controversial one, with a restatement of basic human rights. Perhaps most importantly, the CSCE had several follow-up conferences, thus keeping the dialogue between the participating countries alive and serving as a multilateral forum for East–West *détente* until the present day.

Thus, the relations between East and West were fairly stable during the 1970s despite or because of the existence of the Cold War. Neither of the two superpowers was willing to relinquish its sphere of influence gained during and after the Second World War. Nevertheless, *Ostpolitik* had introduced territorial stability in post-war Europe and compelled the West to face up to the reality of long-term division of both Germany and Europe. In the CSCE Europe had found a means of dialogue which provided for multilateral negotiations on safeguarding the somewhat precarious security of the 1970s. Attempts to overcome the division in Europe had therefore shifted towards seeking improved relations with the countries in the East. The post-war *status quo* had been accepted: this marked the end of the first phase of the post-war period.

Further reading

Barston, R. (ed.) (1991), *International Politics Since 1945*, Aldershot: Edward Elgar.

Black, C. *et al.* (1992), *Rebirth: A History of Europe Since World War II*, Boulder, Col.: Westview.

Calvocoressi, P. (1987), *World politics Since 1945*, Harlow: Longman (6th ed.).

Douglas, R. (1981), *From War to Cold War, 1942–48*, London: MacMillan.

Loth, W. (1988), *The Division of the World 1941–1955*, London: Routledge.

McInnes, C. (ed.) (1992), *Security and Strategy in the New Europe*, London: Routledge.

Mowat, R.C. (1966), *Ruin and Resurgence 1939–1965*, London: Blandford Press.

Wegs, J.R. (1991), *Europe Since 1945*, London: MacMillan.

5 Adaptation and integration in Eastern Europe

The Cold War meant that political life and international relations were far more tightly knit and controlled in the East of the continent than in the West. As will be shown in this chapter, under Stalinism the East was forced to embark on what appeared to be more drastic experiments in political and social organization at home than those in the West, just as was the case in the economic matters described in Chapter 1. Equally, on paper, the Eastern bloc also led the way in international integration. Yet, the bloc's organizations were so much a means of Soviet control, as has already been suggested, that it can fairly be treated together with internal developments.

This points to the fact that, despite the domestic experiments and the imposition of Soviet military control, the post-war years saw neither the quiet pluralism of the West nor its successful integration. Thus, while the West enjoyed a return to prosperity and democracy, the East only experienced a modest economic revival. Coupled with the refusal to allow political pluralism and freedom, this meant that Soviet rule was frequently threatened by protest and revolt in the 1950s and 1960s. Indeed, opposition seemed to be always lurking below the surface, breaking out every time control was relaxed. And, even though such opposition was usually emphatically repressed, the repression often made the situation worse, partly by delaying much needed economic reforms.

Moreover, because the bloc remained much less united than is often realized, the process of integration remained extremely ambiguous. This was partly because the Soviets failed to make real use of the institutions they created, preferring to neglect them rather than risk allowing them a life of their own. It was also partly a result of the constant tension between Soviet desires for enhanced control and attempts by satellite states to preserve a modicum of independence.

Equally, although in the 1970s *détente* gave the East what it sought in terms of recognition and lessened confrontation, the costs involved proved to be much greater than the Soviets had imagined when they initiated the Helsinki process. Hence, the internal situation of the satellite states began to deteriorate drastically when coupled with the debilitating effects of the depression. The Eastern economies proved much less able to cope with the downturn than did their Western counterparts. So, although it was not always realized outside, the Eastern bloc found itself facing a looming crisis. By the 1980s this became a real threat to stability and prosperity throughout the centre and east of the continent.

Stalinist politics in Eastern Europe

The imposition of Soviet rule at the end of the Second World War forced most of Eastern Europe into a new political order. This involved not only the extension of Soviet power to new territories and nations but also, between the late 1940s and the mid-1950s, a profound and violent restructuring of political life. This was the second strand in the Stalinist experiment, following the economic remodelling analysed in Chapter 1. Although experiences varied somewhat between different Eastern European states, all were profoundly, and unhappily, marked by it.

As Chapter 4 has shown, the initial takeover of Eastern Europe took place in the last years of the Second World War as the Red Army moved westwards after Stalingrad. Since the Western allies acquiesced in this expansion the frontiers of east and central Europe were redrawn more extensively than in the West and very much in favour of the USSR. Not merely were Western Karelia, the Baltic coast (including East Prussia), Eastern Poland, Ruthenia, Northern Bukovina and Moldova all annexed by the USSR, but Bulgaria, Poland and Yugoslavia all gained territory.

Full communist government was not immediately installed outside Yugoslavia and the USSR. For the most part Soviet and the relatively small native communist parties sought to establish their mastery behind the large-scale anti-Fascist 'National Fronts' which emerged between July 1944 and March 1945, helping to bring down the remaining monarchies. The Fronts gave rise to coalition governments, dominated by communists. Once in power, the latter were able to implement large-scale purges of the media, non-communists and supporters of the old order through their developing monopoly of courts, police and security forces. Opponents were often sent to prison camps, of which even Bulgaria had 85. In Soviet-occupied Germany up to 200 000 people were sent to such camps. Elections, moreover, were rigged while other parties were, one by one, forcibly merged with the communists. With the application of such 'salami tactics' most countries were turned into one-party states by 1947–48.

If this evolution was not simply the product of superior Soviet military force, there can be little doubt that the nature and policies of the restored states were determined by the Kremlin. In theory the new regimes, often calling themselves 'Peoples' Democracies' were free states run by, and for, the oppressed lower classes of Europe. In actual fact, they represented the imposition of Soviet controls and models; ordinary people had little choice in all this.

The Peoples' Democracies emerged from a complex process in which force was often latent. The Soviets and their associates were able to profit from the fact that the Nazis had already weakened civil society in the East and decapitated actual and potential forces of resistance, notably in Czechoslovakia. Equally importantly, the Communists were able to draw on native admiration for Soviet achievements and distaste for the old social order. Expropriation, land reform, nationalization and economic reconstruction all appealed to previously oppressed groups in the newly occupied countries.

However, the price paid for such gains was immensely high. Not only did Stalinism fail to create both real growth and a successful welfare state, it also focused social aspirations and mobility on the political sector, preventing the emergence of a strong and self-reliant civil society. In any case, in political terms, the Peoples' Democracies under Stalinism had little about them that was either democratic or popular. Because the communist parties claimed to be the true representatives of the working classes the parties ran everything: economy, state and, through the *nomenklatura* system, the rest of society. The system, as Chapter 1 has shown, enabled the party to ensure that all key positions were held by members or trusted sympathizers.

There were few restraints on their authority, the judiciary being entirely subservient to party wishes. Equally, the parties exercised authority with no real reference to popular wishes. Elections became simply a means of justifying their rule by showing that the party enjoyed the support of its citizens. At the same time, the party emerged as a new and bureaucratic ruling class, itself subject to highly personalized control from the top known as 'democratic centralism'.

All this meant the disappearance of real political life outside the ruling Communist party. Meaningful pluralism vanished in politics, society and culture. The influence of Marxist ideology, moreover, was all pervasive in both the media and ordinary life. And, like the enforced restructuring of society and economy along Marxist–Leninist lines, the political transformation was enforced not just by the ultimate support of the Red Army but by massive use of delation, spying and terror. Under Stalinism terror, torture and show trials were directed not just against opponents or relics of the old order, but even against those who actually believed in the changes taking place but who were felt to be deviant or insufficiently devoted to Stalin and his wishes. He wanted pliant tools not enthusiastic zealots with ideas of their own.

This reflected the post-war paranoia of the Soviet people in general and Stalin in particular. Having only escaped total defeat by the skin of their teeth and fearing the power and politics of the West, Stalin was intent on rebuilding the devastated economy without Western aid or contact. He sought to do this partly through reparations and partly by creating a buffer zone on the country's Western frontier. This would not only serve as a glacis against Western aggression, but also enable the country to strike westward should this be necessary. Such a zone would also provide economic benefits and an example of Communist modernization. In order for this to work the Soviets insisted on absolute adherence to their economic and political model as well as on total subordination to the dictates of the Kremlin.

The differing experiences of the satellite states

The transformation entailed by this loyalty did not take place at the same time or in quite the same way in all the countries concerned. First of all, the communists did not come to power at the same time. This happened in 1945 in Bulgaria and Romania but not until 1947 in Poland. In Czechoslovakia, which showed the greatest support for Soviet liberation and for a native communist party, democratic traditions meant that the change only took place in February 1948. Even then it required a cynical coup to ensure communist control. In Hungary, it was another year before the electoral process could be relied on to remove resistances to the creation of a Peoples' Republic.

Partly because of these delays both Czechoslovakia and Hungary suffered especially badly from Stalinist terror and transformation when the developing Cold War speeded these up at the turn of the decade. Czechoslovakia ended up as one of the most totalitarian of the satellites while in Hungary, where the party was divided, one family in three suffered persecution under Stalinism. East Germany was also subject to extreme pressure because of continuing fear of German military potential.

On the other hand, the situation in Poland was both less extreme and less violent. This reflected Western concern and especially the long tradition of anti-Russian feeling amongst the Poles. As a result Stalin, as already suggested, trod carefully so as not to antagonize the largest population in the bloc. He allowed both the Catholic Church and peasant property ownership more freedom than elsewhere. Bulgaria and Romania enjoyed something of a median position between these two extremes. Nonetheless, Stalinism everywhere isolated the East from the West and forcibly homogenized ideological, political and socio-economic structures in the satellite states. This uniformity made the region somewhat more cohesive.

The real exceptions to this were Yugoslavia and Albania, where communists were already in control. Both countries had been liberated by their Communist partisans without any help from the Red Army. In Yugoslavia Tito began to create a fully fledged communist state, in which he hoped to include Albania and other parts of the Balkans. Stalin saw this as a threat to his interests, but he was unable to oust Tito from power. Instead, he expelled Yugoslavia from the Cominform and the communist family, thus propelling Yugoslavia somewhat away from the strict Marxist–Leninist model. The country went on to develop a more devolved system of Communist control, socially and regionally, with more room for private property. It also adopted a non-aligned diplomatic stance and accepted Western economic aid. Furthermore, the split also allowed Enver Hoxha to extract Albania from Tito's clutches. Hoxha went on to create one of the most introverted, hardline and vicious Stalinist regimes in the world.

The CMEA and the Warsaw Pact

The split, along with the outbreak of the Cold War, as well as re-inforcing Stalin's paranoia, led to a further tightening of Soviet control in Eastern Europe. This went beyond imposing direct Soviet influence and models, to establishing formal international structures for co-operation between the USSR and its satellites. This development on paper actually began with the creation of an economic body in 1949. However, it was the establishment of the Warsaw Treaty Organization for military collaboration a few years later, which was the real means of control and the real parallel with integration in the West. However, as has already become clear, the mixture of economic and strategic motives for such experiments was rather different in the East.

Economically the USSR had initially started to control its new glacis bilaterally through such joint ventures as the Sovram firms in Romania. However, this was not very effective and left the reality of Soviet control very much uncamouflaged. Then, as already noted, the Cominform was created in September 1947, which linked parties rather than states. So, in January 1949, a move was made to place Soviet economic supervision on a more systematic, multilateral and legitimate basis with the creation of the CMEA, also known as COMECON. This consisted of the USSR, Albania and the satellites, save for East Germany which did not join until 1950. On one level it was a response to the creation of NATO and the loss of control over Yugoslavia. In a more strictly economic sense, it was a response to the challenge of Marshall Aid, which Poland and Czechoslovakia had not been allowed to accept.

Because the CMEA was envisaged mainly as a forum for the co-ordination of plans, trade and statistics rather than as a means of real integration, its Charter left it up to the individual member states to decide which of the CMEA's provisions to accept and implement. Hence, it started life with a rather limited institutional structure. The key body was the Session of Council which annually brought together delegates from the member countries to discuss policy and to issue recommendations. It was serviced by a Secretariat in Moscow. However, under Stalin it remained little more than an empty shell.

It was this failure to make a reality of economic integration which encouraged the USSR to look to a military means of formalizing its control over its satellites. Until then, the military pillar of Soviet control rested on a series of bilateral mutual defence treaties the first of which had been signed in December 1943 with the Czech government in exile. Such deals helped to provide a basis for the stationing of large bodies of Soviet troops in the satellites. The largest body of these was the 360 000 strong force in East Germany. A military co-ordination committee was then created in 1952 to try and co-ordinate such separate arrangements.

This was not enough for the post-Stalin leadership of the USSR. Krushchev, in fact, was worried about the technological and economic implications of military competition with the West, especially since a re-armed FRG was joining the WEU. He looked for more assistance from the satellites and a more collective security effort. Equally, he was faced with the dual need to withdraw troops from Austria once the State Treaty was signed, and to provide a justification for keeping troops on the borders of a neutralized country. So, the CMEA states went on to sign the Warsaw Treaty in May 1955, with the GDR being allowed in a year later.

The organization created by the Treaty had a more developed institutional structure than the CMEA and included a Joint Military Command, always under a Russian Marshal. Yet, it was neither fully supranational nor all embracing. It was nominally an intergovernmental body even though the USSR always held the upper hand. Moreover, it was superimposed on existing bilateral deals and did not replace them in the way NATO did.

If the Warsaw Treaty succeeded in giving the Soviets more confidence in the military potential and reliability of their satellites so that troops were withdrawn from Romania in 1958, it did not achieve a great deal else to begin with. Indeed, it failed its first challenge of preventing the revolts of 1956 and its early years were another example of what has been called the Kremlin's 'benign neglect' of its institutions of integration. Here, too, the political and integrative efforts of the USSR failed to match up to those of the West despite, or because of, having so much military capacity to back them up.

Movements of revolt

Whereas Western Europe in the 1950s began to adapt to political stability, the new Soviet empire was dogged by a series of revolts. Under Stalin people were too frightened to protest, but trouble started in 1953 with the 'thaw' and, following the beginnings of de-Stalinization, really erupted in late 1956 into a major challenge to Soviet control, notably in Hungary. Moreover, as Chapter 4 has shown, relations with the West deteriorated because of the revolts. Although the challenge was met, opposition was not eliminated. As a consequence the bloc became increasingly unreliable until, in 1968, a further challenge had to be militarily repressed in Czechoslovakia. A crucial factor in all these revolts was the failure of the Communist system to deliver economic and social growth, even when freed of its Stalinist excesses.

Stalin's death in March 1953 had brought to power a less secure, and less extreme, leadership under Malenkov. Faced with unrest among workers in Bulgaria, Czechoslovakia and even in Soviet labour camps, the new rulers tempered the rigours of Stalin's policies. They also cut aid to regimes which were felt to be going too far, too fast. However, in the GDR, which was one of the main offenders in this respect, the local party leader, Walter Ulbricht, twice refused to give way over new purges and the increased production quotas being imposed on workers. As these increased quotas were not accompanied by any increase in wages or food rations they were bitterly resented by a hard-pressed working class. So, on 16–17 June, around 350 000 workers in Berlin and other cities demonstrated against the cuts and in favour of free elections. The Red Army had to be called in to put the disturbances down. Thereafter, the GDR was to prove the most loyal satellite and never again directly opposed Moscow, despite its lasting addiction to hardline communism.

In 1953, the Kremlin could not disavow Ulbricht and the GDR was therefore able to persevere with Stalinism while the rest of the bloc moved away from it. With Malenkov being forced out in February 1955 power in Moscow passed into the hands of the intelligent but unpredictable Krushchev. By February 1956 he felt strong enough to attack Stalin in a secret speech at the 20th Congress of the Communist Party of the Soviet Union (CPSU). He criticized Stalin for excess both in his cult of personality and in his use of terror against people who were essentially good communists. This dramatic shift encouraged internal opposition in the USSR and beyond and also led to moves against hardline Stalinist leaders abroad.

The new policy was to be one of the causes of the troubles of 1956. In Poland, as earlier in the GDR, these had their main roots in worker opposition to wage cuts and Stalinist reforms. In late June trouble developed in the industrial city of Poznan. The combination of government tergiversation and the brutal way the army put down demonstrators caused a wave of dissent and strikes. Liberal elements in the party blamed the problems on hardline policies and, when Krushchev arrived on 19 October 1956, he was persuaded not to call in the Red Army but to allow Gomulka, the recently freed moderate Communist leader, to take over the government. Gomulka, by suspending further collectivization, allowing the Church and workers' councils more freedom and subsidizing the price of food, was able to restore calm.

Just as this was happening the trouble spread to Hungary. There, too, intellectual dissidence against the Rakosi regime emerged. This was not only more hardline than most, but had brutally repressed both people and political rivals. Encouraged by Moscow's displeasure with Rakosi, and by events in Poland, opposition in Hungary mushroomed. Thousands of people demonstrated in favour of increasingly radical demands. Despite many deaths at the hands of the police, street fighting developed. Nagy, the moderate rival of Rakosi, had to be installed as Prime Minister and a coalition government followed. The Red Army partially withdrew at the end of October.

With power slipping from the hands of the party Nagy found himself swept along by the increasingly rebellious popular movement which was turning against communism, the secret police and the whole Soviet connection. On 1 November he gave in and called for a neutral Hungary outside the WTO. This was too much for the Soviets who, aided by Kadar the new Party Secretary, staged an invasion on 4 November. Despite protest strikes and desperate resistance control was restored by the end of the month. Perhaps as many as

25 000 Hungarians were killed in the process and 200 000 fled abroad, an event which had a considerable impact on the West, as has already been noted.

The events of 1956 also shook severely the legitimacy and unity of the Communist bloc. Intellectual dissidence increased and some regimes had to adopt more flexible policies. Encouraged by the way Yugoslavia was developing its own style of self-management socialism with greater openness to the West, countries like Albania and Romania sought to exploit this disarray. The former withdrew from both CMEA and the WTO while Romania created more freedom for itself by insisting on the equality of all communist parties and the principle of non-intervention. On the other hand, in the GDR, the hardline rule of the Ulbricht regime was, as Chapter 4 has shown, embarrassingly unable to win the support of its own people, hence the building of the Berlin Wall to stem the exodus of disillusioned East Germans in 1961. These events helped to bring down Krushchev in 1964, but the Brezhnev regime which followed found itself under continuing pressure.

This was symbolized by the development of new critiques of authoritarian communism in Czechoslovakia which did not draw so much on hardship as in 1956, but stressed how economically unsuccessful the country had been as compared with the West. In the mid-1960s the Novotny regime at first tried to maintain its position by adapting to such demands. However, its ruthless repression of a student demonstration in November 1967 soon led to the appoint-ment of Alexander Dubček as Party leader. The reformist wing of the party then sought to modernize the old communist order. Moscow was very uneasy about this but, for a while, was assuaged by Dubček's protestations of fidelity.

Unfortunately, as in Hungary, once there was the slightest relaxation of control, deep seated disaffection began to show itself. With an explosion of new ideas during the 'Prague Spring' the government found its policy of creating 'socialism with a human face' leading it to challenging the basic ideals of party control in the name of democratic self-government. Failing to browbeat Dubček into abandoning planned purges of hardline personnel and policies, the WTO intervened militarily on a massive scale on 20–21 August 1968. There was little active resistance, especially as Dubček was allowed to continue in office. He was only eased out in April 1969, by when the largely passive opposition had been blunted, as had Czech radical impulses. Large-scale purges of army, party and workers' movement followed with many activists fleeing the heavily occupied country.

With the limits of adaptability of the Soviet-imposed model thus demonstrated, new strategies had to be pursued under Brezhnev. Better relations with the West were also sought through *détente*, so as to reduce pressure from outside and to bridge the growing economic gap between the two halves of Europe. Yet, at the same time Brezhnev refused political liberalization and economic reform.

He also sought, with limited success, to bind the satellites more effectively into the Soviet-controlled international institutions.

The ambiguities of integration in the East

After the revelation of the weakness of the bloc in 1968 came new moves to reform the WTO and, to a lesser extent, the CMEA. The Kremlin sought not merely greater cohesion and effectiveness, but a means of concealing the harsh truths of the Brezhnev doctrine of 'limited sovereignty'. This was enunciated at the Moscow conference of Communist parties in June 1969 and stated baldly that the USSR had the right to intervene in defence of 'socialist internationalism' should party rule be at risk in any of the satellites. However, the attempts to make realities of the two integrative bodies were neither wholly successful nor free from ambiguity.

From 1969 onwards a deliberate attempt was made to restructure the WTO militarily and politically. Militarily there was a new emphasis on quality and efforts were made to upgrade the weaponry used by Warsaw Pact forces. Joint manoeuvres with the Red Army helped to socialize the satellite armies into supporting Soviet aims over national interests. This could include suppressing local disorders and accepting Soviet military privileges. However, in the mid-1970s the Romanians proved very recalcitrant about accepting such controls. Nonetheless, the relatively successful efforts at re-armament led the West to take much more note of the WTO as a body with a life of its own.

It was also given greater political weight in two ways. Firstly, following the Budapest Summit, new structures were created including a standing committee of national Ministers of Defence and a Commission of Foreign Ministers. The latter gave direction to WTO in between meetings of the party leaders on the Political Consultative Committee. This points to the second change, the enhancing of the WTO's political role. It thus played an active part in the Helsinki process.

As a result, although the WTO remained essentially a means by which the Soviets could exert military and political control over the bloc, it did have another side. The WTO, in fact, provided a channel by which the satellites themselves could collectively influence the Kremlin and, to an extent, regularize and contain Soviet absolutism. Hence, even though the Treaty was renewed for a further ten years in 1975, the satellites were able to resist the imposition of financial 'burden sharing' in the late 1970s when the hard-pressed USSR tried to get the satellites to pay more towards their own defence.

This kind of ambiguity over the autonomy of the satellites was even more marked in the CMEA. Reform there had started in 1959–60 with a revised Charter, an executive committee of deputy Premiers, and new banking, standardization and statistical initiatives. More important was the introduction of a transferable *ruble* which facilitated inter-bloc trade. However, ideas of abolishing visas (so as to allow for free movement) and organizing a 'division of labour' amongst the partners were blocked by Romanian fears of being downgraded to a helpless agricultural supplier. Albania withdrew from the CMEA for the same reasons.

Although the domestic economic reforms, already explored in Chapter 1, were put into cold storage after 1968 so as to help normalize life in the bloc, attempts at revivifying the CMEA were intensified. These attempts, initiated by the 1969 summit, had some success. New members joined and further technical bodies, along with an Investment Bank, were established. In 1971, a comprehensive long-term programme for development through co-ordination of plans was launched. Although Romania continued to act as a brake on such ideas there were more joint ventures, notably where the supply of Soviet raw materials was concerned. A certain amount was also achieved in co-ordinating freight transit, research and technical specifications.

Hence, it was still found necessary to make further efforts in the second half of the decade as the economic crisis had its effects. Faced with the double costs of subsidizing oil supplies to the bloc, the USSR sought to make the satellites pay more for access to its oil and gas, including sharing in extraction operations. Not surprisingly, agreement and progress were hard to achieve. Nonetheless, the Charter was twice more revised, in 1974 and 1979, while co-operation was re-focused on such key sectors as agriculture, energy and machinery.

Even so the CMEA remained a body which helped to stabilize bilateral trade inside the bloc rather than one which managed foreign trade, developed growth or encouraged real integration. Recommendations were only binding on those states which chose to accept them and bilateral deals were more common than wider programmes. Fearful of being drawn too far into Soviet control at the expense of their own economic integrity, the CMEA states refused to go beyond low-level contact and co-ordination towards supra-nationality. Hence, integration provided only a limited answer to the economic crisis and the CMEA remained the junior partner to the WTO. This relative failure was typical of the stagnation and internal division which was increasingly affecting the bloc.

Stagnation under *détente*

On the surface, the 1970s in the East were a time of successful adaptation, symbolized more by the process of *détente* than by reform of communism's international institutions. Underneath, however, things were deteriorating. Firstly, *détente* had dangerous side effects within the bloc. Secondly, the Brezhnev regime in the USSR lapsed back into a dangerous combination of internal conservatism and external adventurism. Thirdly, Poland continued to reveal the growing problems within the satellites.

As has been shown in Chapter 4, *détente* was embarked upon in order to cope with the growing political and economic insecurity caused by the arms race. Military costs were squeezing out welfare and investment. This both encouraged dissent and caused non-military sectors of the economy to fall further behind the West. Reassured about his allies by the post-1968 return to traditional policies and the reform of the WTO, Brezhnev felt he could embark on a policy which would allow a decrease in military spending and the beginnings of import-led growth. The latter required better contacts with the West, hence *détente*.

Although Brezhnev achieved his goals in disarmament and diplomacy, there was a high price to be paid for them, although this was not realized at the time. The bloc, in fact, found itself much more exposed to the West than it had imagined. Thus it slipped increasingly into debt to Western financiers. At the same time, it had to relax controls over things like censorship and jamming so that Western influences had an increasing impact notably in the human rights area. Finally, the Helsinki process also provided both a channel and a stimulus for internal criticism, notably from the Czech Charter 77 group and Soviet *refuseniks*.

Coping with this was difficult because the bloc needed leadership from the USSR which was not forthcoming. Not only did the Kremlin throw its weight behind hardline orthodoxy in the satellites, it also showed increasing signs of domestic sclerosis. Ruled by an ageing elite which did well out of the system and which complacently focused on the gains made since the 1930s, ignoring the growing gap with the outside world, Brezhnev's USSR set its face against change. Thus, Western aid was used to shore up the old heavy industrial monopolies rather than to fund innovation. Even so living standards began to drop, with the country often having to buy grain from North America. Pressure on Helsinki monitoring groups increased and, most worryingly of all, *détente* itself came under strain.

This situation very much outweighed the limited economic reforms which were finally allowed to restart in the late 1970s. These were meant to reward firms which improved contract fulfilment, labour flexibility and quality ratings. Some of the satellite states, Bulgaria, the GDR and Czechoslovakia, for example followed the Brezhnevian model with great devotion. Here no political experiments were allowed, but living standards were maintained (sometimes at the expense of investment) in order to head off popular discontent. In the GDR links with West Germany helped to sustain standards. With Honecker remaining a firm opponent of political liberalization, there was less need for the repression of groups like Charter 77, which Husak chose to mount in Czechoslovakia.

Hungary went furthest in this direction since Kadar realized that, after the bloodshed of 1956, he could only prevent further trouble by buying acquiescence. This he did partly by curbing repression and partly by allowing Hungarians the economic freedoms and gains of 'goulasch' communism. Hence, from 1968 the New Economic Mechanism was developed. This was partly modelled on Yugoslavia's market socialism with its attempts at self-management and attracting Western investment. The Hungarian policy allowed for more outside contacts, innovation and retention of profits. Even though this was toned down in the 1970s, it managed to achieve its political goals and without alarming the USSR. The latter even came to terms with the Yugoslav experiment by the 1970s, although the experiment had begun to go off the boil, domestically and diplomatically, even before Tito died in 1980.

The real difficulties came from Romania and, in a different way, from Poland. Under Ceauşescu Romania continued its relatively independent foreign policy, holding aloof from the invasion of Czechoslovakia and developing links with Israel and other outside countries. However, this was accompanied by imposition of ideologically orthodox authoritarianism at home. Behind this sheltered a nationalistic and family-run dictatorship which stressed autarchy above everything else, so as to maintain its freedom of action. Claims of economic betterment were pure propaganda.

In Poland Gomulka's regime soon lost both its economic attractions and its liberalism. After strikes in Gdansk in 1970 were bloodily put down, the party replaced him by another reformer, Edward Gierek. Under his leadership large economic concessions were made to buy acquiescence in both party rule and a dash for industrial growth financed by borrowing from the West. With the recession this policy soon ran into difficulties and by 1975 the regime was facing new labour unrest in Radom over higher prices for food and, significantly, new unrest from intellectuals. Increasingly complaints focused on the corruption and ineffectiveness of the party which had never been renewed as Gierek had promised it would be. With the election of a Polish Pope in 1978 the Communist regime found itself facing a threefold challenge to its very existence.

A looming crisis?

The problems in Poland symbolized the way in which, despite the apparent stability of the Communist bloc in the late 1970s and the general acceptance of the *status quo*, normalization had not really succeeded. The pains and plans inflicted by the Soviet-dominated leaderships, including the original Stalinist transformation, had failed to deliver. The contrast with the West was stark, not just where the political and moral goals of communism were concerned, but also on standards of living, welfare and general economic modernization.

Domestically such gains as there had been had been monopolized by a bloated party and its allies which had failed to adapt to new conditions. Elements of Stalinism remained and continued to complicate the political adaption of the post-war period. Thus, the parties both lost their cutting edge and their contact with the people. States in the East were thus in just as stressed a condition as their Western counterparts. The problem was that the influence exercised by the state went so much further in the East. Although this was not always realized in the West, there was deep popular dissatisfaction in the East. People there adapted, but did not accept.

Externally, integration failed to resolve the problem. Because it essentially aimed at enhancing Soviet control it was often resisted by uneasy satellite leaderships. Therefore, its benefits both to the USSR and, less convincingly, the satellites, were never really obtained. Reliance on military force was equally ambiguous in its effects. All these problems were to come home to roost in the 1980s when they made it almost impossible for most satellites to implement *perestroika*. Moreover, these problems had to be faced in a deteriorating international climate emerging from the limitations of *détente*.

Further reading

Brogan, P. (1990), *Eastern Europe*, London: Bloomsbury.
Holden, G. (1990), *The Warsaw Treaty Organization*, Oxford: Blackwell.
Kaser, M. (1965), *COMECON*, London: Oxford University Press.
Lewis, P. (1995), *Central Europe since 1945*, London: Longman.
Longworth, P. (1992), *The Making of Eastern Europe*, London: MacMillan.
McCauley, M. (1991), *Soviet Politics 1917–1991*, London: Oxford University Press.
Nelson, D. (1989), *The Soviet Alliance*, Boulder, Col.: Westview.
Swain, G. and Swain, N. (1993), *Eastern Europe since 1945*, London: MacMillan.
Young, J. R. (1992), *Cold War Europe*, London: Arnold.
Woodall, P. and Lovenduski, J. (1987), *Politics and Society in Eastern Europe*, London: MacMillan.

PART II

NEW DIRECTIONS
IN THE 1980s

Overview

Nothing in the early 1980s appeared to indicate that this was to become the most extraordinary decade in post-war Europe. Progress in the EC had come to a standstill. The early 1980s were still ridden with economic and political crises: recession, energy problems, rising unemployment, accelerating inflation and growing international tension all eroded the economic and political security the EC had provided during the 1950s and 1960s. Increasing agricultural expenditure had brought the EC to the brink of bankruptcy, while acrimonious debates over resource priority paralysed its decision-making machinery. A search for the solution of conflicts caused by the EC's geographical extension in 1973 dominated the agenda at a time when the EC was faced with its second enlargement: the entry of Greece, Portugal and Spain merely served to underline existing problems. Internal divisions were compounded by fears of a lack of dynamism in the international and European economy. The EC had reached a crossroads and a significant leap forward was needed to improve its somewhat outdated decision-making machinery and encourage new ventures and projects.

On the international level, the Soviet invasion of Afghanistan and the deployment of cruise missiles in Western Europe had led to a cooling in East–West relations. That curious type of stability which had dominated the 1970s, a stability born out of fear and resting on nuclear parity between the two superpowers, was replaced by renewed East–West confrontation. Superpowers' relations, once again, were frozen.

However, by the mid-1980s radical changes took place in both East and West. In the EC, the stagnation came to an end with the arrival of a new Commission in 1985 which, by launching a number of initiatives, lent new dynamism to the process of European integration. The apathetic 1970s gave way to the euphoric 1980s. The ratification of the Single European Act (SEA) provided for the completion of the Single Market by 1992, improvement in the decision-making machinery and the introduction of new policy areas.

At the same time and almost running parallel to the new impetus in European integration, dramatic changes in the Eastern bloc caused a transformation of Europe's political landscape. The advent of Gorbachev in the Soviet Union altered the economic and political environment, not only in that country, but initiated a process of a revolutionary transformation in virtually all Eastern European countries, symbolized most dramatically by the breaching of the Berlin Wall. Each satellite state, in rapid succession, threw off communist dictatorship and embarked on ambitious reform programmes. The speedy unification of the two

Germanies in October 1990 signalled an end of the painful division of Europe. Unprecedented agreements on arms control, the disintegration of the Warsaw Pact and the institutionalization of the Helsinki process, all coinciding in the early 1990s, symbolized the end of the Cold War and 45 years of East–West confrontation. Never before had the political environment of Europe been so hopeful and so promising as the 1980s drew to an end.

6 Politics and policy in Western Europe

By the late 1970s West European states, then largely governed by the Left had, as Chapter 2 suggested, come under increasing strain. Indeed, on the surface, they appeared to be almost in worse condition than their Eastern counterparts. The Eastern bloc seemed to many ultra-stable and, apparently, unscathed by the economic downturn. This contrast was doubly misleading because, on the one hand, a real crisis was looming in the East; on the other hand, the Western democracies were actually beginning to tackle their economic and political problems.

In the early 1980s, Western states were still struggling to cope with the difficulties of the 1970s: continuing depression, an increasingly tense and divided society and a volatile, sometimes even violent, political life. These trends continued well into the new decade, sometimes, as in the case of the economy, in even more acute forms. However, states did begin to adopt new approaches to their economic and other problems. Introduced as a result of recession they were to give considerable support to later growth, and in some cases, and especially – if exceptionally – in Britain, to a swing to parties of the centre right.

Things began to change more markedly, and more rapidly, from the middle of the decade. Economic policy began to converge on traditional free market lines just as the European economy began to pick up. The middle and later years of the decade saw quite rapid economic growth, something which developed from, and consolidated, the new orientation of economic policy. Thanks to the economic revival and the mastering of terrorism states and societies largely regained the confidence they had lost in the late 1970s. However, by the end of the decade, there were signs that things were changing again, and not always for the better.

This Chapter, therefore, starts by analyzing the continuing depression of the early 1980s and the social and political challenges this presented to Western states. Next, it examines political responses to the continuing crisis, notably in Britain. It then suggests that these responses were not the preserve of conservative governments alone, but were shared by socialist-run states, including both the newly restored democracies of southern Europe and, even more strikingly, France where the Socialist party came to power for the first time in the history of the Fifth Republic in 1981.

The emphatic economic recovery from the middle of the decade is the fourth element in this Chapter. However, the social implications of the economic upturn were, in the medium term, to threaten the continuation of the revival.

And, as shown in the last part of the Chapter, issues like immigration encouraged changing political attitudes and re-alignments, often involving emerging Green movements as well as the rise of a new Extreme Right. These were among the harbingers of a new twist in the political story.

Socio-economic and political challenges in the early 1980s

Economically the early 1980s were as much a period of recession as the late 1970s owing to the second oil shock. In 1979 the overthrow of the Shah by the Iranian Revolution meant a sudden cessation of oil exports to the West. Prices soared in July 1979 and continued to do so throughout 1980, in the run up to the Iraqi attack on Iran that September. With the price of a barrel of petrol rising from $14.03 in 1978 to a peak of $36.34 in 1982 the Western import bill doubled, despite previous reductions in overall demand.

Economic growth stagnated after 1980 as it had in the first oil crisis. Indeed, it fell markedly in 1982. And, as before, stagnation was accompanied by rising inflation. Southern Europe and the British Isles were particularly badly hit by this. With interest rates remaining high because of the US deficit, which sucked in foreign money, many firms found themselves forced to lay off workers to reduce their outgoings. Thus, unemployment in Western Europe rose anew after 1979, reaching a peak of 11.5 per cent by 1985.

Old industries were especially badly hit by these developments, notably in Britain. They faced falling demand at home, diminishing overseas markets and increasing competition from imports of automobiles and electronic goods from Japan and low wage 'newly industrialized countries' (NICs) like Malaysia. Such imports continued to pour into Europe despite new attempts at protectionism. These attempts showed how heavily the new situation weighed on most Western states before recovery started, as it did, after about 1983. Even the FRG, which had coped better with the recession than most, was affected.

By 1983 the continuing recession had already had severe social effects as well. Three problems were especially severe. Firstly, there were growing regional imbalances which worsened in the 1980s. Old regions, dominated by agriculture or by heavy industry, were particularly badly hit and began to fall behind more modern regions whose economic strength was in the service sector, which gravitated to more pleasant regions such as Bavaria in the FRG and the Mediterranean coast in France. Unemployment was much higher in old industrial regions, for example the Nord-Pas de Calais in France. Joblessness was generally worst in large cities, as were housing conditions. With unemployment becoming a structural problem society had little to offer alienated young people and the unemployed. Few new jobs were created while even trade unions seemed to offer little real protection. Moreover, growing imbalances in standards of living between regions and classes were bitterly resented.

Secondly, it became increasingly difficult to support the generous levels of social welfare previously made available. Health and welfare costs were already growing because of the ageing of the population brought about by declining birthrates and better living conditions. With most governments running deficits they sought to curb increases in benefits and to increase levies on employers and taxpayers. This, too, was very unpopular, both with those who received the reduced benefits and those who had to pay for them, showing that social solidarity was on the decline. Often this spilled over into resentment of foreign workers and other members of the 'underclass'. For ordinary people suffering from the depression, such people appeared to be abusing the system. In countries like France, the FRG and Switzerland these resentments occasionally encouraged xenophobic attacks on new immigrant communities.

Thirdly, the depression combined with changing social behaviour to create new medical social problems such as drugs and AIDS. Equally notable was the rising divorce rate and the breakdown of the traditional family. The growing number of one-parent households thus created often found themselves in a vulnerable social and economic situation. All this added to the pressures on welfare services and society as a whole became increasingly tense and unequal. It was also less mobile and more prone to divisions and disorder, including terrorism.

If economic difficulties were the most pressing problems facing governments, there were other challenges, including that from terrorism. In the early 1980s, in fact, Western Europe continued to be a favoured target for terrorist groups. Many of these, like the Italian red brigades and their right wing opponents were indigenous. They could also be very violent as when 80 people were killed in the right wing bombing of Bologna railway station in 1980.

However, despite such outrages, the tide had begun to turn. By 1983 counter-measures by the Italian security forces finally led the Red Brigades to give up their armed struggle. Nonetheless, domestic terrorism continued in Northern Ireland, France (both from Corsican nationalists and the left wing Action Directe) and Spain. The continuation of regional–nationalist terrorism shows that not all terrorist violence was the work of left wing extremists. Outsiders, often from the Middle East, were also involved. Thus, 22 people were killed in an attack on Fiumcino airport in Rome in 1983. As late as 1985, before the wave petered out, over 800 terrorist attacks took place in Western Europe.

At the same time several governments faced a further challenge, namely that from the movement against the deployment of cruise and Pershing missiles. This deployment was, as Chapter 9 shows, part of NATO's 'dual track' response to the 'New Freeze' and to growing Soviet military superiority. However, many people in Western Europe sincerely felt that there was no moral, or other reason, for increasing the number of nuclear weapons. Indeed, deployment would add to insecurity. So governments came under great pressure from groups of leftists and others, usually known as the 'peace movement', to reverse the new policy and not to deploy new nuclear missiles. In this they were, of course, encouraged by the USSR.

Belgium, Britain, Italy and the Netherlands all experienced very active and large-scale popular protest, along with the FRG where, as suggested in Chapter 9, there were special reasons for concern. The scale and duration of the process made the adoption of the new policy much more difficult. In the case of the Netherlands public pressure delayed deployment by some two years. Nonetheless, deployment went ahead, even in the Netherlands. So, by the middle of the decade, the movement began to demobilize. This was also true of the urban and youth unrest which affected even ultra-stable countries like Switzerland at the beginning of the decade.

Although pressures from terrorism and the peace movement were dramatic, and often destructive, Western democracy was not really shaken. Thus, just as the Italian state wore down the Red Brigades, so the restored Spanish democracy was able to overcome threats to its existence. In 1981 the new Spain saw off an attempted military coup, led by a disillusioned army officer, in which Parliament was briefly taken over. However, both army and public rallied to the cause of democracy, led by the King, and the rebels surrendered.

Nonetheless, during this first phase of the 1980s, governments remained as overloaded as they had been in the 1970s. They also remained under pressure from electorates increasingly prone to change their minds and vote for new parties. The rise of Progress parties in Scandinavia was one symptom of this new volatility. These demanded an end to taxation and a scaling back of state activities. The initial successes of environmentalist parties in Switzerland, Belgium and especially the FRG in 1983, was another symptom of a trend which was to become increasingly common as the decade advanced.

New policy responses and political re-alignments
In the end, however, it was economic problems which worried electorates most. Generally speaking parties of the left had found themselves dealing with such problems in the 1970s but, by the 1980s, irrespective of who was in power new answers were being sought. Some of the answers advanced were to be quite dramatic in nature. In some countries this led to something of a swing to the right, with Britain leading the way. However, as the involvement of different parties in other countries shows, policies were more significant than parties as such. In both cases it took some time to come to terms with the new social and economic problems, and for recovery to begin. Once it did, however, the load on governments was somewhat reduced. Despite this, public opinion continued to be very changeable which meant that new governments no sooner found themselves in power than their popularity began to decline.

The 1970s had seen many left wing parties return to power, partly because the depression had required large-scale state intervention to try and prop up ailing economies, and they believed in doing this. Things changed considerably in the 1980s. By then pressures on state budgets had become impossibly heavy and many northern countries began to move back towards austerity and government by the right. This was very clearly the case in the FRG. There, the Free Democratic Party (FDP), sensing that public opinion was changing, demanded budget cuts (notably in welfare) in 1982. When these were rejected by Helmut Schmidt's SPD, the FDP controversially renounced its coalition with the former and switched its allegiance to the Christian Democrats. The new coalition was confirmed in power by the 1983 general election which, as Chapter 9 makes clear, reflected the declining appeal of the ideas of the left and the peace movement.

Similar trends were visible in other countries. In Austria the Social Democrats only held on to power after 1983 thanks to a coalition with the far right Freedom Party whose ideas echoed those of the Progress parties which were gaining strength in Scandinavia. However, the orthodox right actually came back to power in Denmark, Norway and Belgium, while the Swiss Radical Democrats re-established their position as the largest single party. In the Netherlands, the Labour Party left government in 1980 rather than agree to budget cuts, allowing the Christian Democrats to ally with the conservative Liberal Party there. By 1987 Fianna Fail government in Ireland and the Finnish conservatives had returned to government, after a long absence, on platforms of budgetary restraint.

It was in Britain, however, that this trend began earliest and went farthest. There, the new Conservative leadership of Margaret Thatcher, which had been brought to power after the Callaghan government had failed to control both industrial and nationalist unrest, believed that there had to be a break with the post-war consensus in order to revitalize the British economy. This meant curbing both the power of the unions to interfere with public finance and, especially, the money supply. Many Tories believed in monetarist economics, the assumption that the economy, and its key problem of inflation, could be managed by controlling the money supply.

Although things did not exactly work out according to plan an attempt was made to put these theories into practice under Geoffrey Howe's chancellorship. Cuts were made in government spending, interest rates were raised to curb inflation, indirect taxes were increased and the pound was allowed to float upward. This had a severe impact on British industry, driving many firms under and raising unemployment from 4.2 per cent in 1979 to 13.3 per cent in 1983. A start was made on curbing local government and reforming the trade unions and other social services. However, state spending remained high because of the costs of unemployment. Such policies, along with deteriorating conditions in ethnically mixed inner city areas, produced large-scale riots in 1981.

By 1982 the new government was one of the most unpopular on record. However, it still went on to win the 1983 general election, thanks to victory in the 1982 Falklands War, the beginnings of economic recovery, aided by North Sea oil, and the attractions of property ownership, which were made available to blue collar workers by the enforced sale of council houses. The divisions in the opposition Labour Party over its shift to the left also played a part. The right wing of the party thus seceded to form the Social Democratic Party (SDP) which worked loosely with the Liberals.

The 1983 electoral victory made it possible to go much further towards fulfilling the initial agenda. The major privatizations of state monopolies such as electricity, gas and telephones were carried through, building up a wider body of shareholders. The power of the unions was blunted by a stream of new legislation and by the defeat of the 1984–85 miners' strike. The number of strikes began to fall drastically thereafter. The Greater London Council (GLC) and other metropolitan councils were abolished and part of the civil service was reorganized on an agency basis. At the same time, the government was able to reduce direct taxation and even to pay off some of the national debt.

These achievements were clearly rewarded in 1987 when voters, and notably those in the south of England, returned the government with another comfortable majority. The Tories were thus able to press ahead with further reforms, notably in education and with privatization of water supply. This third election defeat for Labour finally forced the party to drop its left wing inclinations and embark on a major policy review, which led it to give more room to market forces than to nationalization. Change was also forced on the Liberal–SDP alliance which merged, somewhat uneasily, to form the Liberal Democratic Party, which also began to rethink some of its policies. So, even if government did not change hands, there was some convergence on policy.

The left and policy convergence
This was very much the case elsewhere in Western Europe. For, if governments did not always change, there was something of a shift towards market forces. This convergence was much less drastic than in Britain and was carried out for much more pragmatic reasons. This was the case in Scandinavia and the Low Countries. However, it affected other parts of Europe, including the socialist governments of southern Europe and, particularly, of France. The convergence tied in with the moves to relaunch the EC, considered in Chapter 7.

The extent to which all parts of Europe were affected by these new policy trends stands out in the case of southern Europe. Thus, even Turkey experimented with a very limited amount of privatization. More significantly, controls on banks and foreign exchange dealings were somewhat relaxed in Italy. There was also some success in curbing inflation and tax evasion there. Interestingly, it was Bettino Craxi's Italian Socialist Party which led the way between 1983 and 1987 in getting to grips with the inflationary inheritance of the 1970s, and notably with the indexation of wages. However, despite the claims that Italy had outstripped Britain as an economic power, public finances remained in a sad state.

Greece was another case of very limited adaptation. The left wing Panhellenic Socialist Movement (PASOK) government, which came to power in 1981, started by trying policies similar to those tried in France, boosting pay. However, by 1986, with rampant inflation and a public sector borrowing requirement of 17.5 per cent, Papandreou had to change tack. Salary rises were frozen, higher prices charged for some services and borrowing cut back to 10 per cent. Fierce public opposition prevented much else being done. So the economy remained profoundly uncompetitive and dependent on assistance from an increasingly worried EC.

On the other hand both Spain and Portugal sought to use entry into Europe as a spur to modernization. So when the Spanish Socialist Party (PSOE) came to power under Felipe Gonzalez in 1982 it was much more restrained in its approach. Early attempts at nationalization were soon reversed with firms like SEAT sold off in an attempt to bring in more foreign investment. Wages were also frozen and the school leaving age raised in an attempt to control unemployment. The policy did bring increased growth but unemployment remained high. As a result strikes were common and the party remained in power as much because of the divisions of the opposition and the need to support democracy against dissident army officers and regionalists as because of the attractions of the new policy and leadership.

In Portugal the Socialists had held power in the 1970s but their grip began to loosen in the 1980s. The country chose to back Cavacao da Silva's conservative Social Democrats in their painful attempt to restructure one of the weakest economies in Europe by cutting state intervention, encouraging investment and generally restructuring the economy. Though there was fierce opposition to some aspects of these policies the electorate twice gave the party an absolute majority in parliament. This enabled it to complete the modernization of the constitution, removing the eccentricities left over from the revolution.

However, the most significant example of a socialist government responding to pressure by changing its policies, was in France. As in Britain, the late 1970s in France had been a time of mounting economic difficulties, although the Barre government had some success in bringing the situation under control. However, the long period of right wing government and the divisions between the coalition parties promoted the electorate to give a very narrow victory to François Mitterrand in the presidential election of May 1981. The position of his revived Socialist Party was then confirmed when the legislative elections saw it emerge as by far the largest single party.

Although Mitterrand chose to bring the weakened Communist party into government, it was the Socialists who provided the dynamism for the new Mauroy government. Like the Thatcherites, the Socialists had a very clear view of what they wanted to do once in government. One key element of their policies was to liberalize the structure of the state and this led to the successful decentralization programme after 1982. Even more importantly the PS wanted to revitalize the French economy by using traditional Keynesian and socialist remedies. Consequently, a good deal of the financial and industrial fabric of France was nationalized, consumer spending was boosted through a 25 per cent increase in the minimum wage and other benefits, and taxes on the better off were increased.

The PS soon found that things were not working out as they had hoped. Increased consumer spending did not lead to increased production because so much went on imported goods. With shorter hours leading to higher overall wage costs, French goods became increasingly uncompetitive. So, like the shortfall on the balance of trade, unemployment continued to rise, reaching 16 per cent by 1982. The Franc had to be devalued three times in two years, and the government deficit was spiralling out of control owing to the heavy compensation paid to firms which had been nationalized.

By June 1982 the government realized that traditional socialist economic policies could not easily be implemented in a depression. They also drove down the value of the Franc, presenting the PS with the choice of either seeing this fall, or maintaining its parity with the DM inside the Exchange Rate Mechanism (ERM), which meant following a deflationary economic policy like that of the FRG. Turning their back on the ERM would have been both costly and very damaging internationally. So the government started to change tack in 1982, seeking to curb the deficit, controlling wages and prices, and forcing cost cutting measures on both social services and nationalized industries.

Further U-turns were made in 1983, when the government ceased to try and boost consumption and started to face up to the problems of competitiveness, and in 1984, when the Communists left the government, this was entrusted to a young 'socialist manager' – Laurent Fabius – who was to take France further down the line to what was called *Bundesbank* socialism. Bérégovoy, the Finance Minister, had therefore to cut subsidies, accept enterprise-led restructuring and generally follow austerity policies. This policy switch was also echoed at EC level as Chapter 7 shows.

However, the new policies were not popular at home and industrial unrest continued. Moreover, the PS saw its support plummet both among disillusioned supporters and the uncommitted. In order to try to hold on to power, Mitterrand introduced proportional representation for the 1986 elections. However, given the level of electoral volatility, the right still emerged as the largest force and Mitterrand had to share power, or 'cohabit', with a centre-right coalition government under Jacques Chirac. The new government went somewhat further in privatizing and applying market disciplines than the Socialists, although there was more policy continuity than might have been expected. This was partly due to the deteriorating balance of trade which began to threaten the popularity of the new government, just at the time when new Presidential elections were due. Yet, if Mitterrand and the PS were able to return to power in 1988, they did not find the going easy thereafter. Their electoral victory was paper thin and depended on non-Socialist votes. Economic policy had also to remain fairly tight.

The left in general, faced with a choice between new economic policies or with a spell in opposition, went through a period of painful adaptation in the 1980s. Orthodox Socialist parties thus lost votes throughout the 1980s, even when they were not in government. This was true not just of parties like the British Labour Party and its Swiss and West German equivalents, which lurched to the left (partly because of their opposition to nuclear weapons), but even of more moderate parties. The Swedish model of social democracy in particular came under great pressure. Hence, as in Britain, Germany and the Netherlands, the left was unable to profit from difficulties and divisions on the right. Equally the attempt at 'opening up' to the centre in France, pursued by Prime Minister Michel Rocard after 1988, did not really work.

Furthermore, old-style Communist parties in Finland, France and Italy which had already seen their voters beginning to desert them in the early years of the decade were severely embarrassed by the new line pursued by Gorbachev, as discussed in Chapter 8. This called into question much of what they had previously stood for. Attempts to embrace new causes, such as ecology or resistance to immigration failed to save them. The decline in their political strength could hinder the orthodox left by removing potential allies, at least in France, as well as assisting it by removing a constraint on policy adaption.

Economic recovery and social change

Economic developments also assisted policy adaptation. For while the new policy orientation may have had its roots in the early 1980s, it was to be encouraged by the way in which, from about 1983, the economic situation in Europe began to change markedly for the better. The new policies, in other words, played some part in helping an economic recovery. This had its own spontaneous roots. Nonetheless, the striking nature of the changes in economic climate and policy, had considerable social implications.

The economic recovery of the 1980s dates from about 1983 when reviving world trade and falling oil prices paved the way for a new, and above average, surge in growth. World trade and overseas investment both began to pick up in the 1980s. Trade was encouraged by the new dynamism in the USA and Japan. This produced new markets and opportunities for Europe's manufacturing countries, which were extremely dependent on exports. The easing of the East–West relations after 1985 also played some part in all this. Investment by outsiders in Europe and by Europeans abroad also began to grow rapidly, aiding interdependence and productivity growth.

Oil prices, which had been such a drag on the economy in the 1970s, peaked in 1983. They then began to fall gently, reaching $27 a barrel in 1985. They then fell rapidly to as little as $10 in 1986 before recovering to a relatively stable level of $15 a barrel. The reasons for this were, firstly, that the West had managed to curb its own consumption or replace it by other energy sources. Secondly, some producers produced more than was necessary in order to maintain their income, thereby driving prices down. Although European producing states, notably Britain, the Netherlands and Norway suffered from this, overall the results were positive. Falling oil prices freed some $60 billion for investment and consumption. Governments found they had to borrow less, so that deficits fell from 5.5 per cent of GDP in 1982 to 2.9 per cent in 1989.

As a result of these two factors growth rates began to move upwards, starting in Britain and Denmark. Although rates were less than in the 1950s and 1960s, they could average over 3 per cent, or twice what they had been at the turn of the decade. Rates were even higher in more backward countries like Spain and Portugal. So, overall, between 1985 and 1990 the EC economy grew by 9 per cent. This growth fed through into increased job opportunities. So unemployment peaked in the mid-1980s and then began to fall steadily after 1986, although it remained high. To some extent this decline in unemployment represented not just recovery but the creation of new jobs often in communications and service industries. Equally, inflation, which had already begun to tail off, fell rapidly. Some countries saw a fall of nearly two thirds in the mid-1980s, while in Luxembourg and the Netherlands prices actually declined.

The economy proved itself strong enough to cope with a new financial crisis. In October 1987 the world's stock exchanges experienced a 14 per cent fall in values caused by problems in the financial sector. Although many people feared a horrendous slump, like that started by the Wall Street stock market crash of 1929, in the event there were no further falls. Governments took prompt remedial measures to encourage growth, including making credit more easily available. Confidence soon returned, although new problems were created for the longer term by the way in which governments precipitately lowered interest rates and eased controls on the money supply. This allowed too much money into the system at the wrong time.

The crash of 1987 was also a reflection of the three ways in which changing economic policies had been affecting the European economy. The first was the way in which continuing pressure on state budgets forced a continuation of orthodox fiscal policies. Governments had to control inflation by manipulating exchange and interest rates and curbing budget deficits so as to respond to growing complaints about taxation. This meant cutting subsidies, limiting state sector wages and shaking out labour from state enterprises, as happened in Austria and Belgium.

Secondly, it was increasingly recognized that European industry was uncompetitive on the world market, partly because it was over-regulated. So, along with the EC moves discussed in Chapter 7, there was a gradual domestic move towards deregulation, often encouraged by managers in state enterprises who wanted greater freedom of action. Thus, the French freed up prices, financial markets and stock exchange operations, though not on the scale found in Britain in what was known as the 'Big Bang' when most controls on Stock Exchange operations were lifted.

Deregulation was accompanied by attempts to limit the size of state operations by privatizing some of them. This rarely went as far as it had in Britain but, under Chirac, France did sell off the Paribas bank and firms like St Gobain. In Germany the government contented itself with selling off some of the shares it controlled in companies like Lufthansa and Volkswagen. In Spain marginal state enterprises were sold off. Elsewhere attempts were made to contract out public services or to make consumers pay more for their use. This helped to reduce state outgoings and achieve greater efficiency.

The third aspect of economic policy was its growing European dimension. Both governments and firms, notably Philips, were increasingly aware how the small scale of European markets imposed higher costs on producers as compared with Japan. This was part of the general technological and global challenge to the EC economies discussed in Chapter 7. So, just as large firms began to develop European strategies, whether through joint ventures or acquisitions, so states in response lent their support to the White Paper programme. This was also to affect peripheral and non-member economies, notably in the EFTA states. Equally, the effects of the ERM were to promote growing convergence amongst EC economies.

Changes in the economic cycle and in economic policy also had social implications. They tended to mean that fewer reductions were made in social security budgets than might have been the case. However, the emphasis did change, as it did in education and medical matters. Recovery also lessened, but did not remove either regional problems or fears about migration. Returning economic uncertainty meant that the latter was to become increasingly salient politically.

Overall, Western welfare states found things easier in the 1980s. Though there was much talk of cuts these did not always materialize. Indeed, the fall in the inflation rate meant that the real value of benefits often rose without extra taxation being needed. This was the case in much of Scandinavia. The share of national budgets devoted to social welfare actually went up everywhere except in Britain and Italy. Yet, even in Britain public spending actually increased between 1979 and 1991. Equally talk of privatizing welfare, in line with new economic policies, led to little real change outside Britain. Nonetheless, whereas the French socialist governments had started by trying to reduce the retirement age and increase pensions, by the end of the decade governments were seeking to reduce costs by raising the retirement age and curbing benefits.

Education also received a boost from the new concern for competitiveness. It was brought closer to the market place and, in most countries, more stress was placed on increasing access and training facilities. Training was also seen as a means of coping with unemployment, especially in Sweden. Unemployment remained the major problem facing European welfare states. However, though policies were not very successful, industrial relations did not greatly worsen, reflecting the lower levels of unionization and the growing number of women in the labour force. Female unemployment was an increasing problem.

Housing and poverty also remained major concerns as, for demographic reasons, did medical services. Thus, with ageing populations, increasingly technological forms of medicine and new problems such as drugs and AIDS, medical provision came under pressure. Taxes on cigarettes and alcohol were often raised to try and meet the problems. Both France and Switzerland moved to charging fees for stays in hospital. All this was part of an attempt to place a ceiling on the share of GDP devoted to social welfare.

Recovery did not redress growing regional disparities in Europe. Indeed, the southern agricultural fringes of Europe tended to fall behind in the 1980s and efforts were made to concentrate investment and aid there. However, old industrial regions still had their difficulties and it was there that unemployment and xenophobia were at their worst. Again, this was only partly eclipsed by renewed growth. Therefore, governments began to try and restrict immigration and even, in some cases, to encourage repatriation, especially where migrants came from outside Europe, attracted by its renewed economic success. This reflected the way in which the political climate began to change in the second half of the 1980s.

New political trends
Although free market and sound finance policies were underwritten both by the economic revival and by the way in which most orthodox parties came to terms with the new realities, this convergence did not signify wholehearted or enduring public support for radical market liberalism. Even Britain was bitterly, and sometimes violently, divided in its response to Thatcherism. In fact, electors became increasingly sceptical of state apparatuses and party promises. At the same time public opinion began to be increasingly concerned with new issues and forces. These included the state of the environment, which encouraged the emergence of Green parties across Europe, and re-emerging right wing extremism, fed by new concerns about immigration.

Moreover, the difficulties encountered by the left symbolized a growing scepticism about states and the way they operated. Scandals such as those over the corrupt influence of the P2 masonic lodge in Italy and the secret, illegal files maintained on one in six of the population by the Swiss authorities brought the state a bad name. Turnout at elections thus fell in all countries but Denmark, Luxembourg and Norway during the decade, and especially in France. The reasons for this decline were very different from those which had prevailed in the 1950s and 1960s.

Political parties also attracted an increasingly 'bad press'. They were seen as bureaucratic, ineffective and self-interested. Hence, voters identified with them much less than in the past and tended to switch their voting patterns much more than in the 1970s. Being decreasingly bound by old allegiances to church and class, they profited from the improving economic and diplomatic scene and increasingly voted according to their personal interests, in what is known as 'rational choice' voting. They voted so as to maximize their personal gains and were quick to withdraw support when things did not go as planned. Hence it became increasingly hard to satisfy electorates which, in turn, were quicker to punish governments which did not 'deliver' on their promises than to reward those which did.

As there was an increasing range of parties to which voters could turn electoral volatility rose markedly throughout the decade, as the French example shows. Electors very often switched from established parties to new formations. The 1989 European parliament elections also showed this very clearly. Virtually every party then in government lost votes, often to the benefit of small parties.

To some extent this de-alignment reflected the rise of new issues and forces. At the time the most notable example of this seemed to be the rise of 'Green politics' although, with hindsight, the re-emergence of right wing and nationalist extremism was probably more significant. Concern for the environment had become a major theme in the 1970s, often focused by alarm at the development of nuclear power, and showing itself in direct action. However, despite such anxieties, neither economic life nor government policies changed very much. Hence, some of those who were most concerned about such issues began to develop political parties of their own. Such parties were motivated by new, post-material ideas and very much in favour of grass roots democracy inside both party and society.

These began to enjoy some success in the mid-1980s. Not merely did the West German Greens gain 5.6 per cent of the vote in 1983 and 5.6 per cent in 1987, by when they had 42 members in the *Bundestag*, but many other Parliaments soon had a Green presence. By about 1987 there were 4 in the Finnish *Eduksunta*, 8 in the Austrian *Nationalrat*, 9 in the Belgian Chamber, 13 in that of Italy and 20 in the Swedish *Riksdag*. One of the most successful movements was that in Switzerland. After gaining its first foothold in Parliament in 1979 and 1983, it began to win a considerable number of seats at cantonal elections. By 1987, profiting from the shock caused by Chernobyl and the Schweizerhalle catastrophe on the Rhine near Basle in November 1986 it did even better at the general elections with 9 seats and nearly 5 per cent of the vote.

The key West German party was much more left wing than such parties. It was also deeply split on such issues between so called *Fundis* and the *Realos* who were willing to collaborate in order to achieve their goals. Such divisions were one of the major problems of emerging Green parties. Another was the fact that they remained very small, rarely getting more than 6 per cent of the vote and often less. This limited their effect, although established parties and states, not forgetting the EC, began to try and take environmental issues on board. The great success of Green parties, even in Britain and France, in the 1989 European Parliament elections re-inforced this trend.

All this led to some major switches such as the 1989 Swiss decision to abandon an unpopular plan for a nuclear power station at Kaiseraugst. More significantly, in the same year the Dutch government actually fell over its environmental proposals. The Liberal party challenged tax increases required to finance environmental protection proposed by their coalition partners, the Christian Democrats. However, voters largely rejected the Liberals at the subsequent elections. In other words, by the end of the decade Green issues were rising up the political agenda, and seemed set to go even higher. Yet, at the same time the threat from the Far Right was also re-emerging.

Save perhaps in Italy right wing extremism had been a minor factor in the 1970s, although it did play some role in terrorism, as has already been suggested. However, in the 1980s such extremist movements began to take on a new colouring and a new importance. What changed the parties on the Far Right was the growth of immigration. This initially played no real part in the Scandinavian anti-tax Progress parties or regionalist parties like the Flemish nationalist Vlaams Bloc. However, this began to change, reflecting the concern with immigration at a time of continuing economic difficulties. The growing number of migrants from the Third World who were drawn by the lure of economic revival, many of whom claimed asylum as a means of gaining entry to the labour market, were feared and resented. For, to many self-employed and blue collar workers, the revival was both very fragile and did very little to solve the problem of unemployment which already faced them.

So they tended to see the Tamils, and others who began to arrive in Western Europe in large numbers after 1983, both as a threat to their own job prospects and as a drain on them as hard-pressed taxpayers. They started to believe that overindulgent states provided them with too many benefits. The newcomers could also be seen as a threat to national cohesion and order, as with the murder of a Dutch policeman by a Surinamese in 1985. These kind of events influenced government policies which became notably more restrictive about access, although without really stemming the growing flood of economic migrants and others.

As a result voters increasingly turned either to direct action, with attacks on migrants and their hostels, or to Far Right parties. This happened in Denmark, where the Progress Party became notably more xenophobic under Annette Jost and gained consistently over the decade, as did its Norwegian namesake in 1985. A similar phenomenon was observable in Austria where, after 1986, Jurg Haider took the Freedom Party much further to the right and won many protest votes the following year. The Low Countries also saw the Vlaams Bloc and the Dutch Centre Party make some gains by playing the anti-immigrant card. Finally, in Switzerland, the anti-environmental AutoPartei began to take on an anti-immigrant stance after 1987.

The most notable breakthrough, however, was in France. After failing miserably in 1981 the Front National began to poll over 10 per cent of the vote first in by-elections and then in the 1984 European Parliament. The introduction of proportional representation in 1986 brought them 35 seats in the Chamber of Deputies, as many as the Communists. Although the return to the two ballot system wiped them out in the 1988 general elections, their leader won 14.4 per cent of the vote in the first round of the Presidential elections. This was re-inforced by further success in the European Parliament elections the next year.

The Front National's success was based on much more than PR. First and foremost it reflected abilities of its leader, Jean-Marie Le Pen. Not merely was he a very charismatic figure, who attracted support both as a speaker and a combative TV personality, but he also had remarkable skills of organization. He thus created a network of supporting organizations which have helped to make the party one of the most organized and influential in the country. It was also the one most likely to resort to covert violence. His message, that unemployment could be solved and the security and integrity of the state restored by action against foreigners, went down well in the south of France and many cities with large foreign populations.

Apart from this it was generally the north of Europe which was most affected by the rise of Green and far left politics. West Germany under the CDU/CSU–FDP coalition saw limited moves towards budgetary austerity, although not as much as the FDP would have liked. Unemployment remained a problem. But the Social Democratic opposition was unable to exploit this partly because of the favourable economic and diplomatic conditions, and partly because of its own difficulties. These included having to fend off the challenge from the Greens. As a result the coalition was able to win a fairly easy victory in the 1987 elections.

The Kohl years also coincided with a fivefold increase in the number of refugees who, like the many ethnic Germans returning, swelled the 4.7 million foreigners, many of them Turks. Small right wing parties like the National-demokratische Partei Deutschlands (NPD) and the German People's Union (DVU) began to gain by this, while neo-Nazi movements began to grow, often expressing themselves in skinhead violence against workers and other foreigners. Government attempts to control them were not very successful and, in 1989, the Republikaner, a party led by a former *Waffen* SS officer, made a significant breakthrough in both the Berlin and the European Parliament elections.

Conversely, the Greens seemed to have peaked at this time. They had offended many people by their extremism and refusal to compromise. In any case, because environmental legislation had become almost routine in Germany and elsewhere, there seemed less need to vote Green. And the apparent revival of the SPD, in the wake of the French and Italian parties, offered another outlet for radical voters, just as the Labour party was doing in the UK. This revival of the left seemed to presage a further shift in the political balance.

A watershed?

The growing opposition to the general tolerant consensus on immigration was one of several signs at the end of the 1980s, that the policies which had dominated the decade were being called into question. This was certainly the case with the partial economic and political convergence which had been achieved. Successes in controlling inflation and government deficits while at the same time boosting economic growth began to seem less important than the returning problems of unemployment. At the same time, while there had been no major changes in political control, the monetary policies of the 1980s had been significantly relaxed after 1987.

Although economic growth continued for a while, this relaxation soon came home to roost. Britain thus led the continent into depression as the decade came to an end. This was to have considerable effects on West European politics. However, it was not then clear that Western Europe stood at a watershed of its own. In any case, long before then, the domestic economic achievements of the 1980s had already played a significant part in facilitating other developments, beginning with the considerable progress made in integration after 1985, not to mention perestroika and disarmament. This meant that, overall, the decade was a much better time for the West than had initially seemed likely to some observers.

Further reading

Ardagh, J. (1991), *France Today*, Harmondsworth: Penguin.
Dalton, R. and Kuecher, M. (1990), *Challenging the Political Order*, Oxford: Blackwell.
Dyker, D. (ed.) (1992), *The European Economies*, London: Longman.
Gallagher, T. (1983), *Portugal. A 20th Century Interpretation*, London: MacMillan.
Griffiths, R.T. (1980), *Economics and Politics in the Netherlands*, Hague: Nijhoff.
Harris, G. (1994), *The Darker Side of Europe*, Edinburgh: Edinburgh University Press.
Keating, M. and Jones, B. (eds) (1985), *Regions in the EC*, Oxford: Clarendon.
Muller-Rommel, F. (ed.) (1989), *New Political Movements*, Boulder, Col.: Westview.
Peters, B.G. (1991), *European Politics Reconsidered*, London: Holmes and Meier.

Pettifer, J. (1994), *The Greeks. Land and People Since the War*, Harmondsworth: Penguin.
Preston, P. (1986), *The Triumph of Democracy in Spain*, London: Methuen.
Riddell, P. (1989), *The Thatcher Decade*, Oxford, Blackwell.
Ross, G. *et al.* (1987), *The Mitterrand Experiment*, Oxford: Polity.
Turner, B. (1982), *The Other European Community*, London: Weidenfeld and Nicholson.
Turner, H.A. (1994), *Germany from Partition to Unification*, New Haven, Conn.: Yale University
    Press.

7 The 'relaunching' of the European Community

As indicated in Chapter 3, the 1970s were a critical time for the EC. Many of the new proposals and policies, at which the EC had aimed during the early 1970s, had never materialized. This was partly due to the oil crisis and the breakdown of the Bretton Woods system, but partly also a result of member states' loss of confidence in EC action and their preoccupation with domestic concerns. In the early 1980s, the EC faced a further series of interrelated problems. The threat of bankruptcy loomed large as the result of unlimited expansion of agricultural expenditure. At the same time the EC was negotiating its third enlargement to include Spain and Portugal, while struggling for industrial survival in the face of technological challenges from the USA and Japan. Furthermore, the EC reached this crisis point beset by institutional weaknesses, since, as a result of the Luxembourg Compromise, decisions were still arrived at through time-consuming package deals in an exhausting attempt to achieve consensus between national governments. To remedy this situation, dramatic action was necessary.

This Chapter explains how stagnation in the EC gave way to an economic and political revival in the mid-1980s when, as a result of pressure from leading industrialists, both individual governments and EC institutions submitted proposals designed to revitalize the EC and to spur member states into action. These initiatives centred around two major objectives: firstly, a re-emphasis on the Internal Market and an expansion of the scope of EC policies and secondly, a reform of the outdated decision-making machinery of the EC. Both objectives culminated, in 1987, in the adoption by the EC of the SEA.

Background to the relaunch

In the early to mid-1980s several factors combined to force the EC to take dramatic action to break out of the stagnation that had characterized it in the 1970s. Enormous technological developments and drastic changes in the international setting forced EC leaders to rethink their economic interests, to reassess their social needs and to re-evaluate their political goals. Faced with growing competition from the USA and the emergence of Japan as the world's second largest economy at the expense of all European nations, the EC needed to secure a place for itself in the world of the 1980s. In security terms – particularly in view of the change of leadership in the Soviet Union – the EC had to reconsider its role and its traditional dependence on the USA, once Europe's most important and powerful custodian. The relative decline of the strategic importance of the USA and the emergence of 'new thinking' in the Soviet Union – indicating the end of a bipolar security world – left a kind of power vacuum.

The objectives of the EC had not significantly altered since the 1970s, but continued to be based on national criteria. Moreover, stagnation, recession, rising unemployment and high inflation had not provoked a European response. On the contrary, the protectionist armoury had grown steadily. An exception to the pursuit of national strategies was perhaps the launching of the EMS in 1979 to create, if not full economic and monetary union, at least a zone of currency stability. But the imperfections of the common market in particular showed that member states had not taken advantage of the benefits of integration.

The initial momentum to develop the customs union – completed so successfully in July 1968 – into a truly integrated 'single' market, whereby the freedom to supply goods was to be accompanied by the undistorted movement of labour, capital and enterprise, had been absorbed by economic crises and the EC's first enlargement. While tariffs and quantitative restrictions had been removed between member states, many technical and physical barriers remained, seriously hampering intra-EC trade. It was evident that the EC fell far short of the full common market envisaged in the Treaty of Rome. Europe's decline or at least the necessity to compete with the steady growth of Japanese and American exports alerted national governments and focused their attention on the expansion of the European market.

Industry, being directly affected by these international economic developments, began to favour joint European action. In some ways, Europe's industrial elite was well ahead of EC institutions and European politicians. During the early 1980s Europe's business elite began to lobby national governments and eventually pushed the EC to place market unification on top of its agenda. An increasingly energetic campaign was launched by the 'Roundtable of European Industrialists', an association including influential names such as Philips, Siemens, Olivetti, Volvo, Fiat and Bosch. Philips, in early 1985, published a paper 'Europe 1990 – an agenda for action' which called for collaborate efforts to stem the trend towards stagnation and decline. One of the most important factors in this new domestic political constellation was the realization that the national strategies of the 1970s had failed. This realization led to a weakening of traditional left-wing policies and a shift to a vigorous market-orientated, deregulatory approach in economic management throughout the EC, most notably in France. As Chapter 6 has shown, President Mitterrand, in 1983, abandoned his Socialist agenda of state intervention and regulation and set on a course of neoliberalism, thus encouraging both Spain and Portugal to follow suit. This convergence became instrumental in a new vigorous drive to restore Europe's industrial prowess.

Thus, aided by a favourable domestic setting and pressured by industrialists, the EC institutions, in particular the Commission, seized the opportunity to develop entrepreneurial leadership. The Commission had become increasingly exercised by the lack of a truly integrated market, a concern reflected in the relevant sections of its annual reports. The breakthrough came in January 1985 with the arrival of 14 new Commissioners out of a total of 17, including a new Commission President, Jacques Delors. A former French finance minister, Delors possessed two qualities needed at that time: vision and courage. The presence of this leadership was a necessary condition for the relaunching of the EC. Within days of taking office, Delors mapped out a new plan to spur Europe's economy to new growth by completing the single market and proposing the end of 1992 as a possible target date.

Project 1992
The resulting document, the *White Paper on Completing the Internal Market*, was written within seven weeks, despite having been redrafted 17 times. On June 15th 1985, Lord Cockfield, Commissioner responsible for the Internal Market, presented it to the public. The White Paper identified legislative provisions covering both the remaining barriers to trade and the obstacles to the movement of people. Lord Cockfield set out the two essential ingredients for success of the *White Paper*; which was firstly that a detailed and complete programme was needed involving the removal of all barriers which fragmented the EC economy. The second imperative was a strict timetable and, as a result, the programme was scheduled to be completed by December 1992 – within the eight year lifespan of two Commissions. Since Commissioners are usually reappointed after their first four-year term in office, the timetable proposed would enable them to preside over the entire programme. During that time all controls still affecting the circulation of goods, people, services and capital would be eliminated. Originally 300 proposals, later adjusted to 282, were identified under three specific headings: the physical, technical and fiscal barriers.

Physical barriers
The key physical barriers that affect goods and people alike are essentially custom controls at borders. This leads to unnecessary operational costs and delays caused by administration. The Commission wanted to do away with internal frontier controls in their entirety. However, although the *White Paper* was broadly backed by all member states, people's unhindered passage across the EC's internal borders has been one of the more problematic aspects of completing the Internal Market. Fears of terrorism and drug trafficking, along with differing attitudes to immigration and asylum seekers amongst member states have meant that this issue was hard to resolve.

Nevertheless, some countries were ahead of the programme: thus, on 19 June 1990 the Schengen Convention was signed by France, Germany and the three Benelux countries. Italy followed in December 1990 and Spain and Portugal in June 1991. Greece, having previously been an observer, became a full member in November 1992. The Convention, which was intended to be implemented by 1 July 1993, would lift controls on the movement of people at internal land and sea borders of the EC. (It was to be applicable to airports by 1 January 1994.) However, this was to prove an optimistic timetable. At the same time common procedures for all checks at external borders and airports were to be established. Free movement of people based on the Schengen Convention also includes common visa requirements for non EC-citizens, rules for cross-border operations, surveillance by the police force and common provisions for people requiring political asylum. At present, the UK, Ireland and Denmark remain committed to checking travellers' identification.

By contrast, the free movement of goods is now virtually assured, with control lifted from both individuals and business. It is estimated that the EC has achieved the abolition of some 60 million administrative forms per year.

Technical barriers
Technical barriers refers to the many different technical standards and laws regulating the production and manufacturing of products in each member state. Exporters are therefore forced to undertake alterations to their exported goods, in an attempt to ensure acceptance of their goods by another member state which might have different technical requirements. However, this creates great expense of time and money. The *White Paper* proposed to solve the problem of different rules concerning product standards and controls by common, EC specifications. In the past, the EC has relied heavily on the harmonizing of technical standards of member states. Apart from the fact that this approach is extremely cumbersome, it also smacks of 'uniformity' and the enforcement of 'Euro-products'. A new streamlined method was clearly essential for the huge 1992 legislative programme. In 1980, the Commission had already developed a new strategy and it was this which was to become the keystone of much of the *White Paper*'s legislation: a shift from harmonizing regulations to the principle of 'mutual recognition' of national legislation. The *White Paper* emphasized the principle that goods lawfully manufactured and marketed in one member state, must be allowed free entry into other member states. The idea was quite simple: 'If a Community citizen or a company meets the requirements for its activity in one member state, there should be no valid reason why those citizens or companies should not exercise their economic activities also in other parts of the Community.' Only in a few special sectors, such as foodstuffs where harmonization was deemed to be essential, has EC action concentrated on 'horizontal' directives governing

the use of additives and other regulations in an attempt to protect the health and safety of consumers.

The principle of mutual recognition, originally conceived for the free movement of products, was soon extended to other areas, like financial services, professional qualifications and vocational training. For example, in 1988 a directive covering some 100 professions was adopted by the Council. This stipulated that all educational diplomas following on at least three years full-time study at an institution of higher education, had to be recognized in all member states.

Fiscal barriers

Although the EC, in 1977, agreed on a common basis for assessing VAT, different rates of excise duties and VAT persisted. Fiscal barriers are obstructions to trade such as divergent rates of indirect tax and excise duties and the difficulties in moving capital within the EC. Indirect taxation, whether in the form of VAT or excise duty, enters more or less directly into the final price of the goods or services on which they are imposed. Different levels of taxation are therefore reflected in different price levels.

Cockfield's proposal on indirect taxation in September 1987 called for the harmonization of both VAT and excise taxes. However, by June 1989 the Commission withdrew its proposal for harmonized taxes due to lack of agreement in the Council. The Commission, on 25 October 1989 proposed that, since the imposition of an EC-wide rate of tax as proposed in 1987 was unrealistic, a minimum rate should be applied as from 1 January 1993 for a transitional period. It was hoped that, at the end of the transitional period, namely as from 1 January 1997, a definitive regime would be introduced. During the transition, cross-frontier sales would be taxed in the country of destination of the goods. Under the definitive regime, however, such sales would be taxed in the country of origin. Accordingly, in July 1992, the Council secured a provisional agreement to set a minimum 15 per cent VAT rate for four years as from 1 January 1993 with specific provisions on reduced rates and zero rates. For all its flaws, the transitional regime for VAT and excise duties has done away with the need for basic administrative border controls on all products.

Implications of the White Paper

While the publication of the *White Paper* unleashed a large legislative agenda, it also set in motion other – largely unforeseen – processes. For example, what strategies were necessary to achieve the ambitious project of completing the Internal Market? How could a speedy transposition of necessary legislation into national law be ensured? Certainly, determined and courageous efforts were also needed to reinforce the efficiency of the EC's institutions. As already noted, the unanimous consent of member states enforced by the use of the Luxembourg

Compromise had hampered the EC's decision-making to such an extent that there was serious delay in the adoption of EC provisions. The process of harmonization of regulations and other integrationary measures had become highly cumbersome.

The EC, although still a force at international level, was losing its democratic credentials and was increasingly seen as an organization plagued by 'Eurosclerosis'. Hence, decision-making had to be simplified. A radical departure from previous practise was needed involving majority voting, hitherto the exception rather than the rule. Moreover, the question of further expansion of the EC – Greece had joined in 1981, but the applications for membership from both Spain and Portugal had yet to be dealt with – made effective decision-making in the EC even more imperative. Institutional reform was not only the prerequisite for the realization of the Internal Market, but clearly imperative to meet the challenges of the 1980s.

Furthermore, while the Treaty of Rome had made the completion of the customs union its central objective, it had only given scant attention to other areas and, in some cases, had been silent on important issues. Monetary union, environmental policies, regional imbalances and socio-economic cohesion, not an explicit objective of the Treaty of Rome, were becoming an important element in EC policy-making and had to be given a constitutional base. As EC action became more diversified and membership increased, it became necessary to bring these new policies within the ambit of the EC's constitutional framework.

The most important new area was undoubtedly foreign policy. In the past, member states had sought to harmonize their foreign policies by means of a process, referred to as European Political Co-operation (EPC) established in 1970. However, this was outside the framework of the Treaty of Rome, and co-operation in this area was strictly on the basis of intergovernmental agreements, although managed by the state holding the Council Presidency. The international climate of the 1980s demanded however, that the EC, already the largest single trading unit in the world, should also develop a unified political identity in international affairs.

The challenges the EC was facing, both as a result of internal problems and outside pressures, were compelling. The ever-increasing scope of this huge agenda demanded swift action. This awareness stimulated a debate during the early and mid-1980s involving the European Parliament, the Commission, but also individual governments.

Reform debates

In 1981, the German Foreign Minister Hans-Dietrich Genscher, backed by his Italian counterpart, Emilio Colombo, started campaigning for a new phase in European integration with a view to working towards an EU. The resulting Genscher–Colombo plan was submitted for analysis first to the EC foreign ministers and, in 1983, to the European Council. However, the final version of the paper was considerably watered down by the European heads of state and government and essential questions, particularly in the sphere of foreign policy and institutional reform, were ducked. Virtually all member states were reluctant to increase the role of the EC institutions – a central suggestion of the Genscher–Colombo plan. Britain resented the increase in budgetary resources implicit in the plan – a concern shared by the German Chancellor, Helmut Schmidt. The proposed extension of the use of majority voting was also viewed with suspicion by several member states as an encroachment on national sovereignty. Eventually member states were able to agree on a 'Solemn Declaration on European Union' which was endorsed at the European Council summit meeting in Stuttgart in June 1983. While the declaration fell far short of the aims of the Genscher–Colombo plan, it did keep discussion on political and economic reform at the centre of the EC's agenda.

A key actor in the move towards substantial reform was undoubtedly the EP. Under the leadership of the lifelong European federalist, Altiero Spinelli, an independent member of the Communist group in the EP, and as a result of its newly emerging self-confidence in the aftermath of the first ever direct elections of MEPs in 1979, a comprehensive reform discussion was initiated. In July 1981 the 'Crocodile Club', a group of federalists led by Spinelli, drafted a resolution calling for an EU. Subsequently, an *ad hoc* Committee on Institutional Affairs was set up, charged with the task of drafting a treaty on EU which was completed in 1984.

The draft treaty called for increased powers for the Commission and the EP, the introduction of majority voting and, as noted before, the addition of a number of new policy areas in particular foreign policy to the ambit of EC decision-making. The treaty was adopted by the EP by a large majority on 14 February 1984 and was the most fully articulated plan for a united Europe to date. Moreover, while the treaty was not accepted by the European Council as it stood, it nevertheless significantly influenced subsequent debates.

The real breakthrough, however, turned out to be the European Council meeting at Fontainebleau in June 1984. Member states succeeded in resolving a series of bitter conflicts which had bedevilled the EC for years. These included the granting of a cash rebate to Britain, which had complained about the size of its budgetary contribution to the EC. The question of the British cash rebate had dominated every European Council meeting since 1979. Under the new agreement, Britain would receive an annual rebate based upon 66 per cent of the difference between its VAT contributions and its share of EC expenditure. Much of the credit for the resolution of this long-standing conflict between Britain and the EC, must go to the French President. Having held the presidency of the Council for the first half of the year, Mitterrand was committed to finding a way of solving this issue, before the presidency of the Council passed on to Ireland in July 1984.

The second very important breakthrough at Fontainebleau was an agreement to increase the EC's financial resources. The EC budget was financed at that time from proceeds paid from duties established by the EC in respect of trade with non-member states. These customs duties and agricultural levies were the natural resources of the EC. However, income from these sources fluctuated and were inadequate to finance all the operations of the EC. As a result, provisions were made for the member states to top up the EC's 'Own Resources' by making a financial contribution to the budget based on member states' VAT revenue of up to 1 per cent. As expenditure rose, it became necessary to call on member states to increase their VAT contribution. After extensive negotiations involving several European summit meetings at Stuttgart, Athens and Brussels, the Fontainebleau meeting resolved this issue when member states agreed to increase their VAT contribution from 1 per cent to 1.4 per cent.

The question of increased budgetary resources was closely tangled up with the third crucial issue, namely the finalization of entry negotiations with Spain and Portugal so that these two countries could become members by January 1986. Chancellor Kohl, during the June 1983 Stuttgart European Summit meeting, had insisted that ratification of an increase in the present legal ceiling of 1 per cent VAT would have to be part of a wider 'package', which also included ratification of Spanish and Portuguese membership by 1 January 1986. During the Athens December 1983 summit meeting, Kohl reaffirmed the German position: no increase in budgetary funds without the accession of new entrants. The Brussels 1984 summit paved the way to a broad agreement on this issue which was finally resolved at Fontainebleau.

Having thus cleared a whole backlog of internal problems, the EC was ready to tackle the issue of institutional reform. Two committees were established, the first being a 'Committee for a People's Europe' (the Adonnino Committee). This was charged with examining how a European identity might be developed among EC citizens. The second and more important one was the *ad hoc* Committee on Institutional Affairs known as the Dooge Committee after its Irish chairman James Dooge. Its task was to explore the various proposals for change being put forward and to determine the degree of consensus which might exist among member states.

The Dooge Committee presented its final report to the Brussels summit in March 1985 and outlined a number of main objectives. These included the completion of an 'internal economic area', institutional reform by enhancing the powers of both the Commission and the EP and an expansion of policy activities. Although the report had stayed clear from very contentious issues, being aware of the wide differences in opinion among member states, its very suggestion to convene an Intergovernmental Conference (IGC) to negotiate an

EU treaty drew immediate criticism from Britain, Denmark and Greece. Thus, a split opened up between the federalists of the EC, the so-called maximalists, led by Italy and those who wanted to have as little reform as possible, the minimalists, led by the UK. The conflict reached a climax at the European Council meeting in Milan in June 1985. Differences centred above all on the principle and extent of institutional reform. In an extraordinary move and in an attempt to force the issue, the Italian Presidency called for a vote on holding an IGC. Despite objections from Britain, Greece and Denmark, the majority of member states supported the setting up of such a conference charged with developing a comprehensive reform package based on recent proposals.

The negotiations which followed involved not only the member states, but also the Commission and the EP (which, immediately after the Milan summit, had demanded the right to participate in the conference) as well as the two prospective new members, Spain and Portugal. Finally, at the meeting of the European Council in Luxembourg in December 1985, the EC adopted in principle a text, based on the proposal submitted by the IGC. This document became known as the SEA. It was ratified between June 1986 and June 1987, following referenda in Denmark (June 1986) and Ireland (June 1987) and, as a result of the latter, came into force after a six-month delay, on 1st July 1987.

The SEA

The SEA was a key treaty because it was the first major systematic revision of the Treaty of Rome. It embodied a series of fundamental bargains between member states, which were more than a 'package deal', but were aptly described as the outcome of a 'synergy' between different sectors or approaches to integration. This synergy was most evident in the linkage between unifying the internal market – broadly favoured by all member states – and institutional reform, supported by the 'federalist' countries, in particular Italy. The SEA consisted of a Preamble and four Titles: the preamble reiterated the objective of creating an EU while the Titles provided for the creation of the European Council, covered institutional reform, the extension of policy areas including importantly a commitment to a fully integrated internal market by the end of 1992 and a formal commitment to the co-ordination of foreign policies; it concluded with general and final provisions. In the sense that the SEA merely reiterated the goal of the Treaty of Rome (of creating a full Internal Market), it was not revolutionary. However, the inclusion in the SEA of institutional changes started an evolutionary process.

Institutional reform

The most ambitious objective in this area was the EC's shift to majority voting to facilitate the legislation required to achieve 'the objectives set out in Art. 8A', in other words the creation of the Internal Market. In certain sensitive sectors, especially taxation, free movement of persons and the rights and interests of employed persons, unanimity was retained. The new provisions still fell short of the Commission's proposal which had required majority voting for all measures concerning the creation of the Internal Market. In the event, only 75 per cent of Internal Market legislation were to be adopted by majority vote. Nevertheless, the shift from unanimity previously practised reflected the EC's resolution to break the institutional deadlock of previous decades.

The second provision of institutional reform implied an enhancement of the powers of the EP, although the new role assigned to it may appear very modest. In the past, the EP had acted as a consultative body only. However, the SEA extended the rights of the EP by creating a new 'co-operation procedure' in most fields where majority was possible. This provided for two readings. In the first round of consultations on a Commission proposal, the EP would give its opinion. Parliament's opinion would then be taken into account by the Council in reaching what is called a 'common position'. That common position may be accepted, rejected or amended by Parliament during a second reading which would have to take place within three months. In the event of Parliament's rejection of the Council's 'common position', the latter could only override the rejection by an unanimous vote. If Parliament amended the common position, and the Commission agreed with those amendments, a qualified majority of the Council would be required to endorse the amended proposal. In the case of disagreement between the Commission and the EP, a unanimous vote of the Council would be required to override the Commission and adopt the amendment.

The new provision was designed to set clear limits to Council's powerful role. On the other hand, it did not appreciably alter the latter's authority, since, by acting unanimously, it still had the last word on draft legislation. However, the new provision was important for several reasons. Firstly, it demanded inter-institutional co-operation between the Commission, the Council and the EP. This was likely to alter the character of the tripolar dialogue making for closer contacts between the institutions and ensuring greater transparency of EC decision-making. Secondly, the need for Council to justify its 'common position' during the first reading, forced it to give due considerations to Parliament's opinion. Finally, it soon became clear that the co-operation procedure, limited as it was, had opened the door for evolutionary changes in the legislative process.

New policies
The SEA amended the Treaty of Rome to include six new policy areas, all of which form the bulk of Title II. The most important one was the completion of the Internal Market by 31 December 1992. The SEA defined the Single Market 'as an area without internal frontiers in which the free movement of goods, persons, services and capital is ensured in accordance with the provisions of this treaty'. Although the SEA stipulated a strict deadline for this objective, namely 31

December 1992, a Declaration annexed to the Treaty explained that the timetable was a political aspiration. Hence, it was not legally binding. Significantly, the SEA provided for majority voting covering 75 per cent of the Single Market regulations. The details of what is involved in completing the Single Market have been outlined in the Commission's *White Paper* of 1985 which was discussed earlier in this Chapter.

The objective of completing the Internal Market was flanked by five new policies. The goal of monetary union was reasserted and the EMS, launched in 1979, was given a treaty base for the first time. The SEA laid down provisions for improving the working environment to safeguard the health and safety of EC workers. The peripheral countries (Greece, Spain and Portugal) extracted agreement from the richer member states to develop the regional dimension of the Internal Market. As a result and in order to achieve 'economic and social cohesion', resources for structural funds were increased. At the prompting of the Germans, the SEA demanded co-operation in Research and Technological Development and, for the first time, drew environmental policies into the ambit of the EC's constitutional framework.

Codification of policies and EC 'practices'
The SEA also provided for the codification of certain policies already being carried out by the EC, but which had never been mentioned in the Treaty of Rome. These were the work of the European Council and co-operation over foreign policy issues. The European Council was the only major institution which had no basis in the Treaty of Rome. It had originated in the meeting of heads of state and of government in December 1969 at the end of the transitional phase, when the EC embarked on a new phase of development, as Chapter 3 has shown. Such meetings helped to identify new areas of EC activities. They continued on a regular basis and later were given the title of 'European Council' because, as one observer said, they were meetings of the Council in its 'highest manifestion'. In Art. 2, the SEA recorded the existence of the European Council for the first time. It could be argued that the acknowledgement of a purely inter-governmental body, such as the European Council, counteracts any attempts by the EC to strengthen the supranational nature of the EC. On the other hand, it is fair to say that Art. 2 of the SEA had no further implications for the role of the European Council beyond that of formal recognition of its existence.

Foreign Policy is another area of EC policy which has emerged over the years. It was not an explicit aim of the EC's founding treaties, but had grown over the previous 20 years. It existed in a framework outside the EC, known as EPC, but linked to it both by the Commission's participation and by the fact that the foreign ministers report regularly to the EP. The SEA, under a separate Title III dealing with 'Provisions on European Co-operation in the sphere of Foreign Policy', for the first time explicitly stated that the member states should jointly formulate and implement a European foreign policy. However, the SEA was rather vague on what really was implied when asking member states to 'endeavour jointly to formulate and implement a European foreign policy'. This clearly underscored the extent to which foreign policy was subject to intergovernmental agreements. Since the European Court of Justice (ECJ) was excluded from jurisdiction in this area and member states participating in EPC were referred to as the 'High Contracting Parties', the boundaries between intergovernmental and supranational policy were severely fudged. Furthermore, the SEA did not clarify security issues, agreeing merely to co-operate 'on questions of European security'. However, as this was a highly sensitive area causing serious divergences among member states, even the statement that members are 'ready to co-ordinate their positions more closely on the political and economic aspects of security' was a major breakthrough.

Whatever the drawbacks and weaknesses of the actual text regarding foreign policy in the SEA, it nevertheless codified EPC and was the culmination of a long process of debates. Although foreign policy co-operation in the EC, after the entry into force of the SEA, could not be described as 'supranational', its form reflected the extent to which compromises had been achieved between member states at that time. However, the drawing of EPC into the EC framework indicated the direction European integration might take in the future.

Finally, the SEA provided for the introduction of a new Court of First Instance in an attempt to speed up the judicial process. It was hoped that by hearing certain cases in the first instance, the new institution would be relieving the burden on the ECJ.

The pragmatic line followed in the *White Paper* which contains programme, method and instruments to complete the Internal Market, would nevertheless have been insufficient to reach its objectives, had it not been for a parallel updating of the EC's outdated decision-making machinery. The SEA provided the necessary institutional provisions by the extension of majority voting in the Council and encouraging interinstitutional collaboration. The anchoring of the *White Paper* in a legally binding Treaty, containing a very definite timetable, mobilized political will in the EC.

'Implementing the relaunch' – the verdict
In September 1992 the Commission submitted its seventh (and last) annual report on the progress of the Single Market to the Council and the EP stating that nearly 90 per cent of the objectives of the *White Paper* had been implemented. On 17 December 1992, in their last meeting before the market was formally opened on 31 December 1992, the Council agreed 12 measures bringing the total of 282 provisions to just short of the full programme of the Internal Market legislation proposed in 1985. In the areas of research and development the first programme based on the SEA – an attempt to make European industry more

competitive internationally – was agreed in September 1987. Progress was also made in environmental policies, particularly measures were taken to protect the ozone layer by cutting emissions of sulphur dioxide and nitrogen.

There were important direct implications of the SEA. Firstly, the introduction of a single currency and the creation of a European Central Bank (ECB) – as the crowning of the Internal Market. Under the vigorous leadership of Jacques Delors, this issue was taken up at the Hanover summit meeting in June 1988 when the European Council appointed a special commission chaired by Jacques Delors to devise a plan for complete economic and monetary union. The plan which was submitted to the member states in April 1989 envisaged monetary union in three stages: the first would be completed within the framework of the existing EMS and called for all currencies to join the narrow band of the ERM; the second was a transitional period to coordinate member states' fiscal and economic policies; and the third was to introduce an ECB and a single currency. During the summit meeting in Strasbourg in December 1989 the EC decided to convene an IGC to negotiate treaty amendments necessary for the setting up of the new institutions required in stages two and three.

The second implication of the SEA was financial measures to cost the new programmes. In a special document, entitled 'Making the single act succeed', the Commission, in February 1987, initiated a further round of negotiations. Eventually, under the guidance of the Commission President, a comprehensive package was constructed which included measures to cut agricultural expenditure and reduce surpluses and a proposal to open up a new means of resources, proportionate to member states' GNP. The package also included the doubling of the structural funds (Regional, Social and Agricultural Guidance) and a financial programme for five years ahead. After two abortive attempts by the European Council at the June 1987 and December 1987 summit meetings, the package was finally approved in February 1988 during an 'emergency' summit chaired by Chancellor Kohl. By the end of the FRG's presidency on 30 June 1988 the basic provisions of the 'Delors package' had been turned into binding legal documents.

Thirdly, it was realized that the implications of the Internal Market could be severe in the social area. During 1988, both the West German and Greek presidencies drew attention to this issue. Consequently, in order to give the Internal Market 'a human face', Delors, in May 1989, initiated the drafting of a programme for a minimum set of workers' and citizens' rights, the 'EC Charter of the Fundamental Social Rights of Workers' in an attempt to work for an upward approximation of working conditions throughout the EC. The FRG, at the instigation of its trade union confederation, the Deutscher Gewerkschaftsbund (DGB), had insisted on minimum standards for employees' rights, although Bonn was unsuccessful in promoting the imposition of minimum wage levels throughout the EC. In Strasbourg at the Summit meeting in December 1989 11 member states (because of British objections) approved a watered down version of the original charter.

The impulse for the creation of an Internal Market not only attracted attention in the US and Japan, but also in the EFTA states, the EC's main trading partners in Europe. Access to the EC market was vital for these countries, which in the late 1980s sent some 55 per cent of their total exports to the EC, while about 60 per cent of their imports originated in EC countries. As a result, Jacques Delors, in January 1989, put forward the notion of a European Economic Area (EEA) (or Space), (a phrase coined for the first time in 1984 during an EC–EFTA ministerial meeting) which would allow EFTA countries access to the Internal Market without them incurring obligations of full membership of the EC. Formal negotiations to this effect opened in June 1990. During the negotiations process, it became clear, however, that subsequent developments had overtaken Delors' original plan for an EEA, when some of the EFTA countries led by Austria in 1989 applied for full membership, thus adding to the list of existing applications from Turkey, Malta and Cyprus.

Considering the multitude of political measures adopted between 1985 and 1989, it is legitimate to argue that the EC had made significant progress in its aim to 'relaunch' Europe. The Single Market is beginning to take shape. Mergers, joint ventures and take-over activities have increased since 1985 encouraged by renewed faith in the European relaunch. Since 1984 production has risen by some 20 per cent, while over 8 million new jobs have been created. Intra-EC trade is reviving, while investments from both the USA and Japan have increased since 1985 by 60 per cent and 400 per cent respectively.

The EC has launched institutional reform, although the new provisions still fall short of the EP's demand for co-decision-making with the Council in all EC activities. The EC has also broadened its activities with the inclusion of new policies and codified existing practises. At the same time it has ended the deadlock over agricultural and financial issues which has dominated EC affairs for nearly a decade. Fundamental decisions have been made concerning the flanking policies of the Internal Market, particularly in the area of monetary union. Spain and Portugal have joined the EC on 1 January 1986 thereby doubling the original members from six to twelve.

Internationally, the states of the EC and particularly the prestige of the Commission and its President has grown. This became quite obvious when the EC was asked, in July 1989, to become co-ordinator of Western aid to the new democracies in the East. As political developments in Central and Eastern European came to a head in the autumn and winter of 1989, it was decided, in February 1990, to extend the aid project to other East European countries. In addition, the attraction of the EC was clearly demonstrated by the fact that new applications for membership and associated membership were received, not only from the EFTA countries, but also from the new democracies in Eastern and Central Europe.

Thus, a new dynamism was given to the process of European integration. The EC had surpassed the period of 'Euro-sclerosis' in the 1970s which has given way to the euphoric 1980s. With far-reaching changes in its institutional set-up and new policies adopted, it was clearly demonstrated that the EC was moving towards a federal entity. The adoption of the SEA was a necessary pre-condition in this process. As the decade drew to an end, the political and economic environment of the EC looked hopeful and promising; the EC appeared strong enough to meet the challenges of the 1990s.

Further reading

Commission of the European Communities (1985), *Completing the Internal Market*, White Paper from the Commission to the European Council; Milan, 28–29 June COM (85) 310 final.

Commission of the European Communities (1986), Bulletin of the European Communities *Single European Act*, Supplement 2/86.

Church, C.H. and Keogh, D. (eds) (1991), *The Single European Act. A Transnational Study*, Canterbury: University of Kent.

Vickerman, R.W. (1992), *The Single European Market*, London: Harvester Wheatsheaf.

Williams, A.M. (1991), *The European Community*, Oxford: Blackwell.

Swann, D. (ed.) (1992), *The Single European Market and Beyond*, London: Routledge.

8 The politics of glasnost and perestroika

Gorbachev's coming to power in 1985 with his two-pronged dimensional reform programme 'perestroika' and 'glasnost' was a fundamental psychological shock to a country which was characterized by backwardness, immobility, inertia and a kind of stagnant stability. The impact of these changes on the Soviet people, the East European countries and the world at large was nothing if not spectacular. Gorbachev lifted the lid on a potentially explosive situation, releasing pent up demands, mobilizing hitherto latent talents and encouraging initiative. Gradually, almost imperceptibly at first, these forces transformed the social consciousness of the Soviet people, who began to call their regime to account.

This Chapter traces the dramatic political and economic process set in motion by Gorbachev's reforms which eventually called into question all traditional political dogmas and socio-economic concepts that had been the hallmarks of the system for over 70 years. For a time, it seemed possible that a reform 'from above' might be affected, carried out and controlled by the Communist Party. To this end, a set of measures were introduced, designed to make corrective changes to the existing system without, however, calling it into question. However, towards the end of the decade resistance to Gorbachev's reforms, particularly from conservative circles, grew. His reluctance to deal determinedly with this opposition revealed his own ideological limitations. A committed Communist, he failed to see that Communism had run its course. He wanted to 'reform' the system without abolishing it. In attempting to do this, he encouraged revolutionary changes the magnitude of which even he was unable to foresee. He thus set free forces which eventually led to his downfall.

Nevertheless, as a result of Gorbachev's reforms – as will be shown in Part III, The Challenges of the 1990s – the former Soviet Union is now in a state of transition to democracy and free enterprise, the eastern and central European countries have embarked on their own reform programme, Germany is unified and East–West relations have entered a new and more co-operative phase. Whether Gorbachev had intended this total transformation of post-war Europe, remains – for the time being – an open question.

The Soviet Union in the early 1980s
The Soviet Union approached the threshold of a new era as a country of high international standing. In terms of territory, population and natural resources, it had become one of the most powerful states in the world. Its military capability

was only matched by that of the USA. Its status and wider world influence had gradually been enhanced by its role in the negotiation of the international arms control agreements. And yet, the Soviet Union, by the mid-1980s, was in the grip of a profound economic, political and social crisis.

The bankruptcy of the country, signalled in earlier chapters, might have already been recognized by Yuri Andropov when he became General Secretary in November 1982. He introduced some economic reforms and launched a labour discipline campaign. However, as a result of both his short-lived rule and his own limitations he was unable to envisage and implement truly radical chances. After less than a year in office he retired due to illness and died in February 1984. His successor, Konstantin Chernenko, already in failing health when taking office, only lasted 13 months, during which, however, he was frequently absent from Politbureau meetings because of ill health. He died of emphysema on 10 March 1985.

The economic backwardness of the USSR showed itself in the technological weaknesses, in the poor quality of industrial products, in the low return on investment and in the declining rate of economic growth which had consistently fallen since the 1950s. None of the output targets set by the three five-year plans (1970–85) had been met. The decline was partly due to heavy expenditure on defence during the height of Cold War periods. Falling oil prices and hence a severe shortfall in export earnings – 80 per cent of which was derived from the exports of raw materials – placed an added burden on the badly floundering economy. Readily accessible energy and raw materials were exhausted and now had to be extracted from remote locations at considerable cost. Excessive centralization of economic management, whereby a single centre had a monopoly of decision-making, discouraged enterprise and initiative. This led to inflexibility of both planning and management.

In agriculture, the poor quality of farm equipment and incompetent irrigation led to falling output. The central authorities decided what, where and when to plant and to harvest without consideration for local conditions. A surplus of tractors and combine harvesters (albeit of poor quality) was produced, although there were not enough people to operate them. At the same time, half the grain consumed in the USSR had to be imported and one third of agricultural products never reached the consumer, but was lost in storage or as a result of unreliable transport facilities.

But perhaps even more serious was the moral crisis in the Soviet society, which suffered a progressive psychological alienation. The demoralization of the Soviet society was made apparent by the two extremes in its social spectrum. On the one hand there was the rule of the satisfied, the sordid profiteering of a powerful black market elite and the miserable greed of those who held position and enjoyed privileges. At the apex of the Soviet political and social pyramid was the 'nomenklatura'. This, as already seen, was a privileged group composed of the upper layer of the Party and state apparatus which, by virtue of its political position, had access to goods and services denied to ordinary citizens.

At the other end of the scale, however, there was a widespread layer of the poor and underprivileged: invalids, disabled, alcoholics and single mothers. The destructive monotony and desperate loneliness of modern Soviet life and the struggle for bare necessities often led to alcohol abuse, drug taking and crime. In March 1985 it was estimated that about 30 per cent of the population lived on 60 roubles per month, well below the poverty level, then estimated as being between 50 and 90 roubles, despite state subsidies for food, housing and transportation. The Soviet Union had the highest rate of infant mortality, namely 26 per 1000 in 1985, which was even higher than the 22 in Romania and far higher than in the West where it was only 10. The reasons were excessive and time-consuming bureaucracy in medical health care centres and lack of hygiene in maternity wards. Equally depressing was the fact that life expectancy which had been between 67–70 years in the 1950s, had fallen to 68 years by 1978. During the Brezhnev years life expectancy had not risen at all. For men it was around 62 years, compared with 71 years for men and 78 years for women in the West.

There was a also a chronic housing shortage, while existing buildings were dilapidated. About 50 per cent of families lived in communal apartments shared with other families. The breakdown of social bonds was reflected by an increasing divorce rate, a high suicide rate and 500 000 illegitimate births per annum. About 11 million legal abortions were performed per annum, because other forms of contraception were virtually non-existent. 'What has become of us?' The sorrow and agony behind this question asked by a young Soviet writer forcefully reveals the crisis of the human factor. In fact, the decay of social infrastructure was perhaps the most severe problem facing the Soviet Union when Gorbachev came to power in March 1985.

Gorbachev and the launching of perestroika and glasnost

Mikhail Sergeyevich Gorbachev was born into a peasant family on 2 March 1931 in Stavropol, South Russia. He joined the CPSU in 1952 and rose to power through the party hierarchy. A graduate of law in 1955, he became Central Committee Secretary responsible for agriculture in 1978 and moved to Moscow. He became a full member of the Politbureau (the Soviet cabinet) in 1980 and was promoted to the top ranks of Communist Party leadership by his two predecessors, Andropov and Chernenko. On coming to power in 1985, Gorbachev was 54, the youngest and most educated of the Soviet leaders. As a representative of the generation of post-Stalinist Soviet Communists, who had neither known class struggle, revolution or war, his accession was a turning point in the history of the Soviet Union.

Gorbachev's reforms were conceived in response to the gathering crises already described. In 1985, however, he still appeared to be convinced that a radical overhaul of the central planning system was not necessary and tended to reaffirm traditional values. Initially, therefore, the focus was on improving rather than on eliminating the old social mechanisms which was to have only a temporary and limited effect on the economy. During this first stage, therefore, the reform process, initiated by Andropov, was merely continued.

However, during the second half of 1986, Gorbachev began to realize that 'modernization' or even 'democratization' of the system was not sufficient to eradicate the ills of old structures, nor would it breeze new life into a stagnant political philosophy. His original strategy of *uskorenie* (acceleration) therefore had to be widened gradually and eventually be replaced by more revolutionary changes. From the middle of 1986 Gorbachev exhibited a growing realization that the pace and extent of the development had to be changed if his reforms were to succeed. Progressively, therefore, *uskorenie* was supplanted by the realization that old dogmas had to be cleared away and new mechanisms had to be introduced. As the reform process underwent a radicalization, two new key concepts emerged: perestroika – a programme for a revolutionary restructuring of the entire economy – and glasnost. The latter was a policy of openness, including revelations in terms of past Soviet shortcomings and an expansion of the boundaries of public discussion. Gorbachev had in fact come to the conclusion that it was necessary for the Soviet citizens to understand the political and economic conditions. Only then would he be able to win their confidence and enlist their support for making necessary changes. Glasnost therefore was a necessary extension of perestroika; it overlapped and interacted with the latter. Within a year these two concepts had become household names in Russia and amongst the best known foreign language terms internationally.

Perestroika
Gorbachev's publication *Perestroika: New Thinking for Our Country and the World* was introduced on the occasion of the official celebration of the 70th anniversary of the Bolshevik revolution in November 1987. The need for reform was explained as such: 'Perestroika is an urgent necessity arising from the profound processes of development of our Socialist society. This society is ripe for change …'. The substance of perestroika was a radical decentralization of the economy. Government intervention was to make room for market forces in an attempt to inject new dynamism into the economy. That implied the abolition, or at least a reduction in the suffocating influence of bureaucracy in order to allow personal enterprise, ability and initiative to flourish. The objective was to generate economic growth by introducing structural changes and encourage higher labour productivity. This necessitated the break-up of large monopoly producers and the introduction of a huge privatization programme. It implied price liberalization and currency convertibility, the development of both capital markets and banking systems, and agricultural reform.

The task was enormous: when Gorbachev came to power, there existed some 800 ministries and governmental committees in the Soviet Union employing nearly 16 million bureaucrats. His intention was to reduce the role of the central planning authorities and encourage self-management and self-financing of enterprises. For the first time in Soviet history, citizens were able to make independent entrepreneurial decisions: they were encouraged to plan production, purchasing and selling, regulate prices based on the law of supply and demand and hire labour under the new free market conditions.

Like some of his reform-minded predecessors, Gorbachev emphasized the need to move away from arms production to consumer products. Investment in consumption became a priority and the production of 'luxury' items was encouraged for the first time. But it was not just quantity which was given high priority, but the 'quality' of consumer products assumed a new importance. Another priority was the liberalization of trade. In 1986 and 1988 respectively the Foreign Trade Monopoly and the Ministry of Foreign Trade were abolished and replaced by a new Ministry for External Economic Affairs with the remit to develop a long-term strategy for the reformed economy. The aim was to expand the liberalization of all enterprises, at first by special permit and later with a convertible currency. Foreign equity participation in Soviet enterprises, at first (1987) limited to 49 per cent, was later extended to 100 per cent, so that by 1988 all Soviet enterprises enjoyed the right of direct access to international markets. By 1990, 2000 joint ventures has been agreed, mainly with Western countries. This was all part of an attempt to attract foreign investment and boost exports to enable the Soviet economy to catch up with the Western world.

Agriculture, too, like industry, had been directed from the top and ideologically based resistance to reform was strongest in this area. As late as November 1987, at the 70th anniversary of the October revolution, Gorbachev still defended Stalin's collectivization. However, a year later, he had freed himself from the pressures of old dogmas and, in October 1988, proposed radical changes which, in the long run, implied virtual privatization in this notoriously mistreated sector of the Soviet economy. In April 1989 a law authorizing long-term leases for land of up to 50 years and more was approved by the Supreme Soviet. This meant that, although the state retained ownership of the land, production would be privatized. Finally in November 1990 preliminary approval was given to legislation enabling private ownership of land for the first time in Soviet history. Thus perestroika implied nothing less but a major overhaul of the economy by introducing – for the first time since the Revolution of 1917 – elements of a free market economy.

Glasnost

Gorbachev, as a means to promote perestroika, introduced glasnost, being convinced that a fundamental reform of the Soviet economy could only materialize if he succeeded in generating support from all the country's political and societal structures. In his book he explained his view thus: 'Today glasnost is a vivid example of a normal and favourable spiritual and moral atmosphere in society, which makes it possible for people to understand better what happened to us in the past and what is taking place now, what we are striving for.'

The adoption of this principle implied abandoning the suffocating secrecy which had been so characteristic of Soviet political and cultural life. The new approach was a move away from the intellectual sterility of the past and had particular significance for Soviet domestic politics as well as foreign policy. Glasnost was a political instrument to introduce intellectual and social pluralism in an attempt to lift restrictions on the circulation of information and to encourage debates on previously 'taboo' issues. Government officials and business managers alike made appearances on television and radio programmes and answered consumer complaints. In his book Gorbachev boldly stated 'We cannot move forwards if we do not verify our policy through the participation and criticism, especially from below ... I do not think democracy is possible without it.'

The first big test of Gorbachev's glasnost policy was the accident at the Chernobyl nuclear reactor in the Ukraine in April 1986 which resulted in the world's worst nuclear disaster. The atomic reactor had suffered a melt-down and an explosion spewing radioactive poison far beyond the Soviet frontiers into Italy and southern Germany. Initially, the leadership maintained a cautious silence on the accident. It has been suggested that Gorbachev himself was not fully informed about the disaster initially, but once he had realized the extent of the accident, he grew even more determined to open government policies to public scrutiny. In fact, Gorbachev, although initially embarrassed by it, used the accident to his advantage. He dismissed members of the old guard and replaced them with his own advisers and confidants and made determined efforts to expand the flow of information. In the weeks following the accident, press reports, television coverage and news conferences gradually revealed the events surrounding the accident, although their full extent was not made clear for years. Nevertheless, the Chernobyl disaster gave an enormous impetus to a change in information policy. The incident sparked off a new openness and more candid discussions, in which virtually no subject was taboo, from disclosure of corruption to criticism of political leaders, including Gorbachev himself.

The glasnost campaign continued to gather momentum during 1986 and 1987 with publication of economic data, revelations of past disasters and the reporting of anti-Russian rioting in the central Asian city of Alma Ata. Television coverage now included Western fashion and rock music. Fast-food restaurants sprang up in large cities. In 1986 the Nobel prize winner Andrei Sakharov was released from internal exile and encouraged to appear on television. This was followed by the release of over a hundred other dissidents. The 'new thinking' extended to the arts, where Gorbachev encouraged a major revision of censorship. This meant that long suppressed works such as Pasternak's *Doctor Zhivago* were approved for publication. Editors and publishers no longer needed the approval of the propaganda department of the Central Committee for the publication of material. Previously banned theatre and film productions were now released such as the widely acclaimed film *Repentance* which is an examination of Stalin's purges.

The implications of glasnost, however, were not confined to freedom of the press and opinion. During the late 1980s it deepened into a process of *demokratizatsiya* within governmental institutions, particularly the Party. Gorbachev abandoned the CPSU's claim to undivided power by disassociating himself from the traditional Communist view that 'triumph of Socialism is historically predetermined'. He was convinced that without reform of the political system as a central element, economic reforms were doomed to fail. As a result, he proposed a wide-ranging reform of governmental and Party structures.

On 1 December 1988 the Supreme Soviet approved a series of important amendments to the 1977 Brezhnev Constitution. A new supreme body was created, a 2250 member Congress of People's Deputies in an attempt to shift authority to a semi-elected body. One third (750) of the deputies were appointed by established institutions such as the CPSU, the trade unions or women's councils – all of which were dominated by the 'nomenklatura' – but the remaining two thirds (1500) of Congress deputies were to be elected by secret ballot in the March 1989 general elections. Although no formal opposition parties existed and the Communist Party controlled the choice of many candidates, some regional and cultural groups supported independent representatives. The election, while not truly democratic, nevertheless signalled the end of one-party rule.

The new Congress had two main tasks. Firstly, it was to elect, from its members, a 542 strong permanent Supreme Soviet. This was to constitute a standing legislative, directive and control organ. It was divided into two chambers: the Council of the Union and the Council of Nationalities – the latter representing the interests of the numerous nationalities which made up the Soviet Union. Secondly, the Congress would also be responsible for electing the titular head of state, formally the Chairman of the USSR Supreme Soviet who functioned as the 'state president' along with a 'vice-president' and the members of a new Constitutional Court. The Congress, by a majority of 59 per cent, elected Gorbachev President of the USSR for five years, although future presidential elections were to be by direct popular and secret ballot. The new Supreme Soviet would be a forum for debate and criticism of government policies and would generate new political groupings. It convened for the first time in May 1989 when it engaged in vigorous debates, including admission of Soviet errors and historical distortions.

A major turning point in the Soviet Union's history as a mono-organizational state came on 14 March 1990 when the one-party system was effectively abandoned. This was done by removing Art. 6 of the 1977 constitution, which had guaranteed the leading role of the Party: 'The leading and guiding force of Soviet society and the nucleus of its political system, all of state organizations and public organizations in the Communist Party of the Soviet Union' (Art. 6). However, the CPSU remained the strongest political organization. In fact, an overwhelming majority, 85 per cent of deputies to the new Congress, were members of the CPSU. Gorbachev had every intention to save the Party's face during the transformation. His vision was that of a 'reformed' Party, although it would to a certain degree be accountable to elected bodies. At the same time, he insisted that the Party had to become more open to new concepts and ideas and adjust to new developments. To this end, he demanded tighter discipline among members and there were some dismissals or 'early retirements'. Nevertheless, the retention of the Party's leading role and Gorbachev's defence of it as the 'vanguard of democratization' inhibited the development of a truly parliamentary democracy.

Glasnost and the world

One of the most important by-products of Gorbachev's reform programme was glasnost in foreign policy. This led to a fundamental reassessment and a new appreciation by the international community of the Soviet Union improving its image in the eyes of the world. Glasnost led to the opening up of communications between foreign audiences, Soviet official spokesmen and the Soviet public. By the late 1980s interviews with Soviet leaders in Western countries were regularly broadcast on domestic radio and television. At the same time glasnost brought a somewhat simplified travel procedure for its own citizens and a more liberal issue of exit visas.

Amongst the many far-reaching consequences of glasnost in foreign policy were proposals for nuclear disarmament. These have perhaps had the greatest impact on the world even though cynics might argue that the USSR's new foreign policy was dictated by its need to reduce defence expenditure. Certainly, it would be true to say that the Soviet Union was unable to compete technologically and economically with the USA in the military field. Nevertheless, Gorbachev's new approach represented a radical reversal of traditional Soviet diplomacy. Indeed, both the invasion of Afghanistan and the deployment of the Intermediate Range SS20 missiles were openly criticized by the Soviet leader in 1988 when he stated that these two actions were examples 'of a foreign policy whose goals and methods were ill-conceived'.

The new thinking in Soviet foreign policy led to the signing of the Intermediate Nuclear Forces (INF) Treaty of December 1987 which in turn opened the way for talks on reduction of conventional forces discussed in Chapter 9. In

April 1987 in a speech in Prague, Gorbachev also launched the concept of a 'common European home' clearly implying that, if closer integration with Western Europe was a serious alternative for the USSR, then it was with a free Europe. Europe possessed a 'certain integrity', he declared and 'faced common tasks' and a 'common dedication to avoid war', a point explored in later Chapters.

Furthermore, glasnost was in large measure responsible for the dramatic changes in Eastern Europe. It was due to Gorbachev's decision not to intervene in the revolutionary movements in eastern Europe and a clear indication that he gave to this effect, that led to the replacement of the Communist leadership in these countries. It is still uncertain what role Gorbachev played in the downfall of the eastern and central European regimes. Did he simply observe quietly the demise of the communist parties in eastern Europe, or did he actively play a role in their downfall by preparing the coups in some of these countries? What is certain is that he sent distinct signals to the former satellite states. In July 1989 Gorbachev told the French President Mitterrand that the east European states had to 'decide how to structure their societies and lives' signalling the end of the Brezhnev doctrine (justification of the use of force by the USSR against any Socialist country which intended to move away from orthodox Communism). His message to the GDR leadership left no doubt as to his intentions. In October 1989 on the occasion of the 40th anniversary of the establishment of the GDR he warned Honecker: 'He who comes too late, will be punished by life'. As a result, the former satellites are now in transition from totalitarian regimes to democratic systems.

Last, but not least, glasnost in foreign policy was clearly reflected in the Soviet Union's policy towards Germany. Although the relations between the Soviet Union and West Germany had improved dramatically over the years, especially since the implementation of the *Ostpolitik*, Moscow had always remained inflexible on certain issues. Thus, with regard to the status of Berlin and eventual unification, Soviet policy had been marked by consistency and real single-mindedness over the 'German question'. In fact, despite the conclusion of major agreements during the two summit meetings between Kohl and Gorbachev in 1988 in Moscow and in June 1989 in Bonn, the Soviet leader had left no doubt about the fact that Soviet policy on Berlin was still non-negotiable. Yet, less than two years later, albeit after much soul-searching, the Soviet Union was officially supporting German unification. During a historic meeting with Kohl, Gorbachev in July 1990 dropped his original opposition and accepted the incorporation of unified Germany into NATO, thus removing the last obstacle to German unity. This opened the way for the signing of a treaty on German unification between the four war-time allies and the two Germanies on 12 September 1990. In fact, Gorbachev was instrumental in working out the intricate details of a German settlement such as the schedule for withdrawal of Soviet troops from the GDR. Glasnost, therefore, has had numerous and far-reaching implications, the full extent of which as already noted could not have been foreseen at the time, perhaps not even by Gorbachev himself.

Repercussions of glasnost and perestroika: a dilemma for Gorbachev
Despite the notable achievements of Gorbachev's reform programme, it has to be concluded that it failed. However, it is difficult to pinpoint the causes for the failures. There can be no single explanation for such a complex situation, especially as Gorbachev changed his policies as circumstances dictated. Was the discontent in the former USSR provoked by the maturation of the Soviet people who, once set free, began to call the entire system to account? Or were we simply witnessing the difficulties accompanying the transition from a totalitarian regime to a democratic system based on free enterprise and the rule of law? Perhaps chance was too slow for the increasingly restive Soviet society, no longer afraid to articulate its demands? We are still too close to be able to isolate with any degree of authority and certainty the underlying causes for the failure of Gorbachev's reforms. However, various difficulties and obstacles can be identified in our assessment of what went wrong.

As perestroika and glasnost unfolded, they encouraged reactions which possibly extended beyond the ambitions and intentions of Gorbachev himself. The economic reforms were judged unsuccessful in transforming a centralized economy into a liberal market system as they had not fulfilled expectations. On the contrary, efforts to implement perestroika led to a deepening social turmoil because these reforms undermined the prestige and influence of a particular group, worried about loss of power. The vast personnel of the state bureaucracy had a vested interest in the maintenance of the *status quo*. As a result, resistance grew to the reforms. But not only were the privileged groups or dogmatic party members ambivalent about Gorbachev's reforms, ordinary citizens too felt that perestroika had failed to deliver in terms of living standards. Soviet consumers, accustomed to subsidized food, housing and transportation, resented having to pay market prices for goods and services. Queuing for food continued, as it had been the case under Brezhnev, while at the same time the new 'free market' implied higher prices and harder work.

In 1989 rationing had to be enforced on a larger scale which resulted in panic buying. A year later the Prime Minister, Nikolai Ryzhkov, tried to impose a steep increase in prices for key food products, but this had to be abandoned as a result of the public outcry, while Ryzhkov himself was forced into retirement. Unfortunately, Gorbachev, not always able to balance the urgency of the reform process against its inevitable hardship, tended to pull back in the face of resistance. Thus, indecision at government level combined with continuing economic decline, private hoarding, black market corruption and political dissension all hampered the reform programme.

The failure in agriculture was particularly striking. Grain still had to be imported to make good domestic shortfalls. The 1986 Five-Year Plan had set ambitious growth targets of 4.2 per cent per annum, whereby guidelines adopted at the 27th Party Congress stipulated a growth rate of 5 per cent per annum in order to double national income by the year 2000. As it happened, the rate of growth recorded between 1986 and 1988 averaged only 3.6 per cent – the same as under Brezhnev. Indeed, by 1989 the rate had fallen to 2.4 per cent. Badly organized distribution of essential products such as meat and dairy produce let to food queues and high prices. Few farmers had made use of the new opportunities under perestroika. In addition, there were national catastrophes: from the slump in the price of oil, through the disaster of Chernobyl in 1986 to the earthquake in Armenia in 1988 and the miners' strike in 1989.

By 1989 it was freely admitted that, because of a series of miscalculations, notably during the early reform process, perestroika had failed to bring forth the expected benefits. The notion that the economy could be restructured, at the same time as a new drive for growth was unleashed, proved to be a fallacy. On the contrary, half-hearted liberalization, particularly in the economy, only aggravated existing problems, thus fuelling discontent. Equally, the mixture of central planning and market mechanisms was not a success, but remained an unhappy half-way house with the vices of both. In the event, the discredited system of central targeting for key areas remained in operation. Gorbachev, perhaps with a degree of panic, may have come to the conclusion by that time that the old system had run its course. However, he tried both, to preserve the system and to transform it. This, tragically, was his dilemma and eventually the cause of his downfall. In sum, perestroika appeared to open the way to destabilization, while life under the new regime, at least in material terms, had become harder for many. Perestroika – being a piecemeal reform – had run out of steam.

Glasnost, although remarkably successful in terms of foreign relations, actually exposed a series of the system's domestic shortcomings. This implied revelations about the state of the economy, the poor health provisions, the widespread abuse of alcohol and drugs and the existence of AIDS. While these problems were present in other countries as well, the Soviet Union, in the past had insisted that these were ills of capitalist societies. Glasnost also shed light on the inability of the government to solve its nationality problem. For over 70 years, the Soviet Union had claimed that its many nationalities had been well integrated in an exemplary multinational state comprising a population of 282.5 million. There had already been signs of national or ethnic unrest in the early 1980s, but from 1988 there were mass demonstrations in Armenia, Azerbaijan and in the three Baltic republics where deep-rooted grievances against the centre existed. At first, many of the ethnic conflicts were confined to narrow issues: the central Asian republics complained about discrimination;

discontent in the Muslim republics emerged during riots in 1986 in Uzbekistan; and in 1986 riots in Kazakhstan followed the appointment of a new Russian – rather than a Kazakh – First Secretary in the capital of Alma-Ata. In 1988 war broke out between Azerbaijan and Armenia over the contested region of Nagorno-Karabakh, as further explored in Chapter 13 – and there was nationalist tension in Moldova and the Ukraine. There were demands for the restoration of their national republics from Ukranian nationalists, Russian-Germans and the Tartans.

The most powerful expression of nationalist sentiment was found in the three Baltic states: Lithuania, Estonia and Latvia. They had been overrun by the Red Army in 1944–45 for the second time, after initial occupation in 1939–41 following the Molotov–Ribbentrop Pact, and incorporated into the USSR. These countries were unwilling to make do with the economic autonomy which they were granted. In November 1988 Estonia pressed for a declaration of its sovereignty which meant that the local Supreme Soviet in Tallinn would have to approve any laws from Moscow before they could be applied in Estonia. This action was criticized by the presidium of the USSR Supreme Soviet on the grounds that federal law overrode regional law. On 1 March 1990 Lithuania was the first Soviet republic to declare independence, followed by the other two. To Gorbachev this was a challenge he had to face. How could he give the dissident republic greater autonomy without setting a dangerous precedent? He sent troops to Lithuania and imposed an economic blockade.

Thus, glasnost and the new thinking – so successful in the area of Soviet foreign policy – was far less effective in domestic affairs. It became apparent during the course of 1990 that the central leadership was struggling desperately to retain control over the new aspirations of the republics. It was accepted that the nationalities policy needed an overhaul. As early as his basic policy speech on 30 March 1989, Gorbachev had admitted that the leadership, and thus he himself, had failed to see the full extent of the need for a renewal of the nationalities policy at the beginning of the reform. However, Gorbachev was not prepared to grant the republics the constitutional right to self-determination as this would undoubtedly mean eventual disintegration of the entire empire.

Gorbachev continued to believe that a total system transformation of Communism was possible despite the abolition of a one-party state, the dismantling of a command economy and the discrediting of old dogmas and totalitarian ideology. When he began to encounter major problems, he demanded more leeway for the exectuion of his reforms. In March 1990 he proposed to the Congress that a new post be created, that of Executive President, to be elected by Congress. By September 1990 Gorbachev was given sweeping executive powers which enabled him to force legislation through by presidential decrees. The creation of such extraordinary powers raised the question whether Gorbachev was becoming a dictator! As he underwent what seemed to be a process of radicalization, he alienated gradually even his closest advisers, which eventually led to the resignation of Shevardnadze, his Foreign Secretary, at the end of 1990.

As the economy deteriorated, as unrest in the republic became more widespread, and political discord pushed the Soviet Union to the brink of anarchy two competing forces emerged. Gorbachev was confronted by both the right and the left. The latter pushed for greater reform; in their view perestroika had failed and they demanded a complete break with the old order of Soviet Communism. Gorbachev's main challenger was Boris Yeltsin, the former Moscow Party leader and, from 1990, the President of the Russian Federation. Having thus established an independent power base, Yeltsin made a fierce attack both on the party and on Gorbachev himself pressing for more rapid perestroika.

On the right, Gorbachev faced challenges from anti-reform forces, the hardline Communists and entrenched party bureaucrats together with national extremists and followers of the Orthodox Church – people who had a vested interest in the *status quo*. These groups predicted that the system was not reformable and that any attempts to tinker with it would result in decline or even worse, in total disunity. The anti-reformers were all united in fierce opposition to self-management in industry and agriculture, above all to the introduction of free enterprise. Their resentment of Gorbachev's reforms was deeply rooted and inspired by the Leninist–Stalinist heritage. 'Fear of freedom', a phenomenon which, according to the observations of psychologists, is present in all ages and parts of the world, was the most paramount motivation for their opposition to Gorbachev.

The mood in the 'winter of discontent' (1989–90) was – once the earlier euphoria about the reforms had died – that of widespread disillusion. Output fell, foreign debt increased at an alarming rate and individual regions and republics moved towards autarchy. The Soviet Union on the eve of the 1990s had reached a turning point: would the country continue on the path of reform under the present leadership? Would the struggle between the centre and the republics lead to disintegration or could the federation be contained? Or still worse: would there be a backlash and a re-imposition of totalitarianism? Gorbachev, being torn between the two extremes and being himself unsure of the value of the reform programme, threw in his lot with the conservative wing of his opponents. This proved to be a fatal decision.

Assessment

Unfortunately, perestroika failed to improve living conditions for ordinary Soviet citizens which undermined Gorbachev's personal popularity and thereby his room for manoeuvre. Tragically Gorbachev was caught between forces who accused him of half-hearted reforms and demanded even more radical actions and those who wanted to return to the orthodox way of Lenin–Marxist ideology. The dilemma in which he found himself and his hesitation to side with one or the other of his political opponents – to be either preserver or transformer – clearly revealed his own weakness. He had been brought up with party ideology and, unfortunately, despite his vision and courage, he was never able to shake off the limitations of his political convictions. As a result, the discrediting of his reform policies played into the hands of his opponents. The outcome of this conflict was, as we know, a tragic one for Gorbachev.

And yet, Gorbachev set a train of events into motion which did not only have a dramatic effect on the USSR, but on Europe at large. His achievements are virtually unique in post-war Europe and during his short reign he overshadowed all other statesmen. By initiating a revolution from above and below which went far beyond the national boundaries of his country, he brought a vision of hope to millions of people. He ended the 45-year-old conflict with the West, led the drive for disarmament, undermined the Moscow-imposed system in the East and healed the painful division of the continent by proclaiming and working towards a 'common European home'. These are achievements of major significance which will stand the test of time. Future historians may well pay tribute to this remarkable man who did nothing less than change the course of history by dramatically transforming the post-war political and strategic climate.

Further reading

Cooper, L. (1992), *Power and Politics in the Soviet Union*, London: MacMillan.
Hosking, G. (1990), *The Awakening of the Soviet Union*, London: Heinemann.
Laqueur, W. (1990), *Soviet Union 2000*, London: Tauris.
McAuley, M. (ed.) (1990), *Gorbachev and Perestroika*, London: MacMillan.
MacAuley, M. (1992), *Soviet Politics 1917–1991*, Oxford: Oxford University Press.
Miller, J. (1993), *Mikhail Gorbachev and the End of Soviet Power*, London: MacMillan.
Thom, F. (1989), *The Gorbachev Phenomenon*, London: Pinter.
White, S. (1990), *Gorbachev in Power*, Cambridge: Cambridge University Press.

9 Disarmament, *détente* and beyond

One of the most curious aspects of East–West relations is the fact that the two superpowers, both ambitious and expansive, ideologically opposed and engaged in a deadly arms race, still succeeded in avoiding war for over 45 years. Ironically, it was precisely because of the possession of nuclear weapons and because a roughly equal military balance between the superpowers was achieved that Europe became the most stable area for several decades.

As has been shown in Chapter 4, friction developed between the two new superpowers, the Soviet Union and the USA, almost as soon as military hostilities had ceased. The conflict soon hardened into the Cold War and the two countries became locked in a power struggle, each jealously guarding its own sphere of interests by building up a bloc of allies, both in Europe and elsewhere. Security, it was claimed, meant military strength and, as a result, the two superpowers began to develop deadly nuclear arsenals capable of destroying not only each other, but most of the civilized world.

However, the enormous costs involved in the nuclear build-up, the acceptance of the division in Europe and the gradual relaxation of tensions in the wake of *Ostpolitik* and during the run-up to the CSCE, paved the way for a period of *détente* which lasted well into the late 1970s and led to the first major arms control agreement. Subsequently, the relationship between the Soviet Union and the USA deteriorated and *détente* was stalled. Soviet deployment of modern intermediate missiles, targeted at Western Europe, the invasion of Afghanistan and the imposition of Martial Law in Poland (allegedly encouraged by the Soviet Union) threatened the post-war settlement and led to a 'New Freeze' in superpower relations. The adversarial relations between the two superpowers created a security dilemma for Europe, for it was caught up in the military rivalry between the two belligerents. The security concerns of West European countries – not least because of their geographical proximity to the USSR – changed so as no longer to coincide with those of the USA. This new perception of security by West European countries led, in the early 1980s, to a serious rift between the latter and their powerful American protector. The conflict was resolved when, with the advent of Gorbachev in 1985, a new era in East–West relations began. The results were unprecedented agreements on both nuclear and conventional forces which, underpinned by the institutionalization of the CSCE process, ended East–West confrontation.

The 'New Freeze'
As noted in Chapter 4, during the late 1960s and early 1970s Europe enjoyed a brief period of *détente*. However, the 1979 Vienna summit meeting between

Carter and Brezhnev on SALT 2 was to be the last East–West summit for six years. SALT 2 was never ratified by the US Senate because the late 1970s were the beginning of a new era of conflict. Not only was Europe, once again, caught up in this deterioration of US–Soviet relations, but emerging new conflicts also threatened the rich, if somewhat intangible, rewards from both *Ostpolitik* and the CSCE. The Helsinki Final Act was not a legally binding treaty, but rather a series of aspirations, not enforceable by international law. As a result, the persecution of dissidents in the Eastern bloc continued. In 1979 Czechoslovak leaders of the human rights movement, Charter 77, were arrested. Thus, the violation of human rights in the Communist bloc undermined the Helsinki spirit. Although the first meeting of the CSCE in 1973–75 was followed by a review in Belgrade (October 1977–March 1978), the negotiations failed to achieve anything of substance, except an agreement to meet again. Arms control talks did not fare any better. Mutual and Balanced Force Reduction (MBFR) talks – which had begun in Vienna in 1973 – were deadlocked. It was at that time that a series of events made for a drastic deterioration in US–Soviet relations.

The SALT talks had focused on long-range strategic nuclear weapons, ignoring shorter range weapons. This had always been a matter of deep concern to Western Europe, particularly to the West Germans, since intermediate and short-range weapons, which had been excluded from SALT negotiations, were capable of striking European territories. This concern was brought into sharper relief when the Soviet Union, in 1979, deployed a very modern type of intermediate-range ballistic missiles, the SS20. This replaced the obsolete missiles SS4 and SS5 which had been targeted at NATO Europe since the early 1960s. The deployment of SS20 missiles, with their enhanced capability to strike and destroy all of Western Europe, seemed to confirm that even if, as it had happened in the 1970s, the West relaxed its military build-up, the Soviet Union continued to strive for unilateral advantage, threatening the concept of parity.

The deployment of SS20s came as a profound shock to the West at a time when NATO's own intermediate-range nuclear missiles were becoming quite outdated. This was articulated by American Defence Secretary Brown as follows: 'We build, they build. We stop, they build.' President Carter condemned the Soviet action as 'an extremely serious threat to peace'. SALT 2 was withdrawn from the US Senate although both sides agreed to abide by its (unratified) terms. The climate in East–West relations changed almost overnight, when NATO leaders, in December 1979, decided to deploy new intermediate-range nuclear missiles (INF) in Western Europe unless the Soviet Union agreed within four years to eliminate its new SS20 missiles. The decision to station intermediate-range weapons in five European countries as a retaliatory reaction to the deployment of Soviet SS20s was, to some extent, urged on NATO by West Germany for reasons outlined above.

The tense situation caused by the INF controversy was further aggravated when the Soviet Union, in December 1979, invaded Afghanistan, where a power struggle among the various factions' leaders within the People's Democratic Party (PDP) had developed into civil war. Since the purpose of the invasion was a highly manipulated move to lend support to the leader most favoured by Moscow, Washington interpreted the Soviet invasion as an act of aggression. The response from the West was a US-initiated boycott of the 1980 summer Olympic Games, hosted by the Soviet Union. This was an attempt to humiliate the Soviet Union in the eyes of the world, while a secret US shipment of arms aided the Afghan resistance movement. East–West hostility intensified further during the early 1980s when Polish workers, plagued by food shortages, organized widespread strikes, which eventually led to the foundation of a free trade union 'Solidarity'. Although Soviet forces did not invade this time, the West believed that the introduction in 1981 of martial law by Poland's own leader General Jaruzelski had been initiated by the Kremlin. The West registered a strong response; particularly the new American President, Ronald Reagan, who, representing a more confrontational America, asked for punitive action against both the Soviet Union and Poland.

A rift developed between Washington and the West European countries, when Reagan attempted to obstruct the building of a gas pipeline from the USSR to Europe. The project which would benefit Moscow in terms of boosting its exports of gas and thereby increasing much needed foreign currency, was, however, also important to European businesses which were participating in the construction of the pipeline. Thus, the threat of economic sanctions against the USSR would also extend to European firms. An attempt to resolve this conflict between the USA and West European countries at Versailles in June 1982 was unsuccessful. As a result Reagan imposed sanction unilaterally. Most European countries felt, however, that the pipeline project would help ease East–West relations generally and refused to enact sanctions against Poland on the grounds that this could mean hardship for the Polish people. In the event, more important conflicts overtook the issue of sanctions.

Moscow continued to deploy its SS20s and refused to accept that it was upsetting the military balance in Europe by destroying parity between the two superpowers. Hence, in 1981, the USA offered the 'zero–zero option': all deployment of US land-based intermediate-range nuclear missiles in Europe would be halted provided the Soviet Union eliminated all similar weaponry. The 'zero–zero option' became the central feature of negotiations opening in Geneva a few days later. However, despite several proposals and counter-proposals, no satisfactory solution to the conflict was found and the tug of war between the two superpowers over INF missiles continued unabated.

A further impediment to a reconciliation emerged when President Reagan outlined plans – first unveiled in 1982 – for research into a new Strategic

Defence Initiative (SDI) or 'Star Wars' as it was popularly known which, if successfully developed and deployed, would give the USA the ability to destroy incoming Soviet ballistic missiles in outer space. This was accompanied by large increases in the US defence budgets and a new emphasis on building up conventional forces. While the Star Wars project was an added strain on the US budget, it was hoped that the Soviet Union would be unable to keep pace with the American expansion of its defence programme. Indeed, the US project presented an economic threat to the technologically backward Soviet economy for reasons made clear in Chapter 8 and reactions from the Soviet Union were predictable. It sharply criticized the US actions arguing that they unravelled the limited achievements of the existing arms control agreements and destabilized the arms control process.

The frosty atmosphere between the two superpowers had now reached crisis point. However, in stark contrast to the 1950s and 1960s, the USA failed to win full backing for its anti-Soviet policies from its European allies. Indeed, the position of the USA was becoming weaker than that of the USSR. While SS20s were now stationed in the East, Washington was still waiting for consent from its European allies for the deployment of US missiles on their soil. Clearly, the Western Alliance had underestimated the opposition of their citizens to the renewed arms build-up. European governments were faced with hostile reactions to the NATO proposal to counter the Soviet threat posed by SS20s. Millions of citizens participated in demonstrations in nearly every West European country against the deployment of the very weapons intended to defend them. The movement was particularly strong in the Netherlands, Belgium and Italy.

The INF controversy was very heated in West Germany, where opinions were divided. On the one hand, NATO was still West Germany's long-standing military custodian, seen as the bedrock of West German security policy. On the other, however, the employment of INF weapons on West German soil would damage not only German–German co-operation developed since *Ostpolitik*, but would also undermine German–Soviet relations. The mood of the young and left in Germany had changed significantly since the depth of the Cold War and, for the first time, anti-American sentiments were strongly articulated. This found expression in big demonstrations in 1982–83, the emergence of the Green party and even calls for a state of neutrality, which would have meant an end to NATO membership.

In Britain, too, NATO's decision produced a protest movement by the 'Greenham Common Women', who blockaded the site of the new Euro-missiles in a 'sit-in', which was to last for several years. Thus, the deterioration in East–West relations over INF reflected and intensified a long-term change in the attitudes of European citizens to the importance of *détente* and arms control. Clearly, with the growth of peace movements and rising public interest in the

INF controversy, Western Europe experienced a dramatic change in attitudes to security issues, as shown in Chapter 6.

In an attempt to deepen the rift between the USA and its European allies, the USSR used the peace movement in Western Europe and offered negotiating terms to the latter, particularly to West Germany. However, despite – or perhaps because of – the rise of the peace movement, traditional, conservative forces strengthened and during the early 1980s there was a shift to the right in almost all European countries. This development helped to clear the ground for a more bellicose attitude towards the East. So, after intensive debates, the European wing of NATO agreed to American demands that existing nuclear missiles should be modernized. Even the West German *Bundestag*, in November 1983, voted in favour of the deployment of INF weapons. However, the European wing of NATO had insisted that the US should initiate new negotiations on arms control with the USSR, and, as a result a new round of Strategic Arms Reduction Talks (START) began.

The deployment of 108 Pershing II and 464 cruise missiles in the West in 1983 under US command and control began on schedule. The Pershing II particularly alarmed the Soviet Union, as these missiles were able to reach vital Soviet targets in only a few minutes. Moreover, an additional 162 British and French missiles – not controlled by NATO – were aimed at the USSR and had been excluded from negotiations. In response to NATO's action, the Soviet Union not only strengthened its own nuclear force in East Germany and Czechoslovakia but also stormed out of the new round of START talks which included both a continuation of the original SALT talks and discussions on INF. Meaningful political dialogue had come to a standstill and relations between the superpowers were frozen: the second Cold War seemed set to continue.

However, despite the seriousness of the situation, the new Cold War (1979–86) was not comparable with the Berlin crisis (1948) or the Cuban conflict (1962). Despite the frosty atmosphere as a result of the INF controversy, East–West contacts continued. Importantly, the CSCE process led to a third follow-up meeting in Madrid 1980–83, despite attempts by the Soviet Union to abort it. Negotiations, however, were dominated by arguments over which bloc had failed to live up to the spirit of Helsinki.

From the 'New Freeze' to disarmament

Despite the way in which arms control negotiations had collapsed in December 1983, towards the middle of the decade, the Soviet Union and the USA reaffirmed their interest in bilateral negotiations and agreed to begin another series of talks. For the USSR this was motivated by the necessity of cutting defence expenditure and by an instinctive expectation that a disarmament offensive might yield rich rewards in terms of popularity, both at home and abroad. Similarly, President Reagan's new policy of 'constructual confrontation' with Moscow stemmed from his desire to round off his presidency by making a contribution to peace.

The new climate was even more closely linked to Gorbachev's advent to power in March 1985, which, as Chapter 8 has shown, was the beginning of a new era in Soviet foreign policy. He became the engine for change and, in a dramatic move, called for global nuclear disarmament in three stages by the year 2000. As a first step, and in order to regenerate East–West *détente*, he proposed the immediate elimination of all INF weapons in Europe. The change in the international climate led to three summit meetings between Reagan and Gorbachev.

The first, at Geneva in November 1985, provided an opportunity for a review of progress made at the arms talks and an exchange of views. The atmosphere was friendly, but no tangible progress was made, although a good personal relationship was established between the two leaders and some minor agreements on bilateral co-operation were achieved. In April 1986, however, during a visit to East Germany, Gorbachev proposed the reduction of conventional forces in Europe 'from the Atlantic to the Urals'. Furthermore, in September 1986 a round of security talks under a mandate from the CSCE countries dubbed 'The Conference on Disarmament in Europe' (CDE), which had started in Stockholm in 1984, ended with an agreement on the notification of military manoeuvres between NATO and the Warsaw Pact. Being the first arms control agreement between the two blocs since SALT 2, it was the first clear sign that a change of direction had taken place under Gorbachev.

The second summit meeting between the two superpowers in October 1986 in Reykjavik ended in deadlock. The talks were mainly unsuccessful because the Soviets demanded that all future progress be linked to a limit on American plans for SDI. The Americans were unwilling to restrict their SDI programme, since it was argued that Star Wars was a major US programme for space-based defence to match similar Soviet research efforts. Since Reagan would not accept any cuts in SDI, the Soviets refused to continue discussion on the limitation of offensive weapons. But, although the results of Reykjavik were inconclusive, this meeting marked a consensus between the two superpowers on the principle of nuclear disarmament.

Pressures from the European partners of NATO, who wanted to see significant arms reductions, financial considerations (on both sides) and Gorbachev's need to be able to concentrate on his extensive domestic reform programme paved the way for a third summit meeting between the two leaders. In February 1987, the Soviet leader dropped the Star Wars demand which had deadlocked negotiations. Two months later in a speech in Prague Gorbachev, for the first time, used the concept of a 'common European House' implying that he saw Europe as having a common cultural entity with a common fate. During the same year, the third summit meeting between the Soviet Union and the USA took place, when the two superpowers agreed to eliminate an entire category of nuclear missiles from Europe within three years. This intention was embodied in the treaty formally known as, the 'Treaty between the USA of America and the Union of Soviet Socialist Republics on the Elimination of their Intermediate-Range and Shorter Range Missiles' which was signed by Reagan and Gorbachev in Washington on 8 December 1987 and ratified the following May.

Implications of the INF treaty
It is difficult to appraise the treaty because it caused conflict within the Western Alliance. However, it constituted a turning point in the history of arms negotiations. Firstly, it was the first real disarmament treaty. There was not only a limit on the number of weapons, as was the case with SALT, but missiles were actually destroyed. Secondly, the treaty did not only apply to one category of missiles, but to several categories of weapons, that is to land-based intermediate nuclear missiles with a range of between 500 and 1000 km and to those with a range of between 1000 and 5500 km. Thirdly, the INF treaty constituted a precedent of an asymmetric reduction. In other words, the Soviet Union was prepared to dismantle its arsenal which was larger than that of the USA, by a disproportionate amount. Fourthly, the really novel aspect of this treaty was the establishment of a comprehensive and detailed verification clause, which provided for the first time for on-site inspection. To this end 'each party shall have the right to conduct inspections ... for 13 years after entry into force of the treaty'. Controls had to be accepted not only in terms of the destruction of the missiles, but also on the production plants. This meant that controls were not only exercised in the Soviet Union and the USA, but also in those countries where the missiles had been deployed, that is in the FRG, Britain, Italy and Belgium in the West, the GDR and Czechoslovakia in the East. Finally, a special Verification Commission, a Nuclear Risk Reduction Centre, was set up in the two capitals, in an attempt to institutionalize the verification clause of the Treaty.

Although the INF covered only one third of the INF weapons, leaving air-launched and sea-launched weapons untouched which in turn constituted only 3 per cent of the world's nuclear arsenal, it had an enormous impact on future disarmament treaties. By improving the atmosphere for both START and conventional arms talks, it was undoubtedly a turning point in the transition from Cold War to post-Cold War era. This was because it represented a change in East–West relations. The fundamental assumption of Cold War politics, namely the confrontation of two superpowers, no longer held true. The INF Treaty was the beginning of a sea change, although its eventual significance could only be determined by the repercussions of the Treaty on Europe's overall security.

Having said this, however, the INF Treaty initially engendered anxieties in Europe, particularly in West Germany, since the 'denuclearization' for which the Treaty provided, would eventually leave European countries vulnerable to the superior strength of Soviet conventional forces. The German government was ambiguous on this issue since, in contrast to its original hostility to the stationing of these weapons it now resented the withdrawal of INF systems, arguing that it feared the overwhelming superiority of Soviet conventional arms which were primarily a threat to Europe and notably to the West Germans. The INF agreement also raised doubts about continued American commitment to Europe's security, since a 'limited' nuclear or conventional war would not necessarily extend beyond the European continent and thus need not involve the USA.

The US response to such unease was the concept of 'compensation' for the INF Treaty, a programme of modernizing short-range missiles (SNF) in an attempt to reassure its NATO partners that disarmament and *détente* would not be achieved at Europe's expense. It was argued that, in view of the superiority of Soviet conventional forces, NATO had to modernize its own short-range missiles. This, however, created renewed unease among European countries, who failed to see the logic in eliminating long-range weapons (which had the power to reach the Soviet Union and thus the perceived 'enemy'), while at the same time maintaining and indeed updating short-range weapons, the majority of which were deployed in Europe, particularly in the two Germanies. This would imply that, if war broke out, it would be fought on central European soil. For much of the West German population the existence of short-range weapons was a constant reminder of their exposed position. They had thought that the INF Treaty would also include the destruction of short-range missiles and refused to accept short-range missiles on their territory.

What followed was an acrimonious discussion within NATO about modernization of nuclear weapons. The government of West Germany, taking the lead in the negotiations (supported by Belgium and the Netherlands), in an unprecedented step, challenged the USA on this issue. Determined to resist the modernization of the short-range nuclear force, West Germany argued for negotiations with the Soviet Union. Bonn's reservations, supported by a large cross-section of West German opinion, were expressed by such phrases as 'the shorter the range, the deader the Germans', and 'singularization'. It was argued that this was no longer an equal sharing of risk within the Alliance, but that the two Germanies carried a disproportionate and uniquely dangerous burden. In fact, the former Foreign Minister Genscher declared: 'I have sworn an oath to protect the German people and that includes East Germans.'

However, with the new international climate which had accompanied Gorbachev's advent to power, a major breakthrough was achieved in 1988. On 7 December the Soviet leader took a first step towards reducing the quantitative superiority of Soviet forces in Europe by announcing in his address to the UN General Assembly a unilateral troop reduction of 500 000 men with the corresponding weaponry (tanks, artillery and combat aircraft). He stated: 'Today

I can report to you that the Soviet Union has taken a decision to reduce its armed forces ... Within the next two years their numerical strength will be reduced by 500 000. This will be done unilaterally.' A month later, in January 1989, Gorbachev announced a planned cut in the secret arms budget by 14.2 per cent. Cynics might say that domestic pressures forced Gorbachev to take this step, but his gesture was nevertheless in line with the new thinking in Soviet foreign policies since the mid-1980s.

Furthermore, the new concessions were a clear admission by the USSR that Warsaw Pact forces levels had been far above what was legitimately needed for maintaining 'parity' in terms of defence. The importance of the Gorbachev initiative was therefore that it made negotiations on the reductions of conventional forces feasible for the first time in post-war history. This was another important side effect of the INF treaty: it served to focus attention on conventional arms negotiations. The latter – designated MBFR – had been under discussion between NATO and Warsaw Pact members since 1974, but talks had been bedevilled by disagreements between the two blocs, particularly over the problem of verification. As a result of Gorbachev's concessions, however, and the emerging general change in the international climate, MBFR were wound up after 500 sessions and eventually merged with a new series of talks, dubbed 'Conventional Forces in Europe' (CFE).

The Soviet gesture allowed the US – during the Brussels summit of NATO heads of governments in May 1989 – to compromise on the issue of modernization and delay the eventual deployment of SNF weapons until sufficient progress had been made at CFE talks. This was a distinct move towards the German position and, against the background of tumultuous changes in the political and strategic landscape, the USA, in May 1990, moved to the cancellation of further modernization of the bulk of NATO's SNF capability in Europe. At the same time, the US expressed willingness to negotiate SNF as soon as the CFE agreement was signed. This new climate and the reduced threat perception led, during the July 1990 London summit meeting of the 16 NATO leaders, to a fundamental review of the Western Allies' strategy – which became no longer focused on the Soviet threat. This shift was said by President Bush to be: 'An historic turning point. The alliance has set a new path for peace.'

Against the background of the momentous upheaval in Eastern and central Europe, the CFE negotiations made rapid progress. As part of these, the West German government had pledged to reduce a unified German army to 370 000; a declaration to this effect was subsequently attached to the unification treaty. The settlement of the question of unified Germany's army removed the last impediment to a successful completion of CFE talks. On 19 November 1990, in Paris, negotiations were concluded. The 22 members of NATO and the Warsaw Pact then signed an unprecedented arms control treaty establishing new equal armament ceilings for East and West. The signature of the arms control

Treaty on Conventional Forces in Europe would lead to the elimination of Soviet superiority in offensive weapon systems within a region stretching from the Atlantic to the Urals. The CFE treaty set ceilings for 5 categories of weapons: tanks, artillery, armoured combat vehicles, aircraft and helicopters. Any equipment in excess of these ceilings at the moment of signature must be destroyed, irrevocably converted to civilian use or else transferred to some other category. The treaty, of unlimited duration, also introduced a stringent verification system to ensure compliance with the agreed terms.

The CFE Agreement was the result of one of the shortest ever East–West arms control negotiations, namely 20 months, and – as later transpired – was the last agreement between NATO and the Warsaw Pact, before the latter disintegrated. It thus represented the culmination of arms control talks in Europe and opened a new period in the security climate of the 1990s. The signing of the treaty clearly indicated that the era of East–West confrontation that had dominated post-war European relations was over. However, arms control negotiations had been only one, if major, aspect of the spirit of *détente* that now prevailed. The Helsinki process which had started in the mid-1970s had continued and survived the 'New Freeze' and had served – by complementing and reinforcing the objectives of arms control – as a supportive and necessary pillar of *détente*.

Détente and the CSCE process

Parallel to, and of equal importance with, the arms control negotiations was the legacy from the first period of *détente*, the CSCE process. As outlined in chapter 4, Helsinki was originally an extension of *Ostpolitik* and another affirmation of the territorial and political *status quo* in Europe by pledging to safeguard the inviolability of post-war frontiers. Unlike the arms control treaties, Helsinki was not a legally binding treaty. It could not change the political map of Europe nor could it end the Cold War. After all, the division of Germany, the starkest symbol of East–West divide, remained. Indeed, it could be argued, that the CSCE reflected, in some ways, the East–West conflict and as such was merely a dialogue between opposing blocs rather than a coming together of independent states. More than two thirds of the participating states were aligned to one of the two superpowers. Hence, the CSCE was at worst a forum for East–West confrontation, at best a dialogue between two opposing camps.

However, the CSCE was important in establishing a continuing process of negotiations among 35 sovereign countries, and acted as a bridge across the East–West divide. Despite the 'New Freeze' (1979–86) the very spirit of the Helsinki process survived and continued with several follow-up conferences during the late 1970s and early 1980s, the latter taking place after the Soviet invasion of Afghanistan and in the cool atmosphere of the new Reagan administration. Although not always productive and at times uncertain in its objectives, Helsinki, by institutionalizing the conditions of *détente*, kept the East–West dialogue going. Co-operation, rather than confrontation, became the hallmark of the process and it was in the interest of both, East and West, to continue with the process.

Furthermore, the Helsinki process – particularly its human rights element – played a significant role in bringing about the dismantling of Communist rule in eastern and central Europe by undermining the legitimacy of these regimes, as Chapter 10 shows. The human rights commitments, enshrined in the Helsinki Final Act, encouraged the opposition movement in these countries and afforded dissidents legitimacy. Indeed, the decision by the Hungarian government in September 1989 to open its borders and thereby initiating the mass emigration of GDR citizens leading to the collapse of that regime, was justified on the grounds that the Helsinki Accord obliged member states to respect everyone's rights to freedom of movement.

Similarly, the downfall of the communist Czechoslovak regime in November 1989 had brought into power some of the leading human rights activists, whose activities had been supported and publicized by the CSCE. The revolutions of Eastern Europe in the autumn and winter of 1989 were virtually bloodless and reflected the Helsinki strategy which, by rejecting the use of force, enabled the division of Europe to be overcome by peaceful means.

Not surprisingly, towards the late 1980s, when East–West polarity became increasingly irrelevant, the Helsinki process assumed a new importance. Gorbachev, in November 1989, proposed to convene a CSCE summit to take stock of the revolutionary developments underway in eastern and central Europe. The West agreed, provided that the CFE treaty would be concluded before the date of the CSEC summit. As a result, two very successful CSCE meetings took place during the first half of 1990 demonstrating the new focus in the East–West agenda. Against the background of far-reaching reforms initiated by Gorbachev, the special Bonn meeting on 'Economic Cooperation in Europe' in March and April 1990 produced a document (albeit non-binding) pledging support for free market reforms in the former Communist economies.

The second development was the June 'Conference on the Human Dimension' in Copenhagen, to which Albania was for the first time admitted as an observer. The conference was dominated by the recognition of pluralist democracies and the rule of law 'as essential conditions for peace and security in Europe'. By agreeing on regular free elections, separation of party and state and freedom of expression, the meeting celebrated the political demise of the Communist regimes, after the Bonn meeting had broken their economic legitimacy.

Thus, the Helsinki process was being significantly upgraded and had achieved a new dimension in the wake of the disintegration in the East, the collapse of Communist ideology and the relative decline in the importance or necessity of the Western military alliance. In many respects it had been a unique experience. It had provided the framework for enduring relationships. All that was apparently needed was to formulate and institutionalize the changes which were taking place. In the rapidly changing political climate in Europe with new democracies emerging virtually overnight and German unification a fait accompli, the summit meeting of CSCE members – as suggested by Gorbachev – took place on 19–21 November 1990. Albania participated as observer, while the unification of Germany had reduced the number of members by one (i.e. the GDR). The participating states solemnly proclaimed the 'Charter of Paris for a new Europe; a new era of democracy, peace and unity'. The Charter set out and developed the principles stated by the 1975 Helsinki Final Act although, like the latter, it is non-binding and merely a set of aspirations. A further agreement, the 'Vienna Document on Confidence- and Security-Building Measures', was also signed by the 34 CSCE states; while the 'Treaty on Conventional Armed Forces in Europe' (CFE); and the 'Joint Declaration of 22 States', signed by the two military alliances, welcomed the recent historic changes which had ended their adversary relations.

The Charter of Paris, which in fact institutionalized the CSCE process, consisted of three parts. The first part, 'Human rights, democracy and the rule of law', set out the principles participating states should adopt or adhere to and governed inter-relations. Part 2 on 'Guidelines for the future', dealt with the different aspects of co-operation among CSCE members. Part 3 on 'New structures and institutions of the CSCE process' provided for a permanent institutional structure, including a secretariat located in Prague, to prepare follow-up meetings. Regular meetings of heads of state were to take place every two years, whilst foreign ministers were to meet annually. An 'Assembly of Europe' composed of delegates from national parliaments was to be convened. Two specialist agencies were established: 'The Office for Free Elections in Warsaw' (later renamed Bureau for Democracy and Civil Rights) to promote democratic practices and 'The Conflict Prevention Centre' (CPC) (later renamed European Centre for Conciliation and Arbitration) in Vienna. The Cold War was solemnly declared over. The Charter stated that 'the era of confrontation and division of Europe has ended' and that '... henceforth our relations will be founded on respect and co-operation ...' Undeniably, as President Bush said 'In signing the Charter of Paris we have closed a chapter of history', yet at the same time a new one was being opened.

Aftermaths
The Cold War ended as the result of the interlocking of several forces. Both the CSCE process and arms control talks, apparently quite independent of each other, tended to move and progress simultaneously – each influencing the other – until they virtually converged in 1990. Sometimes the CSCE process and institutionalized arms talks helped to relax tension, while at other times the search for a stable security order was accelerated by a profound transformation of the

international political and strategic climate. Indeed, it has been established how attempts to overcome the division in Europe were at times superseded by or overtaken by momentous historical events.

Yet, although President Bush, in November 1990, declared the Cold War to be 'dead', this was not the end of conflict and change. Certainly, the security structure of Europe had changed from that of a two superpower world order to a multipolar system. Europe is in a state of transition, where new conflicts – once overshadowed by Cold War politics – are now emerging, as shown in Part III. The durability of this new security order remains uncertain. The spectre of profound political and economic changes will haunt Europe in the years to come.

However, despite these uncertainties, the end of the Cold War has been an enormous achievement. No longer is there a Soviet threat. Divided Germany – once the core of East–West conflict – is united. Communism has run its course. Institutional processes set into motion in the 1970s are being consolidated and provide a suitable forum for identifying new conflicts. Given the insecurity and the potential danger of the Cold War, this is a condition worthy of greater appreciation than it has so far received.

Further reading

Buzan, B. *et al.* (1990), *The European Security Order Recast*, London: Pinter.

Calvocoressi, P. (1991), *World Politics Since 1945*, 6th edn, London: Longman.

Heller, A. and Feelieu, F. (1990), *From Yalta to Glasnost*, Oxford: Blackwell.

Laqueur, W. (1990), *European Security in the 1990s*, London: Plenum Press.

Lehne, S. (1991), *The Vienna Meeting of the Conference on Security and Cooperation in Europe 1986–1989*, Boulder, Col.: Westview.

Young, J.W. (1991), *Cold War Europe 1945–1989*, London: E. Arnold.

10 The revolutions in Eastern Europe

The events of 1989 in Eastern Europe came as a considerable surprise to most observers, from academics to statesmen. While there had been evidence of increasing change in Eastern Europe, people still expected only a gradual transition away from rigid Soviet-imposed Marxist–Leninism towards more pragmatic and independent Communism. The collapse of six regimes in three months in the autumn of 1989, starting the unravelling of the Balkans and the USSR, was not foreseen. Moreover, because the revolutions were so unexpected, and so peaceful, they were welcomed euphorically in the West. They were often claimed as the victory of Western democratic values over Communism, even as meaning the 'end of history'.

This was to colour much thinking about the revolutions, encouraging mistaken assumptions about their causes and course. There were at least five of these: that the revolutions had but a single cause – the long repressed desire for free markets and political liberty; that this popular desire exploded, almost out of the blue, in the autumn of 1989; and that the revolutions were inevitable. It is also often assumed that once they had begun they were part of a single movement, which did not vary much from country to country, and that the revolutions were an unsullied success. In fact, the causes of the revolutions were much more complex, both in terms of motivation and timing and were not inevitable. Moreover, there were important differences between the satellites, despite the similar process of revolt through which they went and the difficult legacies they inherited from 1989.

This Chapter therefore looks both at the causes and the subsequent evolution of the revolutions. Firstly, it suggests that the revolutions had complex layers of causes going back to opposition to the regimes created after the post-war takeover. It then goes on to argue that this was not enough to start a revolution. This required, as Chapter 8 has already implied, the destabilizing effects of Gorbachev's reforms in the USSR, reforms which had a particular significance for Poland and Hungary. This was where the revolutionary process examined here really began. However, the wider revolutionary movements were triggered off by short-term causes in the late summer of 1989, notably by the popular exodus from the GDR.

Secondly, the Chapter looks at the way in which, following the crumbling of the regime in the GDR the revolutions began to evolve. They began to spread to other countries, first in central Europe, and then in the south-east. There was also an acceleration of change in the pioneer countries. Yet, the way in which the revolutions seemed to carry all before them, did not prevent an uncomfortable aftermath in many countries.

The causes of revolution

The causes of the revolutions of 1989 were more complex than were initially assumed. In fact, they can best be understood as having three layers of causes: the long, the medium and the short-term. Firstly, the long-term causes, without which there would have been no possibility of revolt: the essential fact was the alienation of the satellite populations. It is crystal clear from both the long series of revolts considered in Chapter 5, and from the regimes' inability to enlist popular backing in 1989, that the Soviet-style regimes were not really supported by their populations. In other words the first, necessary, long-term cause of revolution in Eastern Europe was the underlying popular rejection of the regimes which had been imposed on them. This rejection, however, was not simply because the regimes were not based on Western political principles and relied on massive, Soviet-backed, machinery of military repression. It was also a pervasive popular judgement on the concrete and unhappy experience of life in the Eastern bloc, notably with the way self-interested party elites were rewarded at the expense of ordinary people.

By the early 1980s the problems of poor performance were all too clear. The Helsinki process, with its greater freedom for the media, made it harder for the regimes to conceal the problems caused by political decay and the further impositions made by 'New Freeze' on failing and debt-ridden economies. All this imposed immense strain on the local populations. The regimes were unable to deliver not just on basic provision but also on their own claims to be leading to a better way of life for ordinary people than the West. Indeed, Sir John Harvey Jones once perceptively and pungently remarked that 'the revolts were not about liberty, they were about sausage'. In other words the problem was one of explosive dissatisfaction with Communist rule rather than a positive desire for other values or systems. This was the underlying long-term precondition for revolution. Had there not been this alienation and dissatisfaction, the regimes might not have been at risk.

However, it does not follow logically from such long-term popular alienation that revolution was bound to come in 1989. A second group of medium-term causes actually turned the underlying malaise into a pre-revolutionary crisis. These precipitants were provided by events in the USSR during the later 1980s. It is unlikely that the revolutions would have taken place had it not been for glasnost and perestroika. These turned malaise into crisis by sapping both the structural bases and the vitality of the Eastern leaderships.

Gorbachev's policies cut the ground from under the feet of the bloc leaders. Most of them could not risk the kind of changes Gorbachev wanted, because their position was less secure than his. In any case his ideas called into question all they had been doing over the years. So, rather than being able to rely on the USSR, the leaderships found themselves involved in ideological and policy disputes with a Kremlin whose infallibility they had always praised. They were also worried that they could no longer rely on the latter's unfailing military support. Faced with this, and with pressure from the West, it became increasingly hard to repress dissent.

Equally, the depression prevented them from buying off opposition with economic rewards, even though resentment of disparities between the conditions enjoyed by the elite and those to which ordinary people were subject was ever more apparent. Equally, appeals to national loyalty were falling on increasingly deaf ears. Attempts by the elite to play the national card also had ambiguous effects. Thus, although apparently still imposing, the structures of totalitarianism were in crisis.

The satellite leaderships were reduced to proclaiming allegiance to the new line while actually doing nothing to implement it. Yet, at the same time, because of glasnost they allowed internal reformers and opponents more freedom of action. This posed a second danger of its own, encouraging inertia at the very time when the new spirit of reform was having a dramatic effect on their populations. The latter now found that glasnost both encouraged people to express their grievances, and provided means for them to do so. In fact 'Gorby' offered an attractive symbol of a legitimate alternative vision of Communism. The people saw perestroika as a form of liberation and responded enthusiastically and hopefully.

Outside of Poland and Hungary there was no response to such expectations. So, although as in France two centuries before, a revolution from above and within was needed to avoid a revolution from below or outside, the regimes no longer had the vitality to provide this. Gorbachev's reforms, therefore, although undertaken in order to try and rescue the essentials of Communism, were thus an essential prelude to revolution by sucking the life out of the old regimes.

It was partly because of this that Hungary and Poland began to make significant moves away from Communist orthodoxy in 1987–89. The adventurous – or desperate – regimes in Poland and Hungary tried to reform themselves, aware that they had lost the support of intellectuals and working classes. This was to be an important preliminary stage in the revolutions. Their experiences further encouraged predictions of a gradual evolution away from the rigidities of the past. Events were to belie these expectations in a dramatic way.

This points to the third level of causation, the short-term factors. In other words, while both the long- and the medium-term factors were necessary for revolution, they were not sufficient to bring them about. Crisis and alienation do not inevitably turn into revolution. For this to happen the unexpected and contingent developments of 1989 were needed. These conspired to trigger unstoppable mass disaffection within the satellites.

The triggers involved both the tactical errors made by party leaderships in dealing with the crisis and the way in which events in one country, notably in East Germany, interacted with developments elsewhere in the East. There was a kind of domino pattern as events in one country, sometimes deliberately engineered, triggered change in another, and vice versa. Together they brought the whole structure crashing down in a few short months. So the revolutions were not inevitable in the sense that they actually had to take place in exactly the way, and at exactly the time, that they did. Indeed, as has already been suggested, events in 1988–89 suggested a very different outcome.

The Polish and Hungarian preliminaries

If the initial precipitants came from the Soviet Union, subsequent events in Hungary and Poland also played a significant role in precipitating revolution throughout the Soviet bloc. For it was there that the dissolution of the structures and vitality of the old order really began, partly because of the inherent weaknesses of Communist rule there. Change in Hungary was led by reformist elements inside the Communist party but, after the rise of Solidarity, the Polish United Workers Party was too weak to take similar initiatives. As a result it was in Poland that non-Communist forces first came to power.

Although the crisis in Poland went back a very long way and the alienation of a fiercely anti-Russian population was well established, a new stage began in 1986–87. It was then that the Jaruzelski regime accepted that neither Martial Law nor subsequent attempts to marginalize Solidarity had succeeded. The movement remained a massive threat to government legitimacy and legislation. By the late 1980s this threat could no longer be disregarded because of the accelerating economic collapse.

Drastic steps had to be taken to reform the economy. These would require further increases in food prices. Thus, in 1987, the government sought to gain popular support by inviting the public to choose between various pricing options at a referendum. For the first time in bloc history the vote was lost. Moreover, attempts to push through price rises in 1988 in order to meet the spiralling costs of servicing the foreign debt, were met with widespread strikes first in the spring and again in August.

The strikes brought Solidarity back to life and forced Jaruzelski to stop using the riot police against it. Furthermore, he persuaded the Central Committee that there would have to be talks with Solidarity in order to win approval for reforms, which the Poles liked to call the second stage of perestroika. In August Solidarity accepted the offer of Round Table electoral and constitutional talks. These led, by April 1989, to the legalization of Solidarity, the removal of constraints on the Catholic Church, and the calling of elections both for the Presidency and for a reformed Parliament. The rules provided that a proportion of seats in the lower house or Sejm would be freely elected, as would be all the seats in the restored Senate. In the event Jaruzelski only just crept in as President. Moreover, Solidarity swept the board in all the seats for which it stood, preventing the formation of any government without it. Hence in September 1989 Tadeusz Mazowiecki presented the first ever Solidarity-led coalition government to the nation. With the USSR not intervening and the West offering support, this seemed to open the way for a gradual transition to something closer to plural politics.

Hungary had enjoyed a reputation for being more open and liberal than other Eastern bloc states, with a convertible currency and less repression than elsewhere. This had been the only means by which the regime was able to buy acceptance after the tragedies of 1956. However, by the mid-1980s this 'goulasch communism' was approaching its sell-by-date. Kadar's leadership was losing interest in economic reform at a time when the Kremlin wanted further progress. At the same time the economy was running into real trouble as foreign debt, inflation and unemployment rose and industrial production fell. Domestic support faded as people increasingly judged the regime on what it did and not on what it said about supporting perestroika.

Aided by the limited democratization of the early 1980s intellectuals and reformers inside the party, led by Imre Pozsgay, began openly to campaign for new policies. Their views began to get increasing prominence and encouraged the emergence of a crop of new political movements such as the nationalist Hungarian Democratic Forum (MDF). This pressure, which was in line with glasnost, began to tell on the party leadership. In May 1988 Kadar was kicked upstairs and replaced as Party Secretary by Karoly Groscz, a semi-hardliner acceptable to Moscow. At the same time reformers gained a foothold in the Politbureau.

Over the winter of 1988–89 the reformers began to strengthen their position, talking of seeking a new model of Socialism and responding to popular demands for the rehabilitation of Imre Nagy, the martyr of 1956. In January 1989 Pozsgay spoke out in favour of the 1956 revolution, denying that it had been the illegitimate counter-revolution depicted by the party line. Groscz was opposed to this, but on 10–11 February the Politbureau upheld Pozsgay. The reformers then moved to accept the idea of multi-partyism and, in March, to allow a celebration of the anniversary of the 1849 war with Russia. By April traditionalist Communist opposition in the Politbureau was overcome, and with Kadar being finally removed the next month, the Poszgay faction was, by June, running the government without much reference either to the Party or the Kremlin. Hence, further reforms including the legalization of strikes and the abolition of censorship were begun. Furthermore, in June not merely did 200 000 people take part in the moving rehabilitation ceremonies for Nagy but a Round Table on Polish lines was also established.

Even more significantly, the new government decided to demolish the 'Iron Curtain' along the border with Austria. This signified an attempt to link Hungary to the West. The sight of Hungarian soldiers physically removing the barbed wire fences, so that the borders with the West were opened, was to have dramatic effects. These were reinforced when the government also began to ignore its undertakings to the other satellites on freedom of movement.

Yet, even this failed to satisfy domestic opinion. With by-election victories going to the opposition and popular political activism breaking out everywhere, the gradual evolution within the system desired by Pozsgay and the MDF was increasingly rejected. The two had agreed a revised constitutional deal under which the Party would supply the President and the MDF the Prime Minister. However, public opinion, led by the Free Democrats (SZDSZ), wanted a complete break with the Communist system.

By the late summer things were slipping out of the government's control. Poszgay's ideas of early direct Presidential elections and modernizing the party, met prolonged resistance in the Round Table. So, as autumn began, the political future of both nation and party remained in the balance. However, the effects of the opening of Hungarian frontiers were to tip the scales against the party, just as they undermined the bloc as a whole.

The triggers of revolution

The Hungarian border question was, in fact, the third of the key triggers which, over the late summer of 1989, turned revolt into revolution. Chronologically, the first of these was Gorbachev's renunciation of intervention in satellite affairs in July. The second was the way in which, again during that summer, so many East German citizens chose to desert their regime and state. The Hungarians provided the final element in the process by providing the East Germans with an escape route, by opening the frontiers and later refusing to turn back East German 'holiday-makers', who had started to mass on the border with Austria.

The first element encouraging the move from reform to revolution was the signal that the Kremlin would not intervene to prevent the introduction of pluralism in the bloc. Because of the ultimate reliance of the Eastern European regimes on the USSR the attitudes of the latter were of considerable importance. In late March and April there were rumours that the Kremlin was moving away from the Brezhnev doctrine on the Soviet right to intervene militarily in defence of Communist rule. Then, on 6 July 1989, Gorbachev made a historic speech to the Council of Europe in Strasbourg. He then introduced to a wider audience his 1987 idea of creating a 'common European home' in which all countries could live together in peace. He also implicitly recognized the right of the satellites to choose their own political and social systems, a recognition which was formalized at the Bucharest Summit meeting of the WTO two days later.

This cancelling of the Brezhnev doctrine suggested to Communist reformers, and to the satellite populations at large, that they could alter course without fear of the Red Army invading. Western opinion was very excited by this and began to provide more help for change, notably in Poland and Hungary. All this made life much harder for the very unhappy hardline regimes in the bloc.

However, Gorbachev had merely provided the opportunity for change. It was the reaction of people inside East Germany which was to exploit this and, by so doing, provide the second trigger of revolution. Opposition groups like the Lutheran Church in East Germany were greatly stimulated by changes in the bloc. The emergence of dissent in the GDR which this involved was especially significant for the unfolding of revolution. Not only had the GDR been the darling of the bloc, with its strongest industrial base and the best standard of living, but the party seemed untroubled by divisions between reformers and hardliners. Because of its firm control, there was no challenge to its political authority even when it provocatively came out in support of the Chinese massacre of pro-democracy demonstrators in Tienamen Square that summer. This endorsement suggested that there would be no yielding to calls for democratization.

Underneath this apparent stability, however, was a growing popular malaise. Because of access to Western media and contacts there was keen awareness, in particular, of the increasing gap in living standards between East and West Germany. However, because Erich Honecker the party leader, having set his face against perestroika, would not act on Gorbachev's invitation, and was likely to use force against any dissent, many disillusioned East Germans felt that emigration was the only alternative. They saw no future for themselves living under a regime which neither delivered nor accepted that it could be improved in any way. Hence, there were 50 000 legal departures in the first half of 1989. More significantly, many more began to consider leaving illegally after their holidays and were encouraged in this by events in Hungary, notably the opening of the frontiers.

So, on 29 July East German tourists took refuge in the West German embassy in Budapest, seeking help in getting to the West. Other embassies suffered the same fate. More importantly tens of thousands of skilled craftsmen and intellectuals, and their families, gathered on the Hungarian border with Austria. The Hungarians began to talk of granting them political asylum and did little to prevent their filtering through into Austria. As a result the numbers built up in late August. Many would-be fugitives came through Czechoslovakia, access to which was not cut off by the GDR. All this had an immense psychological effect, underlining the importance of the GDR trigger.

The third trigger came soon after, as already noted, when the reforming Hungarian government lost patience with the East German authorities. Not merely did it refuse to turn people back, but it threatened to let all refugees through if the GDR did not resolve the problem. Because of Honecker's illness the regime was paralysed and so, on 11 September, the Hungarians renounced their agreement with the GDR to let only people with visas out. People began to pour through the now confirmed gap in the Iron Curtain towards the West. Encouraged by this many more left the GDR to take advantage of the open Hungarian frontier. At least 57 000 left in September alone while other countries and embassies also experienced a flood of departures. By the end of the year almost 350 000 had gone.

Although such a haemorrhage was profoundly damaging, the GDR regime continued to mishandle the problem because of its own lack of leadership. After the Hungarian decision it briefly tried to stop trains heading for the West until at the end of September, overwhelmed, it had to allow people to leave, albeit in sealed trains. At the same time, in early October it tried to close its frontiers and call out the army. The latter soon found itself faced with tens of thousands of rioters seeking to leave the country.

By then the general malaise had exploded into domestic political opposition. Hence, the Lutheran Church and a movement known as New Forum organized continuing large-scale political protests in Leipzig and other cities. Intimidation by the security forces merely intensified the dissent. At the same time the long planned 40th anniversary celebrations of the GDR on 6/7 October brought new humiliation for the regime. Not merely was Gorbachev hailed as a liberator by the crowds, but he snubbed Honecker. The latter was also warned both that he would be swept away by history if he did not adapt to democracy and that there would be no military support in case of trouble.

Honecker's reaction was to use force just the same. Already there had been violent clashes between police and the ever growing number of demonstrators, and this fuelled opposition to a corrupt and incompetent regime. Nobody was willing to defend it. So when 70 000 demonstrated for reform in Leipzig on 9 October Honecker ordered the army to fire on them, only to have his orders countermanded by the security forces, intellectuals and elements in the party loyal to Gorbachev.

The ever increasing demonstrations and continuing official disaffection, which produced escalating demands for political change, were to be the prelude to the resignation of the now powerless and discredited Honecker. This came on 18 October. He was replaced by Gorbachev's protégé, the security chief Egon Krenz. Like Pozsgay, he sought to save the system by liberalizing it. However, now that the use of force was denied him, he found he could not control events. His election encouraged demonstrations of up to a million people who wanted a real break with the past. That he had completely lost the initiative was shown first by the re-opening of the GDR's frontiers and then by the acceptance of the right of free travel.

This was followed by the panicky decision on 9 November to open the Berlin Wall. Hundreds of thousands of people poured through, and often out, while Westerners poured in to swell the opposition. The Wall itself began to come down. This, and the enforced onslaught on the crimes of the old order which

Krenz was forced to accept, along with constitutional reform and new contacts with West Germany, showed that the main bastion of the Soviet Empire had collapsed.

The impact of this was enormous. The East German trigger completed the process of starting a real revolution, building on the long-term alienation and the medium-term weakening of the Communist regimes. Not surprisingly other countries began to succumb to the same trends, first in central Europe and then further afield. As they did, the revolutions moved into a new phase of evolution, in which the causal pattern began to change somewhat.

The spreading of revolution: central Europe

Indeed, well before the Wall came down, events in East Germany and elsewhere had helped to trigger off revolts in other satellites. They did this partly through their own direct influence and partly because people elsewhere sought to emulate what was happening there. Errors made in dealing with the growing crisis, notably the use of violence, also played their part in turning dissatisfaction into out and out revolt. It may well also be that the Soviets, whether directly or indirectly, had a hand in manoeuvring some of the more recalcitrant regimes out of office.

Because events in the various satellites were interrelated, the shape of the revolutions had a marked family resemblance. First came a rapid mobilization of popular discontent, like that started in East Germany by the gatherings at the Nikolauskirche in Leipzig. By the end of October similar gatherings were taking place in Wenceslas Square in Prague for instance. Very often this led to the creation of some kind of umbrella movement which organized and represented growing popular anger and dissatisfaction, rather in the way Solidarity had in Poland and New Forum in East Germany. This was the case with Civic Forum in Czechoslovakia and, to a lesser extent, with the National Salvation Front in Romania.

Faced with increasingly organized and large-scale protests the old regimes then very often surrendered their monopoly on power. Only in Romania did this really need force to achieve. However, the Communist leadership also tried to hold on to its leading position. This took two forms. Sometimes it involved no more than trying to reform the party so that it became acceptable again. This was the aim of the Hungarian reformers, as it was to be that of both Hans Modrow in the GDR and the new Bulgarian leadership.

In other cases, the party sought to try and manage the transition towards a more plural society in alliance with democratic forces. This was the case in Bulgaria, Hungary and Poland. However, such half-way houses were inherently unstable. Beginning with Czechoslovakia the old order began to collapse completely, allowing new forces into power. In some cases this was a long drawn out process, as for example in the Balkans. In Czechoslovakia it was remarkably rapid.

Czechoslovakia, like East Germany, had appeared remarkably stable owing to a combination of repression and reasonable living standards. Even Husak's replacement as Party Secretary by Milos Jakes in December 1987 did not bring real change. So, much to Moscow's annoyance, there was only talk about perestroika. However, when student and Catholic disaffection reappeared in late 1988, Jakes then cracked down although his self-satisfied immobility was questioned early in 1989 when he visited Moscow.

With only marginal liberalization, the opposition remained very pessimistic. It was denied the opening provided by the Round Tables in Poland and Hungary. Nonetheless, contact with the latter encouraged the growth of organized opposition organization later that summer. As well as pro-democracy pamphlets and petitions attacking ecological and economic conditions it also successfully celebrated the 21st anniversary of the 1968 invasion in August. Thereafter, a lull followed, because the regime permitted easier contact with the outside world.

By late October, however, news of the fall of Honecker stimulated large-scale protests. Ten thousand people demonstrated in Prague's Wenceslas Square on 28 October, the anniversary of the founding of the First Republic in 1918. The nervous regime also allowed a further demonstration on 17 November, but when 50 000 people turned up, the police attacked them, allegedly killing a student in the process. This may have been an invention to raise the temperature and encourage more opposition.

In any event there was outrage in Prague and other major cities. New groups emerged, demanding an investigation into police brutality and the resignation of hardliners. The developing protests were increasingly co-ordinated by former Czech dissidents who founded the Civic Forum movement on 19 November. Its Slovak pendant, People Against Violence, emerged three days later. These umbrella bodies were to provide both the organization for opposition and a channel for negotiations with the regime.

Negotiation became a necessity after 200 000 demonstrated for change on 20 November. Not merely could the police not control such numbers but they refused to do so. Their violence having been captured on film, they were frightened by the prospect of a public enquiry into their misdeeds. At the same time pro-Moscow loyalists were trying to engineer the replacement of Jakes by somebody more reform-minded. The Czech regime, like others in the bloc, was left too weak and divided to repress the protests. It had to try and temporize.

So Adamec, the Prime Minister, finally agreed to speak to the crowd on 25 November. He at once squandered the chance of accommodation (and an engineered transition) by calling for an end to protest so as to allow government a free hand to reform. This refusal to realize that the people themselves wanted real change, and without the old guard being involved, handed the initiative to

Civic Forum. A general strike was called for 27 November and free elections were vehemently demanded.

Jakes was finally forced to stand down on the day of the strike and a complete reshuffle of the Politbureau followed. Parliament voted to abolish the leading role of the Party and Adamec agreed to form a new government by 3 December. When this turned out to be a very narrow coalition, Civic Forum refused to take part, encouraged by crowds a quarter of a million strong.

Faced with both this unyielding opposition and the evaporation of its own support, the government resigned five days later. On 9 December Husak surrendered the Presidency and two days on a broad coalition cabinet, committed to institutional reform, was formed under the reformist communist Marian Calfa. Parliament's late December choice of Vaclav Havel, the country's leading intellectual dissident, as President, and Alexander Dubček, the man of the Prague Spring, as Speaker, consummated a transfer of power which had taken only 24 days. And, although the party managed to keep going in a revised form, its support continued to crumble, opening the way to free elections in June 1990.

Revolt in the Balkans
Before the Czechoslovak break through was complete, trouble had spread to the Balkans. The revolutions there were to reach a bloody climax over Christmas in Romania. In Bulgaria, on the other hand, the revolution came much earlier. But, like that in Bucharest, it may also have been engineered.

Bulgaria had always been a docile Soviet ally, albeit an underdeveloped one. But with the problems over debt, food supplies and pollution and a new line in the Kremlin, the elderly and ailing leader Todor Zhivkov began to feel insecure. Hence he made a pretence of adopting perestroika while in practice doing nothing to reform the country's superannuated structures. Instead he sought nationalistic support in May 1989 by again turning on the Turkish minority. The regime tried to force Turks to renounce their ethnic identity by forcing them to take Bulgarian names. When this caused protests, some were killed and many were deported. In fact, some 300 000 Turks were forced to leave the country during the year. This was not well received abroad. Yet, in October 1989, Zhivkov did not hesitate to set the police on demonstrators from the emerging opposition *ecoglasnost* movement, protesting against the regime and its abuse of the environment. This was despite the presence of foreign TV cameras covering a CSCE meeting in Sofia.

Such crassness increased disaffection amongst both intellectuals and the populace at large. It also scandalized some of his long-term supporters, not to mention Gorbachev. So when Foreign Minister Peter Mladenov was passing through Moscow he was able to secure the Kremlin's approval for Zhivkov's replacement. Hence, on 10 November, a palace coup forced him to 'offer his resignation' when faced with an alliance of liberal and hardline elements.

As soon as this became known, popular feelings made themselves felt, through new discussion groups and large-scale demonstrations. Thus, on 18 November, a crowd of 100 000 demanded real freedom and the prosecution of Zhivkov. Mladenev was therefore forced to go beyond merely revivifying the party. He had to promise a purge of the Zhivkov faction, the reform of the penal code and free elections. That this was not what the new party leadership wanted was made clear by a Politbureau warning against extremism on 20 November.

By then, however, the populace had got the bit between its teeth. By 7 December the opposition came together in the Union of Democratic Forces (UDF). Although some changes had been made on 25 November, Mladenev was forced to go much further. In December the Zhivkov faction was purged. The party also gave up its leading role, its commitment to Marxist–Leninism and eventually its title. And, on 2 January the anti-Turkish excesses were ended. Paradoxically, this caused a violent nativist protest because many Bulgarians were still very hostile to their minority. The new commitment to Western freedoms was thus called into question by visceral anti-Turkish feelings.

Nonetheless, Round Table talks with the UDF on constitutional change began on 15 January 1990. These were to lead to a more reformist cabinet in February and ultimately to elections in May and June. These were easily won by the Bulgarian Socialist Party (BSP), as the Communist party was by then called, because it still controlled the media and the opposition was very disorganized. However, the party did not want to tackle the transition on its own, so it invited the UDF to join a coalition government. Understandably, the opposition refused, since it was clear that the regime's support was somewhat artificial and it lacked real legitimacy. So the old party found itself facing sole responsibility for such difficult tasks as reforming land tenure, modifying the planned economy and providing real political rights. And it had to do this at a time of gathering economic crisis for which it was forced to take all the blame. So, not merely did the party's attempt to mastermind reform in its own interest backfire, but Bulgarian politics were to remain in an uneasy state of transition for some time.

While events in Bulgaria caused little surprise, many people felt that Romania might escape the contagion of revolution because of its lack of democratic traditions and, especially, because of the effectiveness of dictatorship of the manic Ceauşescu family. Using the innumerable informers, the feared secret police, or Securitate, and the state monopoly of all means of expression they kept the population under almost total control. Indeed, every single typewriter in the country had to be registered to stop their use for subversive purposes. At the same time the dynastic regime deprived its people of electricity, food and health as it exported everything in order to pay off its foreign debts. Having done this it then creamed off what wealth there was into its private coffers and grandiose projects. These included the internationally unpopular attacks on traditional village life and the bulldozing of much of old Bucharest to create a new official quarter with a monstrous Disneyesque palace.

Having thus reduced the country to Third World levels of deprivation, Ceauşescu was very threatened by perestroika. Therefore, he not merely attacked it, but he even demanded that the WTO intervene to prevent reforms in Hungary and Poland. However, apart from increased migration and food riots in Brasov in November 1987, there was, understandably, little public dissent. Inside the party, on the other hand, there were signs of unease. In March 1989, an Open Letter from six founder members of the Party, attacking the way Socialism had been deformed by Ceauşescu's inept dynastic rule, was leaked to the BBC. It is probable that the authors were in contact with an increasingly disenchanted Gorbachev. He found Ceauşescu's antics and opposition to reform unacceptable and internationally embarrassing.

Although rumours of a coup against the dictator circulated in late summer 1989 and again during the November Congress which triumphantly re-elected him as General Secretary, a new crackdown seemed to have allowed the regime to ride out not merely party unease, but also increasing Western pressure on human rights. Despite the upheavals elsewhere in Eastern Europe, trouble in Romania only really began in mid-December 1989 and then in Transylvania where the regime had been oppressing the large Hungarian minority. So, when the Securitate sought to arrest the Timisaoara Magyar leader, Pastor Lazlo Tokes, the populace prevented this. Ceauşescu then ordered the security forces to shoot to kill and, on 17 December, some 90 people were massacred. Since rumour inflated the numbers, the troubles spread. This was true both of Timisaoara, from which an uneasy army withdrew, and of other cities.

On 21 December, the day after Ceauşescu's return from a state visit to Iran, he assembled a handpicked crowd in Bucharest. He meant to deter trouble by making clear his support for the way the security forces had dealt with the so called 'hooligans' of Timisaoara. Instead he found himself howled down and his very position challenged. This was perhaps the clearest and most dramatic example of the way the Communist regimes failed to rally support during the crisis. It left Ceauşescu totally flabbergasted, never having had to face such treatment before.

He was even more bereft when the army refused to fire on the demonstrators as riots began to develop in Bucharest. After the Minister of Defence committed suicide rather than give the orders to fire, the army fraternized with demonstrators rather than attacking them. This was because the soldiers, who were mainly conscripts, had been badly treated by the regime which preferred to rely on the pampered Securitate. The next day the crowds stormed the Central Committee building moments before the Ceauşescus fled by helicopter. The Securitate, fearing that they had been abandoned to popular revenge by the dynasty, then launched a bloody onslaught against army and crowd in which some 700 people died before the army won out. Here too the regime showed that, despite appearances, it no longer had the ability to repress dissent.

Moreover, even then, nobody rallied to the Ceauşescus. The luck of Nicolae and his wife Elena soon ran out, after strange wanderings around the country-side, and they were arrested. Handed over to the army, they were subjected to a farcical video trial for 'genocide'. They were then brutally mown down before they could reach the wall against which they were due to be shot by a firing squad.

This intemperate haste probably had much to do with the fact that the con-spirators inside the party had, by then, started their own coup, somewhat earlier than they had planned. They wished to remove any possibility of the Ceauşescu's remaining a focus of party loyalty. With the Soviets closing the frontiers the plotters created a National Council of the Salvation Front under Ion Iliescu, a former party official, to take over power. Despite promises of food, free elections, free churches and the abolition of the Securitate, this enjoyed only a very brief honeymoon because it was dominated by the hard core of the Party. Some of its more liberal members resigned soon after appointment and student demonstrations against it began in January.

These were to run for months, despite the fact that the new regime bussed in workers to rough up the opposition in January and February 1990. Iliescu's oligarchy also proved adept at controlling the media, playing the anti-Magyar card and rigging the elections in May. As a result the still very disorganized opposition did badly, so that the NSF and its government were confirmed in power. However, rather as in the Bulgarian case, they were left facing continuing popular hostility and accelerating economic difficulties.

Acceleration
Long before the elections, events in Czechoslovakia and the Balkans had helped to carry the revolutionary process forward in the other three satellites. In all three countries the Communist parties imploded as the pressure for change became irresistible. At the same time opposition unity began to diverge and break up once decisions had to be made on the shape of post-Communism society. This was not helped by the growing economic crisis.

In Poland the Mazowiecki government was freed by events elsewhere to start a real remodelling of the country's political structures. It also adopted the radical economic package, proposed by Finance Minister Leszek Balcerowicz, to shift the country onto a market-led basis. This came into effect on 1 January 1990, cutting inflation and making food freely available, albeit at a price. However, industrial output and employment were badly hit. The switch left the Polish United Workers' Party (PUWP) with nowhere to go and it dissolved itself in January 1990. President Jaruzelski also came under pressure to resign, notably from Lech Walesa who also criticized the government, thereby symbolizing the way Solidarity was breaking up because of differences over the pace and effects of decommunization.

Hungary experienced the collapse of the ruling party and the splintering of opposition even earlier than this. Talks on constitutional change went increasingly in the opposition's favour and the Party failed to move to direct election of an executive president, which would have strengthened its position. Equally importantly, members flooded out of the party in the autumn of 1989, despite the fact that, at its October Congress, the Communist Party transformed itself into the Hungarian Socialist Party (HSP), although a rump Communist party continued in existence. Rather than allowing the reformers to continue in power the HSP was sidelined as, during October, Communism was simply dropped. The nomenklatura, the secret police apparatus and the workers militia were all abolished. Even the old Parliament voted to return to older political structures.

The initiative passed to the Round Table parties. Here the pro-Western Free Democrats prevented any chance of a Polish style power-sharing arrangement between Poszgay and the MDF. However, it was the latter with its more cautious and nationalistic solution to the country's growing economic problems, which won the 25 March 1990 elections. This led to the selection of a Free Democrat as President by the new Parliament, with government being entrusted to a coalition dominated by the MDF and headed by its Party leader, Josef Antall.

In East Germany Communism clung to power for a little longer and the shape of the opposition was rather different. In the first instance, however, the opening of the Wall did little to help Krenz. The popular onslaught on the old order gathered pace and despite installing a new government under Hans Modrow, a more open-minded party regional leader, and giving way on one party rule, Krenz was forced to resign on 6 December, after only 44 days in office. This followed a mass demonstration against party corruption on 1 December. Such pressures were reinforced by continuing emigration. This was still continuing at a rate of some 2 500 per day. So, despite calling an early extraordinary Party Congress in mid-December, which transformed the SED into the Party of Democratic Socialism (PSD), Communist hopes of merely reforming the system rapidly faded.

Power was, in fact, shifting away from Party and government to the Round Table. The first Round Table meeting took place on 7 December, and soon began to act as an alternative government, reflecting the growing demands for political change and even unification. On 15 January the Stasi headquarters were besieged, opening the way for further attacks on the old guard. By the end of January Modrow had to form a much wider coalition government, bringing in many members of the opposition, prior to the holding of free elections.

These were held on 18 March 1990 and were, somewhat unexpectedly, won not by old dissidents, the new Forum or the SPD, but by the newly reformed CDU and its allies. Their victory reflected the way in which pressure for unification with the West was becoming irresistible. This had not always been the case. Thus, when, on 28 November 1989, Helmut Kohl had suggested a gradual process of change this was resisted by Modrow. However, the idea caught on. Unification seemed to offer hopes of solving the East's growing economic problems and of providing the same standard of living as the West enjoyed. Kohl proved an extraordinarily successful campaigner in the East elections and this, along with outside support for the idea, helped unification forward. So, things moved fast after the elections, the first free elections in Eastern Germany since the 1930s. The Grand Coalition formed after the elections pushed forward first to economic union and then full union with the FRG. Although the PSD did surprisingly well in the elections with 16 per cent of the vote, it lost all influence on power.

Aftermaths
If, by the summer of 1990 the revolutions as such were largely over, the process of change was only just beginning. The revolutions only changed the visible tip of the Communist iceberg. Even when elections had been held the transition away from the old political order was still not complete. It took some while for the old institutions of integration to crumble for instance. Restructuring the crumbling command economies was only just beginning while achieving Western standards of living remained a distant dream.

Politically the old ruling parties may have been evaporating, but stable pluralist politics had yet to emerge. Political culture remained more coloured by the Communist past than many had imagined. There was often a proliferation of new forces with no ability or desire to combine. Nor was the tolerance, the acceptance of free media, or the respect for the legal system and other social groups, on which civil society depends, always present. Equally, the economic and environmental problems left by the old regime were immense. Yet solving them meant foreign influence, inflation and unemployment. The new societies found this very hard to cope with.

Different countries adopted different strategies for trying to deal with these problems. The East Germans had a 'big bang' approach to economic and political liberalization thrust on them. The Poles initially opted for this as, a little later, did the Czechs. After the June 1990 elections when Civic Forum won a remarkable victory, the majority followed the radical policies of the Finance Minister Vaclav Klaus. However, these were not always acceptable to Havel and some of his supporters or, more worryingly, to the Slovaks. This was to be a prelude to the beginning of deep divisions inside the new federal republic involving parties and, eventually, nationalities.

In the two Balkan states the approach was more gradual, partly because the old parties had succeeded in adapting to the new order. The fact that they stood for continuity and the defence of existing interests helped them to win elections in May and June 1990 with relative ease. They soon found themselves exposed, however, because democratic opinion whether in the UDF in Bulgaria or among the Romanian students who occupied University Square in Bucharest for so long, was bitterly resentful of their links with the past. The reformed parties therefore had to deal with growing economic dislocation alone. And they could not rely on popular consensus when they took harsh decisions. So the post-revolutionary aftermath was an unhappy period almost everywhere.

It was also a period in which the crisis began to spread out beyond the old satellites into the Western Balkans and into the Soviet Union itself. In Yugoslavia, growing Serbian repression in the mainly Albanian province of Kossovo, coupled with the collapse of the League of Communists in January 1990, was starting the process which was to lead to genocidal civil wars as Chapter 15 shows. In Albania itself sheer deprivation was forcing the population to seek sanctuary outside the country. At the same time the USSR was facing growing separatist pressures by the Baltic states.

In all this, as with the revolutions themselves, the national element was becoming increasingly apparent. As well as seeking to reject the alien imposition of Communism and its failure to deliver concretely in environmental and living standards, those who participated in the revolutions were seeking to regain their own national self respect. National feeling was able to feed on the material problems left by Communism. So the post-war era in the East ended with the beginnings of a return to the problems that had led to its collapse in the late 1930s and early 1940s.

Furthermore, the problems of the East were both to influence developments elsewhere in Europe and were to get caught up in other problems. Thus, the revolutions, and especially the unification of Germany, was to encourage a new impetus in European integration. Unfortunately, the economic impact of unification helped to precipitate a new depression in Europe. This made Western states much less ready to respond to the new democracies' desire to 'return to Europe' even though the depression was to make the problems of new democracies even more acute. Thus, notwithstanding the ending of the Cold War and the beginnings of a wider European architecture, the peaceful revolutions of 1989 bequeathed agony as well as ecstasy to the Europe of the 1990s.

Further reading

Ash, T. G. (1990), *We the People*, London: Granta.
Brown, J.F. (1991), *The Surge to Freedom*, London: Adamantine.
Daniels, R.V. (1993), *The End of Communist Revolution in Europe*, London: Routledge.
East, R. (ed.) (1991), *Revolution in Eastern Europe*, London: Pinter.
Fowkes, B. (1993), *The Rise and Fall of Communism in Eastern Europe*, London: Macmillan.
Glenny, M. (1990), *The Rebirth of History*, Harmondsworth: Penguin.
Mason, D.S. (1992), *Revolution in East Central Europe*, Boulder, Col.: Westview.
Prins, G. (ed.) (1991), *Spring in Winter*, Manchester: Manchester University Press.
Stokes, G. (1993), *The Walls Came Tumbling Down. The Collapse of Eastern Europe*, London: Oxford University Press.
Sword, K. (ed.) (1991), *The Times Guide to Eastern Europe*, 2nd edn, London: Times Publishing.
Walker, R. (1993), *Six Years that Shook the World*, Manchester: Manchester University Press.
Wheaton, B. (1992), *The Velvet Revolution: Czechoslovakia 1988–1991*, Boulder, Col.: Westview.

PART III

THE CHALLENGES
OF THE 1990s

Overview

The events of the late 1980s profoundly altered the political and economic landscape of Europe. They brought dramatic and welcome changes as well as revealing many uncomfortable continuities from the past. As a result the decade has already thrown up new difficulties as well as new gains. Together these presented the newly united continent with a series of difficult challenges which few anticipated when the Berlin Wall was breached.

Sometimes histories fight shy of tackling such very recent periods, especially when their nature and prospects are so problematic. However, the issues of the 1990s are precisely those of most concern to students and information on them can be hard to find. So, despite the problems and pitfalls, the effort to define the challenges of the 1990s, their evolution and the issues they pose, is worthwhile. This concluding section therefore looks at some of the challenges of the 1990s.

Initially, between 1989 and 1991, these seemed to be very welcome ones. Thus, integration seemed to be capable of further development, both inside the EC and in relations between the EC and the EFTA states. The Western states seemed to be in a fit state to do this. Economically too, the signs seemed encouraging. At worst, a gentle decline in growth was expected as the Single Market neared completion.

Equally, there was great enthusiasm both about the first stages of transition to both democracy and market economics in the East. Voters there seemed to be happy to turn their backs on hardline Communists and return reformers to power. At the same time the movement towards disarmament was speeding up and extending to the newly independent countries which succeeded the USSR. The Charter of Paris of November 1990, as already noted, also seemed to offer a new harmonious style of international relations in the 'New Europe'.

If all this did not stop the break-up of the Yugoslav Federation, EC mediation seemed at least to have ensured that this happened relatively peacefully. Unfortunately this was not to be. Indeed, the increasingly horrific conflict in former Yugoslavia proved to be one of a number of crises which began to threaten Europe, turning the euphoria of 1989 into increasing pessimism. Ratifying the changes to the EC agreed at Maastricht also proved to be a nightmare in many states whether because of popular opposition or the new instability of the currency markets which hit both the ERM and the proposed EMU. Many Western states, moreover, faced increasingly debilitating economic challenges from rising unemployment and declining growth. Consequently, the domestic political and social climate deteriorated sharply.

In the East of Europe the replacement of Communism did not produce the swift and painless transition expected only a few years before. In fact by 1993–94, the former satellite states found the move to Western norms sufficiently hard and uncomfortable even to prompt the return to power of some former Communists. The successor states of the USSR were plunged into even worse crises. This was especially true of Yeltsin's Russia which began to reassert itself on the international arena, raising fears about the stability of Europe.

All this raised new issues for the West. The disarmament process slowed down and attempts to devise new forms of European security which could cope with an uncertain Russia and new ethnic conflicts as well as with an enlarged Germany, were slow and of limited effectiveness. Equally, developing EC links with the former satellites proved a long and often difficult process. Moreover, the Bosnian tragedy, from which no Western institutions emerged with real credit, continued to drag on. This was but one aspect of the many regional challenges requiring cohesive and flexible strategies for the wider Europe of the 1990s, as the emerging EU in particular found.

By 1994, however, although the new difficulties continued to alarm and depress, there were also hopeful signs of change. The economic recession started to bottom out and more positive European policies toward the wider Europe began to emerge. Nonetheless, such changes, like the continuing difficulties, pose challenges to decision makers and to present and future citizens of Europe. Hence, the last task of *Continuity and Change in Contemporary Europe* is to examine key challenges, and the issues they raise, in more detail.

11   Developing the European Community

During the late 1980s/early 1990s the EC was faced with a number of challenges. Firstly, the implications of the coming into force of the SEA were wider than had perhaps been foreseen. There were important spillover effects from the 1992 programme into monetary and social areas, while the institutional implications of the SEA changed the direction of the EC's legislative process. Having assigned more authority to the EP, it would only be a matter of time before Parliament would make a bid for further power. Thus, the SEA had become a catalyst for change.

Secondly, the peaceful revolutions in eastern and central Europe and the unification of the two Germanies, while dramatically changing the international context, had important repercussions for the EC. A strong, unified Germany needed to be anchored in an equally strong EC framework, while member states felt a special responsibility in the peaceful transition to democracy in central and eastern Europe. Thirdly, the Gulf War and the Yugoslavian crisis had reinforced the collective resolve of the 12 member states to move towards a common foreign and security policy. These internal and external pressures both led to a reconsideration of member states' objectives and a further 'review' of the EC's constitutional bases seemed inevitable.

Within a year of the revolutions in the East and German unification, the EC negotiated yet another amendment to the Treaty of Rome. However, while agreement on the principle of treaty revision was easily reached, conflicts over the extent of the reform soon overshadowed negotiations both prior to the signing of the new 'Treaty on European Union' (Maastricht Treaty) and during the subsequent ratification process, which ushered in a stagnant and particularly acrimonious period. Conflicts over the content of the new treaty were compounded by a general unease accompanying the deep economic recession – which was more acutely felt in some member states than in others – and the rise of instability resulting from the Gulf War and the situation in the former Yugoslavia.

While some of these problems have proved to be ephemeral, the EC, as it approaches the mid-1990s, has entered a somewhat precarious and uncertain period. It remains to be seen whether outstanding problems can be solved at the forthcoming Intergovernmental Conference planned for 1996. Moreover, the inclusion of 'opt-out clauses' in the new treaty for some member states has raised fears among European federalists that a dangerous precedent has been set and that the EC might be entering an era of 'graduated' or 'multi-speed' integration.

Motivations for the second 'relaunch' of Europe

In the late 1980s several factors combined to give weight to the opinion that further reform of EC institutions and an extension of policy areas were necessary. Firstly the SEA, which had issued from extensive negotiations in the early and mid-1980s, had been considered disappointing by many observers, above all by the EP. On the other hand, it could be argued that the SEA, following a uniquely dynamic law, had set the stage for consolidation and extension of the integration process. For example, the introduction of the six new policy areas, and particularly the dynamic effect of the 1992 project, had led to the realization that a common currency was necessary for the Single Market to work effectively. Based on this argument, some member states led by France and Germany, and particularly the Commission under President Delors, demanded further treaty amendments to extend the scope of the existing EMS to achieve full EMU by the end of the decade.

Consequently, the European Council meeting in Hanover in June 1988 instructed a group of experts, chaired by Delors, to study concrete steps that would be necessary to create such a union. The broad substance of the 'Delors Report' mapping out EMU in three stages was accepted by member states in 1989. At the Strasbourg summit meeting of the European Council in December 1989, it was decided to convene an IGC to negotiate treaty revisions necessary for the establishment of complete economic and monetary union. More than any other policy area, the need for a common currency illustrates the spillover effect the 1992 project has created, articulated in the former German Chancellor Helmut Schmidt's comment: 'Who ever heard of a single market with eleven different currencies?'

The need for monetary union as the crowning of the Single Market initiated debate on treaty revisions. However, other pressures, some of which resulted from the changing international context, combined to widen the agenda still further. The EP, while it enjoyed a greater influence on EC activities since the coming into force of the SEA, still felt that its role fell short of that of a full decision-maker. In a series of reports, adopted between September 1989 and November 1990, Parliament – now directly elected for the third time – continually pressed for further moves to tackle the continuing 'democratic deficiency' in the EC's decision-making. It called for substantial constitutional reform and improvement of the legislative procedures including co-decision power for the EP. It also wanted qualified majority voting in most areas, complete economic and monetary union by the mid-1990s and a common foreign and security policy.

Sharing Parliament's concern, some member states felt that a federation of states linked by common economic and social objectives would be incomplete and vulnerable without a common foreign and security dimension. This impulse was reinforced by the Gulf crisis and later by the situation in former Yugoslavia. In fact, the Gulf War, in exposing fundamental philosophical differences between the member states, clearly demonstrated that present mechanisms and practises such as EPC, were not sufficient to deal with the challenges of the 1990s. Nevertheless, the EC drew the lesson from the experience of the Gulf War that as the former German Foreign Minister Genscher put it 'we cannot allow developments over the past months to become a cheap argument against political union. No one should be allowed to hide his reticence towards Europe behind the developments in the Gulf.'

Undoubtedly, the EC drew much inspiration from the provisions of the Single Act, but it would be wrong to suggest that the integrative dynamics of the late 1980s and early 1990s were entirely due to the SEA. The revolutionary movements in central and eastern Europe, which reached a dramatic climax with the dismantling of the Berlin Wall in November 1989, took the EC totally by surprise and had a decisive impact on it. The new eastern democracies looked to the EC in particular as a source of hope and support. This fact raised the possibility of parts of east-central Europe, particularly Poland, Czechoslovkia and Hungary, acceding to the EC. These countries perceived membership of the EC as essential in their long transformation process to a pluralist style of democracy and free enterprise. Meeting this historic challenge required the EC to develop a speedy blueprint and a new strategic concept to deal with these challenges, while it was still grappling with the implementation of provisions arising from the SEA.

The possibility of extensive enlargement – not only from eastern Europe, but from the EFTA countries via the European Economic Area (EEA) – was an additional pressure for reform. Application for membership from Malta and Cyprus had to be examined, while the Commission's opinion on the Turkish application had been negative. Austria had applied for membership in 1989, a move which not only raised the issue of widening versus deepening, but symbolized the likely limitations of EEA membership. Indeed, by the time the IGC had started, Sweden had applied for membership on 1 July 1991 followed eventually by Finland and Norway, in March and November 1992, respectively. The prospect of 16 or more member states in the foreseeable future gave an enormous spur to revision negotiations and particularly to debates on institutional reform. It seeemed clear that the present framework could not function effectively in such an enlarged EC.

The fall of the Berlin Wall on 9 November 1989 added a new dimension to the revision process in the EC. Once again, the 'German problem' became a major concern on the European agenda. Some member states feared that a new German economic giant of 80 million people would upset the European balance. The possibility of unification re-ignited old fears of an assertive, domineering Germany. At the summit meeting of the European Council in Strasbourg in December 1989, the linkage between German unification and deeper integration in the EC emerged clearly for the first time and was to be a constant theme during the months to come. EC leaders attempted to alleviate their anxieties about Germany by in effect exchanging approval for unification for a German agreement to hold an IGC charged with discussing moves toward economic and monetary union. President Mitterrand, uneasy about Kohl's unilateral announcement of a 10-point programme for German unification to the German Bundestag on 28 November 1989, traded France's sovereignty in monetary terms for the anchoring of unified Germany irrevocably in a stronger and more integrated EC.

Against this background, France and Germany in April 1990 called for a second IGC on political union, to run parallel to the EMU IGC. This was partly an attempt to overcome anxiety over German unification and also a move to underline Germany's continued commitment to Europe. Equally, it reflected the German government's determination to extend the mandate beyond mere economic and monetary matters. The Kohl/Mitterrand letter called for the strengthening 'of the democratic legitimacy of the union ...' and for rendering 'its institutions more efficient'. It also wished 'to define and implement a common foreign and security policy'. Jacques Delors, reflecting German sentiments in favour of political union, insisted that treaty amendments would have to include the notion of 'democratic accountability' and the strengthening of the EP's powers.

The run-up to the IGCs
Reform debates, spurred on by these developments, were now underway. Proposals were tabled both by EC institutions and member states. The EP, as already noted, adopted several resolutions, known as the Martin Reports, arguing for further reform beyond the agreed EMU. The Commission President Delors, speaking to Parliament in December 1989, picked up the EP's demand for a second IGC to discuss matters aimed at transforming the EC into a political union. The first member state to come out in support of a second IGC was Belgium, when it submitted a concrete proposal to that effect in March 1990. This was followed by an Italian initiative which advocated institutional reform alongside an EMU. This concept of 'parallelism' between the two IGCs was, as has been noted, taken up by Mitterrand and Kohl in their letter to the Irish Presidency of the European Council in April 1990.

The Kohl–Mitterrand letter was considered by the extraordinary European Council meeting in April. This first Dublin Summit – originally called to discuss German unification – came to no definite decision as to the convening of a second IGC. In the meantime both Spain and Greece came out in favour of a second IGC and the European Council, during its second meeting under Irish presidency in June agreed that two IGCs, one on EMU and one under the broad heading of 'political union' should be opened in December at the Rome summit. The two European Council meetings in Rome, under the Italian Presidency, in October (Rome I) and December 1990 (Rome II) respectively, finalized the agenda for the two IGCs and confirmed the intention to transform the EC into a political union.

During the subsequent discussions, each member state voiced its own objectives and expectations. For Germany, EMU and institutional reform constituted what it called a package. Germany was adamant about the 'parallelism' of the two IGCs to the point of threatening to veto EMU if agreement on political union could not be reached. France was less interested in institutional affairs, but placed high priority on the realization of EMU. The French government regarded EMU as the logical outcome of project 1992, and as a means of overcoming the dominance of both the DM and the German Bundesbank.

These two countries, despite their somewhat different objectives, became the protagonists of reform, backed both by Italy and the Benelux countries. The Mediterranean countries and Ireland were also supportive, although only on the condition that their particular economic problems would be counterbalanced by special aid programmmes. Only the UK – and to some extent Denmark – were neither interested in the EMU nor in the strengthening of the EP. Britain particularly resented the inclusion of a special social chapter and the articulation in the treaty of the principle of federalism. It was only at the last minute during the negotiations that Britain accepted the concept of a single currency and abandoned its own proposal of a hard ECU – a parallel currency to circulate alongside existing national ones – orginally made in June 1990.

The IGCs

The two IGC conferences, which formally opened on 15 December 1990, reflected the previous 15 months of intense debate that had taken place, both within EC institutions and member states, in that two main conflicts emerged. Firstly, the greater degree of consensus on EMU than on political union had already become manifest at the special meeting of the European Council in Rome on 27 and 28 October when it was agreed to launch stage I of monetary union on 1 January 1994 despite British objections. The greater progress of the EMU agenda was understandable, since discussions on monetary union had been underway ever since the April 1989 publication of the 'Delors Plan' for a single currency zone as the next logical step in economic integration. By contrast, political union had only been gradually and reluctantly accepted, although the notion that monetary union needed to be accompanied by institutional reform was supported and indeed pushed by the EP and by some member states. While the conclusions of the Italian Presidency were very clear and precise in terms of the EMU, the objectives of the forthcoming IGC on political union were still imprecise and blurred at that time. Since parallelism between the two IGCs was required, work on the conference on political union had to be accelerated.

Secondly, very soon a gap developed, both between the original objectives of the 1984 EP treaty and the intentions proclaimed in the April 1990

Franco–German resolution, and the final draft of the treaty adopted in December 1991. Both the Commission and the EP had aimed at communitarization of foreign policy, justice and home affairs and wide legislative powers to the EP. However, this proved unacceptable to a number of member states and had to be watered down. The maximalists wanted to see foreign and defence policy brought under the legal umbrella of the Treaty of Rome with qualified majority voting, while the minimalists wanted to keep co-operation in this area on an intergovernmental basis.

Starting from these different bases, the two IGCs adopted different methods of negotiations and advanced at different speeds. As a result of these difficulties, the intergovernmental conferences occupied a period of 12 months, from December 1990 to December 1991 and were not, as some member states had hoped, concluded at the summit of European Council in June 1991. The lack of cohesion between the two sets of reform debates is clearly reflected in the treaty finally adopted in December 1991.

Nevertheless, the first country to preside over the treaty negotiations, Luxembourg, submitted an initial draft treaty after barely three months of negotiations with a view to achieving political union by April 1992. The draft, known as a 'non-paper' because of its informal nature, was of unusual design. Instead of a single structure, the new union would have three pillars, the first one being the provisions of the EC, but with foreign and security policy (CFSP) as the second pillar and Justice and Home Affairs (JHA) as a third pillar. The second and third pillars would be kept outside the EC framework under separate treaty provisions. Hence, they would not be part of the EC legal system and would not be subject to legal review by the Court, while the Commission would enjoy a lesser role in initiating proposals and in implementing policies. The new political union would thus be founded on three pillars co-ordinated by the European Council. The Luxembourg presidency had hoped that such architectual structure would go some way in reconciling the two EC opinions: the federalists with Germany, France, Italy and the Netherlands on the one side, and Britain and Denmark on the other.

However, these hopes were not fulfilled. For the federalists the draft was not ambitious enough, while it went too far for Britain and Denmark. Moreover, the Commission and the EP, supported by the Netherlands and Belgium, found the structure of the draft with foreign and home affairs having a different legal framework, unacceptable. In fact, the Commission, in May, tabled an amendment to the Luxembourg draft, the most important of which was a replacement of the three-pillar structure by a unitary design. This gave rise to extensive criticism by some member states. The Luxembourg Presidency was uncertain whether a majority of member states would be supportive of the Commission amendment. Nevertheless, in trying to take acccount of the Commission position, it made minor amendments to its own draft and reassured the federalist camp that the pillar structure would only be a transition towards full communitarization of all activities including those of CFSP and JHA. This met with broad acceptance by the European Council which felt that the second draft could be a basis for further negotiations. The presidency then passed on to the Netherlands.

The second half of 1991 was overshadowed to a large extent by the events in former Yugoslavia and, as a result, negotiations made little progress. When the Dutch finally produced their own first draft treaty they had, to the surprise of everybody, abandoned the pillar structure in favour of a unitary model incorporating both CFSP and JHA as separate titles of an amended EC treaty. Clearly this was quite ambitious and would have meant that the last two titles would be subjected to EC law and not to intergovernmental agreements. While this was in line with what the EP had specifically requested, the Dutch draft further sharpened the conflicts among member states. A slightly watered down version was presented at a meeting of Foreign Ministers on 30 September, but was rejected almost unanimously, only Belgium accepted it. With time running out, leaving no more room for debating ambitious objectives, a second draft was presented by the Dutch on 8 November returning to the pillar structure as originally proposed by Luxembourg. This provided the basis for the text finally agreed at Maastricht.

The summit opened on 9 December in a highly charged atmosphere, as some contentious issues had yet to be agreed between the heads of governments and state. Predictably, the IGC on political union had not been successful in resolving all institutional and policy issues and therefore some matters had to be referred to the summit for final decisions. Nevertheless, against the background of large international rallies and demonstrations, the European Council, in the early hours of 11 December, was finally able to announce that all outstanding issues had been resolved.

The Maastricht Treaty on EU

Thus, the Dutch draft treaty, based on a three-pillar structure, was ultimately to characterize the Maastricht agreement itself: the first pillar is dealt with through amendments to the existing EC treaties, that is to say the EEC, the EURATOM and the ECSC treaties; the second pillar comprises foreign and security policy, based on intergovernmental co-operation, but with the Commission associated and the EP consulted; JHA constituted the third pillar, operating through co-operation, but with the institutions having no real power of decision-making in this areas.

The Treaty's intention to 'establish among themselves' (i.e. the member states) 'a European Union' may give the impression that a new legal entity, replacing the EC, has been created. However, this is not entirely true. Despite its ambitious label, the Treaty does not set up a 'union', but adds an intergovernmental 'pillar structure' to the EC. At best, the Treaty has created an intergovernmental organization, legally separate from that of the EC, but sharing the same institutions.

The Treaty is introduced by its 'common provisions' (Title 1), spelling out its objectives and principles: 'By this Treaty the High Contracting Parties establish among themselves a European Union, hereinafter called the Union. This Treaty marks a new stage in the process creating an ever closer union among the peoples of Europe where decisions are taken as closely as possible to the citizens.' The German demand for reference to 'federalism' or to the federal goal of the EC did not find acceptance. The Schuman Delaration of 1950 had already spoken of the ultimate federal objective of European integration and the EC system contains a number of federal characteristics such as its legal system, based on the supremacy of EC law, its independent executive branch, the Commission, its elected Parliament and majority voting in Council in some areas. However, the specific reference to the 'federal goal' of the EC was continually contested by the UK which maintained that it would not sign a treaty containing such a reference. Most other member states wished to keep it in, but in the end it was removed at the Maastricht summit meeting itself, in an attempt to satisfy British demands. Instead, the Treaty now mentioned 'a new stage in the process of creating an ever closer union' which picked up the original wording of the Treaty of Rome. Although an ever closer union could, in theory at least, imply a more centralized union than a federal one, this text finally satisfied the UK. In fact, the phrase 'an ever closer union' is open to a more expansive interpretation than arguably a definition of a federal future might have implied since the former conceived the Union not in a static manner, but as a process.

The Treaty also introduces and defines the new concept of subsidiarity, characteristic of all federal systems such as the FRG, where powers and responsibilities are clearly divided between different levels of governments and administration. The new Art. 3b defines subsidiarity: 'The Community shall act within the limits of the powers conferred to it by this Treaty and of the objectives assigned to it therein.' It is explained that, in areas which do not fall within its exclusive competence, the EC will act 'only if and so far as the objectives of the proposed action cannot be sufficiently achieved by the Member States' and can be better achieved by the EC. 'Any action by the Community shall not go beyond what is necessary to achieve the objectives of the Treaty.' Commission President Delors, in his address to the EP following the summit, called for rigorous discipline to ensure that subsidiarity was respected by all EC institutions at a time when criticism of bureaucratic interference in domestic affairs of member states was increasing. The subsidiarity principle is in some ways reinforced by Art. F which states that the 'Union shall respect the national identities of the member states'.

Art. 8 of the EC treaty (Title 2 of the Maastricht Treaty) introduces the concept of citizenship, not of the EC, but of the Union. This means that every citizen holding the nationality of a member state shall be a citizen of the Union and as such is free to move and reside in any territory of the Union, with the rights to vote and stand as a candidate in local elections and to petition the EP or apply to the Ombudsman, appointed by Parliament. This reinforces the rights already contained in the EC treaties.

The Treaty continues with the definition of the first pillar amending the original treaties in such a way to allow for new policy areas to be included. In the economic area, the competences of the EC in agriculture, transport, competition and external relations are now extended. The rules of the SEA concerning economic and social cohesion, research and development and environmental policy are reinforced, while new policy areas – development co-operation, public health, consumer protection and trans-european network – have been added. Some of these policy areas were under discussion when the SEA was negotiated and have been given a stronger emphasis in Maastricht, while others have been introduced. Some of these, for example, culture, development co-operation and consumer protection had already been discussed during the SEA negotiations, but were dropped from the agenda because this proved to be too ambitious at that stage.

A special Cohesion Fund was to be set up by the end of 1993 to help member states whose per capita GDP is less than 90 per cent of EC average to finance through measures aimed at reducing the gap between the prosperity of different regions. This would involve financing projects in the fields of the environment and of transport infrastructure. The concept of cohesion had already been included in the SEA and was then translated into practise in the Delors package of 1988. At the Maastricht European Council meeting, Spain, supported by Greece, Portugal and Ireland, argued for a strengthening of the financial solidarity in the EC by securing a commitment for a 'transfer' of wealth from richer to poorer countries.

In addition, a new institution has been set up, the Committee of the Regions (COR) consisting of representatives of regional and local authorities. This will be consulted by the Council or the Commission and may submit its own opinion on a matter where it believes that specific regional interests are involved. The committee will consist of 189 members ranging from 24 each for the large member states to six for Luxembourg. Further important areas include trans-european networks, education and vocational training, and the environment.

As a result of British opposition, there was no change to existing social policy as laid down by the Treaty of Rome as modified by the SEA. However, 11 of the member states concluded an agreement for implementation of the 1989 Social Charter and attached a special protocol to this end to the Treaty. This agreement is not an integral part of the Union treaty and exempts the UK from any rules applied under the Social Chapter. This situation has no precedent in the history of the EC. It is in fact the first time that the unity of EC law has been breached, although special protocols have of course been added to previous treaties.

The institutional reform contained in the Treaty continued the process which had started with the SEA. Parliament has obtained co-decision rights with the Council in 15 areas which, apart from the Single Market, include new fields such as education, health and trans-european networks. The new legislative procedure, which builds on the co-operation procedure, provides for the convening of a Conciliation Committee and for a third reading of legislation by the Council and the EP. Significantly, the new co-decision procedure reserves Parliament's right to veto – for the first time – legislative proposals. The co-operation procedure introduced in the SEA has been increased and will apply to ten areas, ranging from social security for workers to development co-operation.

The Treaty also extends the areas in which Parliament is required to give its assent. These now extend beyond the budget to the admission of new members and association and international agreements, questions of European citizenship and the structural funds. The Treaty also provides for more effective control by Parliament over the Commission. The EP was successful in achieving the synchronization, in both duration and timing, of the Commission's mandate with parliamentary legislature. The EP is to be consulted with regard to the appointment of the President of the Commission and to give a vote of confidence on the Commissioners as a whole when they are appointed. While the democratic deficit has been visibly reduced, the EP has only made modest gains, since its aspiration to initiate legislation has not been wholly fulfilled.

The most remarkable changes are the inclusion in the Treaty or rather the amendment of existing Treaty provisions which allow for full economic and monetary union to take place in three stages leading to an ECB and the introduction of a single currency. As already noted, concrete plans for monetary union go back to 1988, when it was decided to establish a committee with the objective of studying concrete steps towards EMU. The project, for the first time, has now been solidified within a Treaty base. This section contains much of the solid legal structure of the Treaty of Rome, such as the precision of its timetable and the irrevocable character of the plan. Stage one could be achieved under existing Treaty regulations. Stages 2 and 3, however, required changes in the treaties because they involved setting up new institutions. Stage 2 began on 1 January 1994 with the setting up of a special European Monetary Institute (EMI) charged with co-ordinating member states' monetary policies. At this stage the currencies will be locked and realignment will only be permitted in exceptional circumstances. In 1996 the European Council will decide whether a majority of member states have attained a set of 'convergence' criteria to enable them to proceed to Stage 3 of EMU, namely to adopt a single currency and set up a single European bank. If, at that stage, no majority can be found, monetary union will take place regardless and automatically on 1 January 1999 for those countries who have reached a level of convergence.

The second pillar of the new treaty concerns CFSP. The provisions of Maastricht go appreciably beyond those of the SEA, since the former specifies that member states 'shall define and implement a common foreign and security policy'. Its main objectives, such as: (i) to safeguard common values, fundamental interests and the independence of the Union; (ii) to strengthen its security and that of its members; (iii) to preserve peace and strengthen international security; and (iv) to develop and consolidate democracy and the rule of law, are to be pursued through 'systematic co-operation' between member states. Although the institutional capacity in this area is also somewhat strengthened, since the Commission 'shall be fully associated with the work carried out in the common foreign and security field', CFSP operates outside the supranational structures of the EC. The policy shall be defined by the European Council and implemented through the Council of Ministers thus underlining its intergovernmental character.

The third and last pillar, co-operation in JHA includes asylum, immigration, police and judicial collaboration in civil and criminal matters. These were already subject to political co-operation, but have now been given a treaty base, mainly as a result of pressure from Germany which has been absorbing a flood of migrants, particularly since unification. Like the CFSP, this policy area is based on common positions and joint actions outside the EC framework, although operating through its institutional framework. A common visa policy will be decided by the Council, based on unanimity until 1996 and thereafter by qualified majority. This area, however, will remain an intergovernmental pillar of the Union Treaty, as it will be eliminated from the decision-making competence of the EC.

The 'Final provisions' provide a procedure for the Treaty's ratification which laid down that the Treaty would only come into effect after being ratified by member states in accordance with their respective constitutional requirements. It also included provisions for a revision of the Treaty during a conference of member states in 1996 and describes the process for any other European state which might want to join the EU in the future.

What verdict can be passed on the new Treaty? Maastricht, like the SEA, is clearly a compromise. The walling off of CFSP and HJA is seen as a drawback by federalists because these policy areas remain outside the communitarian structures. On the other hand, the Treaty goes further than any previous EC agreements, extends EC action into areas not previously covered by the EC treaties, builds on the policies and processes which were set in train by the SEA and the creation of the single market. The power of the EP has been extended, while the Commission, although more answerable to Parliament, has become more independent from national governments. Yet the newly created EU is still far from being a federal state. Its budget is minimal – barely 1 per cent of GDP – its bureaucracy smaller than that of most local authorities and a majority of decisions is still in the hands of national decision-makers. At best, Maastricht is a compromise between federalists and intergovernmentalists. Nevertheless, in sheer volume, if nothing else, the Treaty is substantial, extending or amending 150 articles of the original treaties and adding 35 new ones.

Maastricht: the rocky road to ratification

The signing of the Treaty on 7 February 1992 put an end to the period of uncertainty in the EC, but ratification was hampered by many problems in a number of countries. The Treaty on EU could only come into force once ratified by all member states. The target date for ratification was 1 January 1993 – coinciding with the completion of the Single Market programme. The national provisions for ratifications in the 12 member states are, however, quite different. In some cases a simple majority of the respective parliament suffices, in other states a more complicated procedure is necessary. Furthermore, both in Denmark and Ireland a referendum was necessary before further transfer of hitherto sovereign rights to the Brussels institutions could be achieved.

Until the Danish referendum of June 1992 there had been little opposition to the Treaty. Indeed, criticism such as existed emanated mainly from the federal camp: from the EP, which threatened to reject the Treaty because of its pillar structure, and from the Benelux countries, Germany, Spain and Italy – all complaining of the lack of a distinct federal objective in the Treaty. However, when on 2 June 1992 the Danish electorate, albeit by a very narrow margin of 50.7 per cent to 49.3 per cent, voted against the Treaty, the EC was taken by surprise. This was also evident in the fact that in line with previous practice, no provision had been made for non-ratification by one member state. As a result, there was no established strategy to deal with the Danish situation.

The Danish referendum ushered in a period of great uncertainty. In Britain, negotiations of the Maastricht bill, which had already passed its second reading in Parliament, was – in the light of the Danish vote – postponed. In France, President Mitterrand, confident of public support for the Treaty, announced a referendum, although there was no constitutional obligation to do so. He wanted to use the Maastricht Treaty to cause further conflicts among the conservative opposition, which was already divided on the issue of further integration. Ireland was, apart from Denmark, another member state constitutionally obliged to ratify the Treaty by referendum.

Despite the outcome of the Danish referendum, the ratification process continued unabated and, with few exceptions, proceeded smoothly in most countries. It seemed clear that, although the Danish case had sent shockwaves right across the EC, member states – with the exception of the UK – were willing to press ahead with the new Treaty, if necessary without Denmark, although no blueprint for such a possibility had been (officially) worked out.

Nevertheless, the second refendum, on 18 June 1992, that of the Republic of Ireland, was expected with widespread pessimism because it came two weeks after the Danish result. Perhaps more importantly, ratification became mixed up with Ireland's constitutional ban on abortion. This followed an Irish court ruling preventing a 14-year-old rape victim from seeking an abortion in the UK. But the Irish government warned the electorate of impending economic disaster should there be a 'No' vote. While there was no overwhelming enthusiasm for the Treaty, in the end it was impossible for Ireland to ignore the substantial financial benefits EC membership entails and the Treaty was ratified with a majority of 68.7 per cent.

However, the greatest test for the Treaty was the referendum in France set for 20 September. The outcome was unexpected and the timing of the referendum was unfortunate. The French President's popularity was waning as the economy slumped and unemployment rose. The inability of the EC to act decisively over Bosnia and the currency crisis in mid-September which resulted in both the Italian Lira and the British Sterling leaving the ERM strengthened anti-Maastricht groups of both the extreme right and left. The French people – according to opinion polls – did not vote on the merit of the Treaty, but ratification was being threatened by national issues such as opposition to the recent CAP reform. The German Bundesbank's tough policy on interest rates to counter inflationary pressure as a result of unification created resentment against Germany and further fuelled hostility against what appeared to be a German-dominated EMU – the centrepiece of the Treaty. Despite an impressive campaign which even included a televised address by Chancellor Kohl on French television to bolster support for Maastricht, the French people with 51.05 per cent against 48.95 per cent narrowly voted in favour of the Treaty.

A further serious threat to ratification of the Treaty was the controversy and internal division in the British Conservative Party over key policies. When the Danish referendum result became known, the government, as already noted, decided to postpone the Committee stage of the Maastricht bill. As a result of the Danish referendum and the marginal 'Yes' vote of France, the anti-Europeans in the UK grew stronger. On 17 September, the Pound Sterling and the Italian Lira had to leave the ERM of the EMS, because they could no longer keep within the agreed exchange band. This ushered in a period of great instability for the EMS with several countries (Spain, Portugal and later Ireland) having to devalue their currencies. A further cause of conflict was the opposition of the Labour Party to the opt-out clause granted to Britain from the Treaty's Social Chapter. On 4 November 1992 the House of Commons voted by a small majority of only 3 votes to back the government's commitment to the Maastricht treaty and to continue the ratification process. With Liberal Democrats giving crucial support to the government, the MPs rejected by 319 to 313 an amendment tabled by John Smith, the then Labour leader, calling for a halt to ratification until after that month's Edinburgh European Council summit meeting. In the event, the

British government stated that no final decision would indeed be taken until the Danish problem had been resolved.

The rejection of the Maastricht treaty in the Danish referendum meant that a solution to this crisis had yet to be found. Britain, which held the presidency in the second half of 1992 was responsible for taking the lead in resolving the Danish problem. After extensive consultations with member states, Britain proposed that Denmark should be reassured that it would be allowed to remain outside key areas of the Treaty such as monetary union and defence, Union citizenship and police co-operation. The plan, at the insistence of all member states, avoided tampering with the text of the Treaty. This enabled the Danish government to schedule a second referendum to put the amended Treaty before its people.

The provision that the special regime for the Danes should apply exclusively to Denmark and not to existing or acceeding member states was critical. This meant that accession negotiations with Denmark's Scandinavian neighbours would require them to accept not only existing EC law but the full Maastricht Treaty. The UK proposal also required Denmark to give up its right to block its partners' advance towards integration. Not only could Denmark 'opt out' from monetary union, defence, police co-ordination and the concept of Union citizenship, but 'Denmark will not, in any way, prevent other governments from proceeding with the realization of Economic and Monetary Union in conformity with the provisions of the Treaty of European Union'.

On 18 May 1993, the Danish people in a second referendum voted with nearly 57 per cent majority for the amended treaty. This meant that negotiations could go ahead on EC membership by 1995 with Sweden, Norway, Finland and Austria. Two days later, on 20 May 1993, the Treaty passed its third reading in the House of Commons in Britain by 292 to 112. It was then placed to the House of Lords for approval. Despite an abortive attempt by Lord Rees-Mogg to launch a legal challenge to ratification, the Treaty was ratified on 3 August 1993.

Further complications arose in Germany. Although both the Bundesrat (unanimously) and the Bundestag with an overwhelming vote of 543 to 17, had approved the Treaty, ratification was subsequently challenged in the German Constitutional Court by some Green MEPs and Manfred Brunner, the former Chef de Cabinet of Commission Vice President Bangemann, who argued that the Treaty was incompatible with the principles of Germany's Basic Law. However, the Constitutional Court rejected the challenge in October 1993 ruling that no such infringement was involved, although it laid down certain conditions to be met in the event of further advances in the integration process. The last hurdle was therefore cleared and the Treaty became law on 1 November 1993 – 10 months later than orginally planned.

An ongoing debate

The Treaty on EU was preceded by cumbersome, at times acrimonious, negotiations and is the result of complicated compromises. The crisis caused by Denmark's referendum could eventually be overcome by determined efforts on behalf of member states to go ahead with ratification and find a solution to the Danish problem.

To assess the Treaty one has to bear in mind that Maastricht on its own cannot stand, and it cannot be judged on its own. It has to be seen in the light of the development and experiences of the EC of the past 35 years. It has to be set in context of the objectives of the Treaty of Rome. Maastricht fills a gap in the Treaty of Rome, partly because the Treaty could not cover all policy areas, partly because the task of setting up the EC, which is a unique venture to date, was so demanding and left no room for all the tangible and intangible possibilities and opportunities which might arise in the future. The Treaty of Rome setting up the EC is a daring document, but it is not comprehensive and sometimes understandably had to be deliberately vague.

While the Treaty of Maastricht has gone some way to fill the gaps in the Treaty of Rome, it does not sum up the present state of European integration, because the Union is still developing. This process of evolution will gradually crystallize, taking account of all kind of influences, both from internal actors and external pressures such as the changes in the international climate. It is hard to resist the argument that Maastricht is an important step on the road to a federal Europe. Already the Schuman Declaration of 1950 referred to the ultimate federal objective of European integration and subsequently the Treaty of Rome laid the foundation of a federal system such as the setting up of independent institutions and established the supremacy of law. The Maastricht Treaty added further distinct elements such as a common banking system and the co-decision procedure involving the EP to the ambit of the Union.

Further enlargement to include countries from both the southern flank of the EU and from central and eastern Europe will pose new challenges and potential conflicts, stretching the economic and institutional capabilities of the new EU. Austria, Finland and Sweden have become members of the EU on 1 January 1995, while, as Map 3 shows, Norway has – for the second time – rejected membership. A new round of difficult negotiations will take place in 1996. The development of the EU so far has been characterized by alternate periods of progress and stagnation. At this stage, we seem to be in a period of 'mild' stagnation. Whether the IGC planned for 1996 will initiate a third 'relaunch' remains to be seen.

Further reading

Archer, C. and Butler, F. (1992), *The European Community*, London: Pinter.

EC (1992), *Treaty on European Union, Together with the Complete Text of the Treaty Establishing the European Community*, OJC 224.

Gros, D. and Thygesen, N. (1992), *European Monetary Integration*, London: Longman.

Laffan, B. (1992), *Integration and Cooperation in The European Community*, London: Routledge.

Luff, P. (1992), *The Simple Guide to Maastricht*, London: European Movement.

Michalski, A. and Wallace, H. (1992), *The European Community: The Challenge of Enlargement*, London: RIIA.

Rummel, R. (ed.) (1992), *Toward Political Union*, Boulder, Col.: Westview.

Swann, D. (ed.) (1992), *The Single European Market and Beyond*, London: Routledge.

Wise, M. and Gibb, R. (1993), *Single Market to Social Europe*, London: Longman.

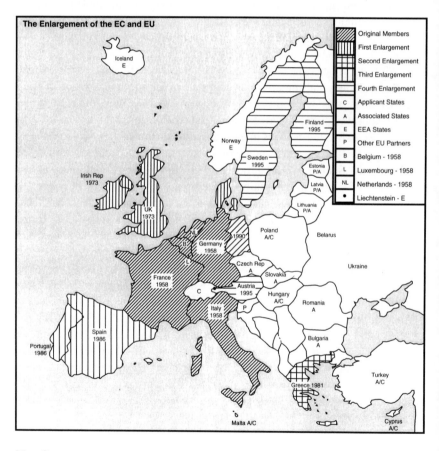

Map 3

12   Political and social problems in
       Western Europe

If Western Europe stood at a watershed at the end of the 1980s, this was not always apparent. Economic and political problems had, to some extent, been obscured by the successful recovery from the 1987 crash, the collapse of the Soviet Empire and the drive to further European integration. However, the problems were to be felt all too painfully in the early 1990s. Three factors in particular contributed to this: (a) the return of economic recession, with all its attendant social difficulties; (b) the increasing influence of European developments on domestic economic and political affairs, making Europe itself an issue; and (c) the interaction of these trends with a growing and corrosive political malaise. As a result the period had much in common with the 1970s. It also disproved assumptions that the fall of Communism would mean an easy ride for liberal democracy.

Yet, if the early 1990s have proved to be a difficult time for most Western European states, they have yet to produce a clear shift in the political balance. What has happened is that very different parties and states have been buffeted by the new problems, including the way in which continuing public scepticism about politics, both European and domestic, has encouraged new political forces and a revived awareness of national identity. So, while many states in the West seem to be suffering from a political crisis, this can take different forms. Furthermore, while some of the policy preferences of the 1980s have been called into question as they approach their sell-by-date, there has been no new clear policy innovation in the West. In other words, so far the 1990s have been dominated by problems to which there are few clear policy answers.

This Chapter therefore looks first at the three related challenges facing Western European states: the socio-economic challenge; the European challenge; and, lastly, the challenge of domestic political malaise. It then goes on to examine their impacts, beginning with that on the political balance, where new forces, mainly of the right, are emerging. Finally, it considers the uncertain evolution of public policy. No very clear patterns seem to emerge in either, suggesting that the West of Europe is in an uneasy period of transition.

The return of depression
The first, and probably the primary cause of the new difficulties experienced in Western Europe has been the renewed and deep economic depression. Growth

had slowed down slightly in the late 1980s but, at first, the downturn seemed both minor and limited. So in 1989 hopes were still for a 'soft landing' of lessened growth without a rise in inflation as Europe exploited the opportunities offered by the Single Market and the rebuilding of eastern Germany. The latter had, after all, begun to offer new export opportunities to other European countries. However, it was not to be. Storm clouds began to gather, notably in Britain, in early 1990. The cold economic winds then began to blow more widely. Even Germany was hit in the second half of 1991 while some countries suffered a real slump. Finland thus found itself facing its worst crisis since the 1930s. Conditions deteriorated further in 1992–93 with a veritable tempest on the exchange markets. Growth in 1993 was largely negative, a worse situation than in the early 1980s, suggesting that there was a depression and not just a recession. Estimates of the nearness and scale of any recovery were therefore continually revised downwards. Although recovery was claimed in the UK during 1993–94, when growth rose by 1.8 per cent compared with the 0.7 per cent fall in 1992, this was limited and neither reversed the trend nor made people confident things were better. On the continent some countries were also beginning to emerge from recession, but generally the downswing was still in evidence. Average growth in Europe during 1994 was not expected to be much more than 1 per cent and unemployment is set to go on rising, reflecting sluggish domestic demand. So the depression is unlikely to end immediately, which suggests that Europe will continue to fall behind other regions of the world.

The causes of this new depression were, at least, fivefold. Firstly, there was the inheritance of the 1980s. Overheating then pushed up wage levels and cut productivity. It also produced a normal cyclical downturn, especially in property where values had soared after the post-1987 relaxation of controls on the money supply. Thereafter, with economic activity and inflation slackening, prices began to fall. Unfortunately many firms and individuals had borrowed when prices were high and found themselves with massive debts which were very hard to pay off in the new climate. Debt meant that firms and individuals sought to pay off their liabilities rather than to invest or consume. This often meant cutting staff and other outgoings or trying to sell property at a time when demand was low. Thus, interest rate cuts did not succeed in preventing contraction let alone in stimulating growth.

Secondly, external factors were at work. Thus, the loss of Communist markets hit some countries badly, while others found that the price of preparing for the Single Market was painful restructuring and lower profit margins. The Gulf crisis and the brief hike in oil prices which followed were also unsettling for Europe. More significantly, Europe suffered because the crisis was almost worldwide. Certainly it affected North America and even Japan, which previously had been immune to such problems. This meant not merely that exports and investment opportunities dried up, but that competition in home markets got ever tougher.

Hence, no single economy was able to play a motor role and give a real stimulus to others. This was a third, acute, cause of recession in Europe because Germany had for long been the dynamo of the wider economy. So, when the twin costs of rebuilding the restored *Länder* in the East and extending West German wage and welfare levels there began to be felt, the rest of Europe, for which Germany was the largest market, was deeply affected. To begin with, hopes of exports evaporated as the German recession began. Thus, for example, even after devaluation in 1992, British exporters were unable to increase market share greatly because the Germans were ordering less.

Later on, unification began to affect the rest of Europe. Because the costs were higher than expected, and because West Germans resisted tax increases, inflation and government deficits both began to rise. This forced the Bundesbank to keep interest rates high in order to defend the DM and curb inflationary pressures. Hence, other countries were also forced to keep their rates high in order to maintain their ERM parities. All this had a detrimental effect on economic activity.

The fourth cause, which was closely related to German unification, was the new instability of currency markets. The abolition in the late 1980s of restraints on European capital exposed the continent to global economic interdependence. Thanks to new technology vast amounts of money now move through the financial markets of the world every day, swirling about to avoid weaker currencies. Such movements are now too large for individual states, with limited reserves, to control.

Such capital movements also proved too much for the ERM. In the 1980s this worked flexibly as a means of moderating exchange rate changes. However, once it became a stage in the monetary unification of Europe it lost its flexibility and realignments became more difficult. Those states which were tied indirectly to the DM, soon found that, to defend their parities, they had to raise interest rates, not cut them as they would otherwise have wished in order to counteract the depression. Such tactics did not always work, for example in the case of Scandinavian currencies, which had to be devalued in 1991.

The problem soon affected ERM currencies themselves. Thus, in 1992, when British economic decline meant that the Pound Sterling was overvalued because of the higher than normal interest rates required to maintain its parities in the ERM, the currency markets turned on Sterling in an attempt to anticipate the expected devaluation. Despite raising interest rates to ridiculous levels, like the Swedes before them, the British failed to stabilize the value of Sterling and were forced to withdraw it from the ERM. Italy did the same so that the Lira, like Sterling, lost an average of 13 per cent of its value after Black Wednesday. The Iberians, and later the Irish, also had to devalue though they remained within the ERM.

Finally, in 1993, the attention of the money markets turned to the French Franc as the French economy began to run into difficulties. In so doing they almost blew the ERM apart in the late summer of 1993. Although currency instability continued for a while after the new, looser bands were introduced into the ERM, most exchange rates were thereafter to settle down in 1994. With the exception of the Sterling rate against the DM many of the pre-crisis parities were restored. However, with the Dollar coming under pressure, the currency turmoil did not vanish altogether. All this change and uncertainty obviously did nothing for economic stability and growth, causing very real problems for investment confidence, not to mention for already hard pressed government finances.

Some authorities would also suggest that the fifth cause of depression is Europe's declining competitiveness. With an increasingly global economy western manufactures have become exposed to competition from low wage, little welfare NICs. Not merely are their costs lower but their use of modern technology and their careful monitoring of western markets means that their quality and service is now reaching European levels. This has further eroded European manufacturing, causing further social and economic problems. Even countries like Germany and Switzerland have seen their competitiveness decline in recent years, allegedly because of their high wage costs, expensive welfare provision and over-regulation. For some, such social interference with market forces is the root of much of the depression.

Whatever the causes, there is no doubt that, in the early 1990s, Europe was indeed again gripped by depression. This showed itself in a variety of ways. Average real growth rates which, as seen in Chapter 6, had been running at about 3.5 per cent per annum in the late 1980s, fell to a mere 0.4 per cent by 1991. By 1993 growth rates were negative for the first time in years, at least in some countries. The German economy actually contracted by 2 per cent in 1993 while Britain experienced a longer period of decline in output than it had in the 1930s.

This reflected the way in which industrial production first stagnated and then, in early 1992, began to decline sharply. Only Ireland managed to buck the trend. Profits also fell and retail trade, outside Germany and the Netherlands, stagnated. Service sectors such as banking and finance were also badly hit. With world trade remaining flat, European external trade, particularly exports, suffered, thus worsening trade balances. As a result bankruptcies multiplied and employment contracted as firms closed or restructured. Restructuring, which was a common response to the crisis, involved cost cutting, reorganization, curbing wages and especially shedding surplus labour. Average unemployment levels, therefore, which had been about 6 per cent in the late 1980s, reached a plateau in 1990 before again rising to over 10.5 per cent in mid-1993. The trend in 1994 was still upward with women and the young suffering particularly badly.

Unemployment, as well as resuming its inexorable rise after the brief intermission of the late 1980s, was also increasingly structural, not cyclical. Even a country like Switzerland, where unemployment had been virtually unknown, has suffered. Thus, the Swiss have seen their unemployment rise from 0.6 per cent in 1989–90 (involving 18 000 people or only 750 more than the number of jobs available) to 5.6 per cent – over 180 000 – at the end of 1993. Numbers were likely to go on rising into 1995, especially where long-term unemployment is concerned. At the same time wage levels ceased to rise and often fell.

However, in line with classic recessions and unlike the 1970s, inflation did not go up greatly. This was in large part due to low-cost competition from abroad. After a modest rise in 1989–90, which encouraged wages to rise, the average EC inflation rate fell continuously from a peak of 9.4 per cent to 3.8 per cent in 1994. Unfortunately, it has shown little sign of moving much below this new plateau and indeed, by 1994, there were again fears of rising inflation. What was new in the 1990s was the combination of low inflation with high debts from the past. This was a problem for both public and private finances.

Share prices and, especially, property prices were particularly affected by this trend, the latter falling significantly. Moreover, if nominal interest rates ceased to rise and then began to ease downward, real rates still remained uncomfortably high. This not only exacerbated the problem of accumulated debt but also, as already noted, affected exchange rates unhelpfully. So it was not surprising that falling interest rates did much less to restore confidence and get economic activity moving again than had been hoped.

Social problems

The sudden downturn in economic fortunes also had an immediate social effect, exacerbating underlying problems. These had never really been resolved because, although the boom of the 1980s brought overall growth, not everyone benefited equally from it. So social inequalities were not redressed, exposing them to the effects of returning depression. Hence, some authorities began to talk of a social crisis. Certainly social services have again come under increasing pressure as demands rise, because of growing unemployment and deprivation, and financial resources contract. Equally, social conflicts have intensified because of the depression.

Social services have come under pressure from both an ageing population and the increased demands made on them by the depression. These are, first of all, the product of rising unemployment which has meant a further drain on the public purse. When countries like Switzerland and Sweden, which had largely escaped unemployment in the past, find themselves with large numbers of jobless, their social insurance systems cannot cope. Unemployment also has a major psychological and social impact, especially on the young. The latter are now suffering disproportionately, not only from unemployment but also from housing problems.

In any case, unemployment insurance does not cover all the costs of those who are out of work. This is one cause of the rising levels of poverty in western Europe. The percentages enjoying less than 50 per cent of average European income range between 6 per cent in Belgium and 33 per cent in Portugal. Such inequalities require more in the way of income support and social transfers. Poverty has direct impacts on educational achievement, health and social mobility. It also reinforces destructive tendencies already at work inside families, including drug addiction and crime.

Such problems have always existed. What is new is the way in which homelessness is becoming a major problem because of the conjunction of the high levels of debt, consequent on the extravagant property prices of the 1980s, with falling inflation and incomes. Many people have thus found that they cannot finance their own housing, especially as falling property prices make it difficult to sell. Equally, many people on low, or no, incomes find they still cannot afford housing in the first place. As well as causing immense personal misery and insecurity this also increases demands on the public purses of Europe.

The latter are also facing rising health care costs as the population ages and medical techniques and services become more expensive. Medical insurance costs have risen more rapidly than general costs and this at a time when states are trying to reduce their outgoings. Generally, states have to try and deal with these escalating problems and demands at a time when not only tax revenues are falling because of the depression, but there are political pressures, including from the EU, to curb public spending. This is because high state expenditure requires higher taxes and interest rates even though reversing the depression seems to require reducing them both.

Attempts to cut back on social services have added to the renewed social conflicts caused by unemployment, poverty and homelessness. A good example of this was the riot in Norrebro, a working class suburb of Copenhagen, at the time of the second Maastricht referendum in 1993. The depression has also led to increasing strike activity not just in countries like France and Spain but even in Finland, Germany and Switzerland as people reacted to threats to jobs, subsidies and wages. Relations between unions and governments generally have often deteriorated sharply as a result. In Spain the fact that government is in the hands of a socialist party has not prevented bitter conflicts. Farmers and others have also resorted to militant action to resist changes in their conditions, in France and elsewhere. This in part reflects the way regional disparities and rivalries have intensified in the depression.

There is also fear of what is known as social dumping, as countries cut their levels of protection in order to attract investment. Equally workers from countries with limited welfare systems can take advantage of the post-1992 opportunities for labour mobility to move to more prosperous and progressive northern countries to take advantage of their social protection. Such fears have had a political impact at the European level. So, all in all, changes in the social setting have added to the economic problems facing politicians in the 1990s. At the same time politicians have also been subjected to new political constraints.

The Europeanization of domestic politics
One of these constraints has been the fact that European states have become increasingly tied into wider international networks. This growing interdependence constitutes the second problem of the 1990s. It has reduced states' freedom of action to the point that some authorities see them as only 'semi-sovereign'. Alongside the global and economic networks already mentioned, there are also political and European links. Indeed, the growing importance of the EC and EU in the domestic politics of European countries, especially of member states, has encouraged talk of the 'Europeanization' of domestic politics. Unfortunately, the way in which interdependence comes into conflict with new political divergences has made western politics much more uncertain.

European issues are, one way or another, increasingly intertwined with domestic politics. This is partly because so many countries are now affected by the actions of the EU. Many of them, even when not members, are also directly involved with the EC's institutions, market and programmes. Even more so are they affected because virtually all domestic policies now have a European dimension. This is especially so after the Maastricht Treaty. The latter meant that the EC was becoming involved, as Chapter 11 shows, not only in more policy areas as such, but with things which were much more directly visible. The EC was brought by Maastricht into increasingly sensitive areas such as citizenship and education. So policy-making can only be done in a European framework, and the desires of domestic lobbies can often be thwarted by EU rules. Even when this does not happen governments are also good at blaming 'Brussels' for unpopular decisions they feel they have to take.

Equally, the way so many things have to be resolved at the European level has implications for the structure and behaviour of governments, parties and other political actors in the member states. Countries like France and Spain have had to change their constitutions to come into line with the requirements of Maastricht. Their parties and parliaments have also had to accept a new European logic in which European law can override their own decisions. So they too need to influence decision-making within the EU. At the same time, the availability of grants and influence at EU level has changed the balance between regional and central authorities inside states, to the detriment of the latter.

Such changes have made the EC much more salient domestically, often raising strongly held fears about the threat its development poses to national identity and sovereignty. The Maastricht ratification process may have meant that ordinary people came to appreciate for the first time exactly what European integration meant. They did not always like it, particularly when the need for

Europe-wide agreement led outsiders to criticize their national political particularities and ways of doing things. Thus, the Danes reacted strongly to criticism of the way their democratic process endangered ratification. Equally there were outside complaints about British parliamentary procedures, German constitutional constraints on military and financial policy, and about the Swiss use of referenda. Such external criticism encourages internal hostility to Europe since outside 'interference' is increasingly resented.

At the same time, developments at the European level can also limit the power of national institutions in two other ways. On the one hand it can mean the transfer of powers to Brussels. The new policy scope of the EC therefore encourages support for subsidiarity as a means of defending apparently threatened national autonomy. On the other, it can mean strengthening the control of one national body over others. In particular parliaments have seen governments monopolize European affairs. Hence, in 1994, the Balladur government in France had to promise to make its policies wait on the advice of the relevant parliamentary committee. All this means that Europe as such has become a destabilizing domestic issue not just inside the EU but also in countries like Norway where the entry issue is bitterly divisive.

There is also a security dimension to this Europeanization. Yugoslavia has made it all too clear that Europe shares in the traditional ethnic hatreds which Communism has so obviously failed to tame. Yet, while there is increasing need for new European security arrangements because of this, as discussed in Chapter 14, some people reject the idea of these being provided by the EU rather than by nation states or NATO. Conversely, many others feel that security can now only come from the EU. Both camps agree that, despite much rhetoric and the creation of a common foreign and security policy in the Maastricht Treaty, the EU has yet to provide meaningful security although they draw different conclusions from the fact. The failure of EC intervention and the role played by individual states in this has thus focused attention on the European dimension. All this has created new problems for Europe and made European integration even more central to Western European politics, placing governments and decision makers under further stress.

The new political malaise

Coping with economic and social problems in this new dimension would be difficult in any circumstances. Unfortunately, states have not been able to rely on the kind of popular support they have previously enjoyed. This is the third challenge to western states. It comes from new domestic political attitudes, themselves a reaction to what is happening in the outside world. External changes have done less to encourage new policies than they have to create a mood of suspicion and volatility amongst the publics of Western Europe.

Instead of political culture being re-inforced and opened up by the events of 1989 attitudes have become more inward-looking and reserved.

This new moroseness, or *Politikverdrossenheit* as the Germans call it, was already visible in the 1980s. It was enhanced by the increasingly bleak economic situation of the early 1990s. Electorates have been led to expect much from governments. The latter have not been able to deliver, partly because of the depression and partly because of the new limitations on their powers. European voters have been quick to disown governments when they fail to deliver on their promises and do not maintain expected levels of governance.

However, there is more to it than this. There seems to be not just a disaffection with government, but an increasing gap between politicians and citizens. Political parties are increasingly seen as offering only discredited answers and, especially, as putting their own interests ahead of those of the general public. They are accused of arrogance and insincerity in changing their tune simply to hold on to power. This, like the growing Europeanization of domestic politics, has encouraged the claim that politicians are not defending the national interest.

Thus, not merely is there increasing pressure to re-nationalize political decision-making but national identity has become a key theme in politics, as it did during the Maastricht debate. The growth of militant regionalist politics has also encouraged this tendency. Virtually all countries in Western Europe have been affected by this revival of national awareness. The most notable example of this has been in Greece. There the recognition of Macedonia as an independent state using symbols and statements which the Greeks feel threaten them, has triggered a wave of chauvinist nationalism. This is underlined by unease about the Thracian Muslims who are now politically organized. Such feelings led some nationalists to secede from New Democracy to form a new anti-Macedonia party, Political Spring.

Moreover, opposition to the diminution of the nation state, which many feel inherent in the 1992 EU Treaty, has not only been very visible in Britain and Denmark, where new political parties have likewise emerged to resist Maastricht. It has also become evident in France and Germany. In France the issue has caused splits in the two main political families and cost them seats in the EP. In the latter, the phenomenon showed itself both in the bitter opposition to the possible disappearance of the DM, which has become a symbol of German stability, and in concerns about threats to the rights of the *Länder*, especially in Bavaria. Fear about institutional identity was also a major element in the Swiss decision to vote against joining the European Economic Area in December 1992.

Parties are also vehemently attacked for using office as a means to private gain. Hence there has been a wave of accusations of corruption, both personal and party based, throughout Europe from Finland to Greece. This has embraced both left and right wing parties, as it has in France where politicians on both sides of the political divide have been accused of awarding public works contracts in return for contributions to their campaign funds. Equally, the PSOE in Spain has been as tarnished by such charges as has New Democracy in Greece, where the former Prime Minister Constantine Mitsotakis faces prosecution for telephone tapping and involvement in a cement sale scandal.

In Italy, literally thousands of politicians were accused of financing their campaigns by taking bribes to award public works contracts, in the so-called *tangentopoli* or backhanders scandal. Faced with the revelations of the crusading judges of the 'clean hands' movement, the electorate insisted on changing the electoral rules and banning public finance for political parties in order to break the power of the parties. Then, having done so, they proceeded to vote for totally new political forces, reducing most existing parties to impotence, only to find that the newcomers also had scandals in their cupboards.

More commonly, however, the new political malaise has encouraged electoral disaffection and volatility. Turnout at elections has often gone down in recent years because of feelings of alienation and suspicion. Voters increasingly vote against governments rather than for them, and are much more willing to change the way they vote. Today's electorate is more educated and less bound to established parties by social and other loyalties. So it is willing to vote in a 'rational choice' way and for new and often untried formations. This was clear as early as the 1989 EP elections and the trend has continued into the 1990s.

Mainstream parties now control a declining percentage of the electorate, while their membership is also shrinking. This makes them, like public opinion, highly dependent on the media as a means of gaining influence. Unfortunately the growing role of the media does not always encourage deep analysis of issues and policies. So public opinion, party systems and parliaments are all very volatile. The number of parties represented in legislatures has, for instance, risen markedly. This may often be because voters switch votes between similar parties, but it does not make government formation any easier. Moreover, their position has become increasingly uncertain. Winning elections has proved only part of the answer as all governments have found control and support slipping, no matter how recent and how convincing their electoral success. As a result European governments face a real political crisis as they try to cope with new conditions and new issues.

The changing political balance

What effect have all these challenges actually had on Western Europe in the early 1990s? The answer is that they have increased uncertainty, shapelessness and diversity. Mainstream parties of right and left have all had their ups and downs. And though new political forces have emerged they have yet, apart from Italy, to achieve power. Equally, policies have oscillated between the ideas of the 1980s and a new interest in economic interventionism. As a result it becomes very difficult to see a single pattern throughout the regions of Europe.

So far the 1990s have not seen any simple dramatic switches of government. Thus, in Scandinavia, the first years of the decade saw conservative parties coming into power. In the case of Norway this happened without an election. Then general elections in Finland and Sweden during late 1991 saw a swing to the right with the Finnish Centre Party gaining more seats than ever before. As the largest single party it provided the Prime Minister for a new centre-right coalition government. In Sweden, the right wing coalition led by the Conservative Carl Bildt won power with a radical agenda for changing Sweden's failing social welfare economy.

More recently, the balance has shifted back the other way, Thus, the Danish Social Democrats who had done well at the 1990 elections, but had been unable to form a viable coalition government came back into power in January 1993 when the Schlüter cabinet fell when convicted of lying to Parliament over the way Tamil immigration had been handled. Later that year the Norwegian Labour party unexpectedly held off its challengers, although the anti-EC Centre party did very well, too. Opinion polls also show that the conservative governments in Sweden and Finland became increasingly unpopular. This helped the Finnish Social Democrats to capture the Presidency in January 1994. Their Swedish counterparts also then returned to government after the autumn 1994 elections as electors found the costs of the attack on the Swedish 'Middle Way' too painful by half.

Conversely, the left has also returned to power in countries as different as Ireland and Greece. In Ireland the Labour Party performed particularly well in the November 1992 elections and was able to form a majority government with the nationalist Fianna Fail. It was able to maintain its position when the Reynolds government fell in late 1994. In Greece New Democracy lost a great deal of ground, allowing Andreas Papandreou and PASOK to return to power in October 1993. The Dutch Christian Democrats were also the main losers in the May 1994 elections allowing the formation of a 'purple' or centre-left coalition led by Labour's Wim Kok so that the Christian Democratic Appeal party (CDA) was excluded from government for the first time in years.

The left also made gains in Britain and Germany, although not enough to enable them to dislodge the Conservatives from power at the national level. Germany, in fact, has begun to shrug off both the depression and divisions over Europe, so that the SPD was unsuccessful in its attempt to unseat Kohl. At the same time the country has freed itself to play a more active security role, both within NATO and without.

On the other hand, in France, the new conservative government won a landside victory over the totally humiliated PS in 1993. It then enjoyed a relatively long honeymoon period. However, this seems to be coming to an end as the government runs into difficulties over the economy which have caused a good deal of social unrest, which the government has sought to conciliate rather than resist. It is also troubled by foreign policy and personal divisions ahead of the 1995 Presidential election.

At the same time, the right has been able to hold on to power not merely in Britain and Germany but also in Malta, Portugal and Switzerland. In Spain, although the Popular Party (PP) failed to overtake the PSOE in June 1993, the latter was forced to rely on Catalan nationalist support to remain in power. And at the 1994 EP elections the PP for the first time outpolled the Socialists.

The same elections also underlined the even more striking electoral victory won by the new forces of the right in Italy three months previously. Thanks to the new electoral system, media magnate Silvio Berlusconi's brand new Forza Italia party and its League and extremist allies were able, as already noted, to defeat both traditional conservative parties and the combined forces of the left in March 1994. After surprisingly long drawn out negotiations, this led to the formation of a right-wing coalition government. Although this enjoyed a honeymoon period, it was not free from accusations of corruption itself, over an amnesty for former politicians, and over Berlusconi's failure to distance himself from his own media interests. This helped to bring his government down in December 1994. Thus, the outcome of the political earthquake is still unclear.

There was also some consolation for the right in recent elections in both Austria and Belgium. This was reinforced by what happened in the EP elections in Denmark and Ireland. However, what comes out of all this is the fact that so many governments have either lost their hold on power very rapidly or have suffered greatly reduced majorities. They have also seen their electorates turn to new and rival formations.

New political forces

Governing Western European states has become increasingly difficult in recent years because of the emergence of new political forces. Alongside the new nationalist forces already noted, at least five other kinds of new political movement have emerged in the early 1990s, beginning with militant pressure for regional autonomy, which often also expresses a desire for a new form of nationhood. This has long been visible in places like Corsica, Northern Ireland and Belgium. By questioning the structure of established states such movements pose a major problem for many governments. Moreover, territorial divisions have re-emerged between England and Scotland, between the East and the West of united Germany and in Switzerland between French and German speakers. At the same time, in the case of Belgium, migration has encouraged some Flemish nationalists to appeal increasingly to xenophobia as well as to separatism.

Southern Europe has also seen two striking developments of this sort. In Italy the disparities between North and South and the failings of the Italian political system helped to produce the Lega Nord. Starting by talking about regional autonomy, if not actual secession, on the grounds that the north is being exploited by the costly and corrupt capital and especially by the south, this has now forced its way into government. In Spain, as well as the various Basque parties there are a whole raft of regional parties who have not resorted to violence in the way ETA has. Their electoral strength has grown as the 1994 EP elections showed, and the Catalans are now vital to the survival of the PSOE government.

Governments of all political persuasions also find themselves facing new challenges from the growth of xenophobic movements on the Far Right. To a large extent these reflect the way the number of foreign refugees has doubled over the last three years. About half came from the former Soviet bloc and the rest from Turkey, Africa and Asia. It is the latter who have caused most concern. They have come partly because of disasters in their own part of the world and partly because of the hopes of sharing in Europe's economic success. All countries have large numbers of such people, with Luxembourg and Switzerland having the largest percentages, and Germany the largest numbers. Latent xenophobia has been brought to the surface by the recession which has exacerbated fears for employment. As well as threatening jobs the influx seems to threaten national identity and integrity, especially with EC developments forcing countries to concede rights to movement, to vote and to receive welfare. Thus, the Mayor of one town in the industrial north of France held a referendum on whether any more foreigners should be accepted.

As a result the old latent threat from extreme right parties may now be becoming a manifest reality. Such parties have achieved considerable success, for example in Belgium, Switzerland and especially France. In Belgium the Vlaams Blok of Karel Dillen, a friend of Le Pen, made major gains in elections during 1991 and again at the EP elections in 1994, when a French speaking Front movement also won a seat. The far right Dutch Democratic Centre also won three national seats in 1994.

In France the Front National may not have made a breakthrough in Parliament but it has established a solid base in popular opinion and large-scale supporting networks. This has had some influence on government policy encouraging Charles Pasqua, the Minister of the Interior, to take firm action against Algerian Fundamentalists. In Germany and Austria recent local elections have also seen a right wing surge, involving the Republikaner in the former and the Freedom party in the latter. However, the extremism of Jörg Haider, leader of the Freedom party, led a substantial minority of his party to secede. This did not stop the Party doing extremely well in the 1994 elections. A crop of right wing parties have done well in Switzerland. Parties like the Leghe and the Scandinavian Progress parties have also made use of the anti-immigrant line.

But the shift to the far right has also shown itself in skinhead and neo-Nazi violence, often aimed at synagogues and hostels for asylum seekers. There were 77 such attacks in Switzerland in 1991 and 54 in 1992, and a number of people were killed for racial reasons. Such assaults have become a major problem in

Germany, especially in the Eastern *Länder*. Despite the general revulsion against such attacks they have become a major concern for many governments.

Stability has also been threatened by a third kind of party, the anti-system party, which has parallels in several countries. Thus, Sweden saw a jokey party called New Democracy establish a foothold in 1991 and the Swiss Lega dei Ticinesi also started life as a populist opposition to introverted establishment parties. The Irish Progressive Democrats, like the British Liberal Democrats, have also attracted votes because they are not the 'old parties'. Equally, unusual special interest groups like the Dutch and Luxembourg pensioners parties and anti-EC forces in Denmark and France have also made an impact. However, the trend was best exemplified by Forza Italia in Italy which, thanks to the total discredit of the old parties and the media skills of Silvio Berlusconi, has turned itself into a new system party.

Ecological parties have been somewhat less of a force than they were, with the German Greens excluded from the Bundestag after failing to get the required 5 per cent of the vote in 1990, a fate shared by the Swedish party the following year. And although Greens made gains in Austria, Finland and Switzerland in 1991 they also failed to make the breakthrough anticipated in France. However, they never disappeared from continental parliaments and Green parties were to score well in the 1994 EP election. This patchy Green performance meant that there was less pressure on established governments even though the problems of the environment remained all too obvious.

Governments also found themselves under varying pressures from the far left. For, although the decline which had already set in during the 1980s was to accelerate after 1989, by 1993–94 the worst seemed to be over for communist parties. The transformation into reformist socialist parties enabled the French and Italian communist parties to limit their losses despite the general humiliation then inflicted on the left. On the other hand some of the far left Scandinavian parties have not done so well. And generally, with the difficulties of many ordinary socialist parties, there has been a continuing crisis in social democracy. This has compounded other economic and political problems presently afflicting western countries.

Policy adaptation
The vagaries and uncertainties of the political balance in Western Europe has been replicated in policy-making. On the one hand, pressures for austerity and liberalization have continued, encouraged by growing government deficits and by awareness of Europe's competitiveness. At the same time, doctrinaire addiction to free market orthodoxies have been queried, but without either a clear switch back to Keynesian approaches or the emergence of new guiding principles. The debate on the key economic policy question of how to combine enhanced competitiveness with maintaining social stability during a depression

is still unresolved. Given that the two imperatives are uneasy bedfellows it is not surprising that clear answers to the problems of the 1990s have yet to emerge. However, the debate has become much more European in nature.

The early 1990s thus saw continuing attempts to cut back taxes, social security burdens and labour market rigidities which were seen as preventing renewed growth and more effective competition with more flexible NICs. There were several reasons for this beginning with the need to combat the depression. The reduction of the soaring costs they imposed on state finances equally required the reduction of such burdens. Otherwise growing deficits would require counterproductive rises in taxes and interest rates. Even a carefully managed country like Switzerland found that federal finances moved from surplus in 1990 to a deficit of 8 billion Sfrs in 1994 and total public indebtedness rose to 30 per cent of GDP. The fact that economic performance could not simply be improved by devaluation because of the ERM was another contributing factor. The growing independence of central banks, whose main concern was the reduction of inflation rather than the stimulation of growth, also played a part.

This, like the need to meet the previously mentioned Maastricht criteria, meant that austerity policies and high interest rates had to continue. This was especially the case in southern economies where further structural adjustment was urgently required to help reduce the disparities with the more advanced economies of the north. This is particularly the case with the new government in Italy which has set itself similar targets to those of the Bildt government in Sweden.

For, although such tendencies were found in most European countries, whether governed by left or right, the most striking example was the Bildt assault on welfare benefits, tax levels and structures, and the size of the public sector. His aim was to reverse the whole drift of the Swedish social economy and to make it a much more open economy. However, such Scandinavian experiments with neo-liberalism have not been well received, especially in Sweden. The recent government changes suggest that the Dutch too have partly turned their back on conservative economic policies.

To the south, the economic crisis has taken an ever heavier toll. In Spain the PSOE has also been subject to fierce criticism over its economic policy. However, in Greece such problems have been largely obscured by national issues which have caused a rift with the rest of the EU. Elsewhere in the south the Social Democrats in Portugal and the new government in Italy have been much less challenged on the issue. However, by the end of 1994 there were major demonstrations against the new Italian austerity budget.

Equally, the commitment of British conservatism to market-driven neo-liberalism still goes far beyond that found in similar parties on the other side of the Channel. This was notwithstanding Mrs Thatcher's replacement by the more pragmatic and emollient John Major. Nor did his appointment give the

Conservative Party the expected boost. Despite the narrow and surprising win in the April 1992 general election, the Government has proved accident prone to a degree, and hamstrung by the failures of its European and economic policies. However, it has, with the new left–right coalitions in the Irish Republic, done something to resolve the Ulster crisis.

At the same time the depth of the economic crisis forced western states, individually and collectively, to try and mitigate the unemployment and poverty arising from depression and restructuring. Such demands have not just come from groups being hurt by the new trends, such as French farmers and lorry drivers, but from voters in many countries worried about the costs of deregulation on employment. This has made unemployment an increasingly important topic, and the OECD has begun to place a new stress on the need for social consensus and protection in the transition to a more flexible economy. Equally the 1994 EU White Paper on *Growth, Competitiveness, Employment*, looking at the need to restore Europe's employment and economic position, argues for a mix of approaches: exploiting the Single Market, helping small businesses, encouraging social dialogue, stimulating growth through new infrastructural networks, and encouraging an information society through advanced training and research. Whether such approaches are adopted remains to be seen. In any case, application is likely to vary considerably between countries.

Europe, however, remains a major issue in many countries and not just in Britain. It was probably even more explosive in Norway as it faced up to the divisive issue of EU entry. Switzerland is also bitterly divided over the question of how far, if at all, to move towards Europe, a divide which also overlaps with debates about economic policy. Austria, however, has been able to preserve consensus and endorse EU entry with relatively little difficulty. Much the same now seems to be true of Germany, despite the challenges to the Maastricht Treaty, discussed in Chapter 11. Equally, Europe has not been an issue for the Benelux countries although the Dutch have some doubts about the Franco–German axis. This has also caused some unease in France, where there are distinct differences with Germany over economic policy and the role of the EP. The situation is further complicated by the jockeying for position ahead of the 1995 Presidential election.

Interestingly, while British Eurosceptics have welcomed the rise of similar movements in France, there are considerable differences in their attitudes to world trade. Thus, the British argued strongly for the conclusion of the GATT Uruguay round as this would mean further liberalization. On the other hand, the French were much more reserved about this because their farmers saw it as an unacceptable threat, a view echoed by some French Eurosceptics who would prefer to see protectionist barriers erected against Japan and the NICs. However, French industry took a rather different view, helping the deal to gain approval.

So, almost without exception then governments have found it increasingly difficult to stay upright in the face of the cold blasts blown by the new international and economic conditions and by the changing internal political climate. Problems abound, but answers to the various crises are in fairly short supply. So far this has only amounted to a grumbling malaise and not to a real threat to democratic stability. Whether this remains the case will depend partly on whether western politics can find new resources of will, aided by the emerging economic recovery, and partly on what happens in the east of Europe and in the development of satisfactory mechanisms for enlarging Western Europe.

Futher reading

Allum, P. (1995), *State and Society in Europe*, Oxford: Polity.

Bell, D. and Shaw, E. (eds) (1994), *Conflict and Cohesion in West European Social Democratic Parties*, London: Pinter.

Bailey, J. (ed.) (1992), *Social Europe*, London: Longman.

Bramwell, A. (1994), *The Fading of the Greens*, New Haven, Conn.: Yale University Press.

Collinson, S. (1993), *Europe and International Migration*, London: Pinter.

Dyker, D. (ed.) (1992), *European Economies*, London: Longman.

Ford, G. (1993), *Fascist Europe. The Rise of Racism and Xenophobia*, Boulder, Col.: Westview.

Gillespie, R. (1994), *Mediterranean Politics, a Yearbook*, London: Pinter.

Hanley, D. (ed.) (1993), *The Christian Democratic Parties. A Comparative Perspective*, London: Pinter.

Keating, M. (1994), *The Politics of Modern Europe. The State and Political Authority in the Major Democracies*, Aldershot: Edward Elgar.

Lewin, L. (1988), *Ideology and Strategy in Sweden*, Cambridge: Cambridge University Press.

Rootes, C. and Richardson, D. (eds) (1994), *The Green Challenge*, London: Routledge.

Somers, F. (1994), *European Economies. A Comparative Study*, London: Pitman.

Varsori, A. (ed.) (1994), *Europe 1945–1990s: The End of an Era?*, London: Macmillan.

Wilson, F. (1994), *European Politics Today. The Democratic Experience*, 2nd edn, London: Harvester Wheatsheaf.

13 The crisis of transition in central and Eastern Europe

As noted in previous Chapters, Gorbachev's reforms were greeted with great expectations, while the revolutionary movements in what used to comprise geo-political Eastern Europe generated much euphoria. Many genuinely believed that the demise of Communism also meant an end to problems and conflicts. However, this has not been the case. In fact, after liberation from Communist rule a period of economic and socio-political instability set in. The revolution-ary movements, both in the USSR and in the former satellites, crucially failed to provide improved living standards. Economic dissatisfaction exacerbated already existing socio-political problems which, in the past, had been disguised and suppressed by dictatorial rule. The resultant crisis spread beyond the old satellites into the Soviet Union itself and undoubtedly contributed to the dis-integration of the empire in 1991. The defeat of the attempted coup of August 1991 and demands for autonomy, most forcefully articulated by the three Baltic states, signalled the end of Communist rule in Eastern Europe.

What has happened in both the former satellites and in the Soviet Union has been rightly called a socio-political revolution. It was a revolution which also swept aside long-standing methods, enduring institutions, deep-rooted values and even people. Consequently, an entirely new political and economic framework had to be constructed, both in terms of institutions and values. Such a formidable task – unprecedented in modern history – is a long-term undertaking. Post-Communist Europe therefore faces challenges on a scale which not only threaten the fragile stability of the new democracies, but present a potential danger to the security of the entire European continent.

This Chapter attempts to explain why the democratic upsurge in Eastern Europe – no matter how welcome – has also heralded a period of socio-political and economic disorientation. The problems started in the new central and Eastern European democracies and then spread to the republics of the former Soviet Empire. There are three major dimensions to the crisis of transition in the East: political uncertainty, economic dislocation and ethno-nationalist conflicts. Although the problems in the old satellites and the former Soviet empire are virtually identical, this Chapter, for the sake of clarity, deals separately with the two regions. Thus, the first part traces the painstaking process of transition from a one-party-state to liberal democracy in the former satellites – which took place against the background of major crises in the Soviet Union. The second part of the Chapter looks at the forces that will shape the future in the newly established independent states of the former Soviet empire. Here too – as in the old satellites – the political climate is very much determined by economic catastrophes and ethnic conflicts. Major obstacles have to be overcome if democracy is to be secured.

The former satellites

The revolutions of 1989 and the subsequent demise of the CMEA and the Warsaw Pact ended 45 years of Soviet domination over central and Eastern Europe, but the collapse of Communism also bequeathed a troublesome legacy. When the dictatorial regimes were removed, the former satellites experienced a brief period of hope as they embarked on the difficult transition from command economies and totalitarian political systems to free enterprise and liberal democratic values. However, a rude awakening often followed the triumph of political victory. Moreover, the pace and intensity of reform differed significantly between the individual states. For example, the reform process, both politically and economically, was much slower in the Balkans, where political leaders were reluctant to embark on a fully fledged Western-type liberal democracy. In these countries, elements of the old system – particularly in the economic sector – continued to exist.

The democratic challenge

All countries wanted to establish liberal democracy and a capitalist market economy. This involved not only a political transformation, but an economic one as well. However, with the exception of Hungary, political change preceded the economic transformation in all countries. The main problem all former satellites faced was lack of democratic political experience and education. Czechoslovakia apart, there was no tradition of democracy, of parliamentary debate or of interaction between governmental and non-governmental actors. Nor was there any model or precedent for this transition from Communism to liberal democracy.

After the revolution, each country drew up its own constitution and legislative procedure, which were variants of Western liberal democracy and the countries' pre-Communist traditions, based on the separation of powers, the rule of law, parliamentary democracy and a market economy. But Western-style democracy might not altogether be the answer for some of these countries which, in essence, were recreating their states. The old system had been destroyed before even the most rudimentary foundation of a new political structure had been laid. As a result, a gap developed between rhetorical objectives and socio-political realities in these countries. This is an intractable dilemma faced by all new democratic states in Eastern and central Europe.

Although all countries have held multi-party elections since the revolutions, the new democratic parties were still immature and lacked mass support. In the beginning they were held together by the need to expel and oust Communist parties from power and thus had unity of purpose and strategy. However, while the revolutionary leadership has been very effective in bringing down the former Communist regime, it was not successful in executing the reform programme or eliciting support for it from the electorate. Moreover, once in government, pressure for a more nationalist programme mounted and distinct left and right wings emerged. This gave rise to tensions and divisions, within both parties and governments. The conflicts centered on the role or power of the state versus that of the individual, collective interests versus civil society, on nationhood versus individual rights and, importantly, on the speed and extent of reform. In the 1989 'movement' material needs had been a minor consideration. But the elation of liberation was closely followed by economic hardship and material concerns became a priority in post-Communist Europe.

In both Hungary and Poland, internal conflicts over the separation of power and speed of reform led to changes in government. These were particularly frequent in Poland. The first completely free parliamentary elections of October 1991 put a centre-right government under Prime Minister Jan Olszewski in power. However, the parliament was fragmented with 29 parties represented in the Sejm, the 460-seat lower house. Tensions built up within the coalition and no consensus existed on the direction and speed of reform. In addition, a power struggle developed between President Lech Walesa and Prime Minister Jan Olszewski over the control of the army. All this merely underlined the fragility of Poland's post-Communist politics.

The dissolution of the first non-Communist government by parliament was followed by several months of bickering, when in July 1992 a new liberal-moderate coalition government led by Hanna Suchocka was elected. For a while, the new government provided a consensus platform for Poland's divergent parties. However, on 28 May 1993 the six party coalition government of Suchocka was defeated on a no-confidence motion tabled by opposition deputies. President Walesa dissolved parliament and called for a general election to be held on 17 September. A new electoral law – passed by the outgoing chamber – barred the way into parliament to those parties which failed to get 5 per cent of the national vote, thus denying entry into parliament to small splinter groups. The September election returned a centre-left government, dominated by Communists, to power.

A similar development took place in Hungary. During the parliamentary elections in March 1990 some 80 parties contested in the first round, although only ten were of any political significance. In the event only six parties received the 4 per cent of votes required by law for obtaining a seat in parliament. The centre-right HDF – led by Josef Antall – emerged as the largest party, winning

165 of the 389 seats parliament, although it relied on the support of two smaller parties, the Smallholders Party and the Christian Democratic People's Party, for its parliamentary majority.

While the transition to democracy was smooth, parties were still immature and lacked mass support. Moreover, internal differences existed within major parties as well as within the coalition government. In 1992, controversy flared up between President Goncz and Prime Minister Antall over whether the former had the ultimate power of appointment over government-controlled media organizations. Development in Hungary showed a striking similarity to that in Poland when, in the May 1994 elections, Hungary's Socialist party, the successor to the Hungarian Socialist Workers' Party which had governed the country in the Communist era, won an outright majority under Gyula Horn, establishing a clear trend towards the resurgence of former Communists in central Europe. The political experience and party organization of former Communists have clearly helped to defeat 'democratic' forces, which had inherited a power vacuum and a devastated economy.

The situation in Czechoslovakia became particularly serious. The country, led by the first post-Communist president Vaclav Havel who – as a result of his involvement in the revolutionary movement – had achieved international standing and prestige, seemed to offer the best chance of stability. Because of the ethnic division between the majority of Czechs (63 per cent) and Slovaks (31 per cent), disputes erupted after the revolution. The Slovaks, traditionally an agrarian people, objected to the domination of the industrial Czech region. Aggravation increased in the autumn of 1990 when the Slovaks called for greater autonomy and the introduction of Slovak as the only official language in Slovakia. Mass demonstrations in March 1991, in support of the 'Declaration of the Sovereignty of Slovakia' demanded complete separation from the Czech republic. In the general elections of June 1992 the pro-independence movement for a Democratic Slovakia won a majority of seats in the Slovak National Council. This led to the resignation of the Czechoslovak President, Havel, and the 'velvet' divorce between the two republics.

The Czech region elected a democratic conservative coalition, while the 'Movement for a Democratic Slovakia' (MDS) emerged as the largest party in the Slovak region. Discussions over the country's legislative organization led to a jointly accepted agenda to divide the country into two autonomous republics and on 1 January 1993 the two republics became independent. The Czech government under Prime Minister Vaclav Klaus embarked on rapid structural reform, while in Slovakia, the government of Vladimir Měciar – leader of the nationalist MDS – was committed to a slower pace of reform.

The process of transition from one party rule to liberal democracy has been distinctly slower in Romania, Bulgaria and Albania, while Yugoslavia, already occupying a different position prior to and during the revolutionary movement, had a wholly different development from that of the six former satellites. The North–South divide, already apparent at the beginning of the transformation process, was subsequently reinforced by political and economic factors. The overthrow of Nicolae Ceauşescu in Romania, the removal of Todor Zhivkov in Bulgaria and the reshuffle in the Albanian government, described in Chapter 10, did not result in a total overthrow of the system and the revolutions in these countries remained incomplete. Former Communist leaders remained and simply changed the parties' names. In all countries in the Balkans, the nomen-klatura still wielded extensive powers. Members of the old elite tried, often successfully, to legitimate their continued access to power and have constituted the main base for the rise of the new middle classes – both developments engendered bitter hostility amongst the people.

Romania is perhaps the weakest and most vulnerable of the former satellites as a result of economic underdevelopment and lack of democratic tradition. Following the revolutions in 1989 and the execution of Ceauşescu on 25 December, the revolutionary movement seized control and the Council of the National Salvation Front (NSF) was formed. Ion Iliescu and Petre Roman – both former Communists – were made President and Prime Minister of the NSF appointed government. The first free elections took place in May 1990, but there was not enough time for opposition forces to organize themselves. Although the NSF had won 65 per cent of the parliamentary vote, giving it 263 of the 387 seats in the Chamber of Deputies and 91 of the 119 seats in the Senate, there were alleged irregularities in the electoral process. Despite growing resentment and the conviction of anti-government protesters that the old power structures had been left intact save by some cosmetic corrections, the NSF remained the dominant force in government.

In September 1991 the government of Prime Minister Roman resigned following riots by striking miners. A new government was formed a month later under Theodor Stolojan at the invitation of President Iliescu. In the run-up to the February–April 1992 local elections, a coalition of democratic parties, the Democratic Convention, provided a challenge to the NSF, which had suffered a decline in popularity. The party split into a pro-Iliescu wing (Democratic National Salvation Front – DNSF) and a pro-Roman (NSF) group. In the September 1992 elections no party gained an overall majority, and Iliescu, with only 47 per cent of the votes cast, failed to win the required majority for election as President. It was only during a run-off for the presidency which took place on 11 October that he was re-elected with a comfortable majority of 62 per cent of the votes.

In Bulgaria too, socialists remain more of a force than elsewhere. Apart from the GDR, the Communist regime in Bulgaria had been, as already noted, the most willing ally of the former Soviet Union. Hence, the upheaval in the USSR in 1991 was of greater significance to Bulgaria than to anywhere else.

The anti-Communist UDF, headed by Filip Dimitrov, had ousted the Communists, but lost power in October 1992 when control passed to a 'non-party government' of technocrats, headed by Lyuben Berov. But the government was supported by the votes of the BSP – successor to the Communists – and this convinced many Bulgarians that the government was still rooted in Communism. Berov became increasingly isolated from the frustrated electorate because of lack of progress in establishing a fully fledged market economy. Although he survived seven no-confidence votes tabled by the UDF during 1993–94, he resigned on 3 September 1994. President Zhelyu Zhelev's invitation made to the main parties in the National Assembly to form a government, was rejected by both the BSP and the UDF. A cabinet crisis followed and led to the dissolution of Parliament by President Zhelev. When early elections were held on 18 December, the BSP won a clear majority.

Albania remained fairly untouched by the revolutions, partly because, following initial demonstrations in late 1989, the government allowed thousands of people to emigrate in an attempt to flush out anti-patriotic elements. Despite this, pro-democratic demonstrations led to a reshuffle of the government. In December 1990 independent political parties were legalized and the first legal opposition party since before the Second World War, the Democratic Party of Albania (DPA), was formed, led by Dr Sali Berisha. In March 1991 the DPA won a landslide victory over the former Communists. However, resentment against the continuing power of entrenched former Communists remained high compounded by mounting opposition in Parliament to President Berisha's increasingly autocratic style. Nevertheless, Albania's conversion to democracy after 45 years of Communist rule was strikingly demonstrated when, in November 1994, Albanian voters overwhelmingly rejected a constitution which would have shifted the balance of power from parliament to the already very powerful president.

The situation in the former satellites is thus mixed: the north has moved ahead with democratization while the Balkans are still beset with political problems. It is interesting to note that, with the exception of the Czech republic, former Communists are now dominating the governments of all former satellites. It would, however, be precipitate to suggest that the post-Communist system has reached its final shape in these countries. Besides, the return of Communists to power may not be a negative trend *per se*. The parties have been much reformed and the system may now be strong enough to re-educate former Communists. Constant observation by the West, on whom the countries are dependent for financial help, could be a further constraint. Indeed, a strident nationalist government – such as that of the Slovak republic after the October 1994 elections – may potentially be a far greater threat to the stability of the region.

Economic transformation – a half-way house?
Political stability in these countries will to a large extent be determined by failure or success of economic reforms. The economic transformation from one system

to another has been different in each of the former satellites – reflecting to a large extent the varying political situation – but all countries have suffered common problems, some of which were 'inherited' from the old system, such as industrial backwardness, foreign debt and low growth while others, such as hyperinflation and unemployment are new phenomena. The countries also face a common task: to transform an inefficient centrally planned economy into a free market system while at the same time maintaining social peace and public support for the reform process.

The problems in all these countries are rooted in the countries' pre-revolutionary systems of central planning and administration in accordance with basic socialist principles. They include low labour productivity, poor return on investment and environmental degradation. All the former satellites had a large backlog of much-needed infrastructure development in transport, telecommunications and housing. In addition, the economic transformation took place against the background of the disintegration of the Soviet Union and that meant the loss of a large market and the end of cheap energy supply. Industrial output fell by 38 per cent in the first two years after the revolution, while unemployment rose from zero to 12 per cent by the end of 1991.

All countries were committed, at least in theory, to introducing a huge privatization programme as part of the transformation from a state-dominated economy to a predominantly private market economy. Privatization is thus a major and important contribution to the type of market economy envisaged. But the programmes underway in Eastern Europe are different in both scale and speed. For example, the 'shock-therapy' strategy of fast privatization to ensure the irreversibility of the process despite short-term, socioeconomic repercussions was undertaken in Poland, Hungary (albeit to a lesser extent) and the Czech republic. A more 'gradualist' approach – building on existing institutions and involving less austere macroeconomic policies and more government intervention – was chosen by the Balkan countries. There are also variants in the method of privatization – for small-scale business it may be sale by auction, for large-scale enterprises the method is usual to transform them into joint-stock companies and then proceed by selling shares. A very common method employed and unique to the East is the voucher system: all citizens are awarded vouchers, which they can exchange for shares of selected enterprises or management companies.

Poland was the first economy to attempt the rapid transition to a market economy: by 1992 many restrictions on economic activities were lifted, the private sector was vigorously developed, monopolies were dissolved and national enterprises were encouraged to seek foreign markets. In 1994 the Polish economy was expected to show the fastest economic growth with GDP rising to 5 per cent topping the 4 per cent reported increase in 1993. Hungary had already introduced some market principles under Socialism and this enabled the country to adopt a more gradual approach to structural reform than Poland or the Czech

Republic, although Hungary should still be considered a 'rapid reformer'. Indeed, the country has undertaken what officials claim is the fastest privatization in the history of the world, although the process is dominated by Western multi-national investors. Top rank multinationals including Electrolux, General Motors, Ford and Unilever have brought technological and managerial expertise. Exports to the West have expanded dramatically and increasing revenues from tourism have helped Hungary to stay in surplus on the current account.

Initially, Czechoslovakia had also implemented a 'shock therapy' programme and there was some success. In fact, in 1992 Czechoslovakia moved ahead of Poland to become the most advanced market economy. But, as already noted, disagreements over the pace of reform contributed to the dissolution of the federation. The Czech government under Vaclav Klaus has been traditionally Western-orientated and hoped that the increasingly privatized Czech economy would respond by building up already growing markets in the EU. By 1994 the Republic was perceived as politically and economically the most stable of post-Communist states. Inflation fell to 9.4 per cent in mid-1994 (against 22 per cent in 1993) and unemployment remained below 4 per cent, partly as a result of a deliberate 'low wage policy' and partly through the creation of thousands of jobs in tourism, banking, retailing and services.

In Slovakia, however, the government of Vladimir Měciar adopted the gradualist approach which involved privatization by more orthodox methods and included direct sales and managerial buy-outs. The country has a much weaker industrial base than its neighbour, the Czech Republic and suffers from a shortage of capital and foreign investment. Unemployment in 1994 soared to 17 per cent. So, while Měciar's behaviour helped to bring down his first government, social unrest played a part in his election victory in the autumn of 1994. The formation of a new coalition government has raised questions about both privatization and foreign policy.

Despite individual differences between these countries, on the whole, the process was strikingly similar. The Visegrad countries are, Slovakia excepted, clearly ahead in terms of GDP and standard of living. However, the shock therapy programme had negative repercussions. This strategy neglected to address the social dimension of reform. As a result of the transformation process, many inefficient enterprises have gone bankrupt and unemployment – virtually non-existent in the former Soviet bloc – has emerged as a major problem in all countries. The principal cause was a reduction in the number of jobs in state enterprises, which were under pressure to shed the excess labour accumulated under central planning.

The rising level of unemployment has placed an additional burden on public finance, when governments are trying to limit the rise in state borrowing for macroeconomic policy reasons. Moreover, high unemployment levels pose political difficulties for governments trying to maintain public support for their reform measures. Finally, widespread unemployment was a major psychological shock to people who had been used to job security. As a result, purchasing power has fallen for the majority and the distribution of income has become less equal. The gap between rich and poor widened. In Poland, for example, of a population of 39 million, three million (15 per cent of the workforce) are unemployed and there is a marked difference in living standards between the urban population – which profited from the reform process – and the countryside where Poland's 'shock therapy' programme generated less prosperity. The dissatisfaction of the poor and unemployed no doubt contributed to the electoral gains of the former Communists in the election of September 1993.

The economic transformation process not only produced a gap between the poor and the *nouveaux riches*, but also a clear North–South divide: while the north fared well, the southern countries, now including the Slovak republic, were reluctant to adopt an effective austerity programme. Despite many differences between the countries of the Balkan, in all cases, the slow progress of reform reflected the greater political uncertainty. Governments in these countries were composed of coalitions dominated by Communists. Privatization of state enterprises, particularly speedy in Hungary, failed to get properly off the ground in the Balkans. The end of cheap Soviet energy supplies and the collapse of Comecon trading was compounded by a world recession and the resultant economic dislocation spilled over into politics. Geographically, the countries are in a less favourable position in terms of trade flows to the EU, while the conflict in the former Yugoslavia has some impact on their economies. Inflation increased, output fell and state budget and hard currency trade balance went into deficit. Falling incomes have kept imported goods out of reach while basic foodstuff, fuel and transport are expensive in relation to wages. So most people spend their disposable income on necessities.

Bulgaria in particular has been hard hit by the UN trade embargo on Serbia and the difficulty of ensuring transit rights it needs for access to Western markets. As already mentioned, a weak government backed by former Communists has been slow in embarking on a process of privatization. Nearly 40 per cent of the working population, or 4.3 million people, live on or below the poverty level. Like in most other satellite states, the situation has been made worse by falling (cheap) oil imports from the former USSR. In Albania the transition to market economy is particularly difficult. The country, burdened by backwardness, still suffers from Communist policies of economic autarchy. There has been an expansion of small-scale private enterprise and agriculture – the principal sector of the Albanian economy – which has shown some improvement, but the lack of technology and foreign investment plus years of isolation have resulted in Albania having the most underdeveloped economy of any European country. Its living standard is well below even that of the poorer other former satellites.

Romania is perhaps the weakest and most vulnerable of the former satellites as a result of economic underdevelopment. The first post-Communist government did introduce some market reforms. The currency was made convertible, a programme of privatization of state enterprises was started, and a law on the decollectivization of land was passed in 1991. But, following a change of government, price control was reimposed in an attempt to control inflation, industrial production fell and the privatization programme stagnated. It was only in November 1994 that Romania attempted to relaunch its privatization programme by inviting public bids for three medium-sized state companies, the first such offerings for 18 months. It is hoped the offers will rekindle the population's interest in privatization and lead to pressure on the government to speed up the process which has been blocked by conservative forces within the governing Democratic National Salvation Front (DNSF).

Ethno-nationalist conflicts

Institutional weakness and economic decline have direct implications for the third problem which has emerged in Eastern Europe: the rise of nationhood. The root of Eastern Europe's ethnic conflicts clearly lies in its history. While the formation of West European states has been a gradual and long-term process, the process in the East, by contrast, has been sudden and of recent origin. At the beginning of the 20th century the people of Eastern Europe were citizens of either the Ottoman, Habsburg or the Russian Empire. After their collapse, the new national frontiers no longer coincided with ethnic distribution. Moreover, most frontiers were arbitrarily drawn by the USSR and many were imposed on the countries after the Second World War. During the Communist regime any expression of ethnic or nationalist consciousness was suppressed. The fall of Communism, however, has exposed long dormant ethnic tensions and has led to a growth of national self-assertion and the emergence of ethnic-based national organizations. In fact, nationalism became a concept which attracted widespread appeal. The focal point is of course Yugoslavia, as Chapter 15 will show. But ethnic tension is also present in virtually all former satellite states. Although of course the conflict is different in each country and concerns differ from one ethnic group to another, the results are very similar throughout Eastern Europe: there is now an acute sensitivity about all questions concerning national and ethnic unity. Any attempt to question or resist that unity has given rise to political crises and, in some cases, has led to armed clashes.

Poland, Hungary and Albania are fairly homogenous ethnically and have escaped the intense inter-ethnic conflicts present in the former Soviet Union and the Balkans. But Poland has a small German and Ukrainian minority. The latter presents a problem, mainly as a result of sectarian factors: the conflict is between Roman Catholics (Polish) and Uniates (Ukrainians) and Orthodox (also Ukrainian) creating a three-cornered struggle over ownership of churches in south-east Poland. In addition there is a Polish minority living in Lithuania, the Ukraine and Belorussia, causing conflicts between Poland and some successor states of the USSR.

In Hungary a dispute has emerged with Romania concerning the collective rights of the Hungarian minority in Transylvania. About 2 million Hungarians live there, in what was once an integral part of Hungary, but which was given to Romania as part of the Versailles settlement. While no territorial revision is advocated, the Hungarian government demands that their compatriots are treated as a distinct legal entity and that their rights be enshrined in an international treaty. However, Romania resents the interference of Hungary in what it considers an internal matter.

While Albania is relatively homogenous ethnically, a significant number of Albanians live elsewhere in the Balkans. Two million ethnic Albanians live in Serbian ruled Kossovo, 700 000 in the former Yugoslav republic of Macedonia, others in Serbia proper, Montenegro, Greece and some 80 000 in South Italy. Many of the Albanians suffer discrimination and Albanian activists hope for a 'united greater Albanian state'. Albania has the highest birth rate in Europe so Serbia and Greece are both fearful that Albanians will shortly outnumber Serbs and rival Greece as the largest Balkan nationality. Relations between Greece and Albania, always precarious because of historical Greek claims to parts of southern Albania, reached a low point in the summer of 1993 as a result of the influx of some 200 000 Albanian immigrants to Greece which the latter wanted to return to Albania. The dispute also involves Albania's Greek minority which, Greece claims, is mistreated by Albania.

The territorial and ethnic conflicts in the other former satellites are far more serious, however. The multinational federation of Czechoslovakia has experienced cultural, religious and linguistic conflicts for many years. The creation of the two new states may have solved some problems, but it also created others. The most problematic relationship for Slovakia is that with neighbouring Hungary involving the joint hydroelectric dam project at Gabcikovo-Nagymaros on the Danube. Hungary withdrew from the project – a 'relic of Communist gigantomania' – for economic and ecological reasons, while Slovakia insists on its completion. The polluted Danube is the main source of drinking water for the two million people of Budapest. However, the diversion of the Danube into a canal would alter the water levels, ruining the purification plants in the polluted Danube and isolating some largely Magyar villages. Slovakia argues that too much finance and prestige has been invested in the project and is going ahead with the dam on Slovak territory. More importantly, however, the project has stirred up dormant ethnic and national rivalries as significant Hungarian minorities live in Slovakia, Yugoslavia and Romania.

Both Bulgaria and Romania define themselves as uni-ethnic states, but each has a large minority which is asserting its identity. In Bulgaria, the legacy of

Ottoman rule includes several Moslem minorities including Pomaks (ethnic Bulgarians converted to Islam) and 3/4 million Turks. On the whole Bulgaria has managed to escape severe ethnic tension, although conflict was caused by the compulsory Bulgarization of Turks in 1984 which led to a mass exodus to Turkey causing worldwide indignation. After the revolution, a large number of Turks returned. However, continued tension between Bulgarians and the Turkish population led to a sharp deterioration in Turkish–Bulgarian relations.

Relations with Romania are also far from cordial. Here, too, the issue is a territorial conflict concerning southern Dobrudja, a region lost by Romania to Bulgaria in the 1940s. A further problem is pollution of the Danube at the Romanian/Bulgarian border. In November 1991 Bulgarian demonstrators blocked the border crossing in protest of the pollution from a chemical plant in Giurgui. Despite these incidents, however, both countries, in a Bulgarian–Romanian friendship treaty of January 1992, have stated that they had no territorial claims on each other. A more serious potential conflict is Macedonia: Bulgaria and Serbia have fought three wars over this region in the last century. A spillover of the war from former Yugoslavia into the newly recognized republic of Macedonia would almost certainly involve not only Bulgaria, but Greece and Turkey as well.

One issue – a potentially most explosive dispute – involves not only a former satellite but also some of the new republics in the old Soviet empire and may therefore illustrate the dangerous 'spillover' effect of territorial–ethnic tensions which have emerged after the end of dictatorial rule. As indicated on Map 4, the conflict involves Romanian demands for the return of territories annexed by the USSR in 1940. Stalin had incorporated parts of Romania (Bukovina and parts of southern Bessarabia) into the Ukrainian Soviet Republic and had annexed the rest of Bessarabia to create the Moldovian Soviet Republic. Its population consists of 3.2 million – about two thirds of whom are Romanian, although there are also Ukrainian, Russian and Turkish minorities. Some 800 000 Romanians live in the Bukovina area and the Danubian district of the Ukraine. The Moldovian Popular Front (MPF) has been active in pressing for restoration of the Romanian language and the national flag. As early as June 1991 the Romanian parliament had condemned the Soviet annexation of Bessarabia and Northern Bukovina, although it had stopped short of making territorial demands on the USSR. Support for reunification with Romania became acute after the declaration of independence by the Moldovian government in August 1991 although there was a split on the issue between the MPF and President Snegur, the latter putting more emphasis on national statehood than on reunification.

A national plebiscite on 6 March 1994 showed over 95 per cent support for Moldovian independence. The plebiscite, together with the February 1994 election result – the pro-independence Agrarian Democratic party gained 43.2

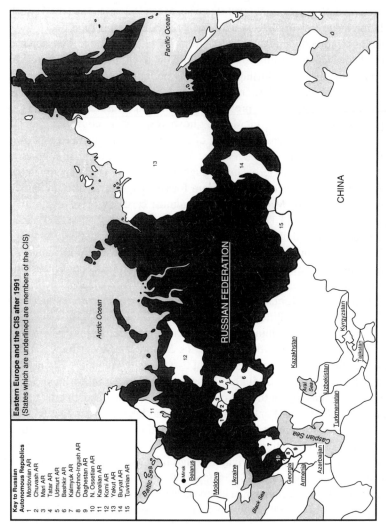

Key to Russian Autonomous Republics

1 Mordovian AR
2 Chuvash AR
3 Mari AR
4 Tatar AR
5 Udmurt AR
6 Bashkir AR
7 Kalmyuk AR
8 Chechno-Ingush AR
9 Daghestan AR
10 N. Ossetian AR
11 Karelian AR
12 Komi AR
13 Yakut AR
14 Buryat AR
15 Tuvinian AR

Eastern Europe and the CIS after 1991
(States which are underlined are members of the CIS)

RUSSIAN FEDERATION

Pacific Ocean

Arctic Ocean

CHINA

Kazakhstan

Uzbekistan

Turkmenistan

Kyrgyzstan

Tajikistan

Aral Sea

Caspian Sea

Azerbaijan

Armenia

Georgia

Black Sea

Ukraine

Moldova

Belarus

●Minsk

Baltic Sea

Map 4

206

per cent of the vote – demonstrated conclusively the lack of support for unification with Romania. Furthermore, the new constitution adopted in July 1994 established the country as a 'presidential parliamentary republic' and defined the state language as 'Moldovian' rather than Romanian, a fact which was 'regretted' by Romania. Nevertheless, the issue of territorial demands and opposition to Moldovian independence among segments of the Ukrainian, Russian and Turkish minorities still present a problem.

Moreover, the Ukraine rejects altogether the demand for the return of the former Romanian regions Bessarabia and Northern Bukovina. Relations between the Ukraine and Romania deteriorated as a result, the former interpreting the Romanian declaration of Soviet annexation of the disputed territories as unjustifiable 'territorial claims' against the Ukraine. The Romanian minority in the Ukraine is subjected to assimilation, emphasizing the seriousness of the situation. An added complication is the fact that the Moldovian region of Transdnestria – with a large Russian population settled by Stalin – has proclaimed independence from Moldova under a special protection of a CIS peace keeping force -an issue which not only involved Ukrainian and Romanian, but also Russian interests. In view of its location and ethnic composition, Moldova is one of the most explosive trouble-spots in Eastern Europe.

In the light of the political, economic and ethnic problems the former satellites are now facing, the future for these countries remains uncertain. Significantly, some of their problems spread into the former Soviet Union and may have contributed to the disintegration of the USSR.

The disintegration of the USSR

While the former satellites embarked on the difficult transformation process, the political situation in the Soviet Union was itself growing extremely tense. By the beginning of 1990 groups across the political spectrum were voicing discontent: on the left democratic and liberal movement demanded more radical measures, on the right conservative and nationalist groups opposed even Gorbachev's moderate reforms. It was not that perestroika was rejected outright, rather that the conservative groups were willing, like Andropov in the early 1980s, to undertake reforms as long as the old structure of power was not jeopardized and, above all, that the Union was retained.

The causes for criticism, as already outlined in Chapter 8, were numerous and varied. Rising prices, the breakdown in the distribution of consumer goods, unemployment, hyperinflation and the reduction or abolition of subsidies were the concern of the ordinary Soviet citizen. The loss of power and privilege aggravated the Soviet political elite. Several republics wanted to establish their own armies, while others demanded outright secession from the Union. Pressure on the government was mounting. The old order was clearly breaking down, but the new structures were not resilient enough to provide for a smooth transition from one system to another. All groups, irrespective of their political persuasion, questioned the legitimacy of Gorbachev and his reform programme. By the early 1990s a 'crisis phenomenon' existed, the country was in a state of decay.

Gorbachev, thus faced with criticism from both the right and the left, also found himself caught between conflicting demands of the various groups. However, he felt that he needed the support of the Right to salvage as much as possible of his reform programme and this made him reliant on the bureaucratic and military elite. In his attempt to compromise he included reactionary forces in his leadership team and thus, inadvertently, contributed to his own downfall. During the winter of 1990–91 his style reflected a new conservatism, which played into the hands of conservative forces.

The *putsch* of 19 August 1991 was directly triggered by the scheduled signing of a new Union Treaty envisaging the creation of a new 'Union of Soviet Sovereign Republics' – the first draft of which had been published in November 1990. The new agreement would redefine relations between the central authorities and the Union Republics and would succeed the 'Union of Soviet Socialist Republics'. The Treaty proposed sweeping away the centrally controlled political system of the USSR and handing a considerable measure of power to semi-independent states. Gorbachev hoped that a voluntary transfer of (limited) power from the centre to the republics would put an end to demands for complete secession. The camp of the old Communists, however, were determined to torpedo the Treaty due to be signed on 20 August. On 13 August, the conservative president Valentin Pavlov, in a televised interview, made a massive attack on the far-reaching reforms contained in the Treaty, while only a few days later the Council of Ministers requested changes in the document.

This led a coalition of conservative forces closely linked with the CPSU, the government bureaucracy and the military–industrial complex, and representing Gorbachev's most strident critics, to try and seize power. On 18 August 1991, Gorbachev, while holidaying in his villa in the Crimea, was confronted with a delegation of the so-called 'State Committee for the State of Emergency' (SCSE) headed by the Vice President, Gennady Yanayev. Refusing to declare a state of emergency and transfer power to the SCSE, Gorbachev was put under house arrest. Tanks and troops were moved into Moscow and Leningrad as well as into the capitals of the three Baltic republics.

However, not only was the *putsch* amateurishly planned, but the plotters had overlooked the fact that five years of glasnost and perestroika had born democratic fruit: Soviet citizens, exhibiting a new awareness of their power defied the illegitimate takeover. During the night of 19–20 August 70 000 Moscovites gathered outside the Russian Parliament building, where their President, Boris Yeltsin, issued a passionate plea to the citizens of Moscow to resist the take-over. Tacit resistance to the coup and mass demonstrations also took place in Leningrad.

On 21 August the coup collapsed, and the Presidium of the Supreme Soviet declared the seizure of power illegal. The plotters were arrested and Gorbachev was freed and (temporarily) reinstated.

However, and even Gorbachev was unaware of it at the time, the failed coup had set in motion a process of disintegration. Key powers and cornerstones of the Soviet system – the Party, the legislative, the executive, the military and the KGB – were suddenly deprived of their leaders. Above all the attempted coup had revealed the extent of betrayal by the party elite. Their support in the coup revealed the need for a radical reform of the political structures. At the same time, the republics, particularly Russia under Yeltsin, gained prestige and influence at the expense of the central authority. Significantly, the three Baltic republics used the crisis to become completely independent from Moscow. Unfortunately, Gorbachev continued to cling to the CPSU, anxious to preserve this major support of the old system. His greatest mistake, indeed his tragedy, was that he was not prepared to realize and recognize the new realities of the situation. During the August–December interregnum the old structure of the empire gradually collapsed. On 24 August, Gorbachev, under intense pressure from Yeltsin, resigned as General Secretary of the Party. The Supreme Soviet, pressured by large demonstrations throughout the Soviet Union, decided to suspend the party and investigate the full extent of its role in the attempted *putsch.* Against this background, the Kremlin recognized the independence of the three Baltic states. This was followed by a wave of declarations of independence from other republics. Between August and October 1991 nine further republics demanded secession from the union (or stated their intention to do so once a referendum had been held). Thus, the failure of the coup accelerated the already developing process of disintegration and was a new impetus to demands for independence by many of the republics.

On 8 December 1991 in Brest-Livosk, Belarus, the three Slav republics, the Russian Federation, Belarus and the Ukraine, as shown on Map 4, founded a new 'Commonwealth of Independent States' (CIS), an interstate body designed to preserve some measure of co-ordination between the republics. Of the 15 Soviet republics only Georgia, where a civil war raged, and the three Baltic states declined to join, although subsequently these four countries sent representatives to some important CIS meetings. In the case of Georgia, it even abided by certain agreements and eventually became a member in 1993. On 25 December 1991 Gorbachev resigned as president, finally grasping that the real crisis of the USSR was the maturation of the republics whose main aim was to become sovereign actors. On 1 January 1992 the Soviet Union ceased to exist.

Problems in the former Soviet Union

The hope that the successor states would move quickly to political and economic unity, has not been fulfilled. Like the former satellites, the 15 republics encountered enormous problems in their difficult transition. The collapse of the USSR meant an end to the cohesion of the Soviet economic and political system and led to the creation of 15 regions struggling toward new statehood against the background of political conflict, economic decline and ethnic strife. No longer was there a co-ordinating centre, either politically or economically, leaving the newly autonomous regions in a state of confusion, with each state desperately attempting to survive in the new order.

The pattern already observed in the old satellites, that of former Communists reasserting themselves against the background of economic hardship, also holds true for most of the former Soviet republics. Four years after the disintegration of the Soviet Union, former Communist parties in many of the new states are back in power and are now adopting a new and fervently nationalistic language. But could it be any different? While in the case of the old satellites, the countries were able to draw on some kind of democratic traditions, no matter how rudimentary, the successor states to the Soviet Union have no such tradition. There has not been enough time to form true liberal democratic parties or, in cases where they did already exist, democratic forces are still too weak to inspire popular appeal. Former Communist parties are by far the best organized political forces in these countries.

The 15 republics have always differed in terms of economic development. However, by the early 1990s, divergence between them seemed to have increased. While all of them, at least rhetorically, had moved to free market economies, they had done so at different speeds and by different routes. The economic process was also hampered by political forces opposed to reform as well as economic difficulties and ethnic strife. These constraints were much more serious in the former Soviet Empire than in the old satellites. The result is not only economic and sometimes political chaos, but, in some cases, armed conflict. Thus, the prospect for economic survival differs from region to region, reflecting not only characteristics of the economic and physical environment, but also the different choices made at political level.

Initially the CIS had been established as a substitute for the defunct Soviet Union to take over essential co-ordinating functions in an attempt to establish a common trading area and a centralized control of strategic forces. Somewhat hastily devised and deprived of any meaningful political substance, it provided for a very loose grouping of the former Soviet republics, but it was not an instrument of political or even economic integration as is the EU. While a central command structure for strategic nuclear forces and joint control of nuclear weapons deployed in Russia, the Ukraine, Belarus and Kazakhstan was established, further military integration was thwarted when the Ukraine went ahead with plans for its own independent army, asserted ownership of all nuclear capabilities located on its soil and claimed the Soviet Black Sea fleet, a development further explored in Chapter 14.

Despite repeated rhetoric support for a market economy, enshrined in CIS documents, none of the states has taken serious steps to implement appropriate policies and all of them have been reluctant to take painful measures. The old elite, the nomenklatura, has managed to retain considerable power in most CIS states and has tried to maintain old production patterns and in some cases, has resisted reform attempts. Many of the CIS states, in an attempt to shield themselves from economic crises, have tended to turn inwards in search of short-term economic solutions and isolate themselves. The task is not an easy one for the young republics, because the transition to economic and political independence took place in a complete institutional vacuum. The absence of a central decision-making power led therefore to economic chaos, while hyper-inflation and unemployment emerged as a typical post-Communist syndrome as it did in the satellites. The ecological catastrophe bequeathed by the old order is also hampering economic reconstruction. As a result, many nuclear and industrial plants have to be shut down or their outdated equipment has to be replaced which in turn requires financial investment.

With the dissolution of CMEA, the states had to establish new trading relations, not only with each other, but also with the West. This is hampered by excessive regional specialization, a continuing legacy of central economic planning. The states looked to the West for help. Membership of the IMF has given the countries access to credit facilities, but this is not sufficient to provide the large foreign currency loans required. Western aid could only satisfy very basic and short-term requirements. In addition, the social factor has to be taken into account: attitudes and experiences may still be based on Socialist ideology, and, in some cases might resist the spirit of free enterprise and entrepreneurial experimentation.

In the event, and contrary to expectations, the CIS proved more durable than expected. This was partly due to the recognition by member states that co-operation within the CIS has distinct advantages not least access to Russian markets. But benefits are perhaps greatest for Russia, which has strengthened its position as leader of the CIS winning formal approval for its role as peace-keeper and guardian of the CIS borders. At the CIS summit in April 1994 Russian influence was reasserted. Moscow won final control of most of the Black Sea Fleet, and persuaded Kiev to associate itself with the 'economic union' established in 1993 that links all 12 CIS states. In September 1994 the CIS states agreed to extend their loose economic co-operation to a payments union and to form an interstate economic committee in a drive to strengthen economic ties. The first is designed to put into effect the economic treaties signed by members of the CIS, but often not implemented, the second to achieve speedy settlement of account between states with independent and non-convertible currencies.

Some of the CIS states, for example the Ukraine, have potentially a relatively strong economic structure with a strong agriculture and a variety of industries.

Despite this, until 1994 the Ukraine, whose political elite was dominated by former Communists, has had a reputation as one of the most mismanaged and economically backward republics in the former empire. One of its problem is sheer size – the Ukraine has a population equal to that of Poland, Hungary and the Czech republic combined. It had also inherited a large share of the Soviet Union's defence industries, which are difficult to convert to more market-orientated production. Finally, it is very dependent on Russia for oil and gas – which has contributed to the country's debt. But, with the election of its new President in July 1994, who vested authority in a small but efficient group of reformers, the Ukraine experienced a belated version of the type of radical reforms which have worked in Eastern Europe. In October 1994, the new president Leonid Kuchma announced a comprehensive and detailed economic reform programme. He promised to liberalize prices, slash the budget deficit, privatize state enterprise, stabilize the currency by pegging it to the dollar, cut subsidies and overhaul agriculture. As a result of these severe measures, the Ukraine is hoping for a substantial $4 billion loan from the IMF and other Western credit institutions.

Russia itself with its own wide regional variation faces the full brunt of the transition process. The Polish style 'shock-therapy' reform, implemented in January 1992, amounted initially not only to a continuing fall in output but also to a steady rise in inflation and unemployment. However, the gloomy position has been eased by a generous Western aid package. Commercial banking is one of the fastest growing sectors in the economy with 2214 banks established by mid-1994. A mass privatization programme, putting 70 per cent of industry into private hands has been concluded with 11 000 state-owned enterprises sold to the public through the 148 million vouchers distributed free of charge to every Russian citizen. The second phase of the privatization plan began on 1 July 1994 and is designed to sell the remaining state-owned shares in privatized companies for cash.

Politically, President's Yeltsin position had been considerably strengthened by the constitution accepted by referendum in October 1993. This conferred most power, including that over the army, to the President and moderated the struggle for primacy between the legislative and executive branches. Even the December 1993 elections – producing a strong showing for right and left national groups – and the departure of senior reformers did not result in the abandonment of the reform programme.

However, the 21 per cent fall in the value of the rouble on 11 October 1994 may prove a serious setback, not only economically, but also politically. The crisis sent that year's inflationary rate to a one year high of 6.8 per cent – the highest since September. Indeed, rising inflation, low bank interest rates, a new tax on bank deposits and a presidential decree ordering all transactions of more than $10 000 to be reported to the tax police – were held responsible for the flight of the rouble. But the government acted swiftly. Determined to pursue its radical economic reform programme, the government committed itself to a monthly inflation target of 2 per cent by 1995, and to refraining from both extending credits from the central banks and from the funding of deficits by the issuing of treasury bills and borrowing from the World Bank and the IMF. Nevertheless, the crisis had political repercussions. On 27 October a no-confidence vote was taken in the Russian Parliament and although the government won, albeit by a slim majority, it is clear that opposition to President Yeltsin is growing. The opposing hard core consists of two groups: the Communist party of Russia, led by Gennady Zynganov and the anti-president group of the Liberal Democratic Party, led by the extreme nationalist Vladimir Zhirinovsky.

Perhaps the most dramatic reform process has taken place in the three Baltic states – non-members of the CIS – which have made the cleanest break with the old order, moving ahead with plans for full marketization and an ambitious privatization programme. Taking advantage of the internal turmoil that followed the coup of August 1991, the three countries immediately declared their independence and moved speedily towards the creation of new constitutions and a multi-party political system. Estonia clearly leads the three countries in terms of economic transformation. The country, led by a broadly based coalition government of centre-right parties, has successfully introduced market-based economic reforms and has shifted trade and investment from the former Soviet Union towards the West and Scandinavia. The national currency, the Kroon, introduced in June 1992, is pegged to the Deutsch Mark and backed by the country's rising gold and currencies reserves. Overall GDP is expected to grow by 5 per cent in 1994 boosted by the explosion of the private sector.

The nationality question and ethnic conflicts
Political and economic disorientation are not the only problems in the former Soviet Union, indeed they may not even be the most serious. Far more dangerous potentially, is the emergence of ethno-nationalism which seems to have replaced Communism as an official ideology. As in the old satellites, the new freedom following the disintegration of the Soviet empire gave rise to racism and xenophobia. Over 60 nationalities live in the former USSR, together with some 100 other minority groups. Apart from Yugoslavia, ethnic tension is most acute in the former USSR, although it is present, as has been noted, in all Eastern and central European states. The re-emergence of the nationality question is one of the most fundamental difficulties facing the former Soviet Union today. In 1991 750 people died as the direct result of ethnic riots, but the figure rose alarmingly to 25 000 in 1992. The changes in economic conditions in the former USSR clearly contributed to the emergence of nationalist sentiment and the relationship between material factors and ethnic conflicts is obvious.

The issue of protecting rights of ethnic groups is the cause of most post-Soviet conflicts. Within days of the abortive coup territorial disputes between the various regions and republics emerged. Once it had become clear that there was no central authority which could suppress inter-ethnic disputes, territorial conflicts emerged. The number of these was said to be over 200 – many were the result of forced population movements in the Stalinist period, others due to the arbitrary drawing of borders by Stalin and his successors. The Chechen problem, discussed in Chapter 14, is a good example of this.

A distinction should be made between the various types of nationalism in the former USSR, all of which require different solutions. Some ethnic and minority groups welcomed the collapse of the Soviet empire as a liberation from foreign rule. However, the situation is different for the 25 million ethnic Russians living in ex-Soviet states who, as a result of the new development, found themselves stranded in ethnically hostile successor states. This conflict is particularly acute in the Baltic states, where the large Russian minority – planted deliberately after 1940 when many Baltic natives were deported to Siberia – have not been granted full citizenship and have been denied the right to vote in elections. Both Estonia and Latvia introduced a citizenship law which stipulated that all non-ethnic Estonians and Latvians must pass a language examination as a pre-condition for continued residence. The Estonian government has argued that its sizable minority – mainly ethnic Russians – are immigrants illegally introduced by an occupying power, the Soviet Union.

At the same time the Russian Federation is home to 20 million non-Russians. The concept of statehood has become a popular theme in the country. A group composed of former Communists and right-wing extremists would like to deny non-Russians their ethnic or national rights while living on Russian territory. At the same time, these forces insist that protection must be afforded to Russian citizens living elsewhere. This group takes for granted that non-Russian nationalities living in Russia should learn the national language and adopt the country's laws and conditions. Yet this would be regarded as an unreasonable demand when it comes to Russians living outside the Federation. Some in this group seek to reverse the process of disintegration, others have clearly imperialist aspirations and even demand the re-conquest of the Baltic states, Poland and Finland with a view to establishing a new Russian Empire. This new revisionism, which appears to be widespread in the new Russian leadership, not only threatens the political development in the former Empire, but is a cause of concern for the West as well.

A second distinct type of ethnic conflict concerns rivalries within and between CIS states or between republics of the former Soviet Union and former satellites. Most involve ethnic groups whose national aspirations or territorial demands cut across not only existing state borders, but also any alternative federal frontiers. The conflicts based on this kind of ethno-nationalist issue are numerous and they cannot all be treated here. However, the longest standing conflict in the former Soviet Union is that between Armenia and Azerbaijan and perhaps best illustrates the seriousness of ethnic issues.

The conflict between the two republics preceded the disintegration of the Empire. It began in 1988 over control over the mountain enclave of Nagorno-Karabakh, which, since 1923, has been an autonomous region of Azerbaijan. In that year Nagorno-Karabakh, with a predominantly Christian Armenian population, requested Moscow to return it to Armenian jurisdiction. The fact that Nagorno-Karabakh had long been administered by Azerbaijan had never been accepted by Armenia. The Armenian population of Nagorno-Karabakh claimed it had the right of self-determination, while the Moslem Azeris insisted that the enclave was part of Azerbaijan. When the Soviet Union disintegrated, Nagorno-Karabakh was part of the Azerbaijan state and the Azeris wished it to remain so. The Armenians, however, claimed that, since the region was predominantly inhabited by Armenians, and far more importantly, because the latter had expressed the wish to belong to an Armenian state – clearly exercising their new right of self-determination – the region should be returned to Armenia or became autonomous.

In response to increased unrest within Armenia, many Azeris fled the region during 1988. Subsequently, and due to rumours of ill-treatment of the refugees riots broke out against Armenians in Sumgait (Azerbaijan), when Azeris attacked Armenians living in the country. In January 1990 a large-scale massacre took place in Baku, the capital of Azerbaijan, which in turn triggered violent clashes between the two republics. The Soviet Union intervened by sending in troops, but was unable to mediate between the two states. The conflict over the sovereignty of the region escalated in 1991 into open warfare between Armenia and Azerbaijan. Several mutually agreed ceasefires were breached by one side or the other and both sides accused the Soviet Union and, after its disintegration, Russia, of aiding the other side. Various attempts were made to resolve the conflict, not just by Russia, but also by the USA, Turkey, Iran, the UN and the CSCE.

The conflict which has now lasted for 6 years, has claimed at least 16 000 lives and created a million refugees. The war caused enormous economic hardship, particularly in Armenia, since its supply route from Russia passes through Azerbaijan. The latter enforced an effective blockade against Armenia. Turkey, on the West of Armenia, was more inclined to support Azerbaijan, while a civil war raged in Georgia, to the north of Armenia. The conflict also destabilized the political situation in Azerbaijan. Failure to secure the Karabakh region culminated in the ousting of governments, which failed to win the war.

Prospects

The demise of Soviet dictatorial rule was an event of epoch-making significance. The task the former Communist countries were facing was formidable as it required a simultaneous transformation on three levels: economic transformation, political democratization, and social peace all at the same time. It would be premature to venture a verdict on the experiments in pluralism being conducted in the former Soviet bloc. However, it seems clear that the future of Eastern and central Europe will to a large extent depend on the degree of success in reforming their economies and their ability to create a stable pluralist democracy. The task may be less daunting for the former satellites than the CIS states. The former, in establishing a system of private law, can refer back to experience before the Soviet takeover. Also, the economic links between these states and the West have become closer and more extensive. Finally, the possibility of assimilating into the West is much greater as these countries have association agreements with the EU and both Poland and Hungary have applied for membership.

For the CIS, however, there are other problems. Faced with the emergence of nationalism – jeopardizing stability and creating new territorial controversies – and the relative frailty of the CIS, the question has to be asked whether a consolidation of the new community of former Soviet republics can be achieved amicably. There are several scenarios possible. One might be that the pendulum swings back to the pre-revolutionary situation resulting in the gradual erosion of democratic rule and a return to dictatorial systems. Another undesirable alternative may be the formation of autarchic regional economies with little interaction, either with each other or with the outside world.

A more hopeful scenario would be that common bonds between the individual CIS states become close enough to forge further integration and that the new economic union established will be durable, to the benefit not only of economic wellbeing, but also of secure inter-ethnic peace. Furthermore, assimilation of the states into the West and its organizations cannot, and should not, be ruled out. It is clearly in the West's interest, both economically and from a security angle, to make concertive efforts in assisting both the former Soviet Union and satellites in their difficult transition to ensure that the dreams which once inspired the revolutionary movements can be fulfilled.

Further reading

Bryant, Ch.G.A. and Mokrzycki, E. (eds) (1994), *The New Great Transformation? Change and Continuity In East–Central Europe*, London: Routledge.

Bugajski, J. (1993), *Nations in Turmoil: Conflict and Cooperation in Eastern Europe*, Boulder, Col.: Westview.

Colton, T.J. and Legvold, R. (eds) (1992), *After The Soviet Union*, London: W.W. Norton and Co.

East, R. (1992), *Revolutions in Eastern Europe*, London: Pinter.

Hosking, G.A., Aves, J. and Duncan, P.J.S. (1992), *The Road to Post Communism*, London: Pinter.

Lapidus, G.W., Zaslavzky, V. and Golerman, P. (1993), *From Union to Commonwealth: Nationalism and Separatism in the Soviet Republics*, Cambridge: Cambridge University Press.

Roucek, L. (1992), *After the Bloc: the New International Relations in Eastern Europe*, London: RIIA, Discussion Paper No. 40.

Schoepflin, G. (1993), *Politics in Eastern Europe*, Oxford: Blackwell.

Taras, R. (ed.) (1992), *The Road to Disillusion*, London: M.E.Sharpe.

14   Post-Cold War challenges – the search for a new security order

The signing of the Charter of Paris in December 1990 and the subsequent demise of the Warsaw Pact, symbolizing the end of the Cold War, radically changed the nature of Europe's post-war security order. The shifts which have taken place in the European landscape have been nothing less than dramatic: German division has ended, the Eastern and central European countries have thrown off Soviet-imposed Communist rule, the USSR has disintegrated and the East–West conflict has abated. However, the end of East–West polarization, which had underpinned and sustained Europe during the second part of the century, also carries the seeds of future conflicts.

This Chapter examines three main developments within the changing landscape. The first assesses the new conflicts and security challenges which have emerged as a result of the drastically changed European landscape: regional wars, a revival of nationalism, massive migration, a deepening economic crisis and border disputes have replaced the hostile bipolarity of the post-war decades. Above all, a new division has emerged, no longer characterized by rigid demarcation between East and West, but by fragmentation into several regions at different stages of economic and political development. Moreover, the attempts by former satellites to seek closer relations with the West has produced a new 'velvet curtain' between the republics of the former Soviet Union, particularly Russia, who resent the assimilation of their former 'allies' into Western-type military and political alliances, and the western and central part of Europe.

The second part of the Chapter traces the period of transition from Cold War hostility to the new peace order in Europe by examining the arms control negotiations of the late 1980s and early 1990s. The progress made in disarmament, remarkable though this was, did not really respond to the new security needs. Indeed, it seemed, that at some points, the pace of events actually overtook the process of arms talks and rendered the latter, to some degree, ineffective.

The final part argues that the abrupt end of bipolarity has created a security vacuum and assesses whether existing security organizations, such as NATO, the CSCE or the WEU are capable of filling this void. It suggests that none of the existing agencies are as yet able to address the many-faceted security challenges which have to be faced in the new multipolar system. The Europe of the 1990s, depicted in Map 5, is thus in a period of transition, where the final framework of future security arrangements has yet to emerge.

Security challenges in the 1990s

Unfortunately, the euphoria which accompanied the disintegration of the post-war power structure soon lost its justification. Already by 1991 – barely two years after the revolutions described in Chapter 10 – the prospects for stability no longer looked good. True, East–West relations were no longer soured by ideological antagonism or rivalries between military blocs, but inter-bloc confrontation had been replaced by dormant and often unresolved inter-state conflicts. In 1993 alone there were 34 military conflicts, most of which took place in Europe and virtually all involved disputes over territories. The defunct Communist regimes gave rise to very diverse state interests which changed traditional security concerns. It is now generally accepted that non-military problems, such as economic decline, ethnic tension, massive migration and unstable political systems in the former Communist bloc are the greatest threat to Europe's peace order. Hopefully, these problems are merely growing pains in the transition from dictatorship to democracy.

The changes in the security situation in Europe have come about as a result of both the speed with which the revolutions in central Europe and the disintegration of the USSR took place and the high degree of unpredictability which followed the end of Soviet rule. The sweeping away of the old power structure in the Eastern bloc left a political and military vacuum. No longer was there a unifying centre. As a result the Eastern bloc's economic, political and military fabric collapsed and has as yet only partially been replaced by new structures. A fragmentation of power began to clear the way for potential conflicts. A number of new states emerged with their own internal problems and their own security concerns. This led to critical changes in the European security climate. The breakdown of the bipolar structure has therefore produced a complex, less stable multipolar system.

Developments in Eastern Europe have not been uniform. Parts of the region have, as Chapter 13 has shown, reached a phase of political and economic development almost comparable to Western levels, other parts, however, are still in the initial phase of new state-building. The former Soviet Union remains an area of instability. The disintegration of the Soviet Union was followed by the creation of the CIS which eventually embraced all former Soviet republics with the exception of the three Baltic states. However, with the exception of the latter, the non-Russian states had never known independent statehood in the modern world. In their attempt to establish new political and economic systems, they are faced with new challenges and problems.

Following the dissolution of the Soviet Union a gap opened between Russia and the 11 other CIS states. As the world's second largest nuclear power, Russia was immediately recognized as the legal heir to the USSR. Its military weight, its role in international relations and its radical economic reformist course – which set it apart from other CIS states – have strengthened its position in

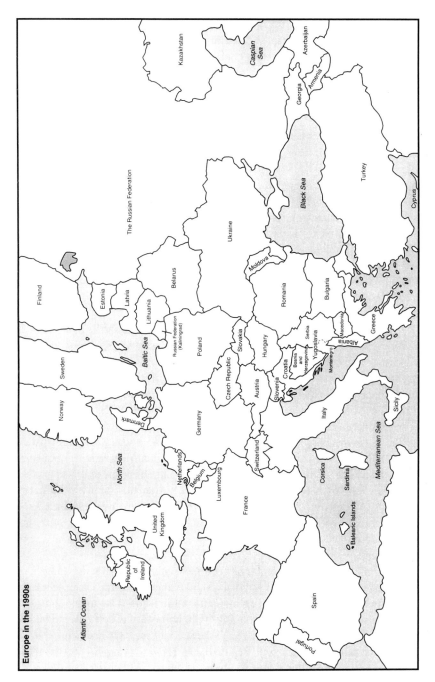

Europe in the 1990s

Map 5

219

relation to the CIS. Such a dominant position carries the seeds of conflict, however, as some countries, the Ukraine in particular, resisted Russian attempts to dominate the CIS. There were conflicts between the two countries over the Black Sea Fleet, the ownership and control of which remained one of the main irritants in Russian–Ukrainian relations. A number of compromises such as joint command or division of the Fleet have not resulted in a permanent settlement of this issue.

Russia itself is a potential source of conflict which might spill over into other regions. Its military and economic weight has encouraged nationalist forces to pursue neo-imperialistic goals. The conflict between president Boris Yeltsin and anti-reformist forces resulted in dramatic civil unrest in the autumn of 1993. Although the national referendum of 12 December confirmed Russia's new constitution, the parliamentary elections showed a high degree of preference (40 per cent) for nationalist and Communists candidate. More importantly, however, the declaration of independence by the breakaway Russian republic of Chechnya led in December 1994 to a clash between invading Russian troops and forces loyal to the republic. The possibility that the forceful assertion of independence by Chechnya is a precedent, and that other provinces of the Russian federation might follow suit, cannot be ruled out.

Conflicts in the former USSR are not confined to Russia and its relations with other members of the CIS. During 1993 the Caucasus was the scene of heavy fighting, where over 40 ethnic and territorial conflicts took place making this region extremely unstable. As already noted in Chapter 13, the worst fighting took place between Armenia and Azerbaijan over the status of Nagorno-Karabakh, a conflict which predated disintegration of the USSR. In Abkhazia – an autonomous territory in Georgia – a domestic dispute turned violent and spilled over the border raising the spectre of another war with Afghanistan. Numerous atrocities were committed against the civilian population with several thousand deaths and one million refugees. Tajikistan suffers the effects of a three-year civil war. With a population of less than 6 million, the country has suffered over 300 000 casualties. Despite the collective security agreement to which some CIS members have become signatories, and the establishment of peace-keeping forces in troubled regions, restoration of peace has not been possible in any of these areas.

Economic decline was sometimes coupled with civil war as in Georgia or inter-state conflict as between Azerbaijan and Armenia. Falling living standards and armed conflicts put the fledgling democratic institutions under considerable strain, especially in those countries with no history of self-determination. The reform-minded leaders in some of these countries have been undermined by fervent nationalists and anti-free marketeers, who attempt to prevent these countries from becoming too Western-orientated. Deterioration of living conditions provided a fertile breeding ground for extreme nationalism, xenophobia and the possible re-emergence of aggressive dictatorships. Most CIS states, economically dependent on Russia, have preserved much of the inherited and outdated economic systems, as have the former satellites in the Balkans. It is imperative to safeguard or consolidate the new fragile democratic structures, as the collapse of these embryonic political systems could give rise to dictatorships and to violation of territorial integrity. There is also a link between security and ecological policies, as environmental damage affects the physical and mental wellbeing of the people through disease and social distress.

In the former satellites, the security climate is less unstable. The reasons for this is that ties have been formed on a regional level: Poland, Hungary, the Czech Republic and Slovakia (the Visegrad group) have signed agreements to begin regular contacts between their armed forces as a replacement to Warsaw Pact co-operation. Moreover, some of these states have also pursued their security through Western alliances, (as shown later in this Chapter), while Poland and Hungary have already applied for membership of the EU. Nevertheless, the security climate is unpredictable here too, because of the various ethnic disputes discussed in Chapter 13, and the civil war in former Yugoslavia with possible repercussions on neighbouring states.

The Yugoslav civil war is, as Chapter 15 shows, one of the worst examples of the new wave of ethno-national conflicts which have erupted in post-Communist Europe. This is to some extent surprising, since Yugoslavia was the first country to embark on its own individual road to Socialism, and had asserted its independence even in the face of Soviet vexation. Furthermore, after the Second World War, Yugoslavia was liberated not by the Red Army, but by internal efforts. However, a weak central authority coupled with social, political, cultural and religious differences between the main national groupings, eventually gave rise to violent conflicts. This not only led to the break-up of the country and civil war, but is threatening the stability of the neighbouring countries. The argument that the Balkan conflict might once again, as in 1914, escalate into a European war, is too simplistic. However, the fear of some spillover drawing in Albania, Bulgaria and Hungary, Greece and Turkey is justified. Importantly, the crisis has put the impotence and weakness of existing security policies into sharper relief.

One factor which raised the spectrum of profound political instability in Europe, albeit only briefly, was German unification. While the goal of a united Germany was set down in the 1949 constitution setting up the FRG, reunification has never been a component of the FRG's official foreign policy agenda. The basic driving force for unification was the East German people, not the Bonn government. Thus, unity was thrust upon a nation which had already resigned itself to division. The fall of the Berlin Wall on 9 November 1989 set the process in motion which led both to speedy unification within 12 months, as well as to a process of accelerated development in the EC, set out in Chapter 11.

Since German unification required the legal approval of the Four Powers, negotiations were conducted within the framework of the 'two-plus-four' (two Germanies and the four allies) conferences which settled issues such as the borders of the united Germany, the size of its army and its alliance membership. These negotiations were completed within six months, and Germany became united on 3 October 1990, barely 11 months after the fall of the Berlin Wall. The East German *Länder* were incorporated into the federal structure under Art. 23 of the Basic Law, which has since become superfluous and has been eliminated from the German Constitution. This also meant that the integration of East Germany into the EC constituted an 'enlargement without accession'. In other words, no modification of the EC treaty was necessary, as no special accession arrangements for a separate state were required. It was simply a matter of an existing state having 'enlarged' its territories.

Because West German laws were immediately applied to the new East German *Länder*, the latter experienced the problems of transformation in a different, and mitigated way from that found in the other former satellites. While there had been an increase in both unemployment and inflation as the direct result of unification, united Germany had, by the winter of 1994, begun to recover from the recession. Real GDP growth has risen from (minus) 1.1 per cent in 1993 to 2.5 per cent in 1994 and is expected to reach 3.0 per cent in 1995. Inflation too, which was at a record high of 3.9 per cent in 1993 has dropped to 3.0 per cent in 1994 and is expected to fall to an estimated 2.5 per cent in 1995. Unemployment is still unacceptably high at 9.6 per cent, albeit with wide regional differences: it is forecast to remain at an average of 8.2 per cent for western Germany, while in the East it will rise to 13 per cent.

While the prospect of German unification had initially fuelled fear and suspicion, the end of the division of the German nation also healed the division in Europe. Germany, which had straddled the border of two different and hostile systems, is now a link between East and West. But because unification also restored Germany's former central political and geographical position, Europe's security very much depends on stability in Germany itself. United Germany, the economic powerhouse of the EU, holds an influential position in the network of European political, economic and military institutions. However, it is also the only EU and NATO country with a direct long border with countries of the former Eastern bloc: as such Germany is very exposed to political and economic instability in the East.

Another reason for concern over security is the massive population movement taking place between East and West in general and between different parts of central and Eastern Europe in particular. The impact of this is socially destabilizing for the countries themselves, but perhaps more importantly, has also precipitated nationalistic counter-reactions from some groups in the host countries. There has been a growth of xenophobic political parties in France,

Italy and particularly Germany, where the influx of refugees resulted in the rise of neo-Fascism, when violence reached a peak in the August 1992 Rostock riots. Germany is particularly vulnerable to unrest in Eastern Europe for historical reasons and, as a result of its geographical location and economic interests, Europe needs German involvement in central European political and economic development as a stabilizing factor in the transition process in the East. Thus the massive refugee flows present one of the most serious threats to Western stable democracies and rates as one of the top security concerns in some Western states.

Thus, the menaces of the 1990s have an entirely different character from those of the past 45 years. The ideological and military division of Europe has been replaced by an economic and sociopolitical one. The focus of security in Europe is no longer on military confrontation, or strategic deterrence, which – no matter how deplorable in moral terms – were easily identifiable. Instead, a range of less tangible factors and problems have to be addressed, such as economic dislocation, extreme nationalism and massive migration. Europe's stability is therefore closely linked to the sociopolitical development in Eastern and central Europe. Much will depend on the speed with which these countries can build strong political democratic systems.

While the East is subjected to forces of fragmentation, the integration process in the West has been consolidated. Military conflicts among these countries are judged unthinkable by virtue of ever closer political and economic links. Ironically, however, as the barriers of the nation-state are gradually abolished in the West, it seems that the East is in the process of erecting new ones. Indeed, one could argue that Europe is still divided, that a new 'velvet curtain' has emerged between the former Communist East and the West. So, although the barriers of the 1990s are less visible than those of the past, they are potentially more dangerous and less controllable than the hostile East–West relations of former years. Thus, the end of the Cold War has given rise to new dangers, which, paradoxically, are all linked to the collapse of Communism and the disintegration of the Soviet Empire. These problems are likely to dominate Europe's new security environment for the foreseeable future.

Arms control: from negotiations to implementation

Between the late 1980s and early 1990s, the security agenda was dominated by the negotiation of several arms control treaties signed in rapid succession. The INF (1987) and CFE (1990) treaties still reflected the Cold War confrontation, while the conclusion of the Treaty between the USA and Soviet Union on the reduction and limitation of strategic offensive arms (START 1) of 1991, followed by START 2 (1993) took place in the new political environment of sweeping changes. These agreements completed the bilateral arms control negotiations between the former hostile blocs which had started 25 years before.

The destruction of INF missiles – as provided for in the INF treaty – was completed in May 1991, making Europe free of nuclear missiles with a range of 500–5500 km. However, by the time the other three treaties were being ratified and implemented, the security situation in Europe had changed. The focus therefore was no longer on arms control negotiations, but on securing the implementation and verification of the various treaty provisions already agreed. However, attempts to do so took place against the background of the disintegration of the Soviet Union and raised questions about the control and security of the former empire's nuclear and conventional arms potential.

The CFE Treaty, although negotiated with remarkable speed, had been overtaken by events, the most spectacular of which were German unification and the collapse of the Warsaw Pact, the latter rendering the content of the Treaty – a balance of forces between NATO and Warsaw Pact – essentially meaningless. Nevertheless, ratification and implementation of the Treaty was deemed necessary as it symbolized the end of post-war military confrontation. However, disagreements among the signatories to the Treaty soon emerged. The dissolution of the Soviet Union into sovereign republics raised the question whether Gorbachev's signature on the Treaty would be binding on those successor states whose territories were affected by the Treaty: the three Baltic states, the Russian Federation, Belarus, the Ukraine, Moldavia, Georgia, Kazakhstan, Armenia and Azerbaijan. Thus, the dissolution of the Soviet Union raised questions of international law.

As a result of the uncertainty over the legality of the CFE treaty, negotiations were conducted in 1991 between NATO and the erstwhile Warsaw Pact members and, in May 1992, the 22 delegations agreed that the Treaty did not apply to the territories of the three Baltic states, but that the weaponry employed there by the former Soviet Union would be included in the Soviet ceilings. Furthermore, the eight former Soviet republics with territories in the CFE Treaty's zone of application reached agreement on how to divide among themselves the allocation of arms limited by the Treaty. Just over half of these went to Russia, a quarter to the Ukraine and the remainder was divided among the five other states. This agreement opened up the way for a special conference of all member states taking part to amend the CFE treaty to take account of the dissolution of the Soviet Union. On 17 July 1992 the CFE Treaty came into force. By the end of November all NATO countries, the five former satellites and the eight republics of the former Soviet Union which lie west of the Urals, had ratified the Treaty. The conference, held under the auspices of the CSCE, also opened negotiations on a new CFE-1A agreement which would set ceilings for military personnel each country can employ within the Atlantic-to-the-Urals area. These were set at levels declared by the parties themselves.

The problems of ratification and implementation of the START treaties were more serious. START 1 was the most significant arms control agreement ever negotiated between the two former blocs. Originally launched on 29 June 1982 by the USA and the Soviet Union in Geneva, the talks – though deadlocked several times – continued for nine years and were concluded at the Moscow summit meeting on 31 July 1991. The Treaty required a significant reduction of strategic offensive arms of approximately 30 per cent in three stages over seven years including a scrupulously developed verification system allowing for on-site inspection. Significantly, entry into force of START 1 was a precondition for the implementation of START 2, signed in January 1993 between the USA and Russia, and reducing the two powers' nuclear arsenals by one third within a decade.

By 1992 the political actors involved in nuclear arms talks had changed, which raised questions about the control of nuclear capacity in the former Soviet Union. The Russian Federation had declared itself the successor to the Soviet Union and, as such, responsible for all international treaty obligations. In the case of START this made sense, as Russia held 83.7 per cent of the former empire's nuclear weapons, but 27.4 per cent were also located in the Ukraine, 5.6 per cent in Kazakhstan and 2.16 per cent in Belarus. This implied that, since the old empire had disintegrated into 15 independent republics, all such states with nuclear capacity had to ratify and implement the Treaty.

However, since then, the three non-Russian republics with nuclear weapons on their soil, particularly the Ukraine, began to object to Russia's assumed hegemony as the 'nuclear successor state' to the Soviet Union and forcefully asserted their right to remain 'nuclear' states themselves. This conflict became the subject of intense negotiations in 1992 making START 1 the first test of arms control in a highly unstable, multipolar international system. In an attempt to resolve the issue, the US and the four CIS states with nuclear capacity met in Lisbon on 23 May 1992 and signed a protocol to the START 1 treaty that identified all four former Soviet republics as bilateral US treaty partners. The three non-Russian states also agreed to sign the NPT and pledged to eliminate all strategic weapons on their territories within seven years of the implementation of START 1 thereby agreeing to move to a non-nuclear status.

For a while, it seemed that the matter had been settled satisfactorily. Kazakhstan, the USA, Russia and Belarus ratified START 1 between July 1992 and February 1993. However, the Ukraine drew back from earlier undertakings and attached 13 conditions to the Treaty, the ratification of which was made conditional firstly, on the receipt of financial compensations for dismantling the weapon systems covered by START, and secondly, on security guarantees from both the USA and Russia in terms of Ukraine's territorial integrity. The Ukrainian case presented a new challenge to the stability of Europe. Not only did the country's reservations jeopardize the START treaties, but it had also consequences for the future of the nuclear non-proliferation regime.

In January 1994 a deal involving the USA, Russia and the Ukraine was struck. The Ukrainian Parliament agreed to transfer all nuclear warheads to Russia within seven years of implementation of the Treaty. In return the Ukraine would be supplied with (Russian) fuel rods for nuclear power, and US financial aid. An undertaking was also jointly given by Russia, the USA, the UK and France in terms of Ukraine's territorial integrity, provided the Ukraine would sign the NPT treaty. As a result of this agreement, the Ukrainian Parliament, on 3 February 1994, voted to remove all the conditions it had previously attached to the Treaty. But it stopped short of approving its former President Leonid Kravchuk's promise that the Ukraine would become a non-nuclear state, by postponing ratification of the NPT.

Yet despite these difficulties, and as a result of budgetary pressures and reduced threat perception, the dismantling of what remains of the post-war military confrontation appeared to be continuing. The terms of the US-Russian START 2 treaty (signed in January 1993) required further significant reductions in the respective numbers of nuclear warheads by the year 2003. This was hailed as a historic achievement. During the same month the multilateral Chemical Weapons Convention was signed. Three months later the newly elected American President Bill Clinton and Russia's President Boris Yeltsin agreed to commence negotiations on a comprehensive test ban (CTB) and to strengthen the 1968 NPT agreement. Both Belarus and Kazakhstan acceded to the NPT in July 1993 and February 1994 respectively, while the newly elected Ukrainian President Leonid Kuchma has expressed hopes that his country would follow suit in due course.

Indeed, the issue was finally successfully resolved by the winter of 1994. On 16 November the Ukraine's parliament ratified the NPT by a comfortable majority and thus improved its strained relations with both Russia and the West. Three weeks later, on 5 December, at the CSCE conference in Budapest, the Ukraine, the world's third-largest nuclear power, formally joined the NPT. Under the agreement, the USA, Russia and Britain pledged to respect Ukraine's territorial integrity, and to seek help from the UN Security Council if it faced nuclear aggression. The agreement was considered a diplomatic breakthrough clearing the way for the START 1 treaty.

While arms control is still a relevant issue, it has become clear that military confrontation and the stabilization of the balance of forces – which have dominated East–West relations for 25 years – have run its course. This would imply that Europe's existing security institutions have become outdated and need to adopt to the new challenges. Cold War organizational structures – well suited to manage arms control issues – lack experience in tackling the new security problems.

The pillars of Europe's new security order
As a result of the dramatic upheavals and tumultuous changes, there is therefore an urgent need to rethink strategies, reformulate concepts and develop existing

organizational structures of Europe's multilateral security institutions. It is against the background of violent ethnic tension and economic dislocation that attention has been focused on building a new European security regime. The revolutions in the East, the civil war in Yugoslavia and the disintegration of the Soviet Union encouraged debates on existing security structures which needed to be reviewed in the light of recent events. Neither NATO, nor the EU or the CSCE had sufficiently developed strategies to either manage the contemporary crises or to prevent further conflicts.

The West's major military alliance, NATO, accepted the need for a redefinition of Europe's security arrangement. Firstly, the military structure of the Warsaw Pact was formerly dissolved on 31 March 1991 and all former Soviet troops were withdrawn from central Europe by 1994 making a surprise attack highly unlikely. Secondly, the collapse of the Berlin wall ended the geographical, political and military division of Europe. Thirdly, East–West confrontation gradually gave way to a new form of partnership between the erstwhile enemies. Virtually every country in central and eastern Europe expressed a desire to join with NATO forcing the existing members to develop new structures to respond to such a sudden shift in allegiances.

Consequently, after the fall of the Berlin wall, the Western Alliance engaged in a strategic review in order to formulate a new purpose for its members. Decisions taken at NATO conferences between July 1990 and December 1991 led to a revision of the Alliance's structure in an attempt to redefine its role in international politics. The command structure was streamlined and the level of forces was reduced. The new strategy removed the idea of 'flexible response' and defined the Alliance's new security policy as one based on dialogue and co-operation with the countries of eastern and central Europe. It was also emphasized that the Alliance was now purely defensive in purpose, and, if attacked, would only act militarily in self-defence.

In an attempt to consolidate *rapprochement* with Eastern Europe, a series of decisions were taken between October 1993 and January 1994. The first was an initiative, launched by the then US Secretary of State James Baker and former German foreign minister Hans-Dietrich Genscher, which led to the creation of the North Atlantic Co-operation Council (NACC) in December 1991. This, alongside with existing Nato members, includes former Warsaw Pact countries, the three Baltic states, and 11 of the successor states to the Soviet Union. NACC is a forum for co-operation between NATO and its erstwhile adversaries, the former members of the former Warsaw Pact. Its purpose is to provide a forum for dialogue between East and West on security issues, although the Alliance resisted pressure from Eastern European states to offer them full membership.

Nevertheless, the possibility of an eastward expansion of NATO remained very much on the agenda and has provoked contradictory responses, not only from the central and Eastern European countries, but also from NATO members themselves. In 1993, as the former satellites progressed on the path to democracy, their desire to be become completely independent of the former USSR increased and so did their interest in joining NATO and the EU. This objective was re-emphasized by the developments in Russia: the countries wanted to avoid being treated as a Russian area of interest. But as Poland, Hungary and the Czech Republic moved towards applying for full membership, problems emerged. Russia became concerned about its territorial integrity and the possibility of isolation and in a letter of 15 September 1993 from Boris Yeltsin to President Clinton and other Western leaders, the Russian President objected to any of the former satellites becoming a member of NATO.

This issue intensified the debate within NATO itself on the development of the Western Alliance and its role in the new security order. Three principal groups, whose views had been largely influenced by political events in Russia and the Yugoslav civil war, thus came into conflict. The first group, led by Germany, desired the immediate enlargement of NATO to include the central European countries. This was to ensure stability during the system transformation in that region. The second group, led by the UK, was determinedly opposed to expansion and argued that the Alliance still lacked a clear vision of a future-orientated security concept. Too radical adaptation and restructuring would be required to cover new areas and extend existing guarantees to new members. Furthermore, an eastward expansion of NATO could be seen by Russia as a forward base from which NATO power would threaten Moscow and might, by encouraging conservative nationalist forces, lead to a new militarization of that country. The third group, led by France, advocated either a gradual expansion of NATO or the provision of associate status, but wanted to attach conditions to the offer, because it was feared that NATO might get involved in national and ethnic conflicts of Eastern and central Europe. France in particular insisted that prospective members must settle their territorial conflicts and minority issues before joining.

In an attempt to bring about a compromise between these opposing groups and positions, a US-inspired 'Partnership for Peace' (PFP) – a military co-operation programme offered to all central and Eastern European nations – was presented at the NATO summit in January 1994. The first to join was Estonia on 3 January. By July 1994, 22 countries including Russia had joined, only Armenia, Belarus and Tajikistan held back, although they are members of NACC. Russia had initially resisted the invitation to join in an attempt to gain a special status in NATO. By suggesting that the CSCE should be the prime security forum, Russia hoped to reduce NATO's role and influence in post-Cold War Europe.

Although Russia joined the PFP on 22 June 1994, it continued to press for the 53-nation CSCE to be upgraded into a European security umbrella. Russia's uneasiness over NATO's planned eastward expansion was further fuelled when NATO, at its 1 December 1994 meeting of foreign ministers in Brussels announced its enlargement programme. In fact, Warren Christopher, the US Secretary of State, had urged his European counterparts to accelerate the process of enlargement and to hammer out criteria and procedures for incorporating newcomers by next spring.

Russia's response was swift. At the Budapest CSCE summit meeting, on 5 December 1994, Boris Yeltsin, sharply denounced NATO's plan to expand into Eastern Europe and warned that the continent could slide from a Cold War into 'cold peace'. Yeltsin also insisted that the CIS be recognized as an international organization that could guarantee security in the former Soviet Union. This was interpreted as effectively Russia's demand for the recognition of its 'sphere of influence'. Yeltsin's speech was in sharp contrast to that of US President Bill Clinton, who, in an address immediately beforehand, had hailed NATO as the 'bedrock of security in Europe' and had emphasized that no country could exercise a veto on its expansion. In an implicit rejection of the Russian demand for supremacy within the former Soviet Union, both President Clinton and Chancellor Helmut Kohl of Germany spoke out against the notion that powerful countries could impose their will over smaller neighbours.

At the time of writing, these issues had not been resolved. Clearly, NATO is still in transition from a Cold War military organization to providing a framework for a pan-European security system. Recent events have raised questions about the whole purpose and future of the Alliance which is still in search of a role.

The collapse of the bipolar international order also gave rise to new expectations about the CSCE's role in a future security framework. As a result of the November 1990 Paris Charter and the July 1992 Helsinki summit, the CSCE process has been institutionalized and strengthened through a parliamentary assembly, a permanent secretariat, an election monitor centre and a conflict prevention centre – all set up in different European capitals. Regular meetings between foreign ministers and senior officials take place to discuss arms control, crisis management and human rights.

After the Paris euphoria, however, the Helsinki process became more elusive and the past years have not altogether justified earlier expectations. No sooner were the new institutions and mechanism established, than they were subjected to a severe test. In the case of Yugoslavia the CSCE failed miserably. Despite the development of the 'mechanism for consultation and co-operation with regard to emergency situation' during the Berlin CSCE Council Meeting in June 1991, the organization has been of little value in solving the crisis. The limitations of the Helsinki process were revealed by Yugslovia's veto in 1991 over a proposed CSCE conference on the future of the country. The Yugoslav experience underscored the impotence of the CSCE. Rather, as Chapter 15 makes clear, it was the EU and the UN who were involved in the Yugoslav crisis, although in terms of outcome they did not fare much better.

Renewed efforts in 1992 resulted in the CSCE playing a more effective role in conflict prevention and crisis management. The process of unanimous decision-making was modified and the principle of 'consensus minus one' was adopted for most decisions. The Office of Free Elections, based in Warsaw, was renamed the 'Office of Democratic Institutions and Human Rights' and given a central role in the sphere of civil liberties, constitutional government and the rule of law. Russia had taken over the USSR seat in the CSCE, but the latter's membership increased from its original 34 members to 38, when Albania and the three Baltic states joined and again to 48, when ten CIS states joined. During 1992 Georgia, Croatia, Slovenia and Bosnia-Hercegovina become full members, while federal Yugoslavia was suspended. At the end of the year, the Czech and Slovak republics were admitted which meant that membership of the CSCE stood at 53.

The fourth CSCE follow-up meeting in Helsinki in the summer of 1992 concluded with the adoption of reformulated aims and structures entitled 'The Challenges of Change'. The council of foreign ministers was confirmed as the 'central decision-making and governing body of the CSCE, while the committee of senior officials was to be responsible for 'overview, management and co-ordination' of CSCE activities. Perhaps most significant was the decision to create a High Commissioner on National Minorities reflecting the view that this presented the major security threat in the Europe of the 1990s. The role of the High Commissioner was to provide 'early warning' and, if necessary, 'early action' with regards to troublespots. A further important initiative of the Helsinki meeting was the decision to provide the CSCE with the capability to undertake operational peace-keeping functions which were to conform to UN principles and resolutions and could if necessary be placed under UN authority. The third important initiative which emerged from the Helsinki meeting was the decision to establish a Forum for Security Co-operation with a 'programme for immediate action'. The latter was allocated three priority tasks: negotiating new disarmament and confidence building measures, harmonizing existing obligations and formulating codes of conduct on civil-military relations.

The Helsinki follow-up appears to have boosted CSCE efforts. In 1992 and 1993 activities concentrated mainly on crisis management, advising democracies on human rights and citizenship and the further strengthening of CSCE institutions. At the same time, the CSCE intensified its relations with the UN, the Council of Europe, NATO and the WEU. In 1992 monitoring teams were employed in countries bordering Yugoslavia, Nagorno-Karabakh, Georgia and Moldova.

During 1993 missions of long duration were employed in Moldova, to effect a settlement of the conflict there and in Estonia and Latvia to advise the governments on questions of citizenship and related issues. A new mission was established for Tajikistan where a civil war raged and, in October 1993, a team of experts was dispatched to Nagorno-Karabakh to prepare a report and make recommendations on the political and military situation there. The setting up of such permanent representation was intended to demonstrate CSCE involvement. The CSCE was also credited, together with the UN and the WEU, with preventing a spill-over of the Balkan conflict into Kossovo and Macedonia and for endorsing sanctions against Serbia and Montenegro. But it was not successful in ending armed conflict in Bosnia-Herzegovina, Georgia, Nagorno-Karabakh or other regions of the former Soviet Union. However, the CSCE has no military power, and relies on persuasive diplomacy only. The creation of the Office of the High Commissioner on National Minorities – which was set up by the Helsinki summit meeting – made headway in addressing ethnic issues in Albania, the Baltic States, Hungary, Macedonia, Romania and Slovakia with all recommendations accepted by the governments concerned.

The limitation of the CSCE progress does not mean that it is becoming obsolete. Perhaps its greatest contribution to Europe's security has been in the past, when it was instrumental in overcoming the division of Europe. As the German Foreign Minister Kinkel said to a CSCE meeting in Vienna on 17 May 1994, the CSCE has 'an overriding responsibility for the prevention of new divisions in Europe'. The new tasks that would have to be tackled are therefore different from those of before 1989. The greatest danger in the 1990s is fragmentation and the splitting of Europe into regions with varying security objectives. The CSCE has made some contribution to Europe's (still fragmented) post-Cold War security concept. The all-embracing character of the CSCE would make it a most suitable forum for discussing panEuropean issues. The increased membership means that the new security area of the CSCE process spans not only Europe and North America, but also Central Asia and the Far East – which is a significant expansion of geographical scope.

Finally, what role, if any, has the EU in the security debate of the 1990s? As the NATO summit in Rome in November 1991 made clear, NATO saw no contradiction between Western European security co-operation and the strengthening of solidarity between NATO members and the emergence of a separate West European security identity. The Gulf crisis stimulated negotiations about the need to develop a European defence system which could cope with crises outside NATO borders. The Yugoslav civil war lent further urgency to discussions on an EC security policy. The latter, however, evolved only gradually and slowly. Originally a loose form of co-operation – known as EPC – which worked on a strictly intergovernmental basis, it was drawn into EC official policy-making for the first time by the SEA. It was then further strengthened by the Maastricht Treaty, which states that there will be 'the eventual framing of a common defence policy which might in time lead to a common defence'. In addition, the Treaty declares that the WEU – revived in 1984 when Spain and Portugal joined – is to be developed as a defence component of the EU and become an integral part of its development.

However, notwithstanding the Treaty, it is still unclear how the EU will play a role in the security of Europe both in the short and long term. It will be extremely difficult to transform the EU into a forum for defense decisions. One of the reason for this is that there are two conflicting views on a common defence policy. The first group, consisting of France, Germany, Spain and Belgium have indicated a support for a 'European model', a desire to develop a fully fledged common defense policy anchored in the EU. According to these countries, WEU should be further developed as a defence arm of a future EU. Against this, the so-called 'Atlanticists', including Britain, The Netherlands, Denmark, Ireland and, occasionally supported by, Italy, oppose any weakening of the Western Alliance, and maintain that a continuing American military commitment to Europe is still a necessary prerequisite for maintaining the stability of the continent. This would imply that NATO's traditional role in Europe's security architecture must be maintained and safeguarded. The WEU could be developed as a 'European pillar' of NATO rather than being developed as the EU's own defence component. While it is generally accepted by this group that some lessons have to be learnt from both the Gulf War and the Yugoslav crisis, there is strong resistance to the EU acquiring an independent defence identity. The conflict between Atlanticists and Europeanists imply that, for the time being neither the EU nor the WEU can replace NATO as the cornerstone of European security.

In the course of 1991, these two competing views collided during negotiations on the Maastricht Treaty thanks to two important initiatives: an Anglo–Italian 'Declaration on European Security and Defence' of 4 October 1991, which supported a reinforcement of the role of the WEU, supplementing but not replacing NATO, and the Kohl–Mitterrand Letter of 16 October 1991. The latter called for 'a genuine European security and defence identity', in which the WEU would be developed into an autonomous defence body of the EU. Subsequent complex and difficult negotiations at the IGC led to the inclusion of a Common Foreign and Security Policy in the Maastricht Treaty and represents a partial gain for the 'Euro-group' since it gives the EU a greater role in security and the right to call on the WEU 'to elaborate and implement decisions and actions of the Union which have defence implications'.

However, as Chapter 11 has outlined, while it was agreed to pursue a common foreign and security policy, this was to remain an intergovernmental process, outside the communitarian structures and with qualified majority voting on certain issues. The Treaty suggested that a common foreign and security policy would include 'eventually the framing of a common defence policy which might in time lead to a common defence' and that the WEU would become an 'integral part' of the Union and would act as its 'defence component'. At the same time in response to pressure from the UK, Maastricht accepted that WEU actions had to 'respect the obligations of certain member states under the North Atlantic Treaty and be compatible with the common security and defence policy established within that framework'.

Nevertheless the 'European model' appears to have gained ground. The WEU, by the end of 1992 had moved its headquarters from London and Paris to Brussels. By April 1993 a small military operations cell was at work. WEU's second enlargement, in November 1992, admitted Greece, Denmark and Ireland as observers, while Iceland, Norway and Turkey became associate members. The WEU, very much like NATO, has developed a partnership scheme with Bulgaria, the Czech Republic, Estonia, Hungary, Latvia, Lithuania, Poland, Romania and Slovakia who have agreed to become associate members of WEU. The new members of the EU, Austria, Sweden and Finland, also have the right to join.

A core group of countries in the EU have already moved ahead in terms of closer co-operation in the area of defence. In 1982, President Mitterrand and Chancellor Kohl, upgraded the 1963 Elysée Treaty by creating a Franco–German Security and Defence Council and a 4200-strong Joint Brigade. The collapse of Communism in Eastern Europe, but particularly the unification of Germany gave a new sense of urgency to French interests in security policies. Paris wanted to lock the newly united Germany into the Western structures. In October 1991 Mitterrand and Kohl announced their intention to establish a Franco–German European Corps, to be placed under the umbrella of the WEU. This 35 000 strong corps is clearly intended to be the kernel of a future European army, although still under NATO operational command in the event of attack. Its membership has been opened up to other Western European states. Spain, Luxembourg and Belgium are now contributing small contingents. But there are still many issues unresolved. The relationship between the Union and WEU and Eurocorps is still too loosely defined. The question remains whether the EU should consider the use of military force to settle the multi-faceted conflicts in Europe. Some member states seem to advocate the use of peacekeeping force under the control of the WEU. However, this could cause resentment, both against EU intervention in principle and against some individual member states, e.g. Germany. On the other hand, for the new CFSP to be taken seriously, the EU needs to develop its military capability.

Another problem is the planned enlargement of the EU to include six former satellites. The principle of membership for these countries has been agreed at the European Council's summit meeting in Essen, Germany, in December 1994, although no date has as yet been set. It is assumed, however, that membership negotiations could be concluded as early as 2000. The question remains, what position Russia would take on this issue, particularly in view of President Yeltsin's firm resistance to NATO's planned expansion towards the East.

Continuing security problems

Despite the fact that East–West confrontation has abated, the security challenges in the 1990s are still grave. Economic dislocation and weak institutional structures could destabilize the fledgling democracies and a return to dictatorial rule is a clear possibility. The socioeconomic divide of Europe entails in itself latent dangers, while the conflict in Chechnya is an unpleasant example of what might be in store. Against these dangers, Europe is making strenuous efforts to establish multilateral fora in which to discuss these problems and find solutions.

Assessments as to what the future holds in terms of post-Cold War security range from predictions of a new system of collaboration to fears of a revival of separatism and fragmentation. At present, security matters in Europe are managed by several and overlapping organizations each of which has a different view of how to deal with Europe's security problems.

The new architecture of European security rests therefore on several pillars: the EU, which, for the time being is not a military power as such, but is debating its strategic role in the new security climate. For it to be viable and effective, it would have to become a federation with a common defence policy and an integrated military force. Secondly, NATO has adapted to the recent changes since the breaking up of the Warsaw Pact and disintegration of the Soviet Union, but a new conflict has emerged centering on the Alliance's planned 'eastward' expansion. At present, it would seem that NATO competes with the EU's embryonic defence system, while a total replacement of NATO with an EU defence regime is as yet not justifiable and would, at any rate, be resisted by some European countries. And finally, could the CSCE, which institutionally is the weakest of the three, but with the widest membership of 53 countries, comprising all Europe, parts of Asia, as well as Canada and the United States, become the umbrella security organization? There is considerable interlocking and overlapping between these various organizations as is emphasized in Chapter 15. However, this would seem to be unavoidable, at least until a new and pan-European security system has fully evolved.

Further progress towards European integration is seen by some observers as an important pillar of a new security architecture. As Vaclav Havel put it: 'Europe should gradually move towards the ideal of an entirely new security system as a forerunner of a future united Europe which would provide some sort of security background or security guarantees. Within some five years a community could be established on European soil that we might call the Organization of European States.' Compare this situation with the Cold War years when Europe was partitioned and divided into two hostile, heavily armed camps. From that point of view the security architecture of Europe has come a long way.

Further reading

Alting von Geusau, F.A.M. (1992), *Beyond Containment and Division. Western Cooperation From a Post-Totalitarian Perspective*, Dordrecht: Martinus Nijhoff.

Buchan, D. (1993), *Europe: the Strange Superpower*, Aldershot: Dartmouth.

Jackson, R.J. (ed.) (1992), *Europe in Transition. The Management of Security after the Cold War*, London: Adamantine Press.

Jopp, M., Rummel, R. and Schmidt, P. (eds) (1991), *Integration and Security in Western Europe*, Oxford: Westview.

McInnes, C. (ed.) (1992), *Security and Strategy in the New Europe*, London: Routledge.

Pugh, M.C. (ed.) (1992), *European Security – Towards 2000*, Manchester: Manchester University Press.

Rummel, R. (ed.) (1992), *Toward Political Union*, Boulder, Col.: Westview.

Waever, O., Buzan, B., Kelstrup, M. *et al.* (1993), *Identity, Migration and the New Security Agenda in Europe*, London: Pinter.

Walker, J. (1992), *Security and Arms Control in Post-Confrontation Europe*, Oxford: Oxford University Press.

15   Inner-European problems

The final challenge facing Europe in the 1990s which has to be considered is one more often treated as a collection of issues rather than as a single problem. Yet the collapse of the old Soviet Empire and the development of EC-based integration has raised a new series of interlinked problems about the management of Europe. In the 1980s these did not really exist. Europe was still too divided economically, militarily and in other ways, for there to be any real contact let alone any comprehensive approach. East–West European relations were largely managed by the superpower-led blocs and mainly through traditional diplomacy which accepted the sovereignty of other states. In the West there was still a considerable distance between EC member states and the other states of Western Europe notably the, mainly neutral, EFTA-countries.

Since the late 1980s, however, the peoples and states of Europe have been brought closer together than at any time since 1945, and in new ways. Physical and political barriers have largely gone, and with them the blocs. So contacts have expanded beyond the merely diplomatic, especially as Western states and organizations find themselves involved in the changes going on in the east and south of Europe. Moral obligation, shared values, fear of backsliding, pressure from the outside and potential gains have all encouraged this. Moreover, Western opinion has become very aware of what has been called 'the cost of half-Europe'. Failure to assist and accept the former satellites could reduce growth and encourage migration, instability and even war. At the same time attitudes to membership of Western institutions has changed dramatically.

Taken all together this means that there is a complex of cultural, economic and political questions to be settled if Europe is to remain a single and harmonious continent. These involve the west, the south and especially the east of Europe. States and peoples in all of them are redefining their relations with other European nations, institutions and processes. Equally, European institutions and their members are having to do much the same. And, although the problems posed by Norway are very different from those presented by Albania, they all raise similar questions about the responsibilities of Europe, about how the continent should be organized and what should happen if countries reject closer ties.

Faced with a similar set of relationships in the past, West Germans used to talk of 'inner-German relations' suggesting that there were also common factors and processes uniting the peoples of the two states. The existence of similar identities underlying differences between states justifies talking of the new problem of the 1990s as one of 'inner-European relations'. Dealing with it would be a complicated matter in any circumstances. In practice, since 1989, there has been a proliferation in the numbers, and types, of countries within the 'New Europe'. Their needs may differ, but they can be very great: for economic aid, political support and market access. Meeting them demands sacrifices of the West at a time of political uncertainty and economic depression. There are few clear policy solutions and no consensus as to which institutions should evolve them. The fact that the 'New Europe' is, as already suggested, more unstable, uncertain and under-employed than the old one, makes things even more difficult.

Given this, inner-European relations ought to be a major concern of the 1990s. Unfortunately, it has taken the West a long time to accept the need for generous and comprehensive strategies. Many people believe that too little has been done too late. President Clinton has recently argued that Europe has not done enough for inner-European relations.

Part of the problem is that it has not been fully appreciated or seen as a whole. This Chapter therefore seeks to examine together what has happened so far in the 1990s to three key groups of states which have largely been outside the nexus of Western institutions: the EFTA countries, Turkey and other southern states, and the central and eastern European states. In the case of the EFTA countries, the experimental special relationship with the EU in the European Economic Area has proved deficient and encouraged many states to seek EU membership as previously noted. Some Mediterranean states have done the same, although most are having to content themselves with a framework agreement with Brussels.

The West has also been slow to open its coffers, institutions and markets to Eastern Europe. The Council of Europe and other bodies have sought to support democracy and slowly new ideas of coping with ethnic rivalries have begun to emerge. The EU has been active in a variety of ways in encouraging the economic and general development of the East, but there has been no new Marshall Plan. Partly because of this the Visegrad countries have sought to join the EU, an aim also shared by other, less favourably placed states, to the south and east. Furthermore, attitudes to Russia have been very hesitant and those to the long-running Yugoslav tragedy, very ambiguous. None of the institutions forced to intervene in the war has been very successful.

Yugoslavia is, in fact, symbolic of the limited progress so far made towards management of the new Europe. As with the other areas, there are still many unresolved needs and questions. Their inter-relations remain somewhat unappreciated. So the problem of inner-European relations remains to be solved.

The EEA and relations with the EFTA states
The place of the EFTA states in an enlarged Europe used to be the least problematical of the three regions. Nonetheless, the EFTA states found themselves forced to make crucial and difficult choices, both about their own roles and about

their relationships with European integration. Their decision to move towards membership offered the chance of a major simplification of inner-European relations in the West. Even so, some difficulties remain.

EFTA had been created in the late 1950s as an alternative to then Common Market. It soon developed into a successful means of handling economic relations between the small states involved, for whom politics ruled out membership, and the EC. With the EC becoming larger, more coherent and more dynamic EFTA found itself in a difficult position, despite the conclusion of a new accord signed at Luxembourg in 1984. So the uneasy EFTAns responded warmly to Jacques Delors' January 1989 suggestion of a jointly managed global association. This seemed to offer them the economic access they wanted without the political costs of membership.

However, the negotiations, in 1990–91, proved long and tortuous, and came within an ace of breaking down because of EC refusal to share decision-making or offer generous policy concessions. In the end the deal struck on 22 October 1991 fell far short of what the EFTAns wanted. The European Economic Area agreement provided for the extension of the four freedoms of the Single Market to the EFTA states through the acceptance of 12 000 pages of the EC *acquis* and participation in flanking policies on competition, company law, consumer protection, environment and social questions. In return the EFTA states were to provide funding for poorer EC states, to speak as one on a joint ministerial Council and to set up an EEA surveillance agency to enforce the agreement. Otherwise their only real influence was on a joint court and in consultation on new policies.

Partly because of these shortcomings, and partly because of economic weakness and the end of the Cold War, which rendered neutrality a much less effective form of security, the EFTAns began to think about membership. The EC seemed to offer a new kind of security. Hence, Austria applied for EC membership in 1989 and Sweden in 1991, as noted in previous Chapters. Then, in 1992, Finland, Switzerland and Norway all tabled their applications. They increasingly felt that only membership would give them the kind of influence they needed for their sovereignty and their security. The EC increasingly came round to accepting the inevitability of their entry, so that negotiations started in early February 1993.

These moves reflected continuing problems with the EEA. Shortly after it was agreed the ECJ ruled that its judicial provisions, which contained safeguards for the EFTAns, were incompatible with EC law, and therefore unacceptable. Re-negotiating these took until May 1992. Then, while ratification in the EFTAn states went well enough at first, the Swiss electorate rejected the deal at a referendum on 6 December 1992. The ensuing Swiss withdrawal required the negotiation of a new protocol eliminating mention of Switzerland from the agreement. Ratification of the latter was then held up by Iberian attempts to gain further concessions on agricultural trade and cohesion payments. All this meant that the EEA did not finally come into being until 1 January 1994. Even then Liechtenstein was not able to take part at once because of technical problems arising out of its 1923 Customs Union with Switzerland.

By then the EEA was being left behind by events. This was because the negotiations on entry were approaching their conclusion. This was despite various delays, policy difficulties and internal EC arguments about the institutional changes necessary to adapt the Treaties to an increased membership. In fact, the bulk of the negotiations was completed in early March 1994 and the Ioannina compromise of 30 March resolved the divisions over voting rights inside the enlarged EU. The agreements were then ratified by the EP in early May with surprisingly large majorities. They were finally signed at the Corfu summit in June 1994 by when the Austrian people had already approved entry in a referendum.

With Finland and Sweden also following suit, the EU became more or less co-terminous with 'Western Europe' as well as opening to the East. Furthermore, by adding stable and wealthy countries it will assist in the funding of the major projects facing Europe's southern and eastern flanks. Several of the EFTA states have also been willing to reinforce their new Europeanization by taking part in the NACC, the Partnership for Peace and the WEU's new consultative body. This reflected a willingness to interpret neutrality more flexibly.

Turkey and the southern 'orphans'

Problems and needs in the south of Europe are greater and more challenging. Yet so far there have been fewer clear-cut answers although without them, Europe risks creating a zone of instability in the Mediterranean. This could seriously threaten much of the rest of the continent through migration and the export of Islamic fundamentalism. Small countries like Malta and Cyprus, and large ones like Turkey look to Europe, and especially to the EU for aid and political support. However, Turkish entry is virtually impossible at present. Nor are there the resources, whether in the EU or beyond, to cope with their needs and those of the rest of the underdeveloped Mediterranean. Hence the south is an important inner-European problem.

By the late 1980s Malta ended its flirtation with Libya and the USSR and re-activated its agreements with the EC. By 1990 it applied for membership. Although the country faces considerable economic restructuring and although there are residual fears about non-alignment and having another very small country in the EU, the 1994 *avis* was relatively favourable. Malta is now pushing for an early start to negotiations, partly for its own interests and partly because it wishes to strengthen the Mediterranean dimension of the EC.

Cyprus is a more complicated problem. This is because the Turkish invasion of 1974 led to the creation of a separate, but unrecognized, ethnic Turkish regime in the north of the island. The island's Association Agreement was also suspended until 1987. Three years later a membership application was tabled, since the Cypriots need EC markets and support. However, the fact that they do not control all their territory poses immense legal and political difficulties. However, the EU eventually decided that if reunification talks – in which the EU is now an observer – made no progress, it would look at the possibility of accepting only the Greek part of the island. The Greek Cypriot authorities welcomed the *avis* and pushed for earlier talks. Negotiations are thus due to start six months after the end of the 1996 IGC. Like Malta they have started preparing for membership although they seek financial support and access to EU programmes, ahead of entry.

The problem of Cyprus is compounded by the fact that Turkey, the only power to recognize the regime in northern Cyprus, has also sought EC membership. This was promised by the 1963 Association Agreement, but the breakdown of democracy in the 1970s caused the Association to be frozen, along with Turkish membership of the Council of Europe. Once the political situation improved in the 1980s the Turks, very aware of their strategic importance to NATO and their need for economic modernization, applied for membership in 1987.

The Commission *avis*, issued at the very end of 1989, turned this down. The worries were that Turkey, though a NATO member, is a very large and under-developed state. Its entry to the EC would be very costly and would totally destabilize the CAP. It could also lead to a massive flood of Turkish labour into the EC, bringing problems of cultural integration. For though the Turkish state is committed to secularism, its population is largely Islamic. At the same time there were major reservations about its poor human rights record, and to a lesser extent, the country's democratic credentials. Greece, as a historic rival and protector of the Greek Cypriots, is also able to use its position as a member to block Turkish aspirations.

The Turks have adjusted quite well to the rejection of their application to the EC, though they still wish to join. Their new role as a bridge to the new Islamic states of Central Asia has encouraged them in this. So too has the chance of increased involvement in Western security through the Gulf War and the post-Maastricht widening of the WEU. The Turks are now demanding an enhanced status in WEU after so many other states are being brought into its orbit. This has led the EC to talk of finding a new kind of relationship with Turkey, and particularly of intensifying political dialogue.

However, finding the necessary structures and resources to do this has not yet got very far. This is because there are problems in the operation of the Association Agreement. There is supposed to be movement towards completing the Customs Union embracing Turkey and the EC. However, on the one hand, there are EU accusations of Turkish protection and economic weakness and, on the other, Turkish complaints about the EU's failure to provide for Turkish workers and financial needs. Direct financial aid is still held up by Greek opposition. Above all, there are continuing worries about Cyprus and, especially, about Turkey's treatment of its Kurdish minority. The human rights problem could well block progress on the Customs Union. All this means that the Turkish relationship with Europe remains undefined and problematical.

In practice the Turks are often forced to rely on the development of programmes to aid the North African and Mediterranean countries whose demographic explosion is beginning to weigh heavily on southern EU states, just as that of Mexico does on the USA. The early 1990s has seen an increasing awareness in EU institutions and states that the EU's southern flank has very real problems, and these ought not to be overlooked because of the new concentration on Eastern Europe. Hence, in 1994 the EU moved towards, on the one hand, entering into new partnership agreements with Morocco and Tunisia and, on the other, to re-evaluating its relationship with the area and taking part in new conferences and institutions for the region. It is possible that an EEA-type framework for the region might emerge from this reassessment. This could involve funding on the scale presently being offered Eastern Europe.

Eastern and central Europe
Because the problems of Eastern Europe pose an even larger threat to European stability and harmony, the region has loomed much higher in the Western consciousness than the south. This also reflects the cultural similarities between the two halves of the continent, the dramatic nature of changes in the East and, especially, the pressures from the East for a 'return to Europe'. To many in central Europe 'Europe' was seen as a symbol of better living standards, stable democracy and general recovery of international status. Hence it became part of the so called 'Triple R' agenda for the East: reintegration, reform and regional security.

All these things, of course, required outside assistance, often on a massive scale, and outside acceptance. Unfortunately, neither have yet been provided. Despite the involvement of a plethora of institutions the former satellites have yet to achieve the kind of regional political and general security they seek. Equally they have only partly won acceptance of the idea that they can participate in Western institutions. There has been, in fact, considerable reluctance to concede this. As bodies of long standing, with a relatively experienced and homogenous membership, many of the international organizations in Europe have been reluctant to accept new states with no recent traditions of democratic self-government and which are dogged by economic, ethnic and political uncertainty. The fact that their participation in Western organizations causes major difficulties with Russia is an additional complication. Hence, the economic and financial aid provided has been much less than needed.

A whole host of Western agencies have become involved with the East, both militarily and politically, which can cause confusion and wasteful duplication. On the military side NATO, as already seen in Chapter 14, has tried to develop its role and become the partner of the new states of central and eastern Europe rather than a rival. Its new form of partnership now looks to limited enlargement as well. NATO's standing has been enhanced by the relative failure of the CSCE to provide the effective framework needed in Europe, notably in the Yugoslav crisis. There are also difficulties between the CSCE and the Council of Europe. On the other hand, NATO's position is complicated by its overlap with the WEU, which is now emerging as the security wing of the new EU.

The EU has also played a major role in developing the new Stability Pact, initiated by French Prime Minister Eduard Balladur, which seeks, as previously noted, to resolve the underlying conflicts of central and eastern Europe, and thus promote stability. The idea took shape at a May 1994 conference in Paris. This created two round tables, one for the Baltic and one for central European states involved with the Hungarian minority problem. The aim is to provide fora for both bilateral agreements about mutual problems and enhanced cross-frontier contacts. Any such agreements will then be underwritten by the CSCE. Such steps mean that, after a long delay, real steps will be made towards regional trust and security.

Western institutions have also been active in trying to encourage democratic reform in the former satellites and beyond so as to deal with the instability discussed in Chapter 13. NATO and the EU have both shown an interest here, the latter having been encouraged by the EP to make this a higher priority within its PHARE programme. The Council of Europe has been very active in encouraging democratization, trying to make up for the way the EC has expanded its own activity in culture, education, local government, human rights and social questions, in which the Council used to specialize. The Council's Lodis, Themis and Demosthenes programmes have tried to develop the practices of democracy and the rule of law. Many Eastern states are now ratifying the Council's many legal conventions which avoid large numbers of bilateral agreements.

The Council's own Parliamentary Assembly also plays a role as a political forum through which new states, from Albania to Andorra, can begin to come to terms with Western norms. Acceptance by the Council is now a *sine qua non* for EC membership. At its Vienna Summit in the autumn of 1993 it pushed forward its rationalization of human rights jurisdiction. This included provision for adapting these to the new problems of minorities, thereby trying to encourage stability within Eastern states. However, the relations between the Council and other organizations remain somewhat unclear while the Council itself, like the EU, is beginning to wonder exactly how far it can safely expand. Reintegration thus has also had its limits.

As well as all these bodies the early 1990s has seen the emergence of non-governmental actors with an interest in the East. These include specific regional institutions, whether large-scale ones like the Pentagonale which embraces countries to the north-east of the Alps or smaller cross-border operations. These include arrangements like the Région Transmanche, stimulated by the Channel Tunnel, which brings together Kent, the Nord-Pas-de-Calais region in France and Belgian regions. There can also be specific policy agreements, often EU-based, and individual social initiatives. All these have helped to make a reality of the interconnectedness of the new Europe.

If such bodies add to the density of inner-European relations, they do not give the firm guarantees of full international participation which Eastern Europe seeks. The EC in particular was very reticent on this, and at first tried to exclude any mention of it from the Association agreements. In the end it accepted that entry was a legitimate aim. Then, as time passed, it came round to accepting, notably at Copenhagen in 1993, that entry could not be denied, and the real question was one of timing.

The EU and the economic transition in Eastern Europe

It was partly because the EU has clear procedures for association and membership that it proved attractive to Eastern countries as Chapter 13 has shown. But it is also partly because the EU is a polyvalent institution which provides the economic aid, model and access which the East needs. Equally it has the capacity to devise effective policy instruments. Hence, the EU has become a major actor in Western approaches to the East, and especially in Western attempts to deal with the economic disorientation already noted. Some countries like Poland, in fact speak of a twin-track approach, looking for NATO entry for military security and the EU for the rest.

This interest in the EU and NATO has eclipsed earlier talk of the Eastern states entering EFTA rather than the EU. Although EFTA signed free trade agreements with a number of states in the early 1990s, its uncertain future now means that this option has lost all credibility. Those who used to argue for it are now talking of amalgamating all Eastern association agreements with the EU and EFTA into a multilateral body. Significantly this is now seen simply as a transitional measure until Eastern countries are fit for EU membership.

The role of the EU, on the other hand, has developed in five ways. To begin with, it was to the EC that the old CMEA had turned, very late in the day, for economic links, in the era of *perestroika*. This led to the first trade and co-operation agreements. These were then refined and extended to new countries once the revolutions had taken place. Enhanced co-operation agreements then led, under pressure from the East, to the signing of 'Europe' Association agreements with most of the former satellites. These have four main elements: bringing in free trade, with the West lowering tariffs first; encouraging general economic co-operation; providing financial aid; and establishing 'political dialogue' between the EU and the associated states. Somewhat reluctantly the EC also recognized that the associated states wanted to become members.

The first Agreements were signed with the Visegrad countries in November 1991. However, they did not come into full effect until February 1994, and then only in the case of Poland and Hungary. This delay, and the relatively ungenerous terms of the Association agreements themselves, was due to Western fears of economic competition from low-wage economies. Indeed, it was often said the EC gained most from them. It was this imbalance which was to push some countries to seek early membership.

Secondly, the EC was invited by the Group of Twenty Four Industrial Countries (G24) in July 1989 to co-ordinate Western aid to Poland and Hungary, through the PHARE programme. The EC has managed the scheme and has also provided most of the basic aid and help with restructuring. The scheme was later extended to virtually all Eastern countries save Croatia and the new Yugoslavia. The EC was also very much involved in the creation of the European Bank for Reconstruction and Development (EBRD) in 1989–91. This was designed to provide pump priming aid for the East in its transition to market economics.

This meant that the Eastern countries have been brought into the wider European economy and encouraged to develop by the EU. This was also true of a third, related, factor, namely the way in which the EU has been actively provided emergency aid to countries in particular distress, first for Romania in December 1989 and then for Albania in 1990. Russia too has, like Bosnia, benefited from such help.

Fourthly, the EC is important because, as well as PHARE, it, like many of its member states, offers general and bilateral schemes to help integrate and modernize the new societies. This includes training and education programmes like the EC's TACIS and TEMPUS schemes and the British 'Know How' Fund. The EC schemes provide links and finance for training, education and technical development in the former CIS and Eastern Europe respectively. TEMPUS is really an Eastern version of ERASMUS. Functional agencies, for instance in the nuclear field, and private sector actors are also active. It reflects the EC's general policy-making role. Eastern countries have, moreover, been invited to join the EC's own programmes such as COST in the way that EFTA countries had previously done.

Lastly, the EU is also increasingly accepting that what matters is not just entry, but the transitional measures to ensure that the countries are brought to a stage where candidate countries are able to cope with the demands of membership. This involves firstly, building on the Association agreements to allow Eastern states to take a larger part in more trade and policy networks and secondly, creating a deeper and more structured political relationship with the EU. This means that the Eastern countries are regularly consulted and able to observe EU meetings. At the same time more support is being given to their economies and to their adaptation of EC legislation. These links extend to the two non-community pillars of Maastricht, foreign policy and judicial matters and are presently being developed by Sir Leon Brittan for the EU.

Other institutions have, of course, played a role. The G24 has, as already seen, provided a framework for economic aid to the East. The Group of Seven (G7) most industrialized nations is also important for setting guidelines for economic policy. However, here again the EC plays an even more important role. The OECD and the United Nations Economic Commission for Europe have a marginal role as monitors of economic progress.

However, neither the deep involvement of the EC nor the sympathetic interest of other bodies has actually produced the cornucopia of aid which some in the East expected. Large promises have often been made, although they fall short of what is needed, let alone of what a new Marshall Aid-type package would have involved. Moreover, not all of the monies promised have actually been delivered. In any case, aid often takes the form of subsidies to help new states buy Western goods and services when their needs are much more to sell their goods freely on Western markets. This has been much less willingly conceded. Such difficulties held up the Association agreements, led to trade disputes, such as the 'cattle war' of 1993, and has encouraged the Eastern bloc countries to go slow on their own opening to Western trade. So, although the EU has provided the bulk of aid to the East, the desires of its institutions to help the East has often been held up by the reticence of member states.

The Visegrad states

Poland, Hungary and the former Czechoslovakia are the states which, having started earliest, have moved furthest towards adapting to capitalism and democratic pluralism, as noted in Chapter 13. They have also gone furthest in developing links with the West. This has taken them into the Council of Europe, into co-operation with EFTA and into both the NACC and the Partnership for Peace. The fact that they are also the most co-ordinated thanks to the Visegrad grouping has enabled them to bring pressure on the EC to consider their case. Although they always resist being regarded as a homogenous bloc, they have co-ordinated their policies, especially where bringing pressure on the EU is concerned. By February 1994 they had also created a free trade area of their own. And although they do have ethnic problems as both the Hungarian minorities and the dissolution of Czechoslovakia show, these have been less threatening than elsewhere.

They have been the most active in pushing for closer links with the EC, first through the 'Europe' Association agreements and increasingly through membership. This reflected the Visegrad countries' growing, and understandable, dissatisfaction with the limited and ungenerous place in the general network of inner-European relations. They looked for at least three things:

greater market access, more appropriate financial and technical aid and political acceptance. At first the EC was very reluctant to accept all this, notably the idea of entry, but increasingly this has been accepted, allowing the Poles and Hungarians to present their applications in April 1994.

However, none of this means that they have overcome their problems. Even here the transition from Communism is proving long and painful, especially in Slovakia. And, although economic progress is slowly being made, some Western opinion has been alarmed by the way in which reformed Communist parties have come back into power in Poland, Hungary and other countries. Nor do the similarities mean that the four countries are identical. Poland's economic reforms were much more dramatic than those of Hungary for instance. Equally, its concerns are very much those of a country with an uncertain Russian neighbour on its eastern border. However, it is very keen to make progress with entry, and wants observer status at the 1996 IGC. The Hungarians, on the other hand, have the complication of having large ethnic minorities in Romania, Slovakia, Serbia and the Ukraine. They too have a carefully constructed timetable which foresees entry by about the year 2000, assuming their economy is then ready for the challenges of membership.

The Czechoslovaks had, like Hungary, secured an Association agreement in 1991 but this was frozen after the country split, as noted in Chapter 13, because of political suspicion and differing approaches to economic reform. Separate agreements have been renegotiated but have yet to come into effect. This has prevented the Czech Republic from presenting its own application for membership, although Prime Minister Klaus believes that the country is ready for membership as early as 1999. This reflects the country's increasingly close links with the West. The Slovak situation is rather different partly because the Slovak economy is so tied to the old fashioned heavy industries of Communist times and partly because of the attitudes of Vladimir Meciar and his wing of Slovak nationalism, the dominant force in Slovak politics.

The Balkans and beyond

To some extent Slovakia reflects the lesser progress made by other more south-eastern countries. All of them suffer from even worse economic problems than the Visegrad states, even Slovenia remaining somewhat vulnerable. The Balkan countries thus took much longer to persuade the West of their democratic bona fides. Further east if the Baltic states have been able to move into the Western sphere, the new countries on the Western border of the new Russia have not been able to do so.

Of the south-eastern countries, Bulgaria found it difficult to negotiate deals with EFTA and the EC. Its loan and association agreements were only achieved in early 1993 and have yet to come fully into effect. And, though it has succeeded in joining the Council of Europe, it has had problems because of the slow transition to full democratic rule and the rather problematic attitudes to its Turkish minority. Hence, it has remained on the peripheries of European co-operation and EC entry is not yet on the agenda.

Romania is yet further behind because of doubts over its democratic nature arising from the continuing rule of ex-Communists. These have been exacerbated both by the Romanians' refusal to grant full civil rights to their Magyar minority in Transylvania and by complications arising from the country's links with Moldova. Despite the fact that much Danube traffic with Serbia crosses its territory, its Association agreement came rather late. Further integration seems some way off.

In the Balkans, Albania poses very different problems. After years of backwardness, isolation and violence, the country fell apart, incapable of feeding itself. So emergency food aid was, for a long while in 1990–92, the main priority. Attention has now shifted to aid which might help to relaunch the economy, but developing more sophisticated links will take a long time. Aid still remains the key concern although there are worries about the extent of democratization and the Albanian relationship with neighbouring countries, notably Kossovo and Greece. Relations with the latter have deteriorated rapidly in 1994 because of the way minorities are treated. Greece has also held up recognition and aid to Macedonia as already noted in Chapter 12.

Slovenia, on the other hand, sees itself as much more advanced and seeks to lock itself into the Western system, including joining EFTA and, perhaps, the EU. However, while it is peaceful and has a better economic base than some, it suffers from its proximity to the Yugoslav war zone. Economically it has not been spared either, with output falling and unemployment rising. So its move into the mainstream of inner-European relations was rather slow. It did enter the Council of Europe and obtained a co-operation agreement in April 1993. This was expected to lead to an association agreement by the end of 1994 but difficulties with Italy, dating back to the last war, have delayed matters. Because of its role in the Yugoslav war Croatia has only recently been allowed to talk about aid and structured relationships.

The Baltic states, on the other hand, are moving faster down this road. Even before their independence they were granted aid from the PHARE programme, as well as by the Nordic states. The new ties with Europe also led to entry into the Council of Europe and accords with both EFTA and the EC, which negotiated co-operation agreements in the summer of 1992. These were seen as evolutionary and likely to lead to political dialogue.

So, once problems over new citizenship laws which discriminate against Russian settlers were resolved, the Council of Ministers in December 1993 urged the Commission to go further in giving the Baltic states more stability and security. This led to the signing of free trade agreements in the summer of 1994, which in turn opened the way to the negotiation of Europe Association agreements.

The West has also been very supportive of the Baltic states' desire to see agreements on the withdrawal of Russian troops fully implemented by the end of August 1994, as they ultimately were. This reflects worries about the prospects of instability in a critical area.

The new states in the west of what was the USSR have found it hard to move away from the old regime. In the case of the Ukraine, while it wants closer links with the EC and the West in general, its stance on nuclear power whether signing START 1 or agreeing to close down Chernobyl, held these up. It was able to secure the continuation of deals formerly agreed with the USSR. Only in March 1994 was a partnership agreement signed. Further contacts with the West depend on the outcome of the uncertain domestic situation.

Much the same is likely to be true of Belarus which, in any case, has been very slow to make itself felt on the international scene. There is a limited agreement such as was also signed with Moldova in July 1994. This too has had difficulties with Russia because of the presence of a dissident Russian ethnic minority in the Transdnester region. With the recent referendum endorsement of independence, rather than merger with Romania, Moldova looks likely to remain another peripheral state.

The EU seems to have decided that the border of Europe will be constituted by the Russian border. However, this does not mean exclusion, but a special kind of relationship with Russia, without which stability will be impossible. Aid was, at first, rather hesitant, but it increased after the 1991 coup. Nonetheless, negotiating an accord with the EU proved long and difficult given the problems discussed in previous Chapters. The new EU 'partnership' agreement with Russia was only signed at Corfu in June 1994. NATO eventually made a similar kind of decision in offering a 16 + 1 dialogue, provided that Russia has no veto on Western policy. This encouraged the Russians finally to sign the Partnership for Peace agreement in 1994. However, this is one of a number of continuing problems which highlight the lack of a co-ordinated approach to inner-European problems.

The former Yugoslavia

What can happen when the West does not have an overall strategy is made tragically clear by former Yugoslavia. This has posed challenges of a very different kind to Europe. Ethnic urges are, as Chapter 13 has shown, more brutal, intransigent and potentially explosive than normal West European politics. They require even more coherent and courageous strategies than the other problems of inner-European relations. New forms of action, including military intervention, are also needed. As a result the Yugoslav crisis has been the greatest test of the new Europe. So far that test has been failed.

Western responses, like the crisis itself, have gone through several phases. The crisis began in Kossovo in the late 1980s with Serbian pressure on the

Albanian majority there. While this was not welcomed in Europe little was done to resist it. The prevailing idea was to hold the country together and help the Markovic government with its much needed economic reforms. In turn, this would give Yugoslavia some hope of fulfilling its aspirations of drawing closer to Western Europe, probably through Association with the EC.

Before this could happen, the Kossovo crisis turned into a general crisis of the Yugoslav state because of Milosevic's exploitation of Serbian nationalism and the rise of anti-Communist separatism in Slovenia and Croatia. Both states then moved towards independence in December 1990. Although there was the possibility of creating a looser confederacy, which might have prevented complete dissolution, differences between the ethnic groups derailed both this and the machinery of Yugoslav federalism. So, when the two northern states finally voted for independence in May–June 1991, the Yugoslav army embarked on its abortive attack on Slovenia in June and July 1991.

By then the EC was seeking to mediate, since the end of the Cold War had created a political vacuum. Intervention by the *troika* during talks at Brioni then brokered a ceasefire and a moratorium on further moves to independence on 7 July 1991. At this point the first 'ice cream men', as the white-coated EC observers were known, were sent to monitor the ceasefire. All this enabled Slovenia to start disentangling itself from Yugoslavia during the autumn.

By then, however, the crisis had entered a new phase with a war in Croatia. Understandably fearing for their future in the new nationalist Croatia of Franjo Tudjman, the ethnic Serbian minority sought to secede, backed by the Yugoslav army. The fighting went very much against the poorly armed Croats who, as shown in Map 6, lost a third of their territory. Many towns were reduced to rubble so as to 'ethnically cleanse' non-Serbs from allegedly 'Serbian' territories.

The Croats looked to the West for support, but the EC still clung to the idea that Lord Carrington, its special representative, might be able to negotiate a confederal settlement. The CSCE also sought to become involved. However, as the 'Croatian' war continued into the winter of 1991–92, European opinion turned increasingly against Serbian non-compliance with the innumerable ceasefires, notably in their bombardment of the historic city of Dubrovnik. Nonetheless, the EC's inability to enforce its wishes became painfully apparent. Sanctions and the use of force were considered while the Council of Europe suspended the rump Yugoslavia from membership. It was only after a fourteenth ceasefire that the war ended, and Croatia was able to become an independent, albeit truncated, state. And even then clashes with both Moslems and Serbs continued, with the latter gratuitously bombarding Dubrovnik again in November 1992.

By then the EC had given up its hopes of keeping Yugoslavia as such together. Indeed, German pressures led the EC to offer recognition to such Yugoslav states as wanted it in December and January 1992. It was hoped that

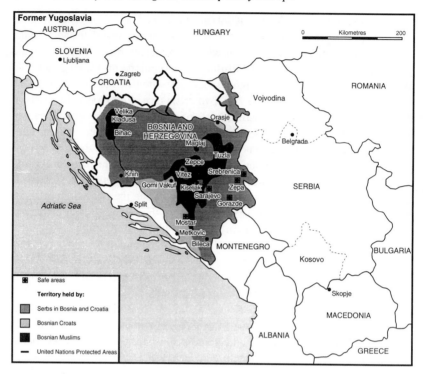

Map 6

this would dowse the conflict and protect the various minorities. In fact, Slovenia
and Croatia were recognized, even though the latter patently failed to fulfil the
criteria for recognition laid down by the EC's own investigating committee.

Recognition allowed Slovenia to finalize its independence and to develop links
with EFTA and the Council of Europe. Croatia was less successful since the
regime's authoritarianism and lack of sensitivity on human rights made much
EC opinion very hesitant about the country. Croat rearmament and intervention in fighting elsewhere did not help matters. Hence, PHARE and other forms
of aid were withheld. Greece complicated the problem by blocking the recognition sought by Macedonia because it saw the name as a threat to its own integrity.
Macedonia was also unsuccessful in its search for an association agreement with
the EC, although it did inherit some of the existing financial aid to Yugoslavia.

Only Serbia and Montenegro rejected the offer of recognition, preferring to
take the crisis into a new phase by overrunning the ethnically very mixed
territory of Bosnia-Herzogevina. This was a response to a successful plebiscite
on independence held by the Muslim-led government on 25 January 1992,
following the invitation to seek recognition. The Serbs refused to accept all this.

Barricades began to go up between the two communities who often lived cheek by jowl. Local Serb forces and the Yugoslav army, which had close ties with the region, then began a ferocious onslaught that April. They targeted Muslim-held areas for bestial ethnic cleansing while mounting an unceasing bombardment of the capital, Sarajevo. This created hundreds of thousands more refugees not to mention a quarter of a million dead and wounded. By the end of the process in the autumn over 70 per cent of the territory of Bosnia was in Serb hands even though they only comprised 35 per cent of the population.

The EC, whose members were still divided about the best course of action, then began to hand over responsibility to the UN and NATO. UN intervention, which followed on the murder of five EC peace monitors in February 1992, did little to remedy things. The Serbs were subjected to economic sanctions, partially enforced at sea by WEU and NATO forces and UN peacekeeping forces were finally deployed in March–April 1992 to bring humanitarian aid to the distressed Moslem population. As with the war in Croatia, ceasefires came and went without really stopping the war. Tightened UN sanctions, the refusal to recognize the 'new' rump Yugoslavia declared in the spring of 1992, and suspension from the CSCE did nothing to stop the horrors. Matters were further complicated by Croatian involvement sometimes alongside the Muslims and sometimes against them.

From the late summer of 1992 until the end of 1993 the crisis settled down into a seemingly interminable banalization of conflict while the UN and the international community sought to persuade the Serbs and others to come to some kind of agreement. Thus, following the London conference in August 1992 Lord Owen and Cyrus Vance, representing the EC and the UN respectively, began negotiations to find a settlement. The aim was to gain agreement on a redrawing of boundaries inside Bosnia which would provide some autonomy for the different ethnic groups who would be divided into ten autonomous cantons within a guaranteed confederal political structure.

The plan, finally presented in January 1993, was accepted by Bosnians and Croats but was rejected by the Bosnian Serbs in May. All sides saw the deal as a second best and preferred to fight on for what they really wanted. The UN response was to try and set up safe havens for Moslem minorities and to threaten to enforce them by air power. This was already being used to drop the increasing amounts of humanitarian aid needed and the situation worsened as the Muslims had to fight off a new Croat attack as well as face increasing pressure in Sarajevo.

A second peace plan involving a three-way partition of Bosnia was then evolved in August and September 1993. This too failed to gain acceptance. So the war continued. The international community was rendered increasingly impotent as peace talks got nowhere and Serbs and others interfered with UN convoys. UN forces seemed increasingly demoralized with only about a fifth of humanitarian aid getting through. This partly reflected disillusion over the unwillingness of NATO and the Western powers to live up to the threats they made.

Things seemed to be changing in 1994. The new UN commander, Michael Rose, began to stand up to the Serbs with the backing of an international community outraged by the massacre of 68 civilians in the market of Sarajevo on 5 February. Serb planes violating the no-fly-zone were shot down and, following the Serb failure to accept an ultimatum to place heavy weapons under UN supervision, they were subject to NATO strikes. The threat of further strikes, together with growing Russian influence, forced the Bosnian Serbs to call off a new attack on Gorazde.

At the same time the USA, reflecting the new role of the former superpowers, brokered a loose union between Croats and Moslems. This changed the military balance to the detriment of the Serbs, thwarting the latter's plans for a final push. Then, in July 1994, a 'contact' group of great power officials came up with a new partition plan which required the Serbs to give up nearly half their gains. This they refused to do, so the Russians persuaded Belgrade to accept and break off relations with the Bosnian Serbs. Milosevic did this to avoid both further sanctions, which would threaten an economic revival, and the lifting of the arms embargo against the Moslems. When they reluctantly allowed outside observers to monitor their closing of their borders with Bosnia, sanctions were partially eased. The Croats also began to try and rebuild bridges with the West as already noted.

The Bosnian Serbs remained defiant and difficult. At the same time the Muslims, with some success, sought to take advantage of the new situation, supported by the Bosnian Croats. However, this went badly wrong in November with a combined Bosnian and Croatian Serb onslaught on Bihacs. Consequently, the UN force remains caught in the middle, subjected to ever increasing attacks, and hamstrung both by Serb intransigence and by increasing differences between the US and its NATO allies. Further difficulties, such as the actual lifting of the arms embargo on the Bosnian government agreed in principle by the UN General Assembly in early November 1994, could lead to Unprofor being pulled out, assuming this is militarily possible. With the Bosnian Serbs threatening total war 'to the death' against both the Bosnian government and the international community, ideas of a wider peace settlement inside the former Yugoslavia again look very problematic, even after the intervention of Jimmy Carter. The West thus remains divided and uncertain in the face of the continuing ethnic crisis in Bosnia.

The present situation: new issues and continuing obstacles

This ambiguity suggests that Europe has not gone all that far in managing its new interrelations, or indeed of appreciating their inner connectedness. States outside and inside the EC have been less willing to change existing policies than rhetoric suggests. The EC too has its own hesitations and problems. So, although strategy is gradually widening at EC level, it has yet to be internalized by all governments or by much public opinion.

In the West, the referenda on EU entry have meant that three states will be joining the EU, but that Norway will stay outside for an indeterminate period. Hence, the future of the rather top heavy EEA looks uncertain because it threatens Iceland and Liechtenstein with domination by Norway, and there are already major disputes over fisheries between the two northern states. In any case, while the Norwegian government is willing to shoulder the costs of the EEA mechanism, some anti-Europeans query both this and the acceptability of any consequential changes to the EEA. However, assuming that it does survive in an altered form, it could provide a framework for the relationships of some of the Western states who do not, or cannot, enter the EU, again presuming that Iceland's interest in entry does not come to anything.

Switzerland is a trickier problem. For while Norway has the UN, NATO, the EEA and the formal and informal support of Nordic co-operation available to it to maintain its place in the continental comity of nations, Switzerland does not. Its interest in EFTA are different from those of Norway. And its needs are, in some ways, more pressing because its integration into the European economy is much greater than that of Norway. As a neutral state in central Europe the Swiss have chosen to stay outside not just NATO but also the UN. Moreover, their friendly relations with Austria cannot be considered the equal of the Nordic arrangements.

Furthermore, in 1992, the Swiss turned down EEA entry because they distrusted their political elite's willingness to defend the political institutions which, like direct democracy, have come to define their identity. Then, having moved cautiously towards starting bilateral talks to resolve some of the problems arising from being outside the EEA, matters were again thrown into disarray in late February 1994. The Swiss electorate then voted to shift all international goods traffic from road to rail within ten years, calling into question an October 1991 transit agreement with the EC. This delayed bilateral talks until the very end of 1994 and raised questions about how successful these were likely to be.

It also provided more reasons for thinking that any second vote on the EEA is not likely to be very productive. Even if agreed by the Swiss, the Swiss–Norwegian combination could prove problematic. Switzerland therefore looks like being an anomaly in Western Europe, which is problematic for the EU, given the country's geographic and economic centrality. Not having it inside the Single Market is inconvenient, but the fierce, if erratic, independence of Swiss electors makes bilateral deals difficult. More formalized arrangements would prove even harder to achieve.

The arguments here are less economic than institutional and policy-based, often relating to identity. The costs of entry would be relatively limited. But for countries like Switzerland, Iceland and Norway entry would impinge on sensitive areas like agriculture, fisheries, oil, property, environment, migration and regional development. It would also mean changes in treasured institutions like neutrality, direct democracy and autonomous decision-making. Hence, there are serious reservations amongst the electorates of such countries about taking part in the EU and other European projects.

The EU is still considering a new policy on southern Europe. However, whether this will lead to the kind of investment in states on the southern shore of the Mediterranean, necessary to increase economic development and thus limit migration is uncertain. The Eastern precedent is not encouraging. Equally, there are problems of adaption for countries like Turkey, notably in economic structure and human rights. There are particular fears about Algeria in all this because of its Islamic fundamentalists' violent hostility to the West.

Although the transition to Western systems is still far from complete, things are looking a little better in the East. The first signs of economic recovery have begun to appear in the former satellites, and there is less concern about instability and the possibility of back-sliding, save perhaps in Russia and the CIS. Moreover, the EC has moved to accept the idea of further enlargement. Nor does it now see this as a panacea and is seeking to prepare the new states for membership by introducing them politically and generally into 'an increasingly unified area'. It has also started to grapple with the problem of ethnic conflict through the Stability Pact, encouraging those countries which are unwilling to concede others the minority rights they themselves have so recently regained. Even in Yugoslavia the fear of exclusion from the new Europe has finally forced Belgrade to halt its support of expansionism, and dampened down fears of a wider Balkan war, even though the Bosnian Serbs remain hell-bent on their own territorial ambitions irrespective of both human life and international opinion.

There are three further problems. Firstly, the economic aid has yet to flow. Secondly, the EU has not resolved its own internal debates between those who believe that deepening should come before any further widening, thereby intensifying the debate about the EC's own nature. Indeed, the EC was, for a long time, reticent about enlargement because of the variety of countries applying, their lack of compatibility, and the costs they might impose. These costs would not only be economic and financial but political. Large-scale enlargement would change the delicate balances between institutions and between large and small states. Even those states most committed to enlargement have been worried by this. This debate, which is likely to flare up again in 1996, complicates both the question of enlargement and the development of a more coherent Europe.

Thirdly, while the EU as such is beginning to take on board the need for a wider approach to all such problems, many states have not done so. Even the German Presidency did not move things on as much as had been expected.

Moreover, there are continuing reservations in southern member states. And the 1994 EP elections suggested that the issue has yet to register with most electors. They remain set in their own domestic political mould, so that there is no clear mandate for new sacrifices in the West and no real awareness of the problem.

So, although there are more contacts between European peoples and states, barriers and differences remain. There are still uncertainties about the responsibilities and organization of Europe, about the balance between traditional diplomacy and institutional arrangements, and about what to do with countries which do not want to participate in the collective enterprise. The new Europe has not moved very far towards a single, well managed area. It is a messy arrangement of bilateral and multilateral arrangements linking an enlarged EU to non-member states and other organizations. Furthermore, its ability to stand up to serious challenge remains in doubt after the Yugoslav debacle.

Further reading
Almond, M. (1994), *Europe's Backyard War: the War in the Balkans*, London: Heineman.
Archer, C. (1994), *Organizing Western Europe*, London: Edward Arnold.
Arter, D. (1993), *The Politics of European Integration in the Twentieth Century*, Aldershot: Dartmouth.
Bennett, C. (1994), *Yugoslavia's Bloody Collapse*, London: Hurst.
Brown, J.F. (1992), *Western Approaches to Eastern Europe*, New York: Council on Foreign Relations.
Buchan, D. (1993), *Europe – the Strange Superpower*, Aldershot: Dartmouth.
Glenny, M. (1993), *The Fall of Yugoslavia*, Harmondsworth: Penguin.
Gow, J. (1994), *Triumph of the Lack of Will. International Diplomacy and the Yugoslav War*, London: Hurst.
Miall, H. (1993), *Shaping the New Europe*, London: RIIA.
Michalski, A. and Wallace, H. (1992), *The Challenge of Enlargement*, London: RIIA.
Norgaard, O. (ed.) (1993), *The EC and the World*, London: Pinter.
Redmond, J. (1993), *The Next Mediterranean Enlargement*, Aldershot: Dartmouth.
Rezun, M. (1992), *Nationalism and the Break-up of an Empire. Russia and its Periphery*, London: Praeger.
Rusi, A. (1991), *After the Cold War. Europe's New Political Architecture*, London: Macmillan.
Van Ham, P. (1993), *The EC and Central Europe*, London: Pinter.

Conclusions

The indeterminate nature of inner European relations is one of the most striking features of the phase of transition and uncertainty into which Europe has moved since 1989. Despite the belief that Europe had entered a drastically new era, drawing a line across the historical ledger, things have turned out differently. The new era has certainly been one of change but there has also been continuity, long-term and short-term. What happened in 1989–90, in other words, does not, by itself explain the issues and challenges of the 1990s.

While there has been welcome change where the Cold War, disarmament and democratization are concerned, there have also been less welcome shifts in attitudes to European integration. Long-term continuities have reappeared in the form of national sentiment and rivalries, the unforgiving social and economic structures of Communist eastern Europe, and the political and social problems of the 1970s and early 1980s. However, the economic policies and political difficulties of the late 1980s have also carried over into the 1990s, along with the dynamic of European integration.

So the story told in the first part of *Continuity and Change* of how the revival, particularly in the West, from Europe's post-war low point in 1945, was partially undone in the 1970s, gains a new significance. The tremendous economic growth and the successful integration of the 1940s and 1950s became the bench-mark for future expectations. It also produced new political movements which were to thrive on the much resented economic depression of the 1970s. In the East the enforced restructuring of state and society created a lasting dilemma. So the continuity with this period is both positive and negative.

In the 1980s the two parts of Europe seemed, as shown in the second part, to be coming together again. In the West there was economic revival and political stabilization. This helped perestroika and glasnost accelerate the implosion of the Soviet Empire and the old Communist forms of politics and society. Yet, as has been suggested, this did not lead to the expected change. Continuity with the 1970s, notably in the economic sphere, together with mistakes made in the 1980s, meant that the gains of the new era were matched by underlying problems. In retrospect the 1980s may seem to have been merely a passing sunny period in the stormy weather which began in 1973.

Given this conflict of change and continuity, the new era has been anything but clear and certain. The process of European integration has thus been furiously debated and its evolution remains undecided. Managing European economies in a rapidly changing global context continues to impose immense stresses on both Western welfare states and the more fragile civil societies of Eastern Europe. Equally, maintaining democracy there in the face of renewed ethnic conflict is an enormous task. But doing this is essential to provide Europe with the wider ranging form of security that has become necessary since 1989. All this is making tremendous demands on the peoples and states of Europe.

Such challenges will continue into the future. They include, firstly, resolving the dilemmas over European integration, notably those inside the EU and coping with the very real difficulties presented by enlargement, especially to the east and south. Secondly, states have to balance increased economic competitiveness with the social solidarity to which Europe has become accustomed. In the East this means pushing forward with economic reform despite the pain this can inflict both on ordinary people and developing stable, pluralist democracies. This will also mean resisting the threat from ethnic and xenophobic forces. Thirdly, it will mean developing appropriate fora and strategies for disarmament and security policies, notably where Russia and the CIS are concerned.

All these things will be costly, politically as well as economically and financially. There is a kind of catch-22 involved here, in that the emergence of European-wide problems demands European-wide solutions, yet many people are unwilling to concede these, even though inward-looking national solutions are likely to worsen the situation for all concerned. The real challenge is to develop both a popular understanding of the difficulties of solving current problems and a mutual respect between people and politicians.

Exactly what will happen depends on a number of outside factors: the evolution of the world economy, the role adopted by the USA, and the pressures on Europe from the former USSR and the deprived south. Within Europe it will depend on the way the policy debate on economic management is resolved and on the willingness of Western electorates to look beyond their own immediate interests. This, in turn, will be intimately bound up with the implementation of the Maastricht Treaty and the outcome of the debate on the future shape of the EU.

At this point in time it is hard, if not impossible to see what the outcomes are likely to be. In overall structure a Europe co-terminous with the EU is unlikely in the near future. What is more likely is a set of complex set of bilateral and multilateral arrangements linking an enlarged EU to non-member states and other organizations. This so-called daisy-flower-model may be messy, but it does cater for the very differing needs of the various parts of Europe. It might also stop the feeling that too much was being centralized too fast in Brussels. In any case, too much institutional simplification could risk both overload and too hard and fast a frontier between states in the EU and those outside.

It is probable that little of this will be the product of some single grand strategy. The development of the differentiated approaches that have already emerged is more likely. Hence, the essential tension between diversity and co-operation in Europe is likely to continue. Whether this will be enough to bring the peace, prosperity and understanding needed to make a success of inner-European relations is another matter. It is a reminder that the future is unlikely to be easy. It is also unlikely to be completely divorced from what has gone before. The seamless web of European history will surely continue into the next century. However, if future citizens can indeed understand the complicated mix of old and new problems which face Europe over the next few years, then these may not prove insoluble. We hope that this text, by setting out the background to contemporary Europe, East and West, within states as well as more generally, and before and after the great watershed of 1989, will make the key issues of the 1990s more comprehensible and thus help the new Europeans along the road they have to travel.

A guide to further reading

The following bibliography is merely selective and is intended to offer the reader a fuller guide to the vast further reading available than that provided at the end of each chapter. While it does not include books in foreign languages and articles in academic journals, it does include all the titles listed as selected readings for individual chapters. It also provides a number of additional titles. For the sake of convenience these are broken down into a series of headings in which works for specific periods and themes are listed in alphabetical order.

Overall historical surveys of the period

Arter, D. (1993), *The Politics of European Integration in the Twentieth Century*, Aldershot: Dartmouth.

Black, C. *et al.* (1992), *Rebirth: A History of Europe since World War II*, Boulder, Col.: Westview.

Calvacoressi, P. (1993), *Resilient Europe: 1870–2000*, London: Longman.

Cipolla, C. (ed.) (1976), *Fontana Economic History of Europe*, Vols. 5 and 6, London: Fontana.

El-Agraa, A.M. (1990), *Economics of the European Community*, 3rd edn, Cambridge: Cambridge University Press.

Gowland, D. *et al.* (eds) (1995), *The European Mosaic*, London: Longman.

Joll, J. (1976), *Europe Since 1870*, Harmondsworth: Penguin.

Lane, P. (1985), *Europe Since 1945*, London: Batsford.

Laqueur, W. (1993), *Europe in Our Time*, Harmondsworth: Penguin.

Lewis, D. (1994), *The Road to Europe*, New York: Lang.

McWilliams, W. and Pitrowski, H. (1990), *The World Since 1945*, London: Adamantine.

Segal, G. (1992), *World Affairs Companion*, London: Simon and Schuster.

Serfaty, S. (1992), *Understanding Europe*, London: Pinter.

Tipton, R. and Aldrich, R. (1988), *Economic and Social History of Europe II*, London: MacMillan.

Urwin, D. (1990), *Western Europe Since 1945*, 5th edn, London: Longman.

Urwin, D.W. (1991), *The Community of Europe*, London: Longman.

Varsori, A. (ed.) (1994), *Europe 1945–1990s: The End of an Era?*, London: Macmillan.

Wegs, J.R. (1992), *Europe Since 1945*, London: St Martins.

Young, J.R. (1992), *Cold War Europe*, London: Arnold.

Reference works

Bullock, A. (ed.) (1990), *Fontana Dictionary of Modern Thought*, 2nd edn, London: Fontana.

Cook, C. and Paxton, J. (1985), *European Political Facts 1918–1990*, Basingstoke: Macmillan.

Dinan, D. (ed.) (1993), *Historical Dictionary of the European Community*, London: Scarecrow Press.

Eastern Europe 1994, London: Europa.

Economist Atlas of the New Europe, London: Economist.

Evans, G and Newnham, J. (1992), *Dictionary of World Politics*, London: Harvester-Wheatsheaf, revised edn.

Pass, C. and Lowes, B. (1993), *Dictionary of Economics*, London: Collins.

Roberts, G. and Edwards, A. (1991), *A New Dictionary of Political Analysis*, London: Arnold.

Robertson, D. (1996), *Dictionary of Modern Politics*, 2nd edn, London: Europa.

Rossi, E. and McCrea, B. (1985), *The European Political Dictionary*, NY: ABC Clio.

Welch, D. (ed.) (1994), *Modern European History 1987–1975: a Documentary Reader*, London: Heineman.

Western Europe 1993 a Survey, London: Europa.

Studies of specific countries

Alderman, G. (1986), *Modern Britain*, London: Croom Helm.

Allcock, J.B. *et al.* (1991), *Yugoslavia in Transition*, London: Berg.

Ardagh, J. (1988), *France Today*, Harmondsworth: Penguin.

Baring, A. (ed.) (1994), *Germany's New Position in Europe: Problems and Perspectives*, Oxford: Berg.

Baudart, M. *et al.* (1990), *Modern Belgium*, Palo Alto, Cal.: SPOSS.

Bennett, C. (1994), *Yugoslavia's Bloody Collapse*, London: Hurst.

Carr, R. and Fusi, J. (1981), *Spain: Dictatorship to Democracy*, London: Allen and Unwin.

Childs, D. (1993), *Britain Since 1945*, London: Routledge.

Clogg, R. (1992), *Greece: A Brief History*, London: Cambridge University Press.

Derbyshire, I. (1990), *Politics in France*, Edinburgh: Chambers.

Fertila, B. (1991), *The Economics and Politics of the Socialist Debacle: Yugoslavia*, Washington: University Press of America.

Fitzmaurice, J. (1988), *The Politics of Belgium*, London: Hurst.

Fulbrook, M. (1991), *Concise History of Germany*, Oxford: Oxford University Press.

Furlong, P. (1994), *Modern Italy. Representation and Reform*, London: Routledge.

Gallagher, T. (1983), *Portugal. A 20th Century Interpretation*, London: MacMillan.

Gillespie, R. (1994), *Mediterranean Politics, A Yearbook*, London: Pinter.

Ginsborg, P. (1990), *History of Contemporary Italy*, Harmondsworth: Penguin.

Griffiths, R.T. (1980), *Economics and Politics in the Netherlands*, Hague: Nijhoff.

Larkin, M. (1988), *France Since the Popular Front*, Oxford: Clarendon.

Lewin, L. (1989), *Ideology and Strategy in Sweden*, Cambridge: Cambridge University Press.

McCauley, M. (1991), *Soviet Politics 1917–1991*, London: Oxford Unversity Press.

Morris, P. (1994), *French Politics Today*, Manchester: Manchester University Press.

Nelson, D.N. (1992), *Romania after Tyranny*, Boulder, Col.: Westview.

Newton, G. (1978), *The Netherlands: An Historical and Cultural Survey*, London: Benn.

Opello, O. (1991), *Portugal From Monarchy to Liberal Democracy*, Boulder, Col.: Westview.

Pasquino, S. (1994), *The End of Post War Politics in Italy*, Boulder, Col.: Westview.

Preston, P. (1986), *The Triumph of Democracy in Spain*, London: Methuen.

Riddell, P. (1989), *The Thatcher Decade*, Oxford, Blackwell.

Ross, G. *et al.* (1987), *The Mitterrand Experiment*, Oxford: Polity.

Sanders, D. (1990), *Losing an Empire. Finding a Role*, London: MacMillan

Strang, M. and Redmond, J. (1992), *Turkey and the European Community*, Brussels: Forum Europe.

Turner, B. (1982), *The Other European Community*, London: Weidenfeld and Nicholson.

Turner, H.A. (1994), *Germany from Partition to Unification*, New Haven, Conn.: Yale University Press.

General Studies
Aldcroft, D.H. (1993), *The European Economy 1914–90*, London: Routledge.

Ambrosius, G. (1989), *Social and Economic History of Western Europe*, Cambridge, Mass.: Harvard University Press.

Armstrong, P. *et al.* (1991), *Capitalism Since 1945 II*, Oxford: Blackwell.

Brassloff, A. and Brassloff, W. (1991), *European Insights: Post War Politics, Society, Culture*, Amsterdam: Elsevier.

Coudenhove-Kalergi, R. (1923), *Pan-Europa*, Vienna: Pan Europa Verlag.

Dorfman, G. and Duignan, P. (1991), *Politics in Western Europe*, Stanford, Cal.: Hoover Institute.

George, S. (1985), *Politics and Policy in the European Community*, Oxford: Oxford University Press.

Graham, A. (1990), *Governments and Economics in Post-War Europe*, London: Routledge.

Harrop, J. (1989), *The Political Economy of Integration in the European Community*, Aldershot: Gower.

Lewis, P. (1995), *Central Europe Since 1945*, London: Longman.

Molle, W. (1990), *The Economics of European Integration*, Aldershot: Darmouth.

Stearns, P. (1975), *Europe in Upheaval*, London: MacMillan.

Van der Wee, H. (1991), *Peace and Upheaval*, Harmondsworth: Penguin.

Woodall, P. and Lovenduski, J. (1987), *Politics and Society in Eastern Europe*, London: MacMillan.

Wyn Rees, G. (1993), *International Politics in Europe – the New Agenda*, London: Routledge.

The post-war background

Ambrosius, G. (1989), *Social and Economic History of Western Europe*, Cambridge, Mass.: Harvard University Press.

Armstrong, P. *et al.* (1991), *Capitalism Since 1945 II*, Oxford: Blackwell.

Baston, R. (ed.) (1991), *International Politics Since 1945*, Aldershot: Edward Elgar.

Brogan, P. (1990), *Eastern Europe*, London: Bloomsbury.

Carr, R. and Fusi, J. (1981), *Spain: Dictatorship to Democracy*, London: Allen and Unwin.

Caute, D. (1988), *Sixty Eight*, London: Hamish Hamilton.

Childs, D. (1993), *Britain Since 1945*, London: Routledge.

Clogg, R. (1992), *Greece: A Brief History*, London: Cambridge University Press.

Dorfman, G. and Duignan, P. (1991), *Politics in Western Europe*, Stanford, Cal.: Hoover Institute.

Douglas, R. (1981), *From War to Cold War, 1942–48*, London: Macmillan.

Enzenberger, H. (1994), *Europe in Ruins*, Harmondsworth: Penguin.

Fowkes, B. (1993), *The Rise and Fall of Communism in Europe*, London: MacMillan.

Fulbrook, M. (1991), *Concise History of Germany*, Cambridge: Cambridge University Press.

Ginsborg, P. (1990), *History of Contemporary Italy*, Harmondsworth: Penguin.

Hallstein, W. (1972), *Europe in the Making*, London: Allen and Unwin.

Hanley, D. and King, A. (1989), *May '68*, London: MacMillan.

Holden, G. (1990), *The Warsaw Treaty Organization*, Oxford: Blackwell.

Kaser, M. (1965), *COMECON*, London: Oxford University Press.

Keating, M. (1994), *The Politics of Modern Europe*, Aldershot: Edward Elgar.

Kitchen, M. (1990), *A World in Flames*, London: Longman.

Larkin, M. (1988), *France Since the Popular Front*, Oxford: Clarendon.

Lewis, P. (1995), *Central Europe Since 1945*, London: Longman.

Longworth, P. (1993), *The Making of Eastern Europe*, Basingstoke: Macmillan.

Loth, W. (1988), *The Division of the World 1941–1955*, London: Routledge.

McCauley, M. (1991), *Soviet Politics 1917-1991*, London: Oxford University Press.

Milward, A.S. (1984), *The Reconstruction of Western Europe 1945–57*, London: Methuen.

Milward, A. (1994), *The European Rescue of the Nation State*, London: Routledge.

Morris, L.P. (1984), *Eastern Europe Since 1945*, London: Heineman.

Mowat, R.C. (1966), *Ruin and Resurgence 1939–1965*, London: Blandford Press.

Narkiewicz, O. (1986), *Eastern Europe 1968–1984*, London: Croom Helm.

Nelson, D. (1989), *The Soviet Alliance*, Boulder, Col.: Westview.

Newton, G. (1978), *The Netherlands: An Historical and Cultural Survey*, London: Benn.

Opello, O. (1991), *Portugal From Monarchy to Liberal Democracy*, Boulder, Col.: Westview.

Pickersgill, C. (1985), *Contemporary Economic Systems*, London: West.

Schiavone, G. (1981), *The Institutions of COMECON*, London: MacMillan.

Smith, G. (1988), *Politics in Western Europe*, 5th edn, Aldershot: Gower.

Stearns, P. (1975), *Europe in Upheaval*, London: MacMillan

Swain, G. and Swain, N. (1993), *Eastern Europe since 1945*, London: Macmillan.

Tipton, R. and Aldrich, R. (1988), *Economic and Social History of Europe II*, London: MacMillan.

Urwin, D. (1990), *Western Europe since 1945*, 5th edn, London: Longman.

Van Brabant, J. (1980), *Socialist Economic Integration*, London: Cambridge University Press.

Van der Wee, H. (1991), *Peace and Upheaval*, Harmondsworth: Penguin.

Western Europe 1993 A Survey, London: Europa (1993).

Weigall, D. and Stirk, P. (1992), *The Origins and Development of the European Community*, Leicester: Leicester University Press.

Williams, A. (1987), *West European Economy*, London: Hutchinson.

Woodall, P. and Lovenduski, J. (1987), *Politics and Society in Eastern Europe*, London: MacMillan.

Young, J.R. (1992), *Cold War Europe*, London: Arnold.

Zeman, Z., (1989), *Pursued by a Bear*, Oxford: Oxford University Press

New directions in the 1980s

Aldcroft, D.H. (1993), *The European Economy 1914–90*, London: Routledge.

Alderman, G. (1986), *Modern Britain*, London: Croom Helm.

Allcock, J.B. *et al.* (1991), *Yugoslavia in Transition*, London: Berg.

Ardagh, J. (1988), *France Today*, Harmondsworth: Penguin.

Ash, T.G. (1990), *We the People*, London: Granta.

Batt, J. (1991), *East Central Europe from Reform to Revolution*, London: RIIA.

Blazyca, G. and Rapacki, R. (1991), *Poland into the 1990s*, London: Pinter.

Brogan, P. (1990), *Eastern Europe 1939–1989*, London: Bloomsbury.

Brown, J.F. (1991), *The Surge to Freedom*, London: Adamantine.

Calleo, D. and Morgenstern, C. (1990), *Recasting Europe's Economies*, Washington: University Press of America.

Cairncross, A. (1992), *The British Economy since 1945*.

Childs, D. *et al.* (1989), *East Germany in Comparative Perspective*, London: Routledge.

Church, C.H. and Keogh, D. (eds) (1991), *The Single European Act. A Transnational Study*, Cork: University of Cork.

Cviic, C. (1991), *Remaking the Balkans*, London: RIIA.

Dalton, R. and Kuecher, M. (1990), *Challenging the Political Order*, Oxford: Blackwell.

Daniels, R.V. (1993), *The End of Communist Revolution in Europe*, London: Routledge.

Derbyshire, I. (1990), *Politics in France*, Edinburgh: Chambers.

Dyker, D. (ed.) (1992), *The European Economies*, London: Longman.

East, R. (ed.) (1991), *Revolution in Eastern Europe*, London: Pinter.

Fitzmaurice, J. (1988), *The Politics of Belgium*, London: Hurst.

Fowkes, B. (1993), *The Rise and Fall of Communism in Eastern Europe*, London: Macmillan.

Fulbrook, M. (1991), *Concise History of Germany*, Oxford: Oxford University Press.

Gallagher, T. (1983), *Portugal. A 20th Century Interpretation*, London: MacMillan.

Glenny, M. (1990), *The Rebirth of History*, Harmondsworth: Penguin.

Griffiths, R.T. (1980), *Economics and Politics in the Netherlands*, Hague: Nijhoff.

Harris, G. (1994), *The Darker Side of Europe*, 2nd. edn, Edinburgh: Edinburgh University Press.

Horvath, A. and Szakolczai, A. (1992), *The Dissolution of Communist Power: the Case of Hungary*, London: Routledge.

James, B. and Stone, M. (eds) (1992), *When the Wall Came Down*, London: Routledge.

Keating, M. and Jones, B. (eds) (1985), *Regions in the EC*, Oxford: Clarendon.

Lewis, P.G. (1994), *Central Europe Since 1945*, Harlow: Longman.

Mason, D.S. (1992), *Revolution in East Central Europe*, Boulder, Co.: Westview.

Muller-Rommel, F. (ed.) (1989), *New Political Movements*, Boulder, Col.: Westview.

Nelson, D.N. (1992), *Romania after Tyranny*, Boulder, Col.: Westview.

Peters, B.G. (1991), *European Politics Reconsidered*, London: Holmes and Meier.

Pettifer, J. (1994), *The Greeks. Land and People Since the War*, Harmondsworth: Penguin.

Pinder, D. (1990), *Western Europe: Challenge and Change*, London: Belhaven.

Prins, G. (ed.) (1991), *Spring in Winter*, Manchester: Manchester University Press.

Preston, P. (1986), *The Triumph of Democracy in Spain*, London: Methuen.

Pryce, R. (ed.) (1987), *The Dynamics of European Union*, London: Croom Helm.

Riddell, P. (1989), *The Thatcher Decade*, Oxford, Blackwell.

Roskin, M. (1991), *Rebirth of Eastern Europe*, Englewood Cliffs, NJ: Prentice Hall.

Ross, G. *et al.* (1987), *The Mitterrand Experiment*, Oxford: Polity.

Rupnik, J. (1988), *The Other Europe*, London: Weidenfeld and Nicholson.

Sjoberg, O. (1991), *Economic Crisis and Reform in the Balkans*, London: Pinter.

Stokes, G. (1993), *The Walls Came Tumbling Down. The Collapse of Eastern Europe*, London: Oxford University Press.

Sword, K. (ed.) (1991), *The Times Guide to Eastern Europe*, 2nd edn, London: Times Publishing.

Thom, F. (1989), *The Gorbachev Phenomenon*, London: Pinter.

Turner, B. (1982), *The Other European Community*, London: Weidenfeld and Nicholson.

Turner, H.A. (1994), *Germany from Partition to Unification*, Newhaven, Conn.: Yale University Press.

Vickerman, R.W. (1992), *The Single European Market*, London: Harvester Wheatsheaf.

Walker, R. (1993), *Six Years that Shook the World*, Manchester: Manchester University Press.

Wheaton, B. (1992), *The Velvet Revolution: Czechoslovakia 1988–1991*, Boulder, Col.: Westview.

Woods, R. (1993), *Revolution in Germany*, London: Pinter.

The challenges of the 1990s

Allum, P. (1995), *State and Society in Europe*, Oxford: Polity.

Almond, M. (1994), *Europe's Backyard War: The War in the Balkans*, London: Heineman.

Alting von Geusau, F.A.M. (1992), *Beyond Containment and Division, Western Cooperation from a Post-Totalitarian Perspective*, Dordrecht: Martinus Nijhoff.

Andersen, S. and Eliassen, K. (1993), *Making Policy in Europe. The Europeification of National Policy-Making*, London: Sage.

Archer, C. (1994), *Organizing Western Europe*, London: Edward Arnold.

Archer, C. and Butler, F. (1992), *The European Community* London: Pinter.

Arter, D. (1993), *The Politics of European Integration in the Twentieth Century*, Aldershot: Dartmouth.

Bailey, J. (ed.) (1992), *Social Europe*, London: Longman.

Baldwin, R. (1994), *Towards an Integrated Europe*, London: Centre for Economic Policy Research.

Baring, A. (ed.) (1994), *Germany's New Position in Europe: Problems and Perspectives*, Oxford: Berg.

Bell, D. and Shaw, E. (eds) (1994), *Conflict and Cohesion in West European Social Democratic Parties*, London: Pinter.

Bennett, C. (1994), *Yugoslavia's Bloody Collapse*, London: Hurst.

Bramwell, A. (1994), *The Fading of the Greens*, New Haven, Conn.: Yale University Press.

Brassloff, A. and Brassloff, W. (1991), *European Insights: Post War Politics, Society, Culture*, Amsterdam: Elsevier.

Brown, J.F. *et al.* (1992), *Western Approaches to Eastern Europe*, New York: Council on Foreign Relations.

Bryant, Ch.G.A. and Mokstycki, E. (eds) (1994), *The Great Transformation? Change and Continuity in East-Central Europe*, London: Routledge.

Buchan, D. (1993), *Europe – the Strange Superpower*, Aldershot: Dartmouth.

Bugajski, J. (1993), *Nations in Turmoil. Conflict and Cooperation in Eastern Europe*, Boulder, Col.: Westview Press.

Buzan, B. *et al.* (1990), *The European Security Order Recast*, London: Pinter.

Cheles, L. *et al.* (1991), *Neo-Fascism in Europe*, London: Longman.

Church, C.H. (ed.) (1990), *Widening the Community Circle*, London: UACES.

Church, C.H. and Phinnemore, D. (1995), *European Union and European Community*, London: Harvester Wheatsheaf.

Coakley, J. (1993), *The Territorial Management of Ethnic Conflict*, London: Cass.

Cobham, D. (1994), *European Monetary Upheavals*, Manchester: Manchester University Press.

Collins, N. (ed.) (1994), *Political Issues in Ireland Today*, London: Manchester University Press.

Collinson, S. (1993), *Europe and International Migration*, London: Pinter.

Colton, T. and Legvold, R. (eds) (1992), *After the Soviet Union,* London: W.W. Norton and Co.

Cviic, C. (1991), *Remaking the Balkans*, London: RIIA.

Dorfman, G. and Duignan, P. (eds) (1991), *Politics in Western Europe*, 2nd edn, Stanford. Cal.: Hoover Institute.

Duncan, P.J.C. (1992), *The Road to Post-Communism*, London: Pinter.

Dyker, D. (ed.) (1992), *European Economies*, London: Longman.

Dyker, D. (ed.) (1992), *The European Economy*, London: Longman.

Ford, G. (1993), *Fascist Europe. The Rise of Racism and Xenophobia*, Boulder, Col.: Westview.

Frankland, G. and Schoonmaker, D. (1993), *Between Protest and Power. The Green Party in Germany*, London: Routledge.

Fertila, B. (1991), *The Economics and Politics of the Socialist Debacle: Yugoslavia*, Washington: University Press of America.

Furlong, P. (1994), *Modern Italy. Representation and Reform*, London: Routledge.

Garcia, S. (1993), *European Identity and the Search for Legitimacy*, London: Pinter.

Gillespie, R. (1994), *Mediterranean Politics, a Yearbook*, London: Pinter.

Glenny, M. (1993), *The Fall of Yugoslavia*, Harmondsworth: Penguin.

Gow, J. (1994), *Triumph of the Lack of Will. International Diplomacy and the Yugoslav War*, London: Hurst.

Gros, D. and Thyessen, N. (1992), *European Monetary Integration*, London: Longman.

Haller, M. and Richter, R. (eds) (1994), *Toward a European Nation?. Political Trends in Europe – East and West, Center and Periphery*, London: M.E. Sharpe.

Hancock, M. *et al.* (1993), *Politics in Western Europe*, London: MacMillan.

Hanley, D. (ed.) (1993), *The Christian Democratic Parties. A Comparative Perspective*, London: Pinter.

Harris, G. (1994), *The Darker Side of Europe*, 2nd edn, Edinburgh: Edinburgh University Press.

Heller, A. and Feelieu, F. (1990), *From Yalta to Glasnost*, Oxford: Blackwell.

Hosking, G. (1990), *The Awakening of the Soviet Union*, London: Heinemann.

Jackson, R.J. (ed.) (1992), *Europe in Transition. The Management of Security after the Cold War*, London: Adamantine Press.

Jakobsen, M. (1992), *Europe in the 1990s. No Stability in Sight*, Geneva: EFTA (Occasional Papers 37).

Jopp, M., Rummel, R. and Schmidt, P. (eds) (1991), *Integration and Security in Western Europe*, Boulder, Col.: Westview.

Keating, M. (1994), *The Politics of Modern Europe. The State and Political Authority in the Major Democracies*, Aldershot: Edward Elgar.

Kirchner, E. *et al.* (eds) (1995), *Britain and Germany in the New Europe*, London: Dartmouth.

Laffan, B. (1992), *Integration and Cooperation in Europe*, London: Routledge.

Lapidas, G.W., Zaslavsky, V. and Golerman, P. (1993), *From Union to Commonwealth Nationalism and Separatism in the Soviet Republics*, Cambridge: Cambridge University Press.

Laqueur, W. (1990), *Soviet Union 2000*, London: Tauris.

Laqueur, W. (1990), *European Security in the 1990s*, London: Unwin Press.

Laqueur, W. (1993), *Europe in Our Time*, Harmondsworth: Penguin.

Lehne, S. (1991), *The Vienna Meeting of the Conference on Security and Cooperation in Europe 1986–1989*, Boulder, Col.: Westview.

Leonardi, R. (ed.) (1992), *Regions in Europe*, London: Cass.

Lewin, L. (1989), *Ideology and Strategy in Sweden*, Cambridge: Cambridge University Press.

Lewis, J. (1993), *Women and Social Policies in Europe*, Aldershot: Edward Elgar.

Lodge, J. (1993), *The European Community and the Challenge of the Future*, London: Pinter.

Ludlow, P. (ed.) (1994), *Europe and the Mediterranean*, Brussels: Centre for European Policy Studies/Brasseys.

Luff, P. (1992), *The Simple Guide to Maastricht*, London: European Movement.

MacAuley, M. (1992), *Soviet Politics 1917–1991*, Oxford: Oxford University Press.

MacAuley, M. (ed.) (1990), *Gorbachev and Perestroika*, London: MacMillan.

Marcus, J. (1995), *The French National Front. The Resistible Rise of Jean-Marie Le Pen*, London: Macmillan.

Marsh, D. (1994), *Germany and Europe: The Crisis of Unity*, London: Heinemann.

Miall, H. (1993), *Shaping the New Europe*, London: RIIA.

Miall, H. (1994), *Redefining Europe: New Patterns of Conflict and Cooperation*, London: Pinter.

Michalski, A. and Wallace, H. (1992), *The Challenge of Enlargement*, London: RIIA.

Miller, J. (1993), *Mikhail Gorbachev and the End of Soviet Power*, London: Macmillan.

McInnes, C. (ed.) (1992), *Security and Strategy in the New Europe*, London: Routledge.

Morris, P. (1994), *French Politics Today*, Manchester: Manchester University Press.

Mortimer, E. (1992), *European Security After the Cold War*, London: Aldephi Papers 271.

Norgaard, O. (ed.) (1993), *The EC and the World*, London: Pinter.

Pavlovic, V. (1992), *Failure of Democratic Transformation*, London: M.E. Sharpe.

Pinder, D. (1990), *Western Europe. Challenge and Change*, London: Bellhaven.

Pinder, J. (1991), *The EC and Eastern Europe*, London: RIIA.

Pugh, M. (ed.) (1992), *European Security – Towards 2000*, Manchester: Manchester University Press.

Ramet, S. (1992), *Nationalism and Federalism in Eastern Europe*, Indiana: Indiana University Press.

Redmond, J. (1993), *The Next Mediterranean Enlargement*, Aldershot: Dartmouth.

Redmond, J. (ed.) (1992), *The External Relations of the EC*, London: Longman.

Rezun, M. (1992), *Nationalism and the Break-up of an Empire. Russia and its Periphery*, London: Praeger.

Rootes, C. and Richardson, D. (eds) (1994), *The Green Challenge*, London: Routledge.

Roucek, L. (1992), *After the Bloc: The New International Relations in Eastern Europe*, London: R11A, Discussion Paper No.40.

Rudig, W. (ed.) (1991–92), *Green Politics I and II*, Edinburgh: Edinburgh University Press.

Rummel, R. (ed.) (1992), *Towards Political Union*, Boulder, Col.: Westview.

Rusi, A. (1991), *After the Cold War. Europe's New Political Architecture*, London: Macmillan.

Sanders, D. (1990), *Losing an Empire. Finding a Role*, London: MacMillan.

Schoplin, G. (1993), *Politics in Eastern Europe, 1945–1992*, Oxford: Blackwell.

Seroka, J.H. and Pavlovic, V. (eds) (1993), *The Tragedy of Yugoslavia – The Future of Democratic Transformation*, London: M.E. Sharpe.

Siebert, H. (1991), *The New Economic Landscape of Europe*, Oxford: Blackwell.

Somers, F. (1994), *European Economies. A Comparative Study*, London: Pitman.

Stares, P. (ed.) (1992), *The New Germany and the New Europe*, Washington, DC: Brookings.

Story, J. (ed.) (1993), *The New Europe*, Oxford: Blackwell.

Strang, M. and Redmond, J. (1992), *Turkey and the European Community*, Brussels: Forum Europe.

Swann, D. (ed.) (1992), *The Single European Market and Beyond – a Study of the Wider Implications of the Single European Act*, London: Routledge.

Taras, R. (ed.) (1992), *The Road to Disillusion*, London: M.E. Sharpe.

Thomas, M. (1993), *The Paper House*, London: Vintage.

Ullman, R. (1992), *Securing Europe*, London: Adamantine.

Van Ham, P. (1993), *The EC and Central Europe*, London: Pinter.

Varsori, A. (ed.) (1994), *Europe 1945–1990s: The End of an Era?*, London: MacMillan.

Waever, O., Buzan, B. Kelstrup, M. and Lemaitre, P. (1993), *Identity, Migration and the New Security Agenda in Europe*, London: Pinter.

Walker, J. (1992), *Security and Arms Control in Post-Confrontation Europe*, Oxford: Oxford University Press.

Wallace, W. (1990), *The Transformation of Western Europe*, London: Pinter/RIIA.

Wallace, W. (ed.) (1991), *The Wider Western Europe – Reshaping the EC/EFTA Relationship*, London: Pinter.

Wallace, W. (ed.) (1992), *The Dynamics of European Integration*, London: Pinter.

Weale, A. (1991), *The New Politics of Pollution*, Manchester: Manchester University Press.

Western Europe 1993, a Survey, London: Europa.

White, S. (1990), *Gorbachev in Power*, Cambridge: Cambridge University Press.

Williams, A. (ed.) (1994), *Reorganizing Eastern Europe*, Aldershot: Dartmouth.

Wilson, F. (1994), *European Politics Today. The Democratic Experience*, 2nd edn, London: Harvester Wheatsheaf.

Wise, M. and Gibb, R. (1993), *Single Market to Social Europe*, London: Longman.

Wyn Rees, G. (1993), *International Politics in Europe – The New Agenda*, London: Routledge.

Glossary

Acquis Sometimes rendered as 'patrimony', and meaning either, or both, the corpus of EC treaties and legislation, and the EC's overall achievements and dynamic.

Atlanticist State or individual who believes that European security is best developed on a transatlantic basis, thus accepting the primacy of NATO and US leadership. Usually contrasted with the 'Europeanist' view that Europe should arrange its own defence.

Association Structured relationship with the EC enjoyed both by former colonies or by European states seeking closer relations with the EC when membership is either expected or not possible.

Benelux Strictly speaking the title of the post-war Economic Union of Belgium, the Netherlands and Luxembourg, but conventionally used to describe anything to do with the three states.

Bipolar Term copied from electricity to describe the state of world politics during the Cold War during which everything turned on the twin poles of the USA and USSR and their relationship. The opposite is multipolar.

Bretton Woods Series of multilateral international agreements on international monetary and economic relations, involving the setting up of the IMF and the World Bank, agreed by the Western Allies in New Hampshire in July 1944. Conventionally used to described the rules regulating Western trade and finance before the 1970s.

Brezhnev Doctrine Soviet doctrine enunciated in Warsaw on 12 November 1968 which stated that the USSR had a right to intervene in any of its satellites should they depart from the fundamentals of Communism. Hence it limited the sovereignty of the satellites. It was used to justify the intervention in Afghanistan and was revoked by Gorbachev in 1989.

Civil Society Term used to describe the general organization of social affairs, run by individuals, and into which the State should not trespass.

Cohabitation French term, copied from married life, to describe the situation in which, as in 1986–88 and 1993–95, there was a President from a different political party from that which, because of its majority in Parliament, nominated the Prime Minister and government.

Cold War American term used to describe the generalized conflict between the Eastern and Western blocs between the 1940s and 1980s when circumstances meant that hostility could not be expressed in a normal 'hot' military war.

Collectivization Policy pursued under Stalin to reorganize agriculture into large-scale units, whether in state, or more properly, collective farms. The latter brought a number of peasant farmers together into a co-operative enterprise in which labour and equipment were shared.

Common Market Technically a more developed form of economic integration than both a Free Trade Area and a Customs Union, in which there is free movement of capital, goods, persons and services within the given area. The term has often been used in British parlance to describe the EEC even though technically the latter was merged in the EC in 1966. The usage carried the loaded (and inaccurate) implication that the EC was, could and should remain an economic entity, not venturing into the political domain.

Convertibility Term signifying that national currencies can be freely exchanged on the open market whether at rates determined by agreement or by the markets. It contrasts with the situation in the Communist world where exchange rates were set by the State which also controlled how, where and when they could be exchanged. Usually such official rates bore no relation to the actual worth of the currencies involved.

Decentralization Process by which specific tasks and responsibilities are transferred from the central authorities of a nation to other territorial bodies within the state, whether regions or local government. Usually restricted to unitary states, such as France after 1981, since the process does not imply that the territorial bodies share in sovereignty as they do in a federal (qv) polity. Often, not wholly accurately, equated with devolution.

Decolonization Process by which the West European nations, mainly during the 1950s and 1960s, allowed their Third World colonies to become independent nations. In theory it also means that the imperial power ceases to exercize influence inside the new nation, but this has not always been the case.

Democratic Centralism Concept used in Marxist–Leninism to describe and justify the fact that decisions were taken at the top and had to be obeyed lower down the hierarchy. The claim was that this was still democratic because the party apparatus represented the people.

Democratic Deficit The claim that the EC lacks the full credentials of democracy, usually because it provides neither proper parliamentary authorization for all its legislation nor real accountability for its executive and administrative bodies. The Parliament is commonly seen as the body representing the ordinary electors of the EU.

Democratization Process of restoring normal democratic institutions and processes to the former USSR and its satellites, replacing the totalitarian one-party states which allowed ordinary citizens no say in the way they were governed.

De-nazification The post-war attempt to cure the former Axis powers etc. of their addiction to Fascist and Nazi ideas. It involved the dismissal of those who had been too compromised by the old regime and a process of re-education for the rest.

De-nuclearization   The move to remove the majority of nuclear weapons from the nations and armed forces of Europe. This was talked about at various times during the Cold War, as in the Rapacki Plan and the proposals for nuclear free zones in particular regions, but only really began to happen at the end of the Cold War.

Détente   Diplomatic term, drawn from the French, and meaning the relaxation of relations between hostile camps, in this case the East and West. It did not mean that there was agreement between the two, merely that there was relatively civilized contact between the two sides. The term can be used to refer either to the process of improving East–West relations or to the period in which this was attempted.

Entrepreneurial   Characteristics of persons or systems which are able to create and develop successful businesses by buying and selling. Claimed by some conservatives to be something lacking in much European business management and policy making and needing to be fostered in order to enhance competitiveness on world markets.

Ethnicity   The quality of sharing in, and believing the overriding value, of the characteristics of a particular ethnic group, whether cultural, linguistic, physical, religious or social.

EURATOM   Colloquial term used to denote the European Economic Energy Community, set up in 1957, and largely merged with the EEC in 1966. The EURATOM Treaty still maintains a quasi-independent existence.

Europeanization   Describes the influencing of states' political and other processes by Western European, and usually EC, developments. Most often used in the post-Cold War context of the transition in Eastern Europe, but can also be used by Western non-member states and in relation to elements of national life in member states which diverged from the EC's policy norms and have to be realigned on the latter.

Euro-sclerosis   The stagnation experienced by the EC from the early 1970s to the mid 1980s when the failure of the ambitious plans of 1969 gave way to increasing divisions and very slow decision making.

Federal   Political science term used to denote a process of governance which seeks to share sovereignty and power amongst different political units, usually within a given state, as in Austria, Germany and Switzerland. Here, the system is understood as essentially decentralizing and not centralizing as in Anglo–American usages. In any case, federal processes do not have to lead to the creation of a single state or federation as implied by many polemical usages (see Federalism qv).

Federalist   Designation used by opponents and supporters of closer integration, not wholly accurately as already noted, to describe those persons, forces and policies seeking to increase the level of cohesion and common decision making in the European Union. By extension **Federalism** is seen as the desire to create a single European state.

Fiscal Having to do with taxation and the raising of revenues by states or international bodies to finance their own activities. Not necessarily a matter of economic management.

Gastarbeiter German euphemism meaning 'guest-worker', used to describe foreign workers brought in to fill labour shortages in the European economy from the 1950s onwards and suggesting that they enjoyed a higher status than was actually the case.

Glacis Term originating in medieval military architecture where it meant a sloping embankment used to protect the bottom of castle towers from being mined. More recently applied to describe the role of the first line of defence in which the USSR cast its satellites.

Glasnost The policy of freedom and openness in Communist life, developed by Gorbachev as part of his reform package in an attempt to enlist support for economic reform, especially from intellectuals. It was also designed to encourage people to feel involved in change particularly by keeping an eye on managers and officials who might otherwise hold up reform.

Governance A wider term than government, meaning the forms, processes and style by which a polity is run, in the widest sense of the term.

Harmonization The process of bringing policies and practices of member states of the EC into line through eliminating major differences so that the rules in all countries all work in virtually the same way. This is more constraining than approximation and especially mutual recognition.

High Contracting Parties Legal phrase used to describe those states which sign an international treaty.

Inner-European relations Concept used here to denote a range of issues concerned with the overall management of Europe in the post-Cold War era, including EC enlargement, but going well beyond this. The basic idea comes from the attitudes the West Germans took towards the East prior to 1989.

Integration The process of bringing economies, individuals or states into a more cohesive and united whole. In economics this involves dissolving all barriers to business activity in a given territory. Politically it can lead to either a new awareness of being part of a single body or the creation of state. The term can also be used to describe the way the EC's institutions operate, that is in a closer mode than that provided by simple co-operation.

Intergovernmental Term used to denote international co-operation by states without any surrender of sovereignty. EFTA is a typical example while the second and third pillars of the post-Maastricht union can also be so described in contrast to the supranational approach which prevails inside the EC pillar. The concept has given rise to theories of intergovernmentalism which suggest that the EC is, or should be, directed by what the members states want and do.

Inter-institutional   Technical EC term to describe an agreement on working practices etc. amongst such institutions as the Commission, the Parliament and the Court.

Internal market   This can mean either the project which emerged in the 1980s to complete the Common Market or the completely free economic area in which all goods, services, capital and persons can move freely which was destined to come into existence by 31 December 1992. It means the same as 'Single Market'.

Iron Curtain   Term first used by Winston Churchill in 1946 to symbolize the new political and economic divide which had come down across Europe because of Soviet policy and power. By the 1960s this had taken on a physical shape as brutal and massive barriers were carved across the face of central Europe to keep the West out and the Easterners in.

Keynesian   Economic and political approach derived from the writings of John Maynard Keynes which argues, amongst other things, that unemployment and depression can be avoided by government control of credit and currency, including using public expenditure to stimulate demand and growth. His views are often contrasted with those of monetarism.

Kremlin   Conventional description of the centre of power of the Soviet system.

Marxist–Leninism   Ruling ideology of the USSR and its satellites prior to 1989, derived from Lenin's reinterpretation of Marx's writings, stressing the dominant role of the Party.

Maximalist   Party or view which wishes to go as far as possible in a political venture, whether communism or integration, often refusing to accept compromises even if this means jeopardizing everything. Usually contrasted with minimalism, i.e. the willingness to settle for the essential minimum of demands, or whatever is realistic.

Mixed economy   An economy which combines private and public sectors and modes of operation, and is not dominated by either. Usually used to describe Western capitalism after the war, in contrast both to early American capitalism and the Soviet style command economy.

Monetarism   Economic theory deriving from Milton Friedman and other American economists and particularly associated with the British conservative government under Margaret Thatcher. The theory argues that inflation – which is seen as the greatest of economic evils – is caused by increases in the amount of money available in an economy. The latter can be controlled partly through high interest rates and partly through other means of management such as reducing public spending, resisting trade union demands and privatizing and deregulating the economy.

Neo-liberalism   The revised form of nineteenth century economic liberalism advocated, and sometimes practised by, the Thatcher and Reagan administrations. It combines tradition, individualism and free trade with new conservative policies such as monetarism and public choice.

New Freeze   The period, and process, of renewed coolness and hostility between East and West which started in the late 1970s, with the troubles in Afghanistan and Poland and ended with Gorbachev's new thinking.

Nomenklatura   Russian word denoting nomination by ruling Communist parties to key positions in state and society. Such nominations were drawn from names on a previously established list of those who were felt reliable. It was a major means of social and political control in the Eastern bloc.

Nordic   Term used to describe the Scandinavian countries, Finland and Iceland and their international organizations.

Ombudsman   Public official responsible for receiving public complaints about administrative maltreatment at the hands of the state. The office was initially a Nordic one but has become commonplace in Europe now.

Ostpolitik   The new German foreign policy conducted by Willy Brandt and the SPD in the late 1960s and early 1970s and based on the willingness both to recognize the existence of the GDR and to come to terms with the Eastern satellites who had suffered at German hands before 1945. It marked a distinct break with the Erhard doctrine which meant that the FRG would not have relations with states which recognized the GDR. It thus played an important part in encouraging *détente* (qv).

Own resources   Term used to describe those sources of income which the EC enjoys as a right including customs revenue, a share of member states' GNP, levies on agricultural imports and a percentage of VAT receipts.

Peaceful co-existence   Doctrine on Soviet international relations espoused by Kruschev and others. While neither accepting capitalism nor giving up the idea of competing with it, the doctrine recognized that this could only be done peacefully. Equally, the two sides would have to live together for long term until Communism eventually triumphed.

Peace Movement   Name given to the radical social movement found in Germany and other Western states in the early 1980s which was agnostic about the Cold War and greatly worried by the risks involved in deploying Pershing and Cruise missiles. It posed a very real threat to Western governments for a while.

Peoples' Democracies   Title arrogated to themselves by the Soviet satellites to signify they enjoyed a truer form of democracy than bourgeois Western democracies.

Perestroika   Russian term meaning 'restructuring' and revived by Gorbachev to describe the kind of economic reforms he sought within the Communist system. Closely linked with glasnost (qv).

Pluralism   Description of a domestic (or sometimes an international) political system in which no one force has a monopoly of activity and authority. The doctrine of pluralism starts from the assumption that societies are inherently diverse and that all elements in the community have a right to take part in the political process. If they do not, Western opinion does not accept the country concerned as truly democratic.

Politikverdrossenheit   German phrase meaning political malaise, nowadays used to describe the bad-tempered nature of Western electorates in the 1980s and 1990s.

Presidium   Key governing committee within Communist parties and parliaments.

Putsch   German term signifying a military *coup d'état* in which one group seizes power from another.

Rational choice   Theory of political analysis which sees electors as motivated essentially by their calculation of which party or movement will reward them most. Linked to ideas of public choice and at variance with the assumption that class and social position determines the way people vote.

Realignment   Process by which social groups, and especially voters, transfer their loyalties to new political forces and parties. Can follow on de-alignment as social change undermines the old cleavages which used to bind voters to traditional parties.

Refuseniks   Soviet Jews who refused to accept peacefully that they would not be allowed to emigrate to Israel.

Regional   Loose geographical term used to describe something related to a sub-division of a larger whole, for instance the EC's regional policy. However, there can be different levels of regions so that Europe can be seen as one of a number of world regions, with its own characteristics.

Relance/relaunch   Conventional terms, the first French, the second English, describing the revival of EC confidence and activity in the mid-1980s, after the long years of Euro-sclerosis (qv). The process, led by Jacques Delors, led to the SEA, 1992 and beyond.

Satellites   Term derived from astronomy to describe the smaller states of central and eastern Europe which fell under Soviet control after the Second World War and were condemned to rotate around the USSR like moons round Jupiter, in other words without a real life of their own. This description excludes Albania and Yugoslavia as was.

Singularization   Term used by nuclear strategists to denote the possible concentration of nuclear war in Europe, and essentially in West Germany.

Sit-in   Popular form of alternative political action of the '68 era involving a largely peaceful occupation of a public space devoted to debate and ended when the police carried away the sitting demonstrators.

Social movements Term used to denote a spontaneous political grouping, usually aimed at achieving a specific political goal with more limited aims and structures than a political party.

Sovrams Soviet-dominated joint enterprises set up after the war in countries like Romania to ensure that the Soviet economy had the access to goods and services it needed.

Stagflation Neologism coined from stag(nation) and (in)flation to describe the unusual economic conditions of the 1970s in which declining activity and growth was combined with rapidly rising prices owing to high energy and labour costs.

Stalinism The economic and political doctrines and practices associated with Josef Stalin involving rapid industrialization and collectivization (qv) in the economic sphere, ruthless centralization and personalization of power, and rule by terror and exclusion.

Stalinization The enforced imposition of a Stalinist style of governance (qv) on a country, as happened after the war in the satellites.

Supranational Opposite form of international organization to the inter-governmental (qv), involving processes, laws and institutions which are superior to those of states usually because the latter have agreed to pool their sovereignty and be guided by commonly decided policies etc. Often used to characterize the EC's institutions.

Synergy A process of mutually advantageous coming together so that the whole becomes greater than the sum of the parts.

Thatcherism Political programme and style, rather than a philosophy of government, said to be that of Margaret Thatcher as leader of the Tory Party. It was seen as including such things as a strongly independent foreign policy in alliance with America, scepticism about European integration, a firm belief in the invincibility of markets and individual freedom, a visceral hatred of all things socialist and an acceptance of monetarist (qv) principles.

Thaw Period following the death of Stalin in which Soviet domestic and external policies were slightly moderated.

Union Either the process of uniting Europe, indicated in the Treaty of Rome and its successors or the new three-pillar institution set up after Maastricht.

Uskorenie An initial, if minor, concept used by Gorbachev to signify the kind of 'speeding up' he felt was needed by the moribund Soviet system.

Volatility Scientific term now applied to the rapidly changing electoral pref-erences of Western voters, which has shown itself in the rapid turnover of parties and governments since the early 1970s. See also de-alignment (qv) and rational choice (qv).

Welfare Providing for the basic wellbeing of citizens through education, food, housing, income and other forms of social security. Because this has become so important a public activity since the war, and one seen as a right by many, it has become a defining characteristic of the modern European state.

Index